Sails.js in Action

Sails.js in Action

MIKE MCNEIL
IRL NATHAN

MANNING
SHELTER ISLAND

For online information and ordering of this and other Manning books, please visit
www.manning.com. The publisher offers discounts on this book when ordered in quantity.
For more information, please contact

> Special Sales Department
> Manning Publications Co.
> 20 Baldwin Road
> PO Box 761
> Shelter Island, NY 11964
> Email: orders@manning.com

Manning Publications Co. 20 Baldwin Road PO Box 761 Shelter Island, NY 11964	Development editor: Marina Michaels Senior technical development editor: Brian Hanafee Technical development editor: Damien White Copyeditor: Linda Recktenwald Proofreader: Katie Tennant Technical proofreader: Jerry Tan Typesetter: Dennis Dalinnik Cover designer: Marija Tudor

ISBN: 9781617292613
Printed in the United States of America
1 2 3 4 5 6 7 8 9 10 – EBM – 22 21 20 19 18 17

brief contents

contents

preface

In 2015, when Manning approached us to write a book on Sails.js, we wanted to take an approach that reflects our background: building real-world applications for clients. And because that was why we built Sails.js in the first place, we wanted to take that experience and weave it into the pages of this book. We feel it's important to teach the theory behind how Sails.js works, but it's even more important to emphasize the *practical steps* involved in building a client-led project using the framework. Fortunately, our publisher agreed, and so we were able to embark on that effort. We hope you have as much fun reading *Sails.js in Action* as we did writing it.

acknowledgements

We first want to thank all the folks at Manning who made this book possible. Marina Michaels was the voice of reason, providing a steady hand in editing this book. Michael Stephens took a leap of faith in allowing us to write the book we wanted to deliver. Thanks go to all of our reviewers: Alvin Raj, Angelo Costa, Damian Esteban, Earl Bingham, Jay Tyo, Jeroen Benckhuijsen, Nick McGinness, Nikander and Margriet Bruggeman, Ozgur Ozturk, Russell Frisch, Sam Kreter, Sergio Arbeo, Stephen Byrne, and Tony Brown. We want to especially thank Jerry Tan for his review of the repos for the book. Also special thanks to bigtunacan for all your hard work in the user forums. And finally, a big thank-you goes to all of our MEAP readers who provided a wealth of feedback, making the book better.

Some icons used in illustrations were made by Freepik from www.flaticon.com.

Irl Nathan

I want to thank my wife Tica for proofreading the early drafts of each chapter. She showed tremendous patience during this process, as did my daughter Zoë and son Jake. I also want to thank my parents and sister for their ongoing support. Thanks go to Scott and Cody for their limitless patience in answering questions. I also thank Rachael and Rachel for transforming my gibberish into readable prose. Finally, thank you Mike, for embarking on this project with me with tireless energy and positivity.

Mike McNeil

I'd like to thank the other core members of the Sails.js team: Cody Stoltman, Rachael Shaw, and Scott Gress. Without their contributions, this book would not have been possible. I also deeply appreciate the editing help from Rachel Kelmenson and from my parents.

about this book

A brief history of Sails

The development of Sails began entirely by accident. Over the course of 2011 and 2012, Mike built several Node.js apps. Like many early Node.js users, he ended up organically accumulating code he could reuse across different projects. As you may already know, that works great for a while, but what he needed was a framework.

But there wasn't an MVC framework for Node.js yet. Most projects at that time directly incorporated two modules—Express and Socket.IO—which are great but were never intended to be used as complete web frameworks. We had to write database queries by hand and make crucial structural decisions on a case-by-case basis. This made it hard to build (and especially *maintain*) Node.js apps without a great deal of prior experience—not only with Node's core libraries and module system but also with backend apps in general.

Not to mention that back in those days the community was full of brilliant hobbyists and tinkerers, but the software industry scoffed at using Node.js on anything serious. Challenging that mindset was the grail for the first years of Sails.js—like many of us, Mike believed in the power of Node.js and wanted to use it at work. He proselytized for months. But alas, some things just aren't meant to be.

So Mike started doing frontend web development in his free time (contracting as a hired gun), in hopes that he'd meet a client with an interesting use case or, better yet, someone who really *got* the promise of Node.js. Fortunately, he found two: first, a guy we'll call "G," who needed help building an entirely realtime cloud storage application for his enterprise customers, and then, a few weeks later, a woman named Jessa, who was building a social chat application but didn't know how to go about it in PHP. Thanks in no small part to these folks, Mike was able to leave his job in 2012, form a team, and start using an early version of Sails on *everything*.

That's when things got serious. Instead of relying on intermittent spurts of productivity to get stuff done, Mike and the core team were driven by paying customers to add new features and fix bugs. And because we were ultimately responsible for making sure everything worked, it meant that we were writing JavaScript on the server every day of the week.

The Sails framework really took off in the spring of 2013 (version 0.8) when Mike created a five-minute screencast that ended up on the front page of the popular tech news website, Hacker News. Almost overnight, Sails was being adopted for real-world projects by developers from all sorts of diverse backgrounds: everything from Django to Java to ASP.NET. The increasing popularity of Node.js itself fueled this even further; as more and more developers tried out Node and inevitably Googled "Node.js MVC framework," they discovered Sails.

The second renaissance in web development

The web has changed dramatically over the past 10 years since Ruby on Rails and other developer-friendly Model-View-Controller (MVC) web frameworks were first introduced. These early projects popularized important ideas that are still prevalent in mainstream web development tools today. They also lowered the barrier to entry for becoming a full stack web developer, making it possible for a larger group of individuals to build web apps.

Because they were designed for building websites, traditional web frameworks needed to support only a single user-agent: the web browser. (A user-agent is a software application—like a web browser—that acts on behalf of a user to send requests to your Sails app. We reference a number of different types of user-agents throughout the book.) But the widespread adoption of mobile devices like the iPhone changed everything. Modern web applications need to support all sorts of different user-agents, from tablets to mobile handsets—even smart devices that don't have screens at all!

Fortunately, the last few years have brought with them a sort of second renaissance in web development. JavaScript frameworks like Angular, React, Ember, and Backbone make it much easier to build rich browser interfaces. Meanwhile, the ecosystem for building iOS and Android apps has tons of great tools, and the manufacturers of new smart devices are making it easier than ever before for developers to build client applications for their platforms. What all of these frontend frameworks have in common is a need for an easy way to prototype and implement the backend of the application.

How this book is organized

The book has 15 chapters:

- Chapter 1 begins by defining Sails.js, what you can build with it, and its core features. The chapter also includes a primer on the fundamental concepts necessary to understand a web application.
- Chapter 2 outlines the tools necessary to create a Sails.js app. After creating and reviewing an initial project, the chapter concludes with an explanation of resources you'll use throughout the book.
- Chapter 3 begins with a discussion of how to set up the frontend static assets in Sails.js. The chapter also discusses the frontend-first approach to API design using jQuery (and later Angular) as frontend examples.
- Chapter 4 illustrates using Sails.js blueprints to prototype an initial API.
- Chapter 5 transitions from automatic blueprints to custom backend code. The chapter also provides an introduction to using third-party npm packages and machinepacks.
- Chapter 6 is an introduction to using databases with Sails.js. The chapter discusses the details of how to model a database and send queries using the Sails.js ORM.
- Chapter 7 goes deep into custom actions, with a few common use cases as examples.
- Chapter 8 provides a detailed understanding of server-rendered views. The chapter marks a transition from building a single-page application, instead applying a hybrid approach. For many apps, this affords some key benefits, including making pages more easily accessible to search engines.
- Chapter 9 describes the relationship between user authentication and sessions. This chapter provides a step-by-step example of implementing a login process.
- Chapter 10 outlines the means to control access to your API through policies.
- Chapter 11 demonstrates best practices for refactoring your Sails app to enhance its maintainability or when faced with inevitable changes to project requirements.
- Chapter 12 expands on chapter 6 to show how to store and retrieve related data through embedding and associations.
- Chapter 13 walks through the implementation of some often-requested features of web applications, including support for ratings, followers, and search.
- Chapter 14 takes you deep into enabling realtime features like chat using Web-Sockets.
- Chapter 15 wraps up the book with a detailed look at what you need to take your web application to production, including a discussion on deployment, security, and testing.

About the code

All of the source code for the book is available for download from the publisher's website at www.manning.com/books/sails-js-in-action and from GitHub at http://sailsin-action.github.io/. There, you'll find links to individual pages for chapters 3–15. Within each link, you'll find, at the least, an ending GitHub repo—that is, a representation of what your source code should look like by the end of the chapter. If the chapter requires that you start from a particular state of code, there will also be a repo for the start of the chapter. Some chapters also include some other reference material.

Author Online

Purchase of *Sails.js in Action* includes free access to a private web forum run by Manning Publications, where you can make comments about the book, ask technical questions, and receive help from the authors and from other users. To access the forum and subscribe to it, point your web browser at www.manning.com/books/sails-js-in-action. This page provides information on how to get on the forum once you're registered, what kind of help is available, and the rules of conduct on the forum.

Manning's commitment to our readers is to provide a venue where a meaningful dialogue between individual readers and between readers and the authors can take place. It's not a commitment to any specific amount of participation on the part of the authors, whose contributions to the Author Online forum remain voluntary (and unpaid). We suggest you try asking them some challenging questions, lest their interest stray! The Author Online forum and the archives of previous discussions will be accessible from the publisher's website as long as the book is in print.

about the authors

Mike McNeil is an open source developer based in Austin, Texas, and the creator of Sails.js, one of the most popular frameworks for Node.js. He is also the CEO and cofounder of Treeline, a Y Combinator–backed startup working to democratize backend development.

Irl Nathan is a recovering lawyer who has worked in technology for 20+ years and started programming in earnest 5 years ago. Over the past 3 years, he's been apprenticing with Mike and the Sails.js team. Irl is a core contributor to Sails, and he produced a successful thirty-plus-part screencast series focusing on web programming using an earlier version of Sails.

about the cover illustration

The figure on the cover of *Sails.js in Action* is captioned "Homme de la Dalecarlie," or a man from Delarna county, located in central Sweden. It borders with Norway in the west and is known for its remoteness, beauty, and wide range of physical geography: deciduous and coniferous forests, plains, lakes, rivers, foothills, and alpine regions. The illustration is taken from a collection of dress costumes from various countries by Jacques Grasset de Saint-Sauveur (1757–1810), titled *Costumes de Différents Pays,* published in France in 1797. Each illustration is finely drawn and colored by hand. The rich variety of Grasset de Saint-Sauveur's collection reminds us vividly of how culturally apart the world's towns and regions were just 200 years ago. Isolated from each other, people spoke different dialects and languages. On the streets or in the countryside, it was easy to identify where they lived and what their trade or station in life was just by their dress.

The way we dress has changed since then, and the diversity by region, so rich at the time, has faded away. It's now hard to tell apart the inhabitants of different continents, let alone different towns, regions, or countries. Perhaps we've traded cultural diversity for a more varied personal life—certainly, for a more varied and fast-paced technological life.

At a time when it's hard to tell one computer book from another, Manning celebrates the inventiveness and initiative of the computer business with book covers based on the rich diversity of regional life of two centuries ago, brought back to life by Grasset de Saint-Sauveur's pictures.

Getting started

This chapter covers

- Reviewing modern web development
- Understanding the architecture of the Sails framework
- Positioning Sails in modern web development
- Installing the necessary components of the technical stack
- Setting up the tools of your development environment

Too often, backend programming is put on a pedestal, where only highly trained and disciplined experts are worthy. That's baloney. Backend programming isn't rocket science—but that doesn't mean it's easy. It means that for those new to it, you just need a healthy curiosity and a powerful framework like Sails to get started. If you already have experience with backend programming in a language other than JavaScript, the transition can also be frustrating. Shifting from synchronous to asynchronous patterns can take some time to master. Whether you're new or experienced, Sails will make this transition much easier. Our goal is to provide an entertaining, practical, gap-free path to understanding Sails as well as modern back-end web development.

1.1   *What is Sails?*

Sails is a JavaScript backend framework that makes it easy to build custom, enterprise-grade Node.js apps. It's designed to emulate the familiar MVC pattern of frameworks like Ruby on Rails but with support for the requirements of modern apps: data-driven APIs with a scalable, service-oriented architecture. It's especially good for building chat, realtime dashboards, or multiplayer games, but you can use it for any web application project, top to bottom.

The book is targeted at two types of developers. First is a developer who has frontend experience and is looking to become a full-stack programmer using JavaScript, a language they already know. Second is a developer who has backend experience in a language other than JavaScript and is looking to expand their knowledge to Node.js. In either case, familiarity with HTML, CSS, and JavaScript is expected, as well as experience with making AJAX requests. Most important is a curiosity about how to build a web application.

1.2   *What can you build with Sails?*

Whether you're a frontend developer seeking to expand your backend knowledge or a server-side developer unfamiliar with using Node and JavaScript on the backend, the common denominator we all share is a desire to create web applications. Sails is designed to be compatible with whatever strategy you have for building your frontend, whether it be Angular, Backbone, iOS/Objective-C, Android/Java, or even a "headless" app that just offers up a raw API to be used by another web service or your developer community. Sails is great for building everyday backend apps that handle HTTP requests and WebSockets. It isn't a good approach for building the client side of your application—that part is completely up to you. If you end up changing your approach (for example, switching from Backbone to Angular) or building a new frontend entirely (for example, building a Windows Phone native app), your Sails app will still work.

> **WARNING**   You're about to experience a buzzword bonanza. If you see a term you don't recognize, don't worry—we'll return to these concepts in detail later in the book.

What types of applications can you build? Sails excels at building these:

- *Hybrid web applications*—These applications combine a JSON API with server-rendered views; that is, in addition to an API, this type of application can serve dynamic (that is, personalized) HTML pages, making it suitable for use cases that demand search engine optimization (SEO). These applications often use a client-side JavaScript framework (for example, Angular, Ember, React, and so on), but they don't necessarily have to. Examples of hybrid web applications you might be familiar with are Twitter, GitHub, and Basecamp.

- *Pure APIs*—These applications fulfill requests from one or more independent frontend user interfaces. We say *independent* because the frontend doesn't have to be delivered by the same server that's providing the JSON API—or even by a server at all. This umbrella category includes single-page apps (SPAs), native mobile applications (for example, iOS and Android), native desktop applications (for example, OS X, Windows, Linux), and the venerated Internet of Things (IoT). Many mobile-first products (think Uber, Instagram, Snapchat) start off as pure APIs.

If you aren't sure which category your application falls into, don't worry: the concepts overlap. A pure API is to a hybrid web application as a square is to a rectangle. We'll spend the first half of this book building a pure API, and the remaining chapters extending and maintaining it as it transitions into a hybrid web application.

1.3 Why Sails?

Sails' ensemble of small modules works together to provide simplicity, maintainability, and structural conventions to Node.js apps. Sails is highly configurable, so you won't be forced into keeping functionality you don't need. But at the same time, it provides a lot of powerful features by default, so you can start developing your app without having to think about configuration. Here are some of the things Sails does right out of the box:

- *100% JavaScript*—Like other MVC frameworks, Sails is built with an emphasis on developer happiness and a convention-over-configuration philosophy. But Node.js takes this principle to the next level. Building on top of Sails means your app is written entirely in JavaScript, the language you and your team are already using in the browser. Because you spend less time shifting context, you're able to write code in a more consistent style, which makes development more productive and fun.

NOTE Both authors of this book can attest to how nice it is to work with *one language* instead of constantly switching back and forth between JavaScript and whatever backend language our company or customers are using. The best part? It means you get *really good* at it.

- *Rock-solid foundation*—Sails is built on Node.js, a popular, lightweight, server-side technology that allows developers to write blazing-fast, scalable network applications in JavaScript. It also uses Express for handling HTTP requests and Socket.IO for managing WebSockets. So if your app ever needs to get really low level, you can access the raw Express or Socket.IO objects. And there's another nice side effect: if you already have an Express app, your existing routes will work perfectly well in a Sails app, so migrating is a breeze.
- *Frontend agnostic*—Although the promise of "one language and/or framework to rule them all" is certainly enticing, it isn't always realistic. Different organizations, technologies, and personalities all have their preferred way of doing things.

It's because of this that Mike McNeil made Sails compatible with *any* frontend strategy, whether it's Angular, Backbone, iOS/Objective-C, Android/Java, Windows Phone, or something else that hasn't been invented yet. Plus, it's easy to serve up the same API to be consumed by another web service or community of developers.

- *Autogenerated REST APIs*—Sails comes with "blueprints" that help jumpstart your app's backend without writing any code. Just run `sails generate api dentist` and you'll get an API that lets you search, paginate, sort, filter, create, destroy, update, and associate dentists. Because these blueprint actions are built on the same underlying technology as Sails, they also work with WebSockets and any supported database out of the box.

- *Use any popular database*—Sails bundles a powerful object-relational mapping (ORM) tool, Waterline, which provides a simple data access layer that just works, no matter what database you're using. In addition to a plethora of community projects, officially supported adapters exist for MySQL, MongoDB, PostgreSQL, Redis, and local disk storage.

- *Powerful associations*—Sails offers a new take on the familiar relational model, aimed at making data modeling more practical. You can do all the same things you might be used to doing in an ORM (one-to-many, many-to-many), but you can also assign multiple *named* associations per model. For instance, a cake might have two collections of people: "havers" and "eaters." Better still, you can assign different models to different databases, and your associations/joins will still work—even across NoSQL and relational boundaries. Sails has no problem implicitly or automatically joining a MySQL table with a Mongo collection and vice versa.

- *Standardization*—When you build a Sails app, you're taking advantage of all sorts of open standards behind the scenes. Almost everything has a specification, from database and file upload adapters to hooks that make up the framework itself. Using the machine specification, you can even make *any function* in your app pluggable, making it easy to switch between different providers for services like email delivery and social authentication. Building on top of well-defined interfaces means that whenever you need to do something custom, your work is self-documenting, quick to implement, and simple to debug.

- *Node machine services*—The Machine Specification is an open standard for JavaScript functions. Each machine has a single, clear purpose—whether it be sending an email, translating a text file, or fetching a web page. Machines are self-documenting, quick to implement, and simple to debug.

- *Realtime with WebSockets*—Sails translates incoming socket messages for you, making them compatible with every route in your Sails app.

- *Reusable security policies*—Sails provides basic security and role-based access control by default.

- *Sails generators*—Sails provides a consistent way of creating projects using reasonable defaults. Sails also contains generators for automating many tasks like creating models and controllers. Generators are built on an extensible architecture, supported by a community of developers.

- *Flexible asset pipeline*—Sails ships with opinionated build scripts and a default directory structure for client-side assets. Out of the box, the asset pipeline provides support for LESS, CoffeeScript, precompiled client-side HTML templates, and production minification. This makes setting up new projects easy and consistent, but it does pose a problem when it comes time to tweak or completely redefine that tooling to fit your personal preferences or your organization's best practices. Fortunately, all the default automation in Sails is implemented as plugins for the Grunt task runner, which means your entire frontend asset workflow is completely customizable. It also means you can choose from the thousands of widely used, open source Grunt plugins already out there.

If you don't understand some of these bullet points, don't worry. Our goal isn't to teach you a bunch of jargon and acronyms. But by the end of the book, you'll have a firm conceptual grasp of each of these topics—and, more important, you'll be able to apply that understanding when building the backend for any of the different types of apps listed.

1.4 Fundamental concepts of a web application

Web application development is riddled with core concepts and terminology that may or may not be familiar to you. It's critical that we have a common frame of reference for them before we begin this extended journey together. This section is a jump-start to your understanding of an important core concept in backend development: the HTTP request/response protocol. If this seems like a review, feel free to skip to section 1.5, "Understanding databases."

1.4.1 Requests and responses

The heart of a web application is handling the conversations made through requests sent by the frontend and responses sent by the backend. We'll ease into this discussion using a tool we're all familiar with: the browser. To start with, let's take a look at the completed version of Brushfire, the application we'll build together throughout the rest of this book. Navigate your browser to https://brushfire.io, as shown in figure 1.1.

The browser just made a *request* on your behalf and the Sails server *responded* with the contents of the home page you now see displayed, as shown in figure 1.2.

When you're talking with a waiter, you might use a *protocol* such as English or Spanish to make a request ("Could I have a glass of water?") and receive a response ("Certainly!"). The same kind of conversation exists between a frontend and your Sails application, but because computers don't have the kinds of mouths, ears, or brains fit

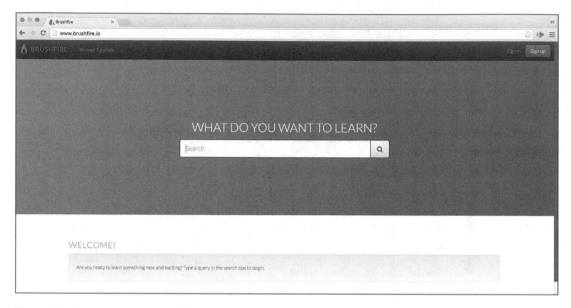

Figure 1.1   The contents of a response from an initial request by your browser to https://brushfire.io

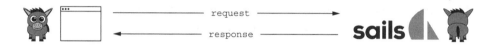

Figure 1.2   The frontend makes a request and the backend makes a response.

for processing human language, the client and server communicate by sending specially formatted strings back and forth. This conversation is called the *Hypertext Transfer Protocol (HTTP)*.

> **TIP**   "Wait, no one said anything about learning protocols!" HTTP is just an agreed-upon set of rules not unlike a rudimentary language. And it is this language that enables different devices that know how to speak HTTP to talk to each other. For the adventurous who want a low-level explanation, check out the Request For Comments (RFC) pages for HTTP found here, http://tools.ietf.org/html/rfc7230#page-5, which are surprisingly readable.

Requests and responses sent back and forth using the protocol comprise the underlying communication bridge between our frontend client and backend Sails server.

    Let's take a closer look at the actual request and the response. Click the Sign Up button in the upper navigation bar of the homepage, and you should see the signup page, as illustrated in figure 1.3.

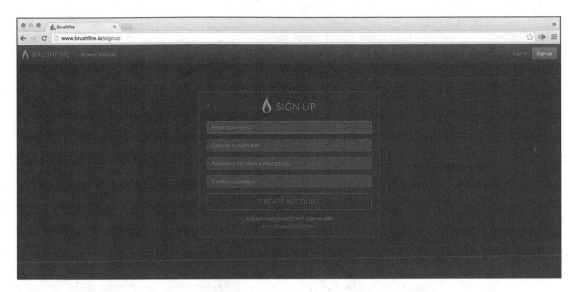

Figure 1.3 **Clicking the Sign Up button generates a request to the Sails backend, which responds with the signup page.**

Once again, the browser makes an HTTP request on your behalf and the Sails server responds, in this case with a string of HTML markup representing the signup page. Figure 1.4 displays an overview of the steps that culminate in the rendered signup page.

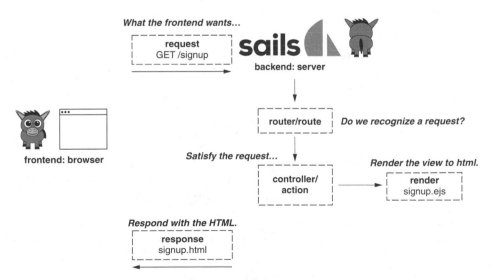

Figure 1.4 **The components necessary for the backend to satisfy the request and deliver the signup page to the frontend**

At a high level, figure 1.4 shows an often-repeated pattern of Sails components you'll use to build the backend. We'll focus on the details of each of these components in chapters 3 through 15. For now, let's concentrate on the request. A portion of the raw request string that was sent from your browser to Sails looks like this:

```
GET /signup HTTP/1.1
```

This is technically called the *request line* or *start line*, but what matters is that it consists of the *method* (GET) and the *path* (/signup).

> **NOTE**   For our purposes, the protocol version (HTTP/1.1) can be ignored— we're interested in just the method and the path. The request contains two other things we care about: *request headers* and a *request body*. We'll discuss them a little later in the book.

Next, let's move over to the response. The Sails server received the GET request to /signup and determined that the intent of the request was to receive a response containing the signup page. The first piece of the raw response string sent from the Sails server to your browser looks like this:

```
HTTP/1.1 200 OK
```

This portion of the response message is called the *response line* or *start line* and consists of the *protocol version*, HTTP/1.1, the *server status code*, 200, and something called the *textual reason phrase*, OK.

> **NOTE**   Naming stuff is probably the hardest thing to do in programming. It's so hard that we get names like *textual reason phrase*.

The important part is the server status code (200), a special number that indicates the status or outcome of the request, like how the code exited. In addition to the status code, the response also contains the HTML of the startup page in a part of the response called the *response body*.

> **NOTE**   The complete response message also contained *response headers*, which aren't part of our example, so we'll postpone discussing them.

Now for some good news! Because requests originate in a limited number of ways, you'll rarely have to work with a raw request or a raw response. Instead, outgoing requests will be generated by one of the approaches in table 1.1.

Table 1.1   Sources of HTTP requests

Approach	Example
A browser URL bar	http://www.myApp.com/signup
An anchor tag	`<a href="http://www.myApp.com/signup"></a>`

Table 1.1   Sources of HTTP requests (*continued*)

Approach	Example
The browser's location property on the `window` dictionary	`window.location = "http://www.myApp.com/signup"`
The browser `window` dictionary `open` method	`window.open("http://www.myApp.com/signup")`

An AJAX request	<pre>$.ajax({
	  url: '/signup',
	  type: 'GET',
	  success: function(result){
	    console.log('result: ', result);
	  },
	  error: function(xhr, status, err){
	    console.log(err);
	  }
	});</pre>

Via an HTTP library (Android example)	<pre>// Instantiate the RequestQueue.
	RequestQueue queue = Volley.newRequestQueue(this);
	String url ="http://www.google.com";
	
	// Request a string response from the provided URL.
	StringRequest stringRequest = new
	StringRequest(Request.Method.GET, url,
	        new Response.Listener<String>() {
	    @Override
	    public void onResponse(String response) {
	        // Display the first 500 characters of the
	response string.
	        mTextView.setText("Response is: "+
	response.substring(0,500));
	        }
	}, new Response.ErrorListener() {
	    @Override
	    public void onErrorResponse(VolleyError error) {
	        mTextView.setText("That didn't work!");
	        }
	});
	// Add the request to the RequestQueue.
	queue.add(stringRequest);</pre>

Incoming raw requests to the backend are parsed and transformed by Sails into dictionaries with properties you can easily access in your backend code.

DEFINITION   What—JavaScript has dictionaries? Because the word *object* is used ubiquitously in JavaScript to describe almost everything, we use the term *dictionary* to refer to an *object* that's declared using {} curly braces. For example, { foo: 'bar' } is a dictionary.

For outgoing responses, you'll rely on Sails' built-in methods for responding to a request with JSON or a dynamic HTML web page. This allows you to focus on how your application is supposed to work, instead of the detailed minutiae of HTTP.

> **NOTE** For 99% of use cases, this level of abstraction is more than flexible enough. But if you ever need lower-level access, don't worry. Sails and Node.js allow you to work directly with the underlying HTTP request and response streams on a case-by-case basis.

Now that you know a bit more about the request and response, let's explore how they're used to successfully fulfill the requirements of our application.

1.4.2   HTTP methods

In section 1.4.1, we introduced HTTP as a way for the frontend and backend to send data back and forth. But requests are useful for more than just transporting data: they also convey intent. The Sails server must interpret that intent and respond with something that fulfills the requirements of the initial request. Let's examine how this communication is accomplished using the signup page as a real-world example. In your browser, fill out the Brushfire signup form you navigated to earlier, and click Create Account. This triggers an AJAX request from the browser. An overview of this request/response can be found in figure 1.5.

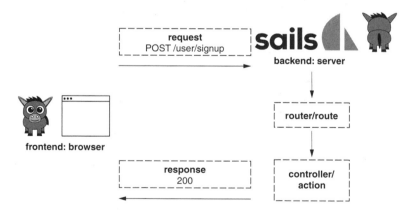

Figure 1.5   The components necessary for the backend to satisfy the request by creating a user and responding with the result

Once again, don't get overwhelmed by the details; we'll reinforce each component many times with examples. If you looked at the raw request string, it would look like this:

```
POST /user/signup HTTP/1.1
```

Because the request included the method, POST, and the path, /user/signup, in this example, you'd say that the browser sent a POST request to /user/signup. HTTP methods (also known as *verbs*) like POST, GET, PUT, and DELETE are simply labels that help indicate the intent of a request.

> **NOTE** The request on the signup page is intended to create a new user. Shortly, you'll see that the frontend and backend have made an agreement that when the frontend makes a POST request to /user/signup, the backend Sails server will create the user. The request is the frontend's portion of that agreement.

The term *HTTP method* can be confusing because it gives the impression that each method has some inherent, specific purpose. The reality is that the method label, POST, doesn't inherently do anything. It can express your intent, but it's up to the backend to determine how to interpret that intent and respond.

For example, you could create a Sails app that interprets a GET request to the path /signup as a request to create a new user. Technically, this would work just fine, but it would be a bad idea, because it would violate a common convention.

> **DEFINITION** We use the term *convention* to mean an informal agreement between programmers for how something is supposed to work. It's usually a bad idea to break conventions. Not only do they make it easier for developers to collaborate and get up to speed on a code base, but they also make it easier for you to remember how your app works as it matures.

The GET method, by convention, is used to indicate that an action is *cacheable* or *safe*, because nothing should change as a result of making a GET request. If your backend interpreted a GET request to the path /signup as a request to create a new user, adding the user would violate this convention. The conventional side effects of each HTTP method are listed in table 1.2.

Table 1.2 HTTP method conventions

Method	Side effects
GET	Should be *cacheable*; that is, sending a GET request shouldn't cause any side effects. Often used for fetching data.
POST	No guarantees. Any given POST request could cause side effects such as sending an email or creating a pet store in the database.
PUT	Should be *idempotent;* that is, sending the same PUT request over and over has the same side effects as sending it only once. Often associated with updating a resource.
DELETE	Should be idempotent (see the previous entry). Often associated with deleting a resource.

But we want to stress again that these are what the methods *should* do according to convention. It will be up to you to implement them in this way on the backend.

The other part of the request is the URL *path*, which looks like a file system path on your computer's local hard disk. Although a path can be anything, more often the path is simply a reference to a *resource* and *action*. For example, the path /user/signup consists of a *user* resource and a *signup* action.

> **TIP**   You can think of a *resource* as a label that groups related tasks together and an *action* as one of those tasks.

By combining the POST method with the path /user/signup, you convey the request's intent—to sign up or create a new user.

Next, let's move to the response. The Sails server received the POST request to /user/signup, interpreted its intent, and as you'll see later, created the user account before responding to the browser like this:

```
HTTP/1.1 200 OK
```

Here, the only part of the response line you're interested in is the status code.

> **DEFINITION**   The conventional meaning of a *status code* is even more ingrained than the conventional meaning behind HTTP method labels. You'll use status codes in your responses as a shorthand way to convey the status of a request. In this case, the Sails server responded with a status 200, signaling that the creation of the user account was successful. For an exhaustive list of conventional status codes, see https://www.w3.org/Protocols/rfc2616/rfc2616-sec10.html.

In our previous example, you learned how the request can convey intent to create a user. But what interprets that intent on the backend? The short answer is that Sails matches the incoming request with a route using its built-in router. We'll explore routes and the router in the next section.

1.4.3   *Routing*

It's easier to examine how Sails interprets the intent of an incoming request using figure 1.6.

Recall that in the earlier example you made an AJAX POST request to /user/signup. Sails "heard" the request via a built-in module called the *router* ❶. The router recognized

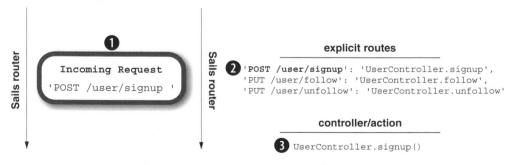

Figure 1.6   Understanding how the Sails router matches the incoming request with routes to trigger an action

the particular request because the request matched ❷ the configured route address of an *explicit route*, and then that triggered an action ❸, as illustrated in figure 1.7.

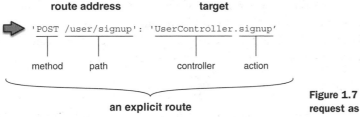

Figure 1.7 The router matched the request as part of an explicit route.

In Sails, explicit routes are configured in a JavaScript file, where they're written as a dictionary with a key for each unique route. The key POST /user/signup is called the *route address*, and it consists of the HTTP method and path. On the right side, every explicit route has a *route target*, special syntax that tells Sails what to do when it receives matching requests. In most cases, this route target consists of a controller, UserController, and an action, signup. When a request is made, the router looks for a matching route address, and if it finds one, it executes the corresponding controller action.

NOTE The action is itself a JavaScript function, and the controller is a name we give the dictionary that aggregates actions under a common resource. So in the signup example, you named the controller UserController because the actions will all concern a user.

It's easy to get lost in all the new terminology, so let's compare a route to something you already understand, a jQuery click event, in figure 1.8.

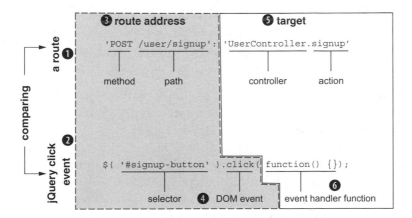

Figure 1.8 A route ❶ operates like a click event handler ❷. The route address ❸ serves a similar purpose to the combination of the DOM selector ❹ and DOM event. And the route target ❺ is similar to an event handler function ❻.

When the Sails router analyzes an incoming request, POST /user/signup HTTP/1.1, and it matches a route's method and path, POST /user/signup, it executes the controller action similarly to the way the browser analyzes an incoming DOM event, matches it against a particular selector, and executes an event handler function.

Now that you can convey intent from the frontend via a request and interpret that intent on the backend using a route and a router, let's explore how to fulfill the requirements of the request on the backend using controller actions.

1.4.4   *Performing actions*

To better understand controller actions (or simply *actions*), let's focus on an example: a signup form. When the user submits the form, a POST request is sent to /user/signup. When it arrives at the Sails backend, the request is automatically compared with your app's configured routes. The first matching route will be triggered, which then calls a controller action. It's the job of this controller action to fulfill the requirements of this request. Recall that actions are just JavaScript functions and that controllers are just dictionaries of related actions.

The requirements for the example endpoint ('POST /user/signup') are to create a new user, store that user in your database, and respond with the status code of 200 to indicate success. If anything goes wrong, you'll want to respond with a different status code, depending on what issue or error occurred. These requirements seem simple, but they bring up some fundamental questions about Sails:

- How do you send the data harvested from your form input elements to the backend, for example, email, username, and password?
- How do you tell Sails where to put the new user's data? And how do you tell it which database to use?
- Speaking of that, what code do you write to store the properties of a user in the database? And where should you write it?
- How do you tell Sails you're finished—in other words, that you'd like to send a response to the requesting user-agent (your form)? And how do you tell Sails what status code and/or data to use?

A significant portion of the book is devoted to answering these questions in detail, so we mustn't get ahead of ourselves. But the least we can do is take a first step toward explaining the answers to these questions right away.

First, a bit about actions: Because you already know actions are JavaScript functions, it probably won't come as a shock that they also receive arguments. The first of these arguments (req) represents the incoming request, and the second (res) represents the eventual outgoing response. Both req and res are special objects called *streams* that come from the depths of Node.js Core. Fortunately, you rarely (if ever) have to think about them that way, because by the time you get hold of req and res in your Sails actions, they've been loaded up with a ton of useful properties and convenient functions that make your life much simpler.

> ### The flexibility of req and res
> One of the great things about Node.js is that even when you hide away complexity with helper methods, all the advanced and powerful features are still there, working their magic behind the scenes. Because `req` and `res` are still technically Node.js streams, you have as much flexibility as you would with Node.js out of the box. Imagine some ridiculously specific use case; perhaps you need to handle strange requests from a legacy point-of-sale system (read: broken-down cash register) in a small fish bait shop. And maybe that PoS system doesn't expect a normal response—instead it expects your server to slowly drip-drop each letter of the alphabet, one every second over the course of two long, excruciating minutes. No problem! You'll write your code to handle the incoming requests from that cash register in the same place you'd write any of your other request-handling code in Sails: an action.

From your action, you can access the data that the user originally typed into the form on your signup page by calling `req.param()`, one of the functions provided on the `req` dictionary. For example, when you call `req.param('username')`, it will return the value from the `username` input element in your form. This begs the question, though, how is the frontend sending these values (called *parameters*) to your action in the first place? If you were sending this request from a native iPhone app or your terminal, the way parameters are bundled would completely depend on the HTTP client library used to create the request. But in this example, because you use a web page as your frontend, you can narrow things down a bit. There are three common ways that parameters are included in a request from a web browser to the backend:

- When using a regular or traditional form submission, the contents of form input elements are included automatically as parameters in the request when the form is submitted. Depending on the method you put in your HTML, these parameters are bundled in either the request's body or in its *URL query string* (sometimes simply called the *query string*).
- When using an AJAX request, the parameters can be included in either the URL query string or in the body of a request.
- When navigating to a URL by pressing Enter in your browser's address bar, including parameters is as simple as typing out a URL query string by hand.

Remember the request line from an HTTP request we looked at earlier?

```
POST /user/signup HTTP/1.1
```

Well, the body is just another line like that in the HTTP request. It's used to transport stuff like the `email` and `password` parameters from your form. Don't overthink the term *body*. Even though it might seem foreign at first compared with something more familiar like a URL, it's just another way to stick data in a request.

The URL query string is similar in that it's another way to transport stuff inside a request, but luckily, it's even simpler to explain. You've probably seen query strings countless times already in your browser's address bar. This is because, as you can see from figure 1.9, the query string is just a part of the URL.

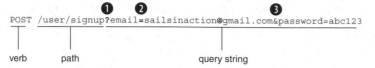

Figure 1.9   **An example of the URL query string that starts with a question mark, contains a key/value pair separated by an equals sign, and is separated by an ampersand**

The URL query string begins with a question mark (?) **❶** followed by parameter key/value pairs, where the name of each parameter is separated from its value by an equals sign (=) **❷**. The key/value pairs are separated from each other by ampersands (&) **❸**.

When do you use the body and when do you use a query string? The short answer is most of the time the frontend framework or utility you're using makes the choice for you. For example, in jQuery if you use the `$.get()` syntax to send an AJAX request, the parameters will be transformed into a query string and tacked on at the end of the URL:

```
$.get('/dogs', {
  page: 4
}, function(data){ ... });
```

On the other hand, if you send a `POST` request using `$.post()` syntax, jQuery will bundle the parameters in the request's body:

```
$.post('/user/signup', {
email: 'sailsinaction@gmail.com',
password: 'abc123'
}, function(data){ ... });
```

So what's the difference? If the URL query string and the body are just two different ways to include parameters in a request, why use one over the other? The truth is that 99% of the time it doesn't have any practical impact on your code. A recurring philosophy in Sails is encapsulation; in other words, it shouldn't matter *how* you send parameters in your requests to the backend; what matters is *what* you send. That said, certain security considerations dictate when you can and can't safely use the URL query string, so we'll return briefly to this subject to cover best practices when we explore shortcut routes and the blueprint API in chapter 4.

We realize that it's a bit of a paradox for us to show you parts of the raw HTTP request but then go on to say that you'll rarely, if ever, interact with them in their raw state. You may be wondering, "Why do I care? You're not my algebra teacher! I don't need to know this!" Fair enough. On the frontend, we could have simply shown the syntax of how to send an AJAX request with jQuery, which demonstrates the verb and the path. We could have turned to the backend and showed the same verb and path in a route address. We could even have pointed you to a video with zooming cloud imagery and whooshing noises, to help you visualize the journey of a request in flight.

But that would be doing you a disservice. It's been the experience of both authors of this book that it was not until we *completely* demystified the raw HTTP request and response that we were able to intuitively understand how servers really work: by slurping up strings and spitting new strings back out. But enough didactics.

An important thing to remember is that you send requests to communicate intent and transport stuff, intent like "Enroll this new user, please" and stuff like { `email:` `chad@hotmail.com` }. When you send a request from a browser or any other user-agent, you're simply generating a string called an HTTP request and blasting it out to the internet. Your request is just like any other string, except that it's specially formatted according to a well-defined standard called HTTP. That means it contains a method (a.k.a. verb), a URL, and maybe some headers and a body.

When your Sails server receives a request, it's parsed and routed to one of your controller actions automatically, at which point Sails runs your code. That backend code tells the server what to do next, whether that's sending an email, saving data, doing math, operating robot arms to play dueling banjos, or a combination of all these. Eventually, this backend code should always send a response; otherwise, the frontend would sit there waiting forever.

When the code in your controller action indicates that it's time to respond, Sails generates a string called an HTTP response and blasts it back out to the internet. This response is—you guessed it—also formatted according to the HTTP standard. It contains a status code and maybe some headers and a body of its own. The status code is used for specifying the outcome of the request, for example, to indicate that a new user was successfully created, or that the provided email address was already in use, or even that some other unexpected error occurred. The response body is used for transporting any relevant data back to the frontend, stuff like JSON data or an HTML web page.

Finally, back on the frontend, the user-agent (browser) receives and parses the response. Then it acts accordingly. For example, if you're using AJAX, jQuery triggers the callback function you provided. And that's it—back where you started!

Now that we've demystified the request and response a bit and set up the related terminology we'll use throughout the book, we're ready to explore what's going on in the backend code itself. We'll start with the most fundamental responsibility of any backend application: working with data.

1.5 *Understanding databases*

Although some experience with a database is helpful, it's not required for you to get through this book. In this section, we'll give a brief introduction to databases in the context of what you'll need to know about them while creating a Sails application.

Specifically, we'll talk about Sails models and the methods used to access various databases. We'll also take a deep dive into the subject of models in chapter 6. If you're already familiar with these concepts, feel free to skip to section 1.6.

A database can seem mysterious at first. But it's just another application: an application that stores an organized collection of data into records. In most cases, but not always, the database stores records in nonvolatile memory like your computer's hard drive. Or, infrequently, the records are stored using volatile memory like the RAM in your computer. A database even has its own API, similar to the one you'll design in the coming chapters. But unlike the web API you'll build in this book, which uses HTTP to communicate between the client and server, the underlying protocol you use to communicate between a Sails app and a database is abstracted away for you by a built-in component of Sails called *Waterline*.

> **TIP**   What's the difference between Sails and Waterline? Sails is composed of many Node.js modules that work together to help you build web applications. Waterline is one of those modules.

Waterline gives your Sails apps an abstraction layer on top of underlying databases like MongoDB or PostgreSQL, providing methods that allow you to easily query and manipulate data without writing PostgreSQL-specific integration code. Sails organizes these methods in a dictionary called a *model*.

1.5.1   *What's in a Sails model?*

A Sails model is a JavaScript dictionary representing a *resource* such as a MySQL table or a MongoDB collection. Every model contains attribute definitions, model methods, and other settings. When you start a Sails app, the framework automatically builds up model dictionaries from a variety of configuration files in your project, adding a whole suite of powerful methods. Your code can then use these methods to find and manipulate database records (a.k.a. rows). Let's look at the PostgreSQL database as an example and use the signup page frontend as a reference. You might define a model called User to store username, email, and password attributes, as displayed in figure 1.10.

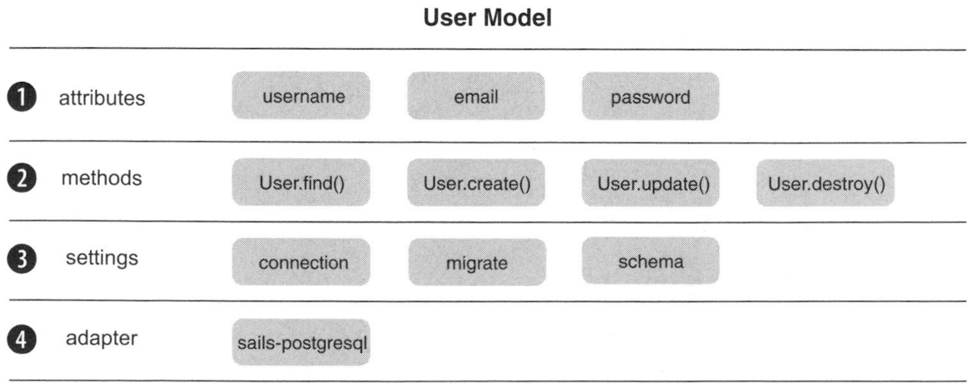

User Model

1 attributes	username	email	password	
2 methods	User.find()	User.create()	User.update()	User.destroy()
3 settings	connection	migrate	schema	
4 adapter	sails-postgresql			

Figure 1.10   The components of a model include attributes, methods, and settings.

The attributes ❶ describe the properties of each `user` record that the database will be tasked with managing—in this case, `username`, `email`, and `password`.

> **NOTE** Attribute definitions are optional when working with some databases like MongoDB, whereas other databases like PostgreSQL require predefined attributes.

Model methods ❷ are the built-in set of functions provided by Sails that you use to find and manipulate records. Model settings ❸ include configurable properties like `connection`, `tableName`, `migrate`, and `schema`. Of particular importance is the `connection` setting, which describes the database the model methods will be run on.

> **NOTE** In Sails v1.0 and above, the `connection` setting for a model is referred to as its *datastore*. To make sure you're comfortable with both terms, we'll use them interchangeably throughout the book.

For example, if you use the `User.find()` method to find a particular record, this option tells Sails which database to search. The `connection` points to a dictionary that contains configuration information like the host, port, and credentials necessary to access the database. If any of that sounds unfamiliar, don't worry—we'll come back to it a few times throughout the book. Another model setting, `migrate`, designates how Sails should handle existing records in the database and whether or not to use auto-migration. As a final example, the `schema` setting allows you to enforce the use of a schema, even if the underlying database would allow you to proceed without one. This is particularly useful for schemaless databases like MongoDB.

The adapter ❹ is a Node.js module that allows your model to communicate with virtually any type of database, whether that's a traditional relational database like PostgreSQL or a non-relational database like MongoDB. As long as you install the adapter for a particular database, your app can talk to it using built-in model methods provided by Sails. Behind the scenes, the adapter takes care of translating code that uses model methods into the specific queries required by the underlying database system. The adapter to use for a particular model is determined by its `connection` setting.

1.5.2 Sails model methods

Earlier we briefly mentioned blueprint actions: `find`, `create`, `update`, and `destroy`. These built-in actions are provided by Sails, but, internally, they use functions we call *model methods* to fetch and manipulate records in a database. These are the same methods you'll call in your custom controller actions later in the book. Table 1.3 displays the most commonly used model methods provided by Sails.

Table 1.3 Common model methods

Method	Description
`.create()`	Creates a new record in the database
`.find()`	Finds and returns all records that match a certain criteria

Table 1.3   Common model methods *(continued)*

Method	Description
`.findOne()`	Attempts to find a particular record in your database that matches the given criteria
`.update()`	Updates existing records in the database that match the specified criteria
`.destroy()`	Destroys records in your database that match the given criteria
`.count()`	Returns the number of records in your database that meet the given search criteria

We'll start messing with databases in chapters 4 and 5 and get immersed in them in chapter 6.

> **NOTE**   In Sails, like most web frameworks, you can write code that works with the database that can be run from anywhere from tests to custom scripts. But for most apps, the overwhelming majority of the data-manipulation code you write will be triggered as the result of incoming web requests.

1.6   *Putting it all together in a backend API*

Now that we've covered the fundamental pieces of any Sails application, let's take what you've learned so far and see how it all fits together. You saw how the frontend talks to your Sails app by sending HTTP requests and how your Sails app replies with HTTP responses. We looked at how every time your Sails app receives a request, it uses your configured routes to determine which controller action to run. And in the last section, we introduced model methods, which are just one example of the many Sails and Node.js library methods you can call from the backend code in your controller actions. But, in theory, you could create almost any imaginable server-side web application with routes and controller actions alone. Routes and controller actions are the fundamental pieces of any Sails application. In practice, controller actions usually leverage many additional library methods provided by Sails and Node.js.

Controller actions can be simple or complex. For example, in the same app you might write one controller action (`PageController.showHomePage`) that simply responds with an HTML web page and another (`CartController.checkout`) that uses model methods to fetch data, calls out to a service with custom business logic, contacts a third-party service to process a bitcoin transaction, and responds with a `200` status code to indicate success. Thinking about the different parts of your application this way can get very complicated very quickly—particularly as time passes and more hands touch the code.

Luckily, there's another, simpler way to reason about the backend that's widely accepted by developers all over the world. Regardless of *what* a particular controller action (or endpoint) does, it's usually pretty easy to discuss *how it responds* and *why it ran* in the first place. Instead of focusing on the code inside the controller action, you can simply consider the request you need to send from the frontend to kick it off and the response you expect to receive in return. In the example of the complicated controller action we mentioned earlier (CartController.checkout), instead of thinking about the mechanics of working with the database and calling a third-party service, you can simply remember that to call the endpoint you need to send a POST request to /checkout and that you can expect a 200 status code in response (provided everything went according to plan).

Any abstraction that allows developers to think about what to call and what to expect in return (instead of having to be aware of the internals of how something works) is called an *application programming interface (API)*. More specifically, when talking about HTTP requests and responses, we call this a *backend API*.

> **DEFINITION**   At times you might also hear the backend API called a web API, cloud API, or even simply the API. No matter the variation in terminology, rest assured that this just refers to the interface exposed by the routes and actions in your Sails app.

Figure 1.11 provides a birds-eye view of how all the pieces we discussed earlier in this chapter work together in harmony to expose a backend API from your Sails app to the world. When Sails receives an incoming request ❶, it matches it against one of your app's routes ❷. Then, it runs the appropriate controller action ❸, whose job it is to send some sort of response ❹.

You'll see this pattern repeated throughout the book.

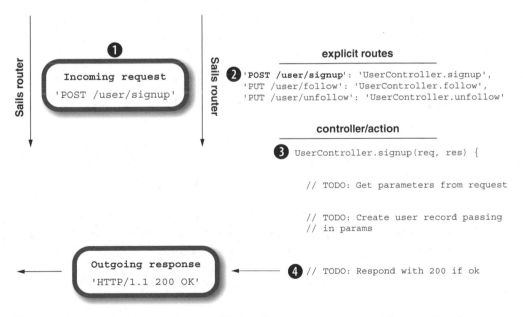

Figure 1.11   An endpoint from a backend API in action, processing a request from a signup form

1.6.1 Other types of routes

In addition to the explicit routes you define for serving web pages or working with the database, Sails includes some additional routes of its own, named *shadow routes*. Unlike explicit routes, which you write yourself, shadow routes are exposed automatically behind the scenes. Many web frameworks have a similar concept of automatic routing, specifically for assets. For example, adding a file called foo.jpg to the folder configured as the web root for an Apache web server implicitly causes GET requests to /foo.jpg to respond with the contents of that file. As you might expect, Sails provides a similar abstraction for static assets like images and client-side JavaScript files, sometimes called *asset routes*. These routes are exposed automatically and map directly to any files in the configured web root folder (.tmp/public/ by default). We'll examine asset routes extensively in chapter 3.

The framework also exposes a couple of other important shadow routes that we'll cover in this book:

- *Blueprint routes* automate the prototyping phase of backend development by providing an easy way to work with blueprint actions through a conventional API. We'll cover blueprints extensively in chapter 4.
- The *cross-site request forgery (CSRF) token route* is a built-in utility designed for use as part of an overall protection technique to prevent CSRF attacks. We'll cover this shadow route when we show how to secure your applications against CSRF vulnerabilities in chapter 15.

> **TIP** Like any of the other "magic" features in Sails, you can use as many or as few of them as you like. Every shadow route can be disabled via configuration or overridden on a case-by-case basis by defining an explicit route with the same HTTP method and URL pattern.

1.7 Our backend design philosophy

Now that you have a better understanding of both the components of a backend API and how they function, it's worth spending a moment on the overall approach we'll take in this book. When you set out to build a web application, it's difficult to know exactly where to start. Conventional wisdom is mixed on the subject; some books suggest starting with UML diagrams and data modeling before you write a single line of code. More recently, the "Ship early, ship often" mantra (for example, Facebook's "Move fast and break things" motto) is becoming increasingly popular. This approach suggests getting to a first prototype as quickly as possible.

We've built many startup products and enterprise tools, and in every case we've found that the best place to begin is from the user's perspective. We call this a *frontend-first* approach to backend design; see figure 1.12.

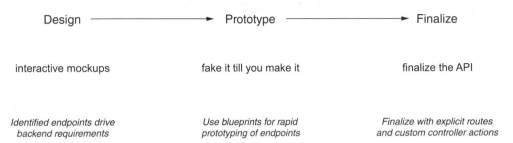

Figure 1.12   The frontend-first approach to backend development

Too often, development can get mired in what-if backend programming, that is, programming the backend to handle all of the things that the user *might* do rather than figuring out what the frontend will actually *allow* them to do and implementing only those features. Without direction, you can waste a lot of time creating things that are either unnecessary or aren't compatible with how the user will ultimately engage the frontend. Even worse, once created, backend code must be maintained—whether it's used or not! It's critical to spend the time necessary to identify the requirements for each of the API endpoints you build. Even if you think that an endpoint might be used in more ways down the road, the important thing is to optimize for the frontend you have today. It's always better to build the simplest, most specific API that meets your needs, even if it might need to be changed substantially someday as new features are added to the user interface.

If you come from a design or user experience–design background, this may sound familiar. When designing user interfaces, we always prioritize the needs of human users before making decisions on the implementation. Similarly, as backend developers, it's our responsibility to make sure that user interaction drives backend functionality and not vice versa.

1.7.1   *Starting with just the frontend code*

The easiest way to make sure you build exactly the backend API you need is to build the frontend part of your app first. Until you add the real backend, this will feel more or less like a fake, interactive mockup. But it captures the basic functionality of the interface you're trying to build, and it ensures that you've taken all the requirements into account before you begin. For example, the signup form in figure 1.13 inspired the design of the POST /signup endpoint we showed previously in section 1.4.

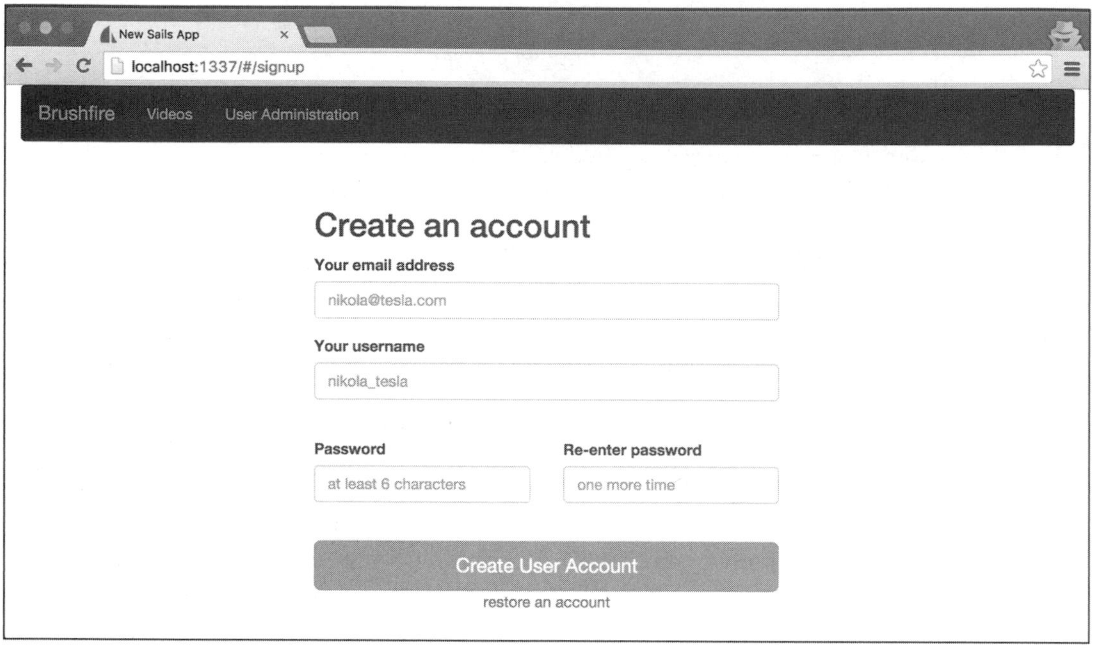

Figure 1.13 An interactive mockup of a signup form. The fields in this form help determine the request parameters you should expect when designing the API endpoint to process it.

This interactive mockup consists of the code necessary to drive the frontend user experience. For websites and single-page apps, this is HTML, CSS, images, and client-side JavaScript files. For an iOS native app, it's the .nib files, Swift scripts, and other assets you need to compile your project in Xcode. The goal is to finalize the key pieces of the frontend of the user interface, because that will identify all the requests that will need to be made from a particular screen, as well as the requirements of each request. Figure 1.14 shows an annotated example of how you might design your API endpoints based on the requirements of this page.

Not only does this approach help you notice inconsistencies in requirements and catch gaps in the feature set early in the process, but it also allows you to punt on critical architectural decisions until you know more about how your application will work. Once you've created interactive mockups and used them to identify the requirements of your backend, you can use tools that Sails provides to quickly transform those interactive mockups into working prototypes.

1.7.2 *Prototyping with blueprints*

So far, we've focused on how you can create your own custom routes and controller actions to create backend APIs in Sails. Recall that in section 1.5, we showed how you might combine an explicit route and a custom action to expose an API endpoint for

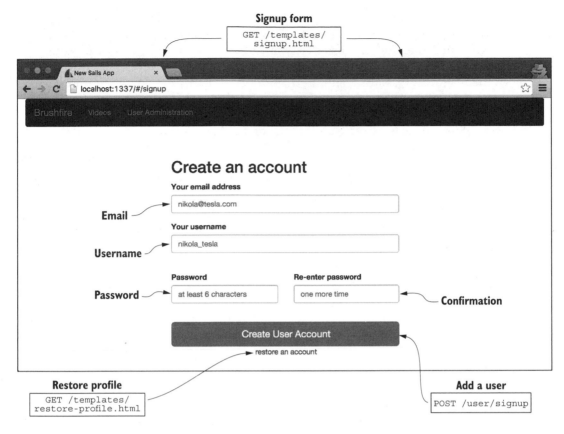

Figure 1.14 An annotated mockup showing the requests this user interface will send to your Sails app

handling new user signups. Under the covers, it's hard to say exactly what this API endpoint might need to do; you don't know enough details just by looking at the form in isolation. It might send a welcome email, encrypt a password, or even send a confirmation text message. But even without knowing all of the details, you can at least assume that it would need to create a new record in your database.

Traditionally, in this scenario, frontend developers were forced to use setTimeouts or to create a dictionary to fake a response with some JSON data. This allowed developers to test loading spinners and gave the user interface code some data to use temporarily until a backend API endpoint similar to the one for the signup page was available. Fortunately, for many use cases, Sails blueprints make this kind of temporary, throwaway code unnecessary. Instead, frontend developers can just set up a quick set of API endpoints (a JSON CRUD API) around a particular resource, such as a user. Those endpoints are then immediately available to use from frontend code, meaning that the frontend code can be finished and hooked up to the server ahead of any custom backend work.

NOTE JSON is called a lightweight data-interchange format. What that means for you is it's a way to safely transfer data from the client to the server and vice versa. In Node.js or the browser, you can take almost any JavaScript value stored in memory (for example, a variable containing a dictionary with an email address, password, and username) and stringify it, converting it into a specially encoded string. That string can then be transported over the network from the backend to the frontend or vice versa. On the receiving end, the JSON string is parsed back into the original JavaScript value.

Because you can create them very quickly, blueprints are incredibly useful during the prototyping phase. Instead of having to manually create the routes, controller actions, and model methods necessary to create an API before you even understand what it needs to do, you can use Sails' blueprint API to supply similar functionality. To set up blueprints for your signup example, you need only issue a single command in the terminal window:

```
~/sailsProject $ sails generate api user
```

Then, the next time you start the Sails server with `sails lift`, you'll have access to a JSON CRUD API around the `user` resource. Table 1.4 shows the shadow routes and built-in controller actions that this exposes automatically.

Table 1.4   Shadow routes and built-in controller actions exposed by the blueprint API

CRUD operation	Blueprint shortcut route			Blueprint RESTful route		
	Route address		Target	Route address		Target
	Verb	Path	Blueprint action	Verb	Path	Blueprint action
Read	GET	/user/find	find	GET	/user	find
Read	GET	/user/find/:id	find	GET	/user/:id	find
Create	GET	/user/create	create	POST	/user	create
Update	GET	/user/update/:id	update	PUT	/user/:id	update
Delete	GET	/user/destroy/:id	destroy	DELETE	/user/:id	destroy

In chapter 4, we'll examine what each blueprint action can do. For now, just note that each action corresponds to a CRUD operation. So, instead of creating a custom route and controller action to handle form submissions from the signup page, you just ran a command on the terminal, and Sails took care of setting all that up for you.

Why not use blueprints for everything? The truth is, for most applications, CRUD alone isn't enough, and you'll need to write a custom controller action for most if not all of your endpoints. For example, your signup endpoint will eventually need to encrypt the user's password, and as we mentioned earlier, you might also want it to send a welcome email (or someday, even a text message). Fortunately, when the time comes, overriding blueprint actions is just as easy as making your own custom controller action. And, in the meantime, your frontend code has gone from an interactive mockup to a full-fledged, server-driven prototype.

> **Shortcut blueprints**
>
> You might have noticed a subset of blueprint routes known as *shortcut blueprint routes* (or just *shortcut blueprints*). These are just more shadow routes that point to the same, built-in blueprint actions. The only difference is that you can access all of them from your browser's URL bar. Seems like a bad idea, right? That's why you should *never* enable shortcut blueprints in your production application.
>
> What makes shortcut blueprints so insanely useful is that they allow you to quickly access and modify your data during development without needing to rely on a database-specific client like phpMyAdmin. As you build your application throughout this book, you'll take advantage of this Sails feature frequently.

1.7.3   Finalizing your API

There comes a point when blueprint actions alone are insufficient to meet the requirements of the frontend. Fortunately, transitioning to custom controller actions is easy: as we discussed earlier in this chapter, you just write code for the actions and then define explicit routes that point at them. As you can see in figure 1.15, the implementation of your Sails app doesn't affect the interface. In other words, as long as

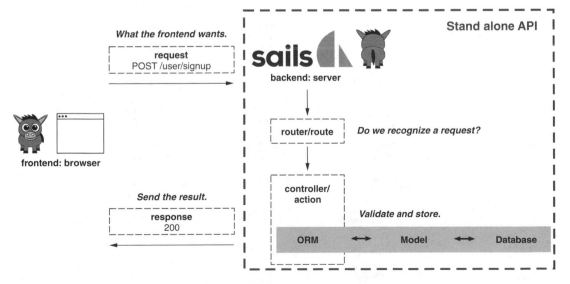

Figure 1.15   As long as the expected request and response for an API endpoint remain consistent, frontend code doesn't need to change.

your custom controller actions are written to be compatible with the requests that your frontend sends and the responses it expects, then your frontend code doesn't need to change at all.

Remember, controller actions are just JavaScript functions. This makes them incredibly powerful, because they can do anything that a JavaScript function can do. But with such great power comes great responsibility. You'll want to protect some of your actions, so that only certain logged-in users are allowed to run them. Fortunately, Sails provides a powerful feature for managing access to controller actions called *policies*. We'll explore and implement policies in chapter 10.

1.8   *Delivering frontend assets*

Now that you understand how clients and servers communicate and how to design and build backend APIs, we'll turn our attention to the frontend itself. *Wait a second, isn't Sails a backend framework?* It is! But for certain kinds of apps, the backend is responsible for *delivering* frontend assets. Whether that fits your Sails app depends on the types of frontends you're building or, more specifically, the types of *user-agents* your application will need to support.

> **DEFINITION**   A *user-agent* is any program that makes a request, such as browsers, spiders (web-based robots), command-line tools, custom applications, and mobile apps.

When we use the term *frontend*, we're talking about the user interface elements of your application. Figure 1.16 depicts the universe of common frontend user-agents for web applications.

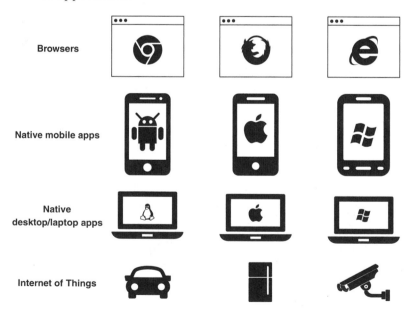

Figure 1.16   Examples of frontend user-agents used in web applications

If you were building a smart toaster or a native mobile or desktop application, you could skip ahead to chapter 4 and jump right into building and integrating a stellar, standalone API with Sails. Why? Because the frontend assets for Internet of Things (IoT), native mobile, and native desktop applications usually aren't distributed on the web. Instead, they're downloaded from an app store or bundled on a piece of hardware. Therefore, Sails can be blissfully unconcerned about their delivery. In that case, as shown in figure 1.17, all your Sails app has to worry about is requests for data (like a high score list) and behavior (like sending a text message or processing a signup).

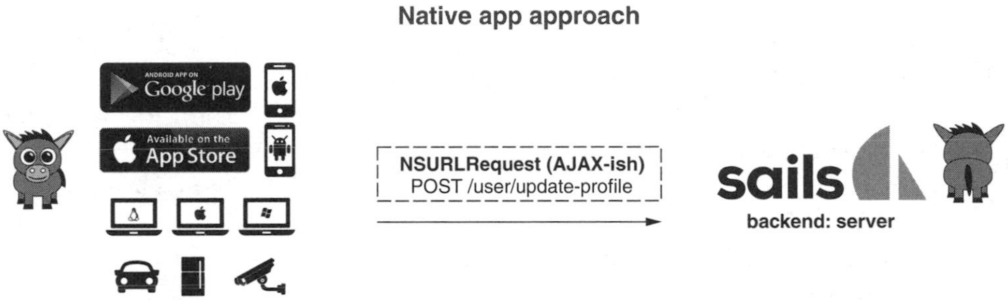

Figure 1.17 Sails used as a pure API with no responsibilities for delivering frontend assets

> **NOTE** There are two cases that may necessitate Sails delivering native app elements: for example, apps built using a frontend wrapper framework like PhoneGap or Electron. PhoneGap uses a browser within a native mobile app to display the UI. Some native app developers opt to deliver some or all frontend assets (for example, HTML, CSS, and JavaScript) via Sails because it allows for a greater degree of flexibility. In this case, treat the frontend like a browser user-agent and a single-page app.

Once installed, native and IoT applications make normal requests to Sails endpoints that fulfill backend requirements like storing and sharing data.

On the other hand, browser user-agents rely on some combination of HTML, CSS, and JavaScript for the frontend user interface. Instead of visiting an app store, users download the frontend app (or web page) by visiting a URL in their browser. If you plan to build an app that will support web browsers, then you need to decide how each page or view in the app will be delivered and ultimately rendered. There are two basic approaches: single-page apps (SPAs) and hybrid web applications. Figure 1.18 illustrates the two kinds of requests you can expect to see when building an SPA.

This approach is not too different from the approach for native apps because it relies on client-side rendering. The only real difference is that in addition to exposing endpoints for fetching data and triggering backend logic, Sails may also need to deliver static assets: files like images, HTML templates, client-side JavaScript, and style

SPA approach

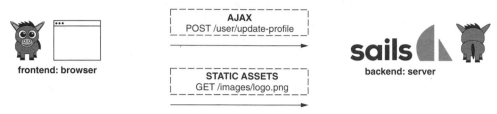

Figure 1.18   Typical frontend requests to the backend using the SPA approach

sheets. Using this approach, Sails delivers the initial HTML page as a static asset, and then client-side JavaScript (running in the browser) is responsible for making intermediate changes to the view via AJAX requests to the backend API. Wholesale page navigation, if any, is managed by special client-side JavaScript code (sometimes called a *client-side router*).

The second approach, a hybrid web application, relies (at least to some degree) on server-side rendering. That means Sails is responsible for preparing personalized, dynamic web pages on the backend from special templates called *views* and then delivering the personalized HTML to the browser. Figure 1.19 illustrates the kinds of requests you can expect to see if you're building a hybrid web application.

Hybrid approach

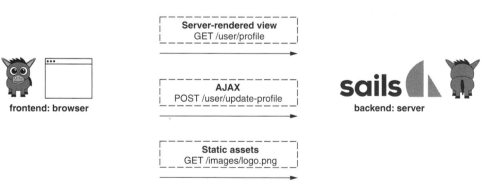

Figure 1.19   Delivering personalized HTML and static assets to a hybrid web application

Using this approach, Sails provides the initial server-rendered view for some or all of the pages on a website. Client-side JavaScript *might* also update the DOM by making calls to the Sails app, but most or all navigation between pages in a hybrid web application is handled by allowing users to navigate between different URLs in the browser, fetching freshly personalized HTML from the server each time.

Our experience, based on many client projects, has shown that when in doubt, the hybrid approach provides the best overall results. But in an effort to give you a broad knowledge base, we'll demonstrate both the SPA and hybrid approaches. We'll start by building an SPA in chapter 3. When it comes time to incorporate user authentication, access control, and SEO in chapter 8, we'll transition to the hybrid approach.

1.9 Frontend vs. backend validations

We'll address security throughout the book, with some extra emphasis on the subject in chapter 15. But in the meantime, we need to focus on an important security concept before you start building your application: whom can you trust? There are two basic realms in a web application: the frontend and the backend. Each of these realms guarantees a different level of trustworthiness and therefore requires a different degree of rigor when it comes to security, as depicted in figure 1.20.

Figure 1.20   The two security realms of a web application

We'll address the implications of this security reality as they come up periodically throughout the book. For example, in chapter 7, we'll introduce frontend validations to restrict users from creating a password with fewer than six characters. But because you can't trust the frontend, it's important to be aware of the possibility that the same user could maliciously use a tool like Postman or cURL to make any conceivable request from outside the browser, thus completely bypassing whatever frontend validation you put in place.

> **NOTE**   Another example of a security concern is a frontend that won't let the user submit a form until they fill out a required field. This is good UX, but your controller action on the backend still needs to do its own check, because it can't trust that the corresponding parameter will exist in the incoming request.

If you've done any sort of backend development, this concept might be old hat, but it's important enough that we wanted to address it up front. If this is a new concept for you, just remember this: you have to design your backend applications under the assumption that any given request *might* be malicious and could contain anything.

1.10 Realtime (WebSockets)

So far in this chapter, we've used HTTP to communicate between the user-agent (frontend) and the Sails server (backend). For most traditional web applications, this is all you need. The frontend always initiates requests, and whenever it receives a request, the backend responds. But for some apps that rely on features like chat (Slack), schedules (Nest thermostat), and realtime location tracking (Pokémon Go), this isn't enough.

Sails apps are capable of full-duplex realtime communication between the client and server. Instead of always having to initiate requests itself, client-side code can establish and maintain a persistent connection to a Sails server, allowing your backend code to send messages to individual clients or to broadcast messages to whole segments of your user base, at any time. In chapter 2, when you generate a new Sails app, start it up, and open your home page in the browser for the first time, you'll witness this behavior firsthand.

Sails implements support for realtime messaging and persistent connections using Socket.IO, a popular MIT-licensed open-source tool that helps ensure a wide array of legacy browser support, including Internet Explorer 7 and up. We'll explore WebSockets extensively in chapter 14.

> **DEFINITION**   In this book, we'll use both the terms *sockets* and *WebSockets* to refer to a two-way, persistent communication channel between a Sails app and a client. Communicating with a Sails app via WebSockets is really a form of AJAX, in that it allows a web page to interact with the server without refreshing. But sockets differ from traditional AJAX in two important ways: First, a socket can stay connected to the server for as long as the web page is open, allowing it to maintain state. Traditional AJAX requests, like all HTTP requests, are stateless. Second, because of the always-on nature of the connection, a Sails app can send data down to a socket at any time, whereas AJAX allows the server to respond only when a request is made.

1.11 Asynchronous programming

One of the highest hurdles for most new Node.js developers is learning how to write asynchronous code. Even if you're already familiar with AJAX callbacks, timeouts, and event handlers from client-side JavaScript, the sheer number of nested callbacks that show up when writing JavaScript on the server can be a bit intimidating at first. There are also new patterns to learn: concepts like asynchronous loops (`async.each`), asynchronous recursion (imagine building Dropbox in Node.js), and asynchronous conditionals (`if/then/finally`); or doing something asynchronous under some conditions and something synchronous under others.

In this book, we don't expect you to have any past experience writing asynchronous functions. We'll cover that in depth throughout the coming chapters. But before you start, it's a good idea to get familiar with what it means to use an asynchronous function and what that looks like.

Asynchronous JavaScript programming is very similar to web programming on the frontend. In a browser, you might want to trigger a function each time a button on the page is clicked. So you bind an *event handler* (a.k.a. *event listener*), which is just a callback function that will be executed whenever the button is clicked. Let's look at an example using jQuery.

Listing 1.1 jQuery callback pattern

```
$('#my-button').click(function whenClicked (){
  $.get('some3rdpartyAPI', function(data) {
    $('.result').html(data);
  });
});
```

⟵ **Sets up a callback function
(whenClicked) that will run anytime
the DOM element identified by
#my-button is clicked**

Listing 1.1 shows code that binds a callback as an event handler. Whenever the user clicks the specified button, the callback function (`whenClicked`) will run.

Now let's look on the backend for something similar. Let's say you want to create a user in a database. The time it takes to create the record in a database can vary, and you don't want every incoming request to your app to have to wait. Herein lies the beauty of Node.js, Sails, and server-side JavaScript in general: instead of blocking all incoming requests while the server communicates with the database, file system, or other third-party APIs, Node.js keeps working, allowing other requests to be processed while it waits, granting Node.js apps a huge scalability and performance boost.

But like everything in life, this comes with a price: instead of simply returning a value or throwing an error like normal code you might be used to, asynchronous function calls in Node.js expect you to provide a callback function. When Node.js hears back from the database, whether good news or bad, Node.js triggers the callback function you provided. If something goes wrong, the first argument (`err`) will be truthy. The pattern you'll see repeatedly is something like what's shown here.

Listing 1.2 A typical Node asynchronous callback pattern

```
User.create({name: nikola}).exec(function userCreated(err, newUser) {
  if (err) {
    console.log('the error is: ', err);
    return;
  }
  console.log("The result: ", newUser);
  return;

});
```

In this example, you want to create a user named `nikola`, and then once the user record has been created, you want Sails to log a message to the console. You provide a callback function, `userCreated`, that will be called once `User.create()` has finished. If anything goes wrong, your callback will receive a truthy `err`, which it will log to the console and then bail. Otherwise, everything works out, so a different message will be shown with the result from `User.create()`.

The important thing to recognize as a consumer of asynchronous functions in Node.js is that your later callback will always have at least one argument: `err`. And if the asynchronous function you're calling has output (as is the case with `.create()`), then you can expect a second argument: `newUser`. You can name these arguments whatever you want; it's often useful to name the second argument something that represents the expected result. By convention, the first argument is typically named `err` and it contains what you would think: a JavaScript error instance or at the very least some truthy value. This allows you to simply check `if (err) {…}` to find out if anything went wrong.

This pattern differs considerably from traditional synchronous programming, where you would do something like this:

```
var keys = Object.keys({name: 'nikola'});
```

In this example, when `Object.keys()` runs, the process is completely blocked until the JavaScript runtime can calculate an array consisting of all the keys from the specified dictionary. In the meantime, no other code runs, no callbacks are fired, and no new requests are handled. If everything works out, the synchronous instruction (a.k.a. function call), `Object.keys()`, returns the result (`['name']`). If something goes wrong (if this was `Object.keys(null)`, for example), then `Object.keys` will throw an error.

Handling uncaught exceptions

Possibly the most important thing to remember about writing code for Node.js is that throwing uncaught exceptions inside any callback from an asynchronous function *will cause your server to crash*. So it's imperative that, when writing code inside an asynchronous callback, you wrap anything that might throw in a `try/catch` block.

But don't worry! We'll reiterate this again and again throughout the book to help drive the point home. And once you've gotten used to this style of coding, you'll protect yourself by instinct. Eventually, you may even find, as we did, that writing code like this makes you a more efficient programmer (because it forces you to think about error conditions from the very beginning).

Finally, let's take a look at one last example that puts it all together. The next listing demonstrates what it looks like to use multiple asynchronous instructions (function calls) in a row.

Listing 1.3   Nesting other functions in an asynchronous function

```
Request.get('http://some3rdpartyAPI.com/user', function(err, response) {
  if (err) {
    console.log('the error is: ', err);
    return;
  }
  User.create({name: response.body.name}).exec(function(err, newUser) {
    if (err) {
      console.log('the error is: ', err);
      return;
    }
```

```
        console.log('The new user record: ', newUser);
        // All done!
        return;
    });//</after creating new user>
});//</after receiving response to 3rd party request>

// No code should go down here!
```

Here, you're doing a GET request to some other API, some3rdpartyAPI.com. You don't know when the response will come back, so you provide a callback that will be triggered when the request is completed. Then (in *that* callback), you create the user based on the response you got back. Notice that instead of writing one line of code after another, when using asynchronous instructions, you'll want to nest whatever comes next within the callback of the previous instruction.

In Node.js, like in most programming languages, in synchronous instructions time flows from top to bottom. If you write two instructions, one on line 3 and one on line 4, then the instruction on line 3 will run first, followed by the instruction on line 4. But in asynchronous instructions, time flows from *left to right*. If you write two asynchronous instructions, then the second instruction must be nested inside the callback of the first.

New Node.js developers often refer to this as *callback hell*. Some developers find several strategies helpful when attempting to mitigate the amount of nesting in Node.js code (promises, fibers, await, and so on). There are also some trusted tricks and indispensable tools, such as an npm package called async. We'll cover some of our own tricks, as well as best practices for working with async, on a few occasions throughout the book.

For now, bear in mind that like most hells, callback hell is subjective. Asynchronous callbacks are a reality of Node.js. And until you've accumulated some serious experience working with them, they can feel a bit clumsy. But you may find that after a few months you feel just as comfortable using them as you do writing traditional synchronous code.

Mastering callbacks

We can't stress enough how important it is to master the basic use of callbacks *before* attempting to learn technologies like promises, async/await, or fibers. We've seen and dealt with countless timing issues and memory leaks introduced in Node.js apps. The vast majority of them could have been easily avoided by following this advice. So please learn callbacks first. It's far too easy to introduce bugs in a well-intentioned attempt to reduce the number of callbacks in your code.

The examples in this book are designed to give you plenty of reps with callbacks. If you follow along, you'll be more than prepared to make an informed decision about whether to use callbacks or promises in your own application.

Okay, enough asynchronous programming theory. Even if your head is swimming with all the new vocabulary, don't despair! We promise that in a few chapters you'll look at asynchronous functions and marvel at how much you know and how easy they are to use.

That about wraps up our primer. We're almost ready to start building stuff! But first, in the final section of this chapter, we'll outline the recurring scenario and example application that we'll use throughout the remainder of the book.

1.12 Meet Chad

This book would be boring if we just droned on and on about "feature this" and "feature that." So, to keep you on the edge of your seat (and to keep us motivated) we invented a fictional character—a friend named Chad. Likely, you're thinking: "Been there, done that. No more books about invisible friends." Don't worry. We won't make a habit of it.

Chad considers himself quite savvy in the ways of social and viral media. He explained to us that he has a vision: "I'm going to build the most virally adopted web app in history." Clearly, what Chad lacks in development experience, he makes up for in confidence. Normally, we avoid partnerships like these, but Chad is a nice guy. He even referred us to a couple of clients, and he *is* letting us sleep in his house for a couple of weeks. Long story short, we agreed to help build his vision. The only problem is that Chad's vision changes from week to week. Currently, the only thing he's sure about is that "the app *must* include YouTube video clips."

Armed with those detailed requirements, we're sure to build a prototype of something amazing. We'll pick back up on that in chapter 3 when we explore static assets. But before bringing Chad into the mix, you need to get your environment ready and take Sails for a quick spin.

1.13 Summary

- The heart of any web application backend is in handling incoming requests.
- The anatomy of a backend API includes its routes and controller actions, which deliver on the requirements of an incoming request.
- The ORM tool in Sails, called Waterline, allows you to communicate with databases like MySQL or MongoDB using JavaScript.
- Three common types of applications whose assets are delivered in different ways by Sails are native apps, SPAs, and hybrid web applications.

First steps

2

This chapter covers

- Installing the necessary components of the technical stack
- Setting up the tools of your development environment
- Creating your first application
- Cloning your first repository

To get things started, you'll set up your development environment. This will consist of installing the necessary tools and underlying software to build Sails applications. You'll then generate a Sails app to apply what you learned in chapter 1. This chapter will also provide an opportunity to demystify the process of backend app creation and dismiss the idea that it has to be a long, drawn-out process. The first application you'll generate will be disposable. Yep, we said it—disposable. But that's not a bad thing. It's actually a feature. Sails is all about rapid development—the ability to have an idea or concept, act on it immediately, create the app, and explore your idea. The bottom line is this: don't be afraid to experiment. Nothing is wasted. Just relax, explore, and have some fun!

2.1   *Tools of the trade*

Fortunately, developing modern web backend applications doesn't require a lot of tools. In fact, you just need a few:

- Node.js
- Sails.js
- A text editor/integrated development environment (IDE)
- A command-line terminal (shell)

Once these are installed, the underlying applications require very little in the way of configuration. So let's get busy.

2.1.1   *Mac, Windows, and Linux … oh my!*

The decision to develop your application on a particular operating system is a matter of personal choice. We use OS X El Capitan on a MacBook. Most of the examples will be in this context, but if you're a Windows or Linux shop, they'll work just as well.

2.1.2   *Choosing a text editor vs. an IDE*

A text editor is a program that allows you to create and edit files that are stored as plain text. A traditional word processor like Word or Google Docs adds special formatting characters that aren't displayed but are stored when the file is saved. These special characters can interfere with the computer's ability to interpret your source code. Therefore, it's important that any text editor you decide to use stores its files as plain text.

Like your choice of operating system, the choice of a text editor and/or IDE depends on your coding style. We use Sublime Text, but there are many options:

- *Text editors*—Sublime Text, TextMate, Notepad++, Vim, Atom, Emacs
- *IDEs*—WebStorm, Komodo IDE, Visual Studio, Aptana Studio, Koding (cloud-based)

What's the difference between a text editor and an IDE? Traditionally, an IDE will have additional tools to automate your coding process like code completion, integration with version control, and added debugging. Over the last several years, the lines between a text editor and an IDE have blurred.

> **BOTTOM LINE**   If you're not already hooked on a particular editor, start with Sublime Text (there's a free trial) and then experiment with other choices until you find something that best fits your coding style.

2.1.3   *Must-have tools*

In the OS X world, ShiftIt has become an essential part of the development workflow. Through the use of hotkeys, you can control the placement of windows in your text editor, browser, or any other application. For example, suppose you want to compare two different files in different projects in Sublime Text. You can quickly use the hotkey Ctrl-Option-⌘-↑ to position the first window in the upper half of the screen and

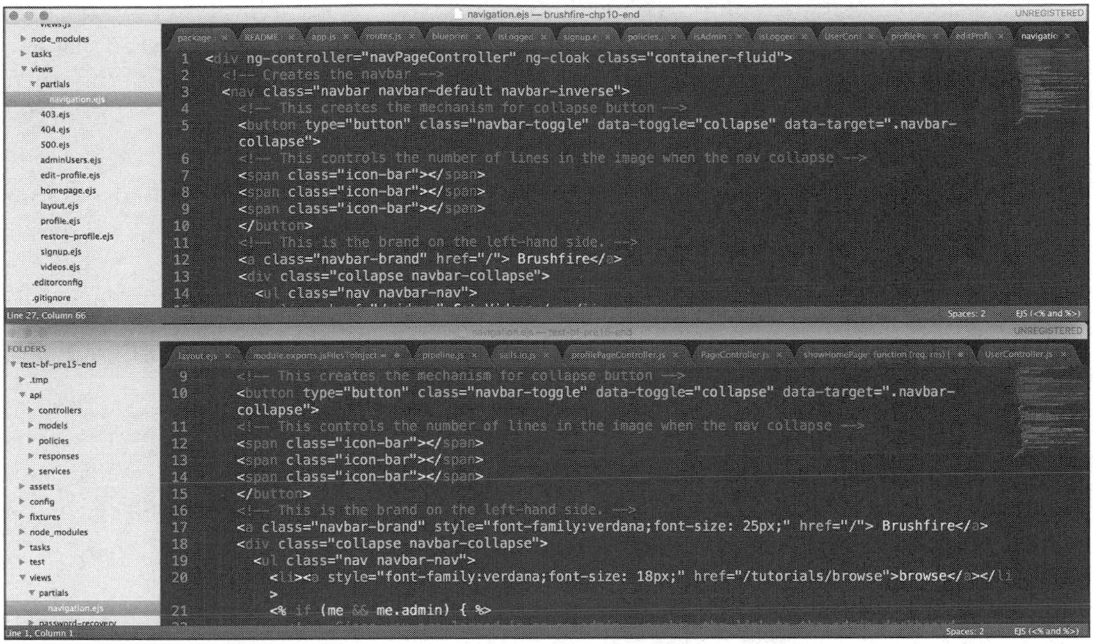

Figure 2.1 Comparing the code of two different projects in Sublime Text with ShiftIt

Ctrl-Option-⌘-↓ to position the other window in the lower half of the screen. Now these files are positioned so you can easily compare the code. See figure 2.1.

You'll constantly move around code windows and browser windows during development, and having ShiftIt makes this process a breeze. You can find ShiftIt at https://github.com/fikovnik/ShiftIt/releases.

Another indispensible tool we use on a daily basis is Postman. Postman makes it super easy to test your backend endpoints via a simple user interface. In addition, Postman allows you to group often-used requests into collections that can be accessed at any time. Collections are not just stored but also synced in realtime. If you work on multiple machines, you can use your Postman account to keep them in sync. Having an account allows you to manage collection links. You can upload collections and get a link that you can give out to others. Postman comes in two versions—a Chrome extension and an OS X installed application. We use the installed application version in the examples in this book. The Chrome extension mirrors all the features that we use in this book with the installed version. To install Postman, navigate your browser to https://www.getpostman.com/apps. You'll use Postman later in this chapter.

2.1.4 Whoa, command line? Terminal? W-what?

For those not familiar with the *command-line terminal* (commonly referred to as the Unix shell), this next section is for you. The terminal is a magical place where you can issue commands to your machine without the clutter of a graphical user interface. As a developer, you spend a large portion of your life at the terminal. I realize that may sound depressing, but you'll soon discover how productive you can be with this essential tool and wonder how you existed without it.

WHERE'S THE TERMINAL?

On a Mac (OS X v10.11.2) you can find the terminal in Applications/Utilities/Terminal.app. When you first launch the terminal, you'll see something like what's shown in figure 2.2.

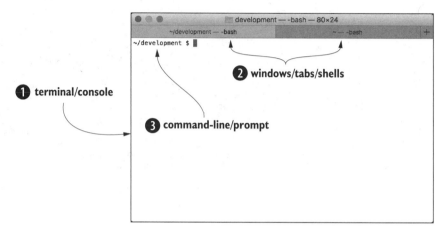

Figure 2.2   The terminal consists of one or more windows or tabs. Each window or tab contains a command line, where you type commands.

In figure 2.2, the terminal ❶ is the application you launched. You can open multiple windows ❷ or tabs from the terminal, which gives you access to the command line ❸, where you issue commands. Note that your command-line prompt will likely look different from what's pictured in figure 2.2.

2.1.5   *Installing Node*

The best way to install Node for OS X or Windows is to use one of the installers shown in figure 2.3.

If you're partial to Linux or SunOS, you can find the binaries for those operating systems as well. Once the installation is complete, open a terminal window and type

```
~ $ node -v
```

This command will serve two purposes: verify that Node is installed, as well as provide the version of Node. Now you're ready to install Sails.

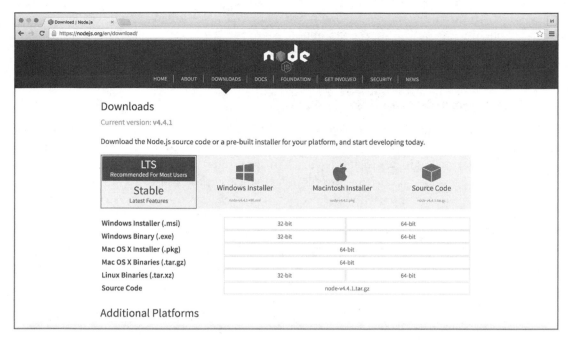

Figure 2.3   The Node installation page for Windows, OS X, and Linux operating systems

2.1.6   *Installing Sails*

You'll use the Node package manager (npm) to install the Sails framework. The Node package manager is included when you install Node and is a way for developers to share and reuse code. Node applications are made up of these packages (or modules) that are stored in various JavaScript files. You can set up a list of files, called *dependencies*, that you rely on for a given module in a file named package.json. The list of dependencies in package.json will be used by npm to install the necessary files and folders. We'll explore npm in more detail in the next section. Go back to the terminal window and install Sails from the command-line by typing

```
~ $ npm install sails –global
```

> **Using sudo**
>
> You may have to use `sudo npm install sails -g`, where `sudo` refers to *super user*. The user you normally log in as might not have the rights necessary to install something into a root folder. Using `sudo` allows you to temporarily take on super user rights during installation. In Windows, you may have to open the command prompt as a system administrator.
>
> The `-g` flag means that npm will install Sails globally, allowing you to generate Sails projects from anywhere in your file system.

At this point, the many files that make up Sails are downloaded and installed on your machine. With one simple command, npm install Sails -g, the package manager determines all the necessary files to install Sails, finds them on the npm registry (npmjs.org), and installs them on your device.

2.2   *How code is organized in Node.js*

It's difficult to start a discussion about Node modules, packages, dependencies, and npm because all the concepts are dependent on one another. The Node package manager makes it easy to aggregate, share, and reuse existing JavaScript. npm enables you to aggregate JavaScript into modules, which expose functions and properties you can easily install and use in your project. In fact, Sails is an npm package. Hundreds of thousands of packages are warehoused on registries like www.npmjs.com and available for inclusion in your apps. Even better, once you install a package into your project, npm makes it easy to check for updates and install any dependencies that have changed. npm consists of the three different technologies depicted in figure 2.4.

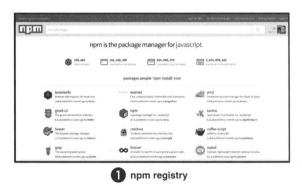

1 npm registry

2 npm CLI application

3 npm package

Figure 2.4   npm consists of a registry with hundreds of thousands of packages ❶, a command-line-interface application ❷, and individual packages ❸.

2.2.1 *What is a Node module?*

A Node module aggregates related JavaScript code into a single unit. Technically, a module is just a file that exports something. A Node.js file that doesn't export anything is usually called a *script*. An npm *package* is a directory of files that you install from npm. But because npm installs packages into a folder named node_modules/, many Node.js developers (including Isaac Schlueter, the creator of npm, and us) have become accustomed to using the terms *npm package*, *npm module*, *package*, and *module* interchangeably.

> **NOTE** In case you couldn't guess, we'll use the terms *package* and *module* interchangeably too.

Node modules make source code reusable. Instead of taking a chunk of JavaScript and copying it from one project to another, you can put the code into a module and then require that module from another file. For the most part, we'll be consumers of modules in this book. Still, to really understand this concept, let's look at a simple module we built. Here's the source code of our module.

Listing 2.1 `the-ultimate-question` Node module

```
module.exports = {

  answer: function() {
    return 42;
  },

  question: function() {
    return 'Sorry, Earth was destroyed before I was able to calculate the
    ➥ question.';
  }
};
```

Instead of getting caught up in the details, just know that this file, named index.js, creates a dictionary with two methods, `answer` and `question`.

> **DEFINITION** Remember, our definition of a *dictionary* refers to the *object* that's declared using curly braces—{}. For example, { `foo: 'bar'` } is a dictionary.

There's one other file in the module folder named package.json.

Listing 2.2 The package.json file of `the-ultimate-question` module

```
{
  "name": "the-ultimate-question",
  "version": "1.0.0",
  "description": "A method to determine the meaning of life",
  "main": "index.js",
  "author": {
    "name": "Irl Nathan"
  },
```

```
    "license": "MIT"
}
```

The package.json file contains information about the module such as name, version, author, and licensing. So this awe-inspiring module consists of two files: index.js and package.json. The repository can be found at https://github.com/irlnathan/the-ultimate-question. Publishing a module goes beyond the scope of the book, but all it would take to publish it to the npmjs.org registry is issuing the command npm publish at the root of the module. Now let's use our module in a Sails project.

2.2.2   *Creating your first Sails application*

Let's create your first application in Sails. Head back to the terminal window and from the command line type

```
~ $ sails new firstApp
info: Created a new Sails app `firstApp`!
```

> **NOTE** In the example in this section, we displayed what you need to type, sails new firstApp, as well as what was returned, info: Created a new Sails app `firstApp`!.

The new command is part of the Sails command-line interface. We'll introduce other commands like sails generate in the next section. The command sails new generates the file and folder infrastructure of a boilerplate Sails application. Automating repetitive tasks like generating boilerplate code in your development workflow is a core feature of the Sails framework.

Note that earlier you installed the Sails framework globally on your device. Each time you create a new Sails project, Sails installs itself as a dependency of your project; see figure 2.5.

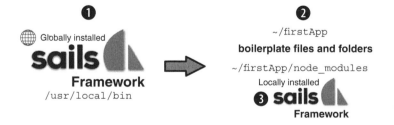

Figure 2.5 The globally installed version of Sails ❶ generated a new Sails application ❷ and installed itself as a dependency of the new project ❸.

Your new project is completely self-contained and doesn't rely on you packaging up some other source files in addition to your project folder to deploy it. You can see the Sails dependency by looking at the firstApp package.json file.

Listing 2.3   firstApp's package.json file

```
{
  "name": "firstApp",
  "private": true,
  "version": "0.0.0",
  "description": "a Sails application",
  "keywords": [],
  "dependencies": {
    "ejs": "2.3.4",
    "grunt": "0.4.5",
    "grunt-contrib-clean": "0.6.0",
    "grunt-contrib-coffee": "0.13.0",
    "grunt-contrib-concat": "0.5.1",
    "grunt-contrib-copy": "0.5.0",
    "grunt-contrib-cssmin": "0.9.0",
    "grunt-contrib-jst": "0.6.0",
    "grunt-contrib-less": "1.1.0",
    "grunt-contrib-uglify": "0.7.0",
    "grunt-contrib-watch": "0.5.3",
    "grunt-sails-linker": "~0.10.1",
    "grunt-sync": "0.2.4",
    "include-all": "~0.1.6",
    "rc": "1.0.1",                        Sails is a dependency
    "sails": "~0.12.1",         ◁──────   of firstApp
    "sails-disk": "~0.10.9"
  },
...
```

What is the impact of a dependency, and how do you use a third party module? Glad you asked. Let's put the-ultimate-question module to use in your new app.

2.2.3 *Using a module from npm*

In chapter 1, you learned that a user-agent could make a request that triggers a route that executes a controller action. The controller action can do stuff and then ultimately respond to the requesting user-agent. Most of the book expands on this process of satisfying requests with controller actions.

Now that you have a project, go to the command line, make sure you're in the root of the project, and type

```
~ $ cd firstApp
~/firstApp $
```

Next, install the-ultimate-question module into the firstApp project by typing

```
~/firstApp $ npm install the-ultimate-question –save
the-ultimate-question@1.0.0 node_modules/the-ultimate-question
```

You can see the module as a dependency by reopening the firstApp/package.json file in Sublime, similar to the following listing.

Listing 2.4   firstApp's package.json with dependency `the-ultimate-question` module

```
{
  "name": "firstApp",
  "private": true,
  "version": "0.0.0",
  "description": "a Sails application",
  "keywords": [],
  "dependencies": {
    "ejs": "2.3.4",
    "grunt": "0.4.5",
    "grunt-contrib-clean": "0.6.0",
    "grunt-contrib-coffee": "0.13.0",
    "grunt-contrib-concat": "0.5.1",
    "grunt-contrib-copy": "0.5.0",
    "grunt-contrib-cssmin": "0.9.0",
    "grunt-contrib-jst": "0.6.0",
    "grunt-contrib-less": "1.1.0",
    "grunt-contrib-uglify": "0.7.0",
    "grunt-contrib-watch": "0.5.3",
    "grunt-sails-linker": "~0.10.1",
    "grunt-sync": "0.2.4",
    "include-all": "~0.1.6",
    "rc": "1.0.1",
    "sails": "~0.12.1",                        the-ultimate-question
    "sails-disk": "~0.10.9",                   module is now a
    "the-ultimate-question": "^1.0.0"   ◁──   dependency of firstApp.
  },
...
```

TIP   By making the module a dependency, you can copy the project without the node_modules folder and later install all the necessary dependencies by using npm install.

Now, generate a controller by typing

```
~/firstApp $ sails generate controller life?
info: Created a new controller ("life") at api/controllers/LifeController.js!
```

In Sublime, open firstApp/api/controllers/LifeController.js and add the following code.

Listing 2.5   Adding an action to the `LifeController`

```
var Meaning = require('the-ultimate-question');   ◁──   Using require provides access
                                                          to the methods in the module.
module.exports = {

  purpose: function(req, res) {          ◁──   The action is just a JavaScript function
                                                that's triggered by the route.
    return res.json({          ◁──
      answer: Meaning.answer(),          You respond by executing the
      question: Meaning.question()       two module methods and
    });                                  returning the results as JSON.
  }
};
```

Okay, let's see all of this in action.

2.2.4　*Starting the Sails server*

To start the Sails server, head back to the terminal window and type

```
~/firstApp $ sails lift
```

Your terminal window should look similar to figure 2.6.

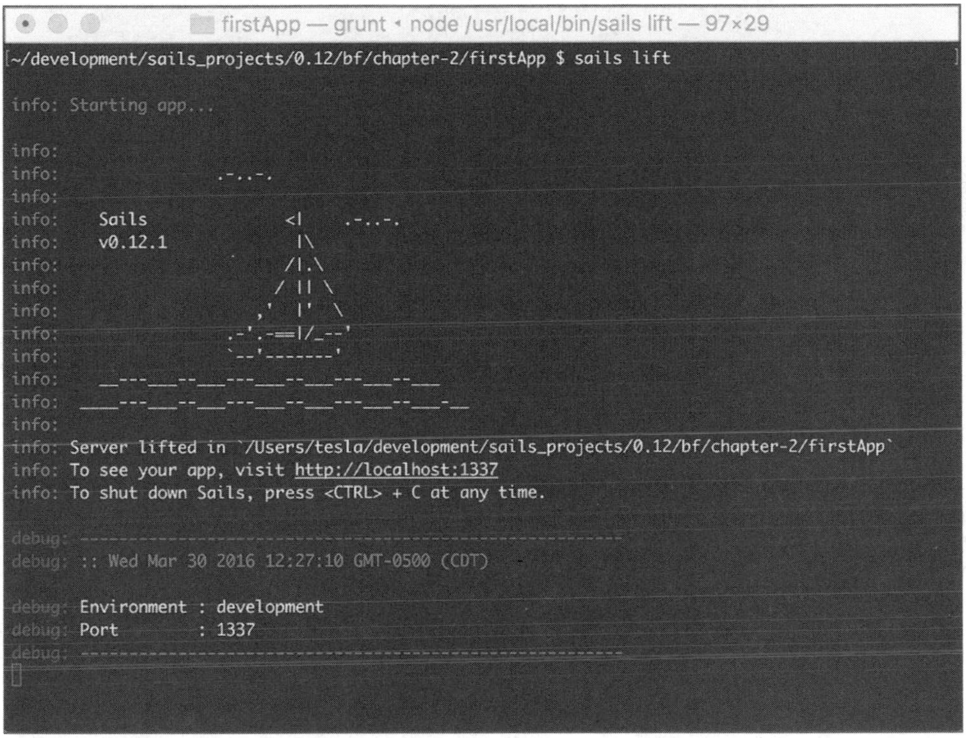

Figure 2.6　The Sails server up and running

The Sails server is now listening for requests. Navigate your browser to localhost:1337:
/life/purpose and your browser should look similar to figure 2.7.

You're also using the Chrome extension JSONView, which adds syntax highlighting. Figure 2.8 provides an overall illustration of what just happened.

To recap, your browser made a GET request ❶ to /life/purpose on your behalf, which matched a blueprint route ❷ and triggered the purpose action ❸ in the Life-Controller. The purpose action, which is a JavaScript function, gained access to your previously installed the-ultimate-question module by using the require method ❹ and assigning the results to a dictionary you imported as Meaning. You then used the

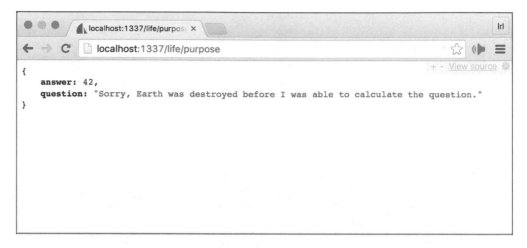

Figure 2.7   The JSON response from the `purpose` **action.**

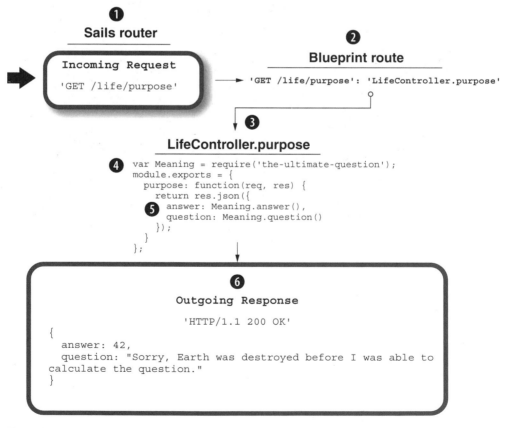

Figure 2.8   An overview of the GET **request to** /life/purpose

Meaning dictionary ❺ to execute two methods from the module and responded to the request ❻ using the results of the methods formatted as JSON. This flow, in a nutshell, is the foundation of creating a web application backend.

2.2.5 *What is localhost:1337?*

The hostname *localhost* is shorthand for accessing your computer's local network services. Using localhost usually resolves to the address 127.0.0.1, which is a way of bypassing the outside network. What is the number 1337? Think of the hostname, localhost, as the name of a city and a port number, 1337, as a street address. Separate port numbers are a way to differentiate between applications that are trying to access your computer's resources. So localhost:1337 is a way to access your device and, more importantly, your project, firstApp, at a particular port.

2.2.6 *Killing the server*

Now that you understand how to *lift* a Sails server, let's see how to *lower* or close it. From the terminal window, press Ctrl-C, and the terminal window then looks similar to figure 2.9.

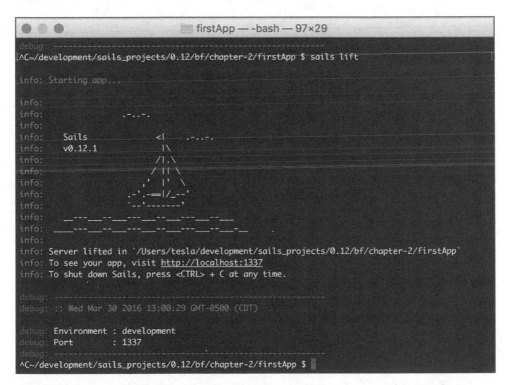

Figure 2.9 The terminal window responds with the command prompt after you close the Sails server with Ctrl-C.

What would happen if you typed `sails lift` in two different tabs of the terminal window? Try it and see what happens. Restart Sails in this tab using `sails lift`. Next, open a new tabbed window by pressing ⌘-T.

> **NOTE** ⌘-T opens a new terminal window tab, placing your command-line prompt at the root folder of firstApp.

Now start Sails in this new tab using `sails lift`, and your terminal window should look similar to figure 2.10.

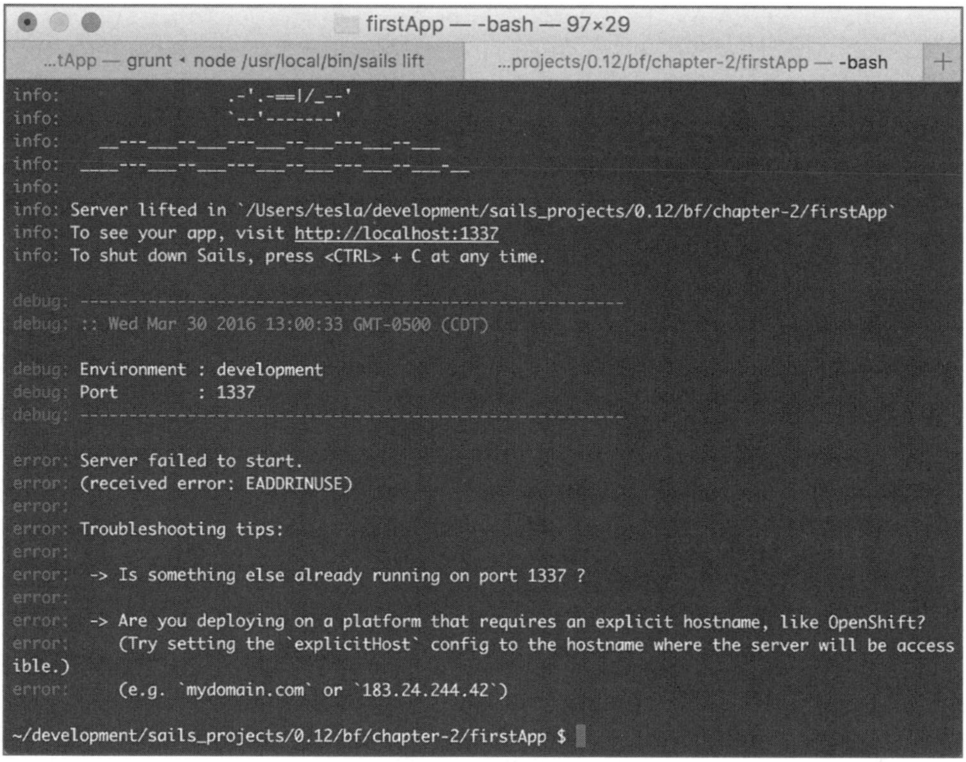

Figure 2.10 Only one node application at a time can be running on a particular port.

What happens is you can't run more than one Node application on a particular port at the same time, and if you try to do so Sails produces an error.

2.3 *Online resources for this book*

The bulk of *Sails.js in Action* teaches concepts through progressively building an application. To prevent the book from becoming a multivolume set, we've provided some additional resources online. The central aggregation of links to all resources can be found on the *Sails.js in Action* hub: http://sailsinaction.github.io/. The hub contains links to the following:

- Source files for each chapter stored on the popular Git repository-hosting site GitHub.
- Gists, which are code snippets that correspond to each program listing in the book. For example, the book might list a small portion of the code to add to an existing source file. The gist will provide the entire file, including the added portion for context.
- Mockup designs for pages of the application.
- API and endpoint references.

The main hub contains links for each chapter.

2.3.1 Git and GitHub

Git is another technology that we use day in and day out. It's an indispensable part of our development flow, and, coupled with GitHub, it's possible to easily collaborate with others on projects. Version control is a way for you to track the state of one or more files over time and then restore a particular version to some prior state at will. Because this book isn't about version control, we'll give you enough information to install Git and clone existing repositories of the source code for each chapter of the book.

2.3.2 Installing Git

Like installing Node, the easiest way to install Git is by using one of its installers. The installer for OS X can be found at http://git-scm.com/download/mac. Once it's installed, you'll want to configure Git to identify yourself with your comments. From the terminal window type

```
~ $ git config --global user.name "Humphrey Bogart"
~ $ git config --global user.email hbogart@casablancaway.com
```

For more extensive information about using Git, check out the great guide at https://git-scm.com/docs.

2.3.3 What is a GitHub repo?

GitHub provides a secure backup of a local repository. It also has a powerful social network of developers with tools that make it easy to collaborate on a repository with people around the world. You'll use GitHub primarily for copying source files and folders that correspond with each chapter of the book.

The *Sails.js in Action* hub, http://sailsinaction.github.io/, contains links to an overview page for each chapter. Within each chapter is a link to one or more GitHub repositories. Most chapters will have a beginning repo to clone to your local machine and an ending repo that contains all the activities completed for that particular chapter. Why can't you simply follow the examples in the book? We wanted to provide you with meaningful frontend source code to utilize while learning backend development. If we attempted to explain and provide the source code for the entire frontend, we could have easily added hundreds of pages to the book. Therefore, for most chapters, we provide the fully baked frontend example before starting the chapter and leave backend development to the pages of the book. If we don't add assets at the beginning of a chapter, you'll be given the choice of continuing with a project from the previous chapter or cloning a repository that gets you up to date before starting a chapter.

2.3.4   *Cloning a repo*

Copying a remote repository is known as *cloning*. By cloning a repository, you can rapidly obtain all the files of a particular project. Give it a try. Open a browser and navigate to https://github.com/mikermcneil/cursors. Your browser should look similar to figure 2.11.

This repo contains files and folders ❶ of a Sails app that you'll install and briefly explore. Copy the link, https://github.com/mikermcneil/cursors.git ❷, in figure 2.11.

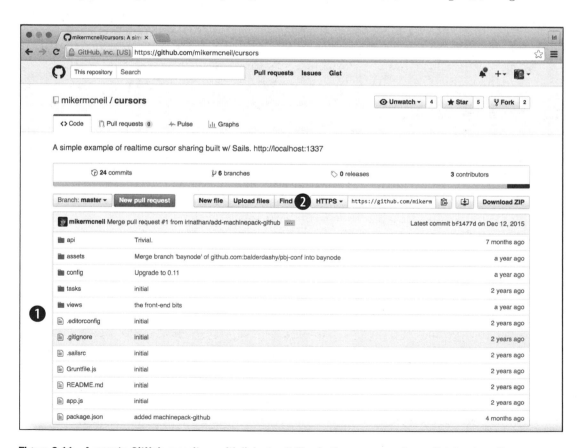

Figure 2.11   A remote GitHub repository with links to all files in the repo as well as a link to clone the repo

Open the terminal window and `cd` to a folder where you'd like to place this project. After installing Git, use the following command to clone the remote repository:

```
~ $ git clone https://github.com/mikermcneil/cursors.git
Cloning into 'cursors'...
remote: Counting objects: 260, done.
remote: Total 260 (delta 0), reused 0 (delta 0), pack-reused 260
Receiving objects: 100% (260/260), 373.27 KiB | 0 bytes/s, done.
Resolving deltas: 100% (92/92), done.
Checking connectivity... done
~ $
```

Note that the number of files in your count might vary. Next, `cd` into the cursors folder and type

```
~/cursors $ npm install
```

The command `npm install` will look for the dependencies in the package.json file in the root of the `cursors` module and install the necessary dependencies. The cursors application is an example of using WebSockets, which we introduced in chapter 1. Start the application by typing

```
~/cursors $ sails lift
```

Now open a browser and navigate to localhost:1337. Open another browser window in incognito mode and navigate to localhost:1337. Enter a phony name when prompted for each browser window. Your browsers should look similar to figure 2.12.

Figure 2.12   The cursors Sails project in action

Every time you move the mouse, Sails sends the position of your cursor to the other browser. This simple example demonstrates the power of WebSockets within Sails. Now that you know how to clone a repo, you're almost ready to start exploring Sails in earnest by building a real-world application.

2.4   *Documentation and community support*

Sails has a growing community of developers. Some of the more heavily trafficked areas include these:

- *Official documentation*—http://sailsjs.org/documentation
- *Stack Overflow*—Use the sails.js tag.
- *Gitter (chat)*—https://gitter.im/balderdashy/sails
- *Google Groups*—sails.js
- *IRC*—#sailsjs

2.5   *Summary*

- The Sails technical stack consists of Node.js, Sails.js, a text editor, and the command-line shell.
- Start the Sails server via `sails lift` and close the server with Ctrl-C.
- Use `npm install` to install Node modules into a project.
- Sails applications can incorporate other Node modules by using the `require()` method.

Using static assets 3

Your development environment is installed, and you've taken Sails for a quick spin. You're now ready to get down to the business of creating an application. You need to answer some initial questions:

- What types of user-agent will your application need to support?
- Will Sails be responsible for delivering frontend assets and, if so, how?

This chapter will help you answer those questions and explore in detail ways Sails can deliver frontend assets in a web application. Many great libraries and frameworks work well with Sails. We chose jQuery as a proxy for client-side DOM manipulation tools and Angular as a proxy for client-side frameworks. In this chapter, we'll use both to demonstrate how to integrate DOM manipulation tools like jQuery and client-side JavaScript frameworks into the static asset pipeline. The remaining chapters will focus on Angular on the frontend.

We have limited information from our new client, Chad. He's provided us with a name for our application, Brushfire, and the following specifics: "I want a homepage and a videos page where I can add highly viewed YouTube clips." Not exactly a requirements document, but it'll suffice during our initial design phase.

In chapter 1, we discussed a variety of different user-agents that can be used in web applications. Because Brushfire will support the browser as a user-agent, your next decision will be whether to implement the frontend as a single-page application (SPA) with Sails responding to requests as a standalone API, or as a hybrid application combining Sails server-rendered views, client-side JavaScript, and requests fulfilled by a Sails API.

> **DEFINITION**   Sails can supply a backend API separate from the frontend; hence, the phrase *standalone API*. As mentioned in chapter 1, standalone APIs are typically used with native mobile, native desktop, IoT, and SPA applications, where the frontend of the application comes from a source other than Sails.

Starting in this chapter, you'll first build Brushfire using the SPA approach on the frontend and then integrate with the standalone Sails API you'll also develop. The SPA will use client-side routing and rendering for chapters 3 through 7. Starting with chapter 8, you'll transition Brushfire to use the hybrid web application approach that uses server-side routing and rendering for the frontend. That way, you'll have experience with both approaches depending on your application's requirements. You'll also understand the pros and cons of each approach.

In chapter 1, we also examined the general mechanics of integrating an SPA into the Sails ecosystem, as depicted in figure 3.1.

Using this approach, Sails or a content delivery network (CDN) ❶ delivers the initial HTML view, JavaScript, and CSS ❷ as static assets in response to a GET request to the root route. (The root route, or web root route, is simply / with nothing following it.) Then, the JavaScript on the frontend is responsible for making intermediate changes to the view ❸ while also handling page navigation ❹. Separate AJAX requests can be used to access the Sails backend API ❺. The second approach involves server-side rendering and routing, where Sails renders all the application views on the backend and then delivers them to the browser user-agent to be displayed. With this approach, page navigation requires a refresh of the entire page.

In this chapter, we'll focus on how to deliver HTML, CSS, and JavaScript assets, as well as the initial *entry point* of an SPA using the Sails *static-asset pipeline*. Before we get too far, let's make sure we're on the same page (pun unintended) where we use the term *static assets*. What are static assets? You're already familiar with accessing web

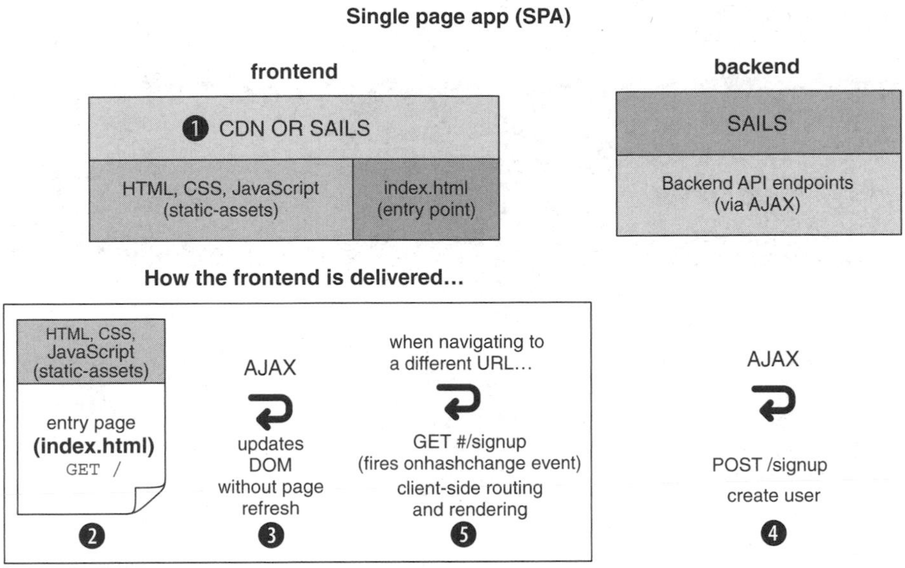

Single page app (SPA)

frontend

❶ CDN OR SAILS

HTML, CSS, JavaScript (static-assets)	index.html (entry point)

backend

SAILS

Backend API endpoints (via AJAX)

How the frontend is delivered...

HTML, CSS, JavaScript (static-assets)

entry page **(index.html)** GET /

❷

AJAX ⤸ updates DOM without page refresh

❸

when navigating to a different URL... ⤸ GET #/signup (fires onhashchange event) client-side routing and rendering

❺

AJAX ⤸ POST /signup create user

❹

Figure 3.1 Delivering assets and endpoints to a single-page application

pages (.html), images (.png, .jpg, and so on), JavaScript (.js), and stylesheets (.css) as static assets from a browser. What makes something a static asset is not its file extension but rather the fact that the content of the file doesn't change between the request from the user-agent and the response from the Sails server. Instead of jabbering on about this in a theoretical way, we'll let you get your hands dirty with a real use case. To begin, you'll create your initial Brushfire project in Sails.

3.1 Introduction to static routing

In this section, you'll generate a new Sails project. This process will create the necessary files and folders of a default Sails project and will also install Sails itself. This makes the project a self-contained, independent unit. It will be your blank canvas on which to develop Brushfire. Create or move to the folder where Brushfire will live, and from the terminal window type

```
~ $ sails new brushfire
```

Now move into the root of the project by typing

```
~ $ cd brushfire
~/brushfire $
```

Finally, start the Sails server by typing

```
~/brushfire $ sails lift
```

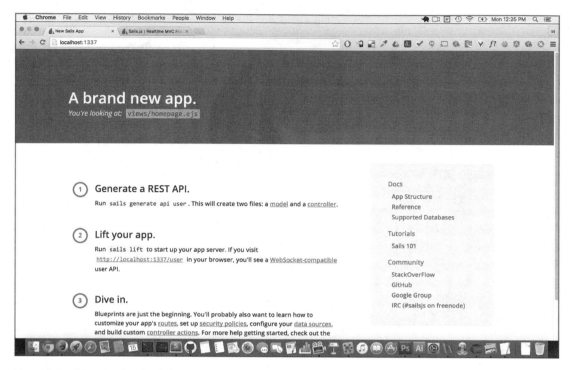

Figure 3.2   After starting the Sails server and navigating to the root route of the project, Sails responds with the default homepage.

To access the default homepage generated with each new Sails project, navigate your browser to localhost:1337. Your browser window should look similar to figure 3.2.

The request triggered a response that contained the necessary assets to display your homepage. Where are your static assets located in the project? It's easy to find them in a Sails project because they're in a folder named brushfire/assets/. By default in a new project, Sails creates a few subfolders of assets/ for convenience, including images/, js/, and styles/ as well as a favicon.ico file and a boilerplate robots.txt file.

> **DEFINITION**   The *favicon.ico file* is the icon that can be displayed on a browser tab in Chrome and in other browsers in the address bar and task bar. The *robots.txt* file is used to control how search engines index your live URLs.

Your current homepage isn't in the assets folder. Instead, by default, Sails created an explicit root route and a server-rendered homepage view when you created the project. We'll explore both in the next section.

3.1.1   The default homepage

Let's explore the default behavior of the root route generated in a new Sails project. You learned in chapter 1 that Sails uses explicit routes and shadow routes to manage incoming requests. When Sails generates a new project, by default it sets up an explicit route to handle GET requests to the root path (/) of a project. In Sublime, open brushfire/config/routes.js to see this default explicit route, which is similar to the following listing.

Listing 3.1   The Sails default root route

```
module.exports.routes = {
  '/': {
    view: 'homepage'
  }
};
```

A GET request to the root path triggers a response that contains a server-rendered view of the homepage, as shown in the route in figure 3.3.

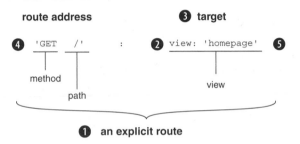

Figure 3.3   In addition to an action, an explicit route ❶ can have a view ❷ as its target ❸. When a request matches the root address ❹ of this route, the Sails server responds with a view ❷. In this case, the view is the homepage ❺.

This is new. In chapter 1, you observed explicit routes that triggered actions as their target. Explicit routes can also contain server-rendered views as the target. You'll learn more about these later, but for now you'll use the SPA approach for your frontend. Therefore, you need to change the default behavior of your Brushfire project from using explicit routes and server-rendered views to using asset routes and client-side rendering.

3.1.2   Replacing the default homepage

You'll use a generator to modify your existing Sails project files, changing Brushfire's default behavior to use asset routes as the entry point for your application.

> **DEFINITION**   The *entry point* of an application means the response to a GET request to the root route of a project.

You need to change a number of files to set this up. You could manually change those files, or you can use a Sails *generator* to modify the files automatically. You've already used a generator without knowing it: sails new, the command you used to create the initial Sails project, is a generator. The sails new command generated the files and folders necessary to create a default project. Although it's beyond the scope of the book, you can create your own custom generators and then execute them via the `sails generate` command. For a complete list of available generators, visit http://mng.bz/Aoxs. In this section, you'll install an existing generator.

In chapter 2, you learned that npm enables developers to easily share reusable JavaScript code via packages. Because this generator is implemented as an npm package, you'll use the npm command-line application in the terminal window to install it from the npmjs.org registry. If the Sails server is running, press Ctrl-C to stop the server, and then type

```
~/brushfire $ npm install sails-generate-static -save
```

> **NOTE**   Earlier, when you installed Sails, you used the `-g` or global argument to install Sails globally on the machine. That made Sails available from anywhere on your machine. Here, you install the `sails-generate-static` module locally.

Executing this npm command installs the generator into brushfire/node_modules/.

> **DEFINITION**   The *brushfire/node_modules/ folder* is where all Brushfire dependency files are installed. This makes each project self-contained and very portable.

When you used the `--save` parameter, npm also added the generator as a dependency in your brushfire/package.json file.

> **NOTE**   The brushfire/package.json file has a section that contains the names and versions of all your Brushfire module dependencies. Inevitably modules are upgraded with breaking changes. Having a file that tracks the working versions of the modules you use in your application is a lifesaver when it comes to debugging.

Now that the module is installed, you can use the generator by typing

```
~/brushfire $ sails generate static
```

The generator removes the explicit route in brushfire/config/routes.js and copies most of the contents of the current homepage located in brushfire/views/homepage.ejs to a file located in brushfire/assets/index.html.

> **NOTE**   We say *most of the contents* of the current homepage are copied because some of the tags used in server-rendered views are not used in plain HTML. We'll take a detailed look at these special tags in chapter 8.

Head back to the terminal window and restart the Sails server by typing

```
~/brushfire $ sails lift
```

Refresh your browser, which should have localhost:1337 in the URL navigation bar. Figure 3.4 illustrates the homepage before and after using the static generator.

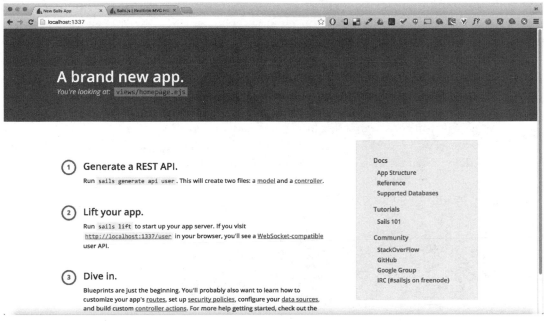

Before the static generator

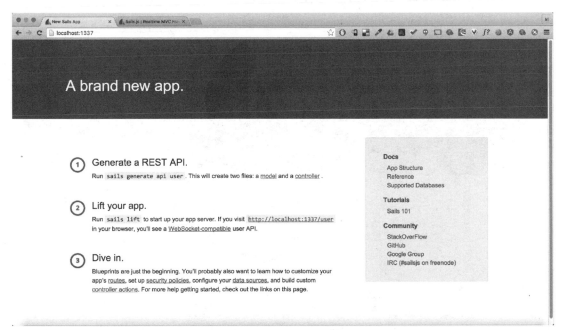

After the static generator

Figure 3.4 The homepage before and after running the static generator

Although the pages look similar, there are three subtle but important differences. The first difference isn't apparent from viewing each page. When your browser made a GET request to the root route, Sails tried to match it to an explicit route that contains the *route address* 'GET /'. Since that explicit route no longer exists, Sails used another type of route, an *asset route*, to deliver the homepage located at brushfire/assets/index.html. Moving the contents of the homepage view to brushfire/assets/index.html automatically created an asset route. Therefore, a GET request to / now responds with the contents of brushfire/assets/index.html, a.k.a. the homepage.

The second difference is that the path to the homepage isn't displayed as it was for the default server-rendered homepage. When Sails used the explicit route, the path was added to brushfire/views/homepage.ejs before the server responded with the view, as shown in figure 3.5.

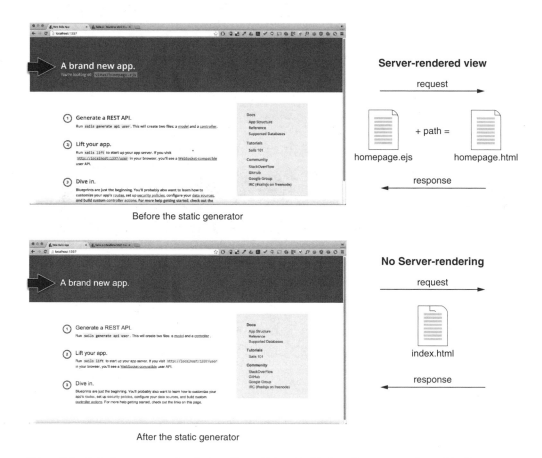

Figure 3.5   Using a server-rendered view, the path is added before the response is sent to the requesting user-agent. Using a static asset, the index.html page isn't changed between the request and response.

Because you're now using an asset route to deliver the entry point to Brushfire, the contents of brushfire/assets/index.html didn't change between the request and the response. That is, the path wasn't added to index.html and therefore wasn't displayed on the homepage like in the server-rendered view.

The final difference is that with the server-rendered approach, the homepage was initially an EJS file before being rendered as brushfire/views/homepage.html. We'll cover EJS and its use of tags to add data in chapter 8, which is on server-rendered views. For now, let's take a closer look at the asset pipeline.

3.2 The asset pipeline

In addition to responding to asset routes with static assets, the Sails server may also be called on to perform some preprocessing tasks on these assets. These tasks are contained in the static-asset pipeline, as illustrated in figure 3.6.

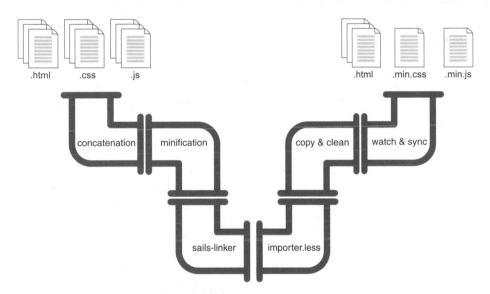

Figure 3.6 The static-asset pipeline aggregates preprocessing tasks to assets.

TIP "I thought you said static assets don't change!" They don't change between the request and the response, but some performance and utility tasks can occur before a request/response transaction is initiated.

The asset pipeline bundled in Sails is a set of tasks configured with conventional defaults designed to make your project more consistent and productive. The entire frontend asset workflow is completely customizable but also provides some default tasks right out of the box. Sails also makes it easy to configure new tasks to fit your needs. A full list of default tasks can be found at http://mng.bz/X2rL. We'll examine tasks in the order in which they come up in Brushfire, including these:

- How Sails uses a .tmp/ folder as an equivalent to the public folder on a typical web server
- How the Sails asset pipeline uses Grunt to execute necessary pipeline tasks
- Adding Brushfire frontend assets from a GitHub repository
- Integrating a content delivery network into the asset pipeline
- How naming a file index.html impacts how it's accessed
- Adding images to the asset pipeline
- Understanding relative paths

First, we'll look at where the asset files are actually served from with a Sails project.

3.2.1 *A quick look at the .tmp/ folder*

With all of this talk of the assets folder, you might think Sails was serving up brushfire/assets/index.html from the brushfire/assets/ folder. Out of the box, the Sails asset pipeline pulls files from brushfire/assets/, does transformations in the brushfire/.tmp/ folder, and then dumps the result into the brushfire/.tmp/public/ folder.

> **NOTE** The .tmp folder is a hidden file in the operating system. This means that if you search a folder using the `ls` command, the file won't be returned. To list all files and folders, including hidden folders, you can use `ls -a`.

Separating /assets from .tmp/public enables Sails to perform different pipeline transformations that do handy things like compile LESS stylesheets.

Compare the brushfire/assets/ folder and the brushfire/.tmp/public/ folder in figure 3.7.

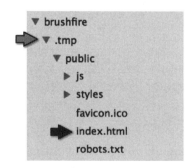

Figure 3.7 The brushfire/assets/ folder synced with the brushfire/.tmp/ public/ folder

Talking about this can take us only so far. To see how the files are automatically copied in action, make sure Sails is running via `sails lift` and that both the brushfire/assets/ and the brushfire/.tmp/public/ folders are open in Sublime. Within Sublime, create an empty file named brushfire/assets/videos.html. You should see videos.html magically appear in the brushfire/.tmp/public/ folder, similar to figure 3.8.

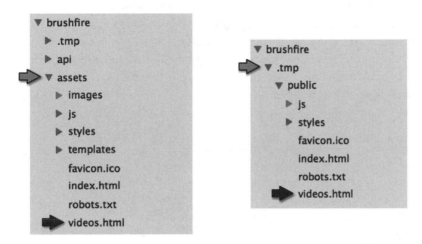

Figure 3.8   The videos.html file synced in both the assets/ and .tmp/public/ folders

How did videos.html suddenly appear in the brushfire/.tmp/public/ folder? The short answer is Grunt copied it for you.

> **NOTE**   The ability to view the brushfire/.tmp/ folder in Sublime was great for this example, but there's a dark side. It's easy to confuse the two folders when editing your project. Irl has probably taken several years off Mike's life asking him why a file hasn't updated, only to find out that he was editing it in the brushfire/.tmp/ folder, and the file was getting overwritten each time he restarted Sails. Bottom line: do yourself a favor, and configure Sublime to ignore the .tmp/ folder.

Okay, Grunt copied it for you. So what is Grunt?

3.2.2   *Grunt: the other white meat*

Grunt calls itself a "JavaScript task runner." We think that's pretty accurate. It allows Sails to set up repetitive asset pipeline management tasks, which are then executed automatically or manually, depending on the task. You saw earlier that there's a Grunt task that looks for changes in brushfire/assets/ and syncs them to brushfire/.tmp/public/.

> **NOTE**   Grunt is also optional. If for some reason you enjoy doing manual repetitive tasks, simply delete brushfire/Gruntfile.js from the root of your

project. No more Grunt. When you restart Sails via `sails lift`, warnings saying "Gruntfile could not be found" and "No Grunt tasks will be run" are displayed in the terminal window.

3.2.3 *Putting it all together: Chad's sweet homepage*

Using the default project-generated files is a good first step, but it's time to get to the real work. Chad has a specific vision laid out for the sweet homepage. Let's create custom assets that match the design mockups. In keeping with our *frontend-first* approach to design, let's take a look at the mockups of Brushfire's homepage and video page for chapter 3. Because Brushfire currently has relatively few pages, we'll display the mockups in the book as well as online.

> **NOTE** As the application grows over the next few chapters, the mockups will be available online only to minimize their impact on the page count of the book.

Navigate to http://sailsinaction.github.io/chapter-3/mockups.html to access the mockups for chapter 3. As shown in figure 3.9, the mockup page contains thumbnails for each Brushfire page with a larger modal view that can be accessed by clicking the thumbnail.

Figure 3.9 Interactive mockups are an essential part of the frontend-first approach to development. Each chapter has an online hub that contains mockups. The homepage mockup from the chapter 3 hub is pictured here.

Based on Chad's mockups, add your own markup to the generated homepage in brushfire/assets/index.html. Open brushfire/assets/index.html in Sublime and replace the current markup after the <body> tag with the HTML shown here.

Listing 3.2   Adding markup to the homepage

```
...
  <body>
    <div class="container-fluid">
      <!-- Creates the navbar -->
      <nav class="navbar navbar-default navbar-inverse">
        <!-- This creates the mechanism for collapse button -->
        <button type="button" class="navbar-toggle" data-toggle="collapse"
        ➥ data-target=".navbar-collapse">
        <!-- This controls the number of lines in the image when the nav
        ➥ collapse -->
        <span class="icon-bar"></span>
        <span class="icon-bar"></span>
        <span class="icon-bar"></span>
        </button>
        <!-- This is the brand on the left-hand side. -->
        <a class="navbar-brand" href="/#"> Brushfire</a>
        <div class="collapse navbar-collapse">
          <ul class="nav navbar-nav">
            <li><a href="/videos">Videos</a></li>
          </ul>
        </div>
      </nav>
      <div class=" col-md-8 col-md-offset-2">
        <div class="jumbotron">
          <h1>Chad's Viral Videos Emporium</h1>
          <h2>Viral Videos since 2015</h2>
        </div>
      </div>
    </div>
  ...
```

This markup uses classes from the popular Bootstrap styling framework, which you'll include in your project using a content delivery network to deliver the dependencies.

3.2.4   Using a CDN

It can be advantageous to host *static assets* on a CDN, where distributed servers put the assets closer to the end user. The goal of a CDN is to deliver web assets as fast and reliably as possible. In this section, we use a CDN to host dependencies like jQuery, Angular, and Bootstrap. First, head over to http://getbootstrap.com/getting-started/#download and grab the link from the Bootstrap CDN section.

   As a sanity check, copy and paste the CDN link (in the href) in your browser's URL bar to confirm that this is simply pointing to the minified Bootstrap CSS file. Next, manually add the bootstrap CDN reference to the homepage markup so that it can benefit from Bootstrap styles. In Sublime, open brushfire/assets/index.html and place the link reference above the STYLES tags as follows.

Listing 3.3   Adding a manual reference to the Bootstrap CDN

```
...
<link rel="stylesheet"
href="https://maxcdn.bootstrapcdn.com/bootstrap/3.3.6/css/bootstrap.min.css"
    integrity="sha384-
       1q8mTJOASx8j1Au+a5WDVnPi2lkFfwwEAa8hDDdjZlpLegxhjVME1fgjWPGmkzs7"
    crossorigin="anonymous">
<!--STYLES-->
<!--STYLES END-->
</head>
...
```

Make sure Sails is running via sails lift and navigate to localhost:1337. With Bootstrap added as a dependency, the page should look similar to figure 3.10.

Figure 3.10   The homepage with Bootstrap styling added as a CDN dependency

3.2.5   *Why index.html?*

Sometimes, you may want to link to a folder instead of directly to a file. As a convenience, files named index.html have a special status within the brushfire/assets/ folder. If a request is made to a subfolder of brushfire/assets, the Sails server will look for and display a file named index.html in that subfolder. If index.html doesn't exist, the server will respond with a 404 Not Found status.

Let's set up the videos page to see how this special status works. First, head back to the mockups section of chapter 3, and take a look at the videos page mockup depicted in figure 3.11.

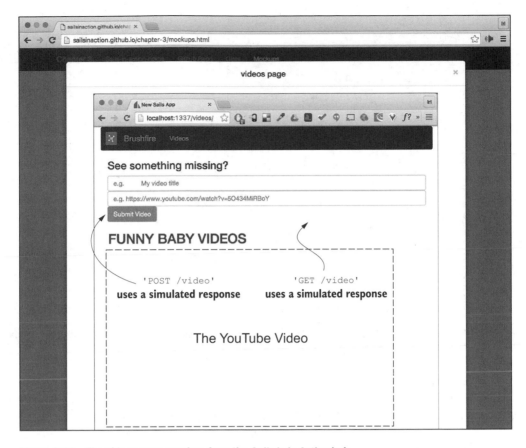

Figure 3.11 The videos page mockup from the *Sails.js in Action* hub

Now, return to the terminal window and create a new tab using the shortcut Cmd-T (on OS X). Next, move into the brushfire/assets/ folder:

```
~/brushfire $ cd assets
```

Create a new subfolder named videos/ within brushfire/assets:

```
~/brushfire/assets $ mkdir videos
```

In Sublime, create a new file named index.html for your videos page and save it in brushfire/assets/videos/. You can access the HTML for the page from the following gist: https://gist.github.com/sailsinaction/b77772769f28112247bc. Copy the source from the gist into brushfire/assets/videos/index.html. Now, let's see the videos page in action, which will also demonstrate the special status of index.html. Ensure that Sails is running, and then navigate to localhost:1337/videos in the browser, and you should see the videos page displayed, as shown in figure 3.12.

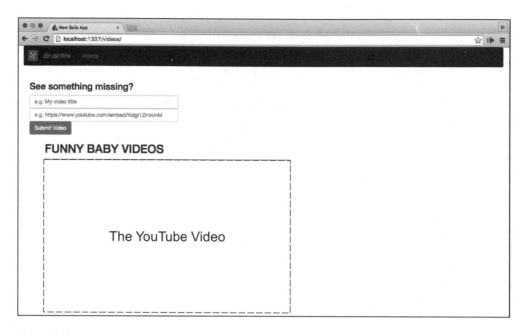

Figure 3.12   A GET request to /videos triggers a matching asset route, which displays index.html from brushfire/assets/videos/index.html.

When the browser made a GET request to /videos on your behalf, Sails first looked for an explicit route that contained the route address 'GET /videos'. Finding no matching explicit route, Sails then looked for an index.html file in the brushfire/assets/videos/ folder. Because one exists, Sails displayed the videos page. Next, we'll explore how Sails delivers images in the asset pipeline.

3.2.6   An <img> is worth a thousand words

Based on the mockup, you need to add an image to the left of the logo in the navbar. You'll use an image from the Sails website. Navigate your browser to https://placekitten.com/g/250/250. Right-click the image, save it in the brushfire/assets/images/ folder, and name it logo.png. In Sublime, open brushfire/assets/index.html and add the following tags, similar to listing 3.4.

> **NOTE**   Each partial code listing is shown in context through a GitHub gist. For example, listing 3.4 can be found at https://gist.github.com/sailsinaction/628731cc9683256f8cc9. Each chapter has its own gist with a link on the chapter hub page similar to http://sailsinaction.github.io/chapter-3/.

Listing 3.4 Adding an image tag using a relative path in the homepage

```
...
<!-- This is the brand on the left-hand side. -->
<a href="/#" class="pull-left"><img height="29" width="25"
    src="images/logo.png" style="margin-top: 10px; margin-left: 10px;"></a>
<a class="navbar-brand" href="/#">Brushfire</a>
<div class="collapse navbar-collapse">
  <ul class="nav navbar-nav">
    <li><a href="/videos">Videos</a></li>
  </ul>
</div>
...
```

Add the image via an image tag using a relative path.

With the Sails server running via sails lift, navigate your browser to localhost:1337, and you should see something similar to figure 3.13.

Figure 3.13 The homepage with an image in the navbar using a relative path

3.2.7 Relative paths

The logic behind relative paths isn't very intuitive, so let's dig a bit deeper. Earlier, you used images/logo.png as the source path for the img tag in the navigation bar. This is a *relative* path. That is, images/logo.png will be appended to the location of the page that contains the img tag, brushfire/assets/index.html. So in this case, images/logo.png will be appended to brushfire/assets/, resolving to brushfire/assets/images/logo.png.

> **NOTE** Those of you who are really paying attention might be asking, "Because we're syncing these files to brushfire/.tmp/public, doesn't the path ultimately resolve to brushfire/.tmp/public/images/logo.png?" And the answer is yes. But because we're hiding the .tmp folder, we're looking at this from the perspective of brushfire/assets being the asset root route.

But using a relative path can be problematic. Let's look at another example to see why. In Sublime, open brushfire/assets/videos/index.html and add the same img tag to the videos page, similar to the next listing.

> **Listing 3.5   Adding an image tag using a relative path in the videos page**
>
> ```
> ...
> <!-- This is the brand on the left-hand side. -->
> <a href="/#" class="pull-left"><img height="29" width="25"
>    src="images/logo.png" style="margin-top: 10px; margin-left: 10px;"></a>   ⊲─┐
> <a class="navbar-brand" href="/#">Brushfire</a>
> <div class="collapse navbar-collapse">
>   <ul class="nav navbar-nav">
>     <li><a href="/videos">Videos</a></li>
>   </ul>
> </div>
> ...
> ```
> **Add the image via an image tag using a relative path.**

Make sure Sails is running via sails lift and navigate your browser to localhost:1337/videos. You should see a broken image link in your browser similar to figure 3.14.

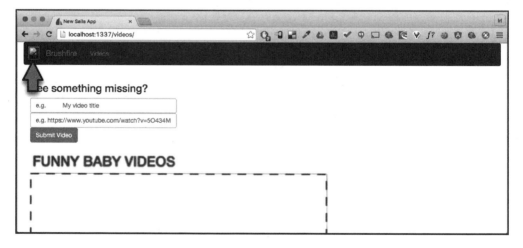

Figure 3.14   The source path within the image tag used a relative path that didn't exist and resulted in a broken link.

Why did the image tag break? This time the img tag is located in brushfire/assets/videos/index.html. The source path images/logo.png gets appended to brushfire/assets/videos/, resolving ultimately to brushfire/assets/videos/images/logo.png. Because that path doesn't exist, you get the broken link.

The solution is to add a leading / (slash) in front of the source path. Placing a leading / before the folder name changes the relative path to an absolute path. That is, the source path /images/logo.png will now be appended to the asset root or web root folder. Because the web root folder is brushfire/assets/, this will resolve to brushfire/assets/images/logo.png, which will display the image properly. Let's propagate this change to the videos page in brushfire/assets/videos/index.html, similar to the next listing.

Listing 3.6　Adding an image tag using an absolute path to the videos page

```
...
<!-- This is the brand on the left-hand side. -->
<a href="/#" class="pull-left"><img height="29" width="25"
  src="/images/logo.png" style="margin-top: 10px; margin-left: 10px;"></a>    ◁┐
<a class="navbar-brand" href="/#">Brushfire</a>
<div class="collapse navbar-collapse">
  <ul class="nav navbar-nav">
    <li><a href="/videos">Videos</a></li>
  </ul>
</div>
...
```

Add the image
via an image
tag using an
absolute path.

3.3　*Managing scripts and stylesheets*

It's often better to have all your dependencies available locally while developing an application. That, for example, allows you to develop without the dependence of an internet connection. You also get to take advantage of another aspect of the Sails asset pipeline called the `sails-linker` task. The linker will automatically add CSS and JavaScript file links to the asset folder, which can save considerable time compared to manually adding them. To illustrate how `sails-linker` works, you'll trade out your Bootstrap CDN link for a local copy of the Bootstrap library.

To do this, first remove the CDN links from brushfire/assets/index.html and brushfire/assets/videos/index.html. Next, go back to http://getbootstrap.com/getting-started/#download and download the Bootstrap distribution zip file. Uncompress the zip file and copy the bootstrap.min.css and bootstrap.css.map files into the brushfire/assets/styles/ folder. Make sure Sails is running via `sails lift` and navigate to localhost:1337. The homepage doesn't seem to have changed, but take a closer look at the page source, shown in figure 3.15.

```
<!--STYLES-->
<link rel="stylesheet" href="/styles/bootstrap.min.css">
<link rel="stylesheet" href="/styles/importer.css">
<!--STYLES END-->
</head>
```

Figure 3.15　The page source reveals the reference links to the Bootstrap and importer.css files.

In the page source, you can now see the links to brushfire/assets/styles/bootstrap .min.css and brushfire/assets/styles/importer.css. But how did these files get linked to the home page? (*Hint*: insert grunting sound.) That's correct, another Grunt task to the rescue. In fact, we've grouped a special collection of Grunt tasks introduced earlier as the `sails-linker` into the asset pipeline.

3.3.1 *Automatically injecting <script> and <link> tags*

The `sails-linker` task is one of the most powerful utilities in the built-in asset pipeline. It's one of the Grunt tasks: brushfire/tasks/config/sails-linker.js. Instead of having to manually insert `<script>` or `<link>` tags for file dependencies like in jQuery or Bootstrap, `sails-linker` automatically injects them for you. All you have to do is add some special `sails-linker` tags in the files where you want the dependencies added. For example, any files with a .css extension placed in brushfire/assets/styles will automatically be linked to any page that contains the special `sails-linker` tags:

```
<!--STYLES-->
<!--STYLES END-->
```

> **NOTE** As long as the Sails server is running, the injection takes place automatically via a `watch` Grunt task that monitors any changes to the brushfire/assets folder and updates any link as needed.

The same is true for files with a .js extension placed in the brushfire/assets/js/ folder. The script tags for those JavaScript files will be automatically included on any page with the `sails-linker` tags:

```
<!--SCRIPTS-->
<!--SCRIPTS END-->
```

> **NOTE** The Sails linker also takes HTML files from the /assets/templates folder and precompiles underscore templates into a JST file. These precompiled templates are placed in /.tmp/public/jst.js. We won't be using precompiled templates in Brushfire.

This is another concept that's better understood via an illustration. Figure 3.16 illustrates what happened when you added the bootstrap.min.css file to brushfire/assets/styles.

When you added bootstrap.min.css to the brushfire/assets/styles/ folder, Sails linker inserted a reference to it in brushfire/assets/index.html. This makes it much easier to maintain dependencies on the frontend, because you don't have to remember to manually add them. A quick look at the homepage reveals that a script has also been added to the page, as shown in figure 3.17.

By default, sails.io.js is generated by each project.

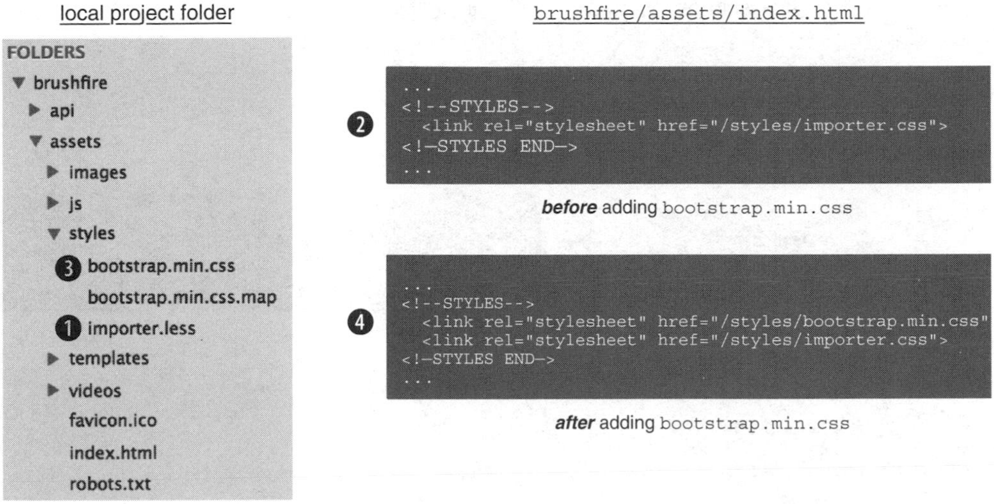

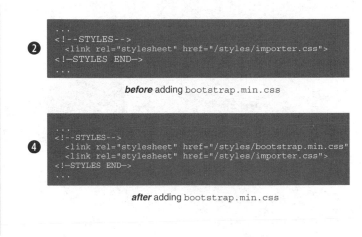

Figure 3.16　By default, an importer.less file **1** is generated for each new Sails project. You'll see later how importer.less is compiled into importer.css. What's important here is that the compiled importer.css file **2** was injected into brushfire/assets/index.html because it contains the special Sails linker tags. After adding bootstrap.min.css **3** to the brushfire/assets/styles folder, a link **4** was also automatically added to brushfire/assets/index.html for the bootstrap.min.css file.

```
<!--SCRIPTS-->
<script src="/js/dependencies/sails.io.js"></script>
<!--SCRIPTS END-->
```

Figure 3.17　The page source reveals the reference script tag to the sails.io.js file.

TIP　You'll explore sails.io.js in chapter 14 when you learn about WebSockets. For now, just know that any file added to brushfire/assets/js/ will be linked to in HTML files that contain the special `<!--SCRIPTS-->` tags.

Figure 3.18 illustrates how `<script>` tags were added to the homepage in the same way `<link>` tags were added earlier by `sails-linker`.

sails.io.js located in the brushfire/assets/js/ was automatically added as a dependency via the `<script>` tag by `sails-linker`.

3.3.2　Built-in LESS support

The following may disturb those of you who are CSS experts. We recommend averting your eyes when viewing Irl's styles—or rather his lack of style. We could use plain-ol' CSS for our styles, but we're fans of LESS. We like the way we get benefits from LESS without having to change much of how we use CSS. By default, a file named importer.less was created in the brushfire/assets/styles/ folder. In order for LESS files

local project folder

❸ brushfire/assets/index.html

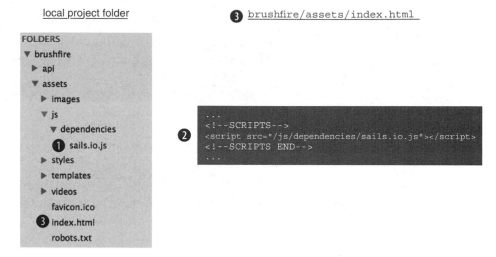

Figure 3.18   By default, a sails.io.js file ❶ is generated by each project and placed in the brushfire/assets/js folder. `sails-linker` ❷ inserts a reference to it in brushfire/assets/index.html ❸.

to be compiled and included automatically in the markup, you must first import them via importer.less. The imported LESS files are then compiled and included in the order in which they're listed each time the Sails server is started. So mixins, variables, and the like should be imported first so that they can be accessed by subsequent LESS stylesheets.

> **TIP**   If mixins and variables are foreign to you, we'll explain what you need to know to use them as they come up in the project.

Let's add some styles to a .less file and then import that file into LESS. In Sublime, create a new file named brushfire/assets/styles/custom.less and add the styles shown in the following listing.

Listing 3.7   Adding an external LESS file to brushfire/assets/styles

```
/* Center the logo*/
img {
  width: 100px;
  margin: 30px auto 0px auto;
  display: block;
}

/* Center the heading */
.jumboHeading {
  text-align: center;
  padding: 20px 0;
  font-size: 2.5em;
}
```

```
/* Center the heading */
.jumboSubHeading {
  text-align: center;
}
/* Don't display bullet points in list */
.the-list-of-videos {
  li {
    list-style-type: none;
  }
}
```

Next, open brushfire/assets/importer.less in Sublime and add

```
@import 'custom.less';
```

Make sure Sails is running via sails lift and navigate your browser to localhost:1337. The homepage should look similar to figure 3.19.

Figure 3.19 The homepage with the new styles in custom.less

If you look at the page source, you'll see that importer.less has been compiled into importer.css. As a sanity check, click the path to importer.css, and, as expected, you'll find the styles you just added as plain-ol' CSS.

3.4 *Frontend-first API design*

You're now ready to start preparing and designing the backend. In chapter 1, we emphasized the importance of identifying the requests made by each page in your application to guide backend development. Traditionally, requests can be faked on the frontend using a combination of techniques. It's useful to explore this traditional approach before we demonstrate, in chapter 4, how you can start with prototyping an actual backend at this phase of development using blueprints. First, we'll identify the requests for each page of Brushfire. Then, we'll use an array of dictionaries to simulate backend responses to each request.

3.4.1   *Identifying backend requirements*

Navigate back to the chapter 3 mockups, http://sailsinaction.github.io/chapter-3/mockups.html, and check out both the homepage with requests and the videos page with requests mockups. The homepage has two endpoints, which both make requests using anchor tags that are satisfied by asset routes. Therefore, the homepage doesn't have any additional requirements for your backend.

As shown in figure 3.20, however, the videos page has two requests that require you to simulate backend responses—one for video submissions and the other to load the initial video list.

Figure 3.20   The videos page has two requests, one for new video submissions and the other for the initial videos of the page.

Each request requires a visual mechanism for a loading state and a means for adding a new video to the page after a submission.

> **NOTE** Because we're faking the response, we won't implement the error states until we start making AJAX requests in the next chapter.

3.5 *Using Sails with jQuery*

Integrating jQuery as a dependency is easy. Head over to http://jquery.com/ and download the latest production/compressed version of jQuery. Copy that file into the brushfire/assets/js/dependencies/ folder, name it jquery.min.js, and you're finished. The jQuery library will now be added automatically to brushfire/assets/index.html and brushfire/assets/videos/index.html. You'll also use a popular JavaScript utility library called lodash.js. Navigate to https://raw.githubusercontent.com/lodash/lodash/4.5.0/dist/lodash.core.min.js and copy the contents of the page to a new file in brushfire/assets/js/dependencies/lodash.js.

3.5.1 *Example: listing data with jQuery*

Currently, the initial videos are hardcoded in the markup. Instead, you'll load them from an array using jQuery. Let's first alter the markup a bit to account for the classes you'll need to select elements with jQuery. In Sublime, open brushfire/assets/videos/index.html and alter the list-of-videos section to reflect the code that follows.

> **Listing 3.8 Adding classes to make selecting elements easier in jQuery**

```
...
<!-- LIST OF VIDEOS -->
<section class="the-list-of-videos col-md-12">
  <div class="loading">Loading videos...</div>
  <ul>
    <!-- VIDEO DATA INSERTED HERE AS HTML -->
  </ul>
</section>
...
```

Notice that you add an element for your loading state. You also remove the static YouTube video iframes, which will be replaced by dynamic-loading iframes via jQuery.

Next, create a new file for the jQuery code that will load the video list. In Sublime, create a new file named brushfire/assets/js/videos-page.js and add the jQuery shown in the next listing.

> **Listing 3.9 Adding jQuery to load the video list**

```
$(function whenDomIsReady(){

  $('.the-list-of-videos .loading').show();          ❶ Displays the
                                                         loading spinner

  setTimeout(function afterRetrievingVideos() {      ❷ Simulates a delay in
    var videos = [{                                      fetching the fake data
      title: 'FUNNY BABY VIDEOS',
```

```
      src: 'https://www.youtube.com/embed/_FvTVWjLiHM'
    }, {
      title: 'Justin Bieber - Baby ft. Ludacris',
      src: 'https://www.youtube.com/embed/kffacxfA7G4'
    }, {
      title: 'Charlie bit my finger - again !',
      src: 'https://www.youtube.com/embed/_OBlgSz8sSM'
    }];
    $('.the-list-of-videos .loading').hide();

    var videosHtml = _.reduce(videos, function(html, video){
      html += '<li class="video">' +
        '  <h2>' + video.title + '</h2>' +
        '  <iframe width="640" height="390" src="' + video.src + '"
        frameborder="0" allowfullscreen></iframe>' +
        '</li>';
      return html;
    }, '');

    $('.the-list-of-videos ul').replaceWith(videosHtml);

  }, 750);
});
```

❸ Hides the loading spinner

❹ Merges simulated data with an inline template

❺ Inserts videos into the DOM

The intent is to add a loading state and to simulate a response from the backend when the page loads. To accomplish this, when the page loads you first display the loading spinner ❶. You then simulate a delay ❷ in fetching the fake data so you can see the loading spinner in action. After receiving a simulated response from the backend, you hide ❸ the loading spinner. Next, you merge ❹ your simulated data with an inline template using the Lodash library. Finally, you insert ❺ the videos into the DOM.

> **TIP**   The `_.reduce()` method is handy for iterating through an array. It reduces the array of dictionaries to a value (merging your markup with the fake data), with the accumulated result being your list of videos.

This approach is just as an example—you should be HTML-escaping user input to prevent a possible script injection attack. Even better would be using a more structured frontend framework on top of (or in lieu of) jQuery. You'll be using Angular for Brushfire. We'll discuss XSS attacks and their prevention in chapters 9 and 15.

3.5.2   *Example: jQuery form*

For the videos list page, you needed to add a couple of classes to select elements via jQuery. The submit video form doesn't require any additional classes, but you do want it to perform the following tasks:

- Enable the loading state and disable the Submit button to prevent double submissions
- Harvest the `title` and `src` of the YouTube video from the form
- Extract the YouTube ID of the video
- Add the new video title and iframe to the DOM
- Disable the loading state and enable the Submit button

Head back to Sublime, open brushfire/assets/js/videos-page.js, and replace the current source with the following code.

> **Listing 3.10 Adding jQuery to process the submit video form**

```
$(function whenDomIsReady(){
  ...
  $('.the-submit-video-form').submit(function (e){        ← ① Binds a submit event on submit-video-form

    e.preventDefault();

    var newVideo = {                                      ② Harvests the data from the form
      title: $('.the-submit-video-form input[name="title"]').val(),  ←
      src: $('.the-submit-video-form input[name="src"]').val()
    };

    $('.the-submit-video-form input').val('');            ← Clears the data and displays the loading state
    $('.the-submit-video-form button').text('Submitting...');
    $('.the-submit-video-form button').prop('disabled', true);   ③

    var parser = document.createElement('a');

parser.href = newVideo.src

var youtubeID = parser.search.substring(parser.search.indexOf("=")+1,
  parser.search.length);
                                                          ④ Simulates a delay in fetching the fake data
    newVideo.src = 'https://www.youtube.com/embed/'+youtubeID;

    setTimeout(function (){                               ←
      var newVideoHtml = '<li class="video">'+
      '  <h2>' + newVideo.title + '</h2>'+
      '  <iframe width="640" height="390" src="'+newVideo.src+'"
      frameborder="0" allowfullscreen></iframe>'+
      '</li>';

      $('.the-list-of-videos').prepend(newVideoHtml);     ← Inserts the HTML
      $('.the-submit-video-form button').text('Submit Video');   ⑤
      $('.the-submit-video-form button').prop('disabled', false);

    }, 750);
  });
```

First, you bind a submit event ① on your submit-video-form and prevent the default browser from handling—this is 2016, after all. Next, you harvest the data from the form in the DOM ②. Now that you have the data from the input fields, you can clear them out and display the loading state ③. You also want to disable the Submit button to prevent double posting while loading. Because you need only the YouTube ID, you need to parse the URL provided for the ID. As you did for the video list, you can simulate the delay ④ your eventual request will cause, which gives you a chance to see the loading state. Next, insert the HTML ⑤ for the newly added video into the DOM. Then hide the loading state and reenable the Submit button.

Although it's not completely bulletproof, you have enough here for a user to submit a YouTube URL to Brushfire and for Brushfire to display the submission. The videos page is also backend ready with loading states and simulated delays to aid in testing those states. You'll postpone the creation of the error state until you actually make a request. With the Sails server running via `sails lift`, navigate to local-host:1337/videos. The videos page is rendered with the video list. Open a second browser tab and navigate to http://youtube.com. Search for a video, and then select and copy the URL of that video into the form on the submit videos page. Add a title and click Submit Video. The new video will be added before the first video on the page, similar to figure 3.21.

Figure 3.21   The added video from the `video-submit-form` using jQuery

Now that you know how to do this using jQuery, you'll transition your frontend to use Angular to do the same thing.

3.6   *Using Sails with Angular*

Adding Angular as a dependency is as easy as it was with jQuery. Head over to https://angularjs.org/ and download the latest stable uncompressed version of Angular. Copy that file into brushfire/assets/js/dependencies/, and you're finished. Angular will now be added as a dependency to any page that contains the `sails-linker` tags.

3.6.1 Example: listing data with Angular

You'll continue to load the video list from an array. First, you'll change the markup and add the necessary Angular files to display the list of videos. Open brushfire/ assets/videos/index.html in Sublime and replace the markup in the list-of-videos section, similar to what's shown in the following listing.

Listing 3.11 Adding Angular markup to load the video list

```
...
<body ng-app="brushfire_videosPage" ng-controller="PageCtrl">      ◁─── Adds ng-app and
...                                                                       ng-controller to
    <!-- LIST OF VIDEOS -->                                          ❶   the body tag
      <section class="the-list-of-videos col-md-12">
        <div class="loading" ng-if="videosLoading">Loading videos...</div>   ◁───
        <ul>                                                            Adds ng-if
          <li class="video" ng-repeat="video in videos" ng-           to toggle
      ➥    if="!videosLoading">                                       the Loading
            <h2>{{video.title}}</h2>                                  videos...
            <iframe width="640" height="390" ng-src="{{video.src}}"   indicator  ❷
      ➥      frameborder="0" allowfullscreen>
            </iframe>
          </li>
        </ul>
      </section>
...
```

Adds ng-if that toggles whether the video list is displayed ❸

First, add the standard Angular `ng-app` and `ng-controller` directives to the body tag ❶. Next, add an `ng-if` directive ❷ to toggle the Loading videos... indicator. The Boolean value of this directive toggles whether the loading indicator is displayed. Last, add another `ng-if` directive ❸ that toggles whether the video list is displayed.

> **TIP** You display the video list via the `ng-repeat` directive, which iterates through a $scope variable named `videos`.

Next, you'll create the necessary Angular code to simulate a request that fetches the initial list of videos.

> **NOTE** Because this book is primarily about the backend, we won't be teaching you Angular, but we want to show a few examples to get you comfortable with integrating it with Sails.

In Sublime, open brushfire/assets/js/videos-page.js and replace the jQuery code with the following Angular code.

Listing 3.12 Adding the Angular code to list videos in the videos page

```
angular.module('brushfire_videosPage', [])
.config(function($sceDelegateProvider) {           ◁───  Whitelists
  $sceDelegateProvider.resourceUrlWhitelist([           www.youtube.com in
    'self',                                         ❶   the .config function
```

```
    '*://www.youtube.com/**'
  ]);
});

angular.module('brushfire_videosPage').controller('PageCtrl', [
          '$scope', '$timeout',
  function ( $scope , $timeout ){

    $scope.videosLoading = true;

    $timeout(function afterRetrievingVideos (){
      var _videos = [{
        title: 'FUNNY BABY VIDEOS',
        src: 'https://www.youtube.com/embed/_FvTVWjLiHM'
      }, {
        title: 'Justin Bieber - Baby ft. Ludacris',
        src: 'https://www.youtube.com/embed/kffacxfA7G4'
      }, {
        title: 'Charlie bit my finger - again !',
        src: 'https://www.youtube.com/embed/_OBlgSz8sSM'
      }];

      $scope.videosLoading = false;
      $scope.videos = _videos;

    }, 750);
  }
]);
```

2 Creates a controller and passes in $scope and $timeout

3 Displays the loading spinner

Simulates a delay in the request to **4** the backend

5 Hides the loading spinner

Adds the returned **6** videos into the DOM

Sets the simulated **7** amount of delay

When the module first loads, it's necessary to whitelist www.youtube.com in the `.config` function **1** or errors will occur.

> **NOTE** The need for whitelisting is an issue with the use of an iframe in Angular; see https://docs.angularjs.org/api/ng/provider/$sceDelegateProvider.

Create a controller **2** and pass in two dictionaries: `$scope` and `$timeout`. You'll use Angular's `$timeout` **4** to simulate the delay you can get from a request to the backend. Adjusting the amount of this timeout is useful for being able to see the loading states in action. Next, display **3** a loading spinner by setting the value of the `videos-Loading` parameter to `true`, which connects to the `ng-if` directive in assets/videos/index.html. Then, simulate a delay **4** in the backend request while declaring an array that will contain your fake video titles and URLs. After the simulated response delay, hide the loading spinner **5**. Finally, add the returned videos to the DOM **6** through the magic of two-way data binding. You can also increase the delay in `$timeout` **7**. Let's see this in action. Make sure Sails is running via `sails lift` and navigate to localhost:1337/videos.

When the page loads, the video list is displayed, but the string interpolation `{{video.title}}` can flash briefly on some browsers before the actual titles are displayed. This is easy to fix with yet another Angular directive: `ng-cloak`. This directive ensures that an Angular HTML template isn't in its raw (uncompiled) form until the page loads. In Sublime, open brushfire/assets/videos/index.html and add `ng-cloak` to the `body` tag as follows.

Listing 3.13 Adding `ng-cloak` to the body tag in the videos page

```
...
   <!--STYLES-->
   <!--STYLES END-->
 </head>
 <body ng-app="brushfire_videosPage" ng-controller="PageCtrl" ng-cloak>
   <div class="container-fluid">
     ...
```

The directive has a corresponding bit of styling, so open brushfire/assets/styles/custom.less and add the styles shown here.

Listing 3.14 Adding `ng-cloak` styles to custom.less

```
...
[ng\:cloak], [ng-cloak], [data-ng-cloak], [x-ng-cloak], .ng-cloak, .x-ng-cloak {
  display: none !important;
}
...
```

3.6.2 *Example: Angular form*

To process the submit video form and display the videos list, you need to add some markup to the video page. In Sublime, open brushfire/assets/videos/index.html and replace the current markup under `<!-- SUBMIT NEW VIDEO -->` with this new markup.

Listing 3.15 Adding Angular markup to process the submit video form

```
...
 <!-- SUBMIT NEW VIDEO -->
   <section class="the-submit-video-form col-md-4">
     <h3>See something missing?</h3>
     <form ng-submit="submitNewVideo()">
       <input class="form-control" type="text" ng-model="newVideoTitle"
         ng-disabled="busySubmittingVideo" name="title" placeholder="e.g.
         My video title"/>
       <input class="form-control" type="text" ng-model="newVideoSrc"
         ng-disabled="busySubmittingVideo" name="src" placeholder="e.g.
         https://www.youtube.com/embed/Kdgt1ZHkvnM"/>
       <button class="btn btn-success" type="submit"
         ng-disabled="busySubmittingVideo">{{busySubmittingVideo?
         'Submitting...':'Submit Video'}}
       </button>
     </form>
   </section>
...
```

Annotations:
- ❶ **Adds an ng-submit directive** (points to `<form ng-submit="submitNewVideo()">`)
- ❷ **Adds the ng-model directive to the title input element**
- ❸ **Adds the ng-model directive to the src input element**
- ❹ **Adds the loading state**

Add an `ng-submit` directive to the form ❶ to submit it the Angular way. Next, add the `ng-model` directive to the `title` input element ❷, which connects the values to your

$scope. You also add the ng-disabled directive to prevent changing the field while it's being submitted. Similarly, add the ng-model directive to the src input element ❸, which connects the values to your $scope. Also add the ng-disabled directive to prevent changes to the field while it's being submitted. Finally, add the loading state to the button element ❹ when busySubmittingVideo is set to true, and add the ng-disabled directive to prevent multiple submissions while the form is being processed.

Now that the submission form markup is prepared for Angular, you need to update the Angular controller to reflect the new submit video form. Head back to Sublime, open brushfire/assets/js/video-pages.js, and add the following code.

Listing 3.16   Adding the Angular code for submitting a new video

```
...
$scope.submitNewVideo = function() {                          ❶ The submit event will
    if ($scope.busySubmittingVideo) {                            fire this function.
      return;                                                 ❷ Spin lock to prevent
    }                                                           double submission
    var _newVideo = {
      title: $scope.newVideoTitle,                            ❸ Harvests the data
      src: $scope.newVideoSrc,                                  out of the form
    };

    var parser = document.createElement('a');                 ❹ Creates an anchor
                                                                placeholder
    parser.href = _newVideo.src

    var youtubeID = parser.search.substring(parser.search.indexOf("=") + 1,
➡ parser.search.length);

    _newVideo.src = 'https://www.youtube.com/embed/' + youtubeID;

    $scope.busySubmittingVideo = true;                        ❺ Sets busySubmittingVideo
                                                                to true to display a
    $timeout(function() {                                       loading state

      $scope.videos.unshift(_newVideo);                       ❻ Simulates a delay

      $scope.busySubmittingVideo = false;                     ❼ Inserts HTML for the
                                                                newly added video
      $scope.newVideoTitle = '';      ❾ Clears form
      $scope.newVideoSrc = '';          inputs              ❽ Hides the loading state

    }, 750);
  }
}
]);
```

When new video is submitted, your form's submit event is bound to this function via ng-submit="submitNewVideo($event) ❶ in the HTML. You also add a little spin lock to prevent double submission ❷ because disabling the Submit button still allows a double post if a user submits using the Enter key. Harvest the data from the form ❸, and, thanks to ng-model, it's already in the $scope object. Because you need only the YouTube ID, you need to parse the URL provided for the ID. To do this, first create a placeholder anchor element ❹ and assign the entered URL to the attribute `parser.href`. Next, parse the URL using some string methods until only the YouTube `ID` remains. Update the `src` attribute of the `_newVideo` dictionary with the correct embed `Path`. Next, set `busySubmittingVideo` to `true` ❺ so you display a loading state and also disable form submission. Simulate a delay ❻, and then insert HTML for the newly added video ❼ on the `videos` array of the `$scope`. This will update the new values in the DOM. Next, hide the loading state ❽ and reenable form submission. Finally, clear out form inputs ❾.

With the Sails server running via `sails lift`, navigate your browser to local-host:1337/videos. The video list should be displayed. Open a second browser tab and navigate to http://youtube.com. Copy another YouTube video URL and use it to submit your updated form on the videos page. The new video is added before the first video.

3.7 Summary

- Server-rendered views combine backend data with EJS before being sent via a response to a requesting user-agent.
- Sails uses asset routes to respond to requests for static assets.
- The asset pipeline allows you to perform tasks for file concatenation, minification, dynamic linking, and it speeds up development by automating what would otherwise be manual tasks.
- It's important to set up loading states via a framework like jQuery and Angular to simulate requests.

Using the blueprint API

This chapter covers

- Expanding your understanding of the relationships among requests, routes, and actions in a Sails API

- Generating a backend API with blueprint routes and blueprint actions

- Integrating frontend requests with the blueprint API

- Using blueprint shortcut routes to access data from the browser

- Upgrading with WebSockets to provide realtime features

Chad loved Brushfire's ability to display and add YouTube videos. He soon discovered, however, the limitations of the simulated backend. When he refreshed his browser, all of the videos he added were no longer listed! We explained that this was because the links to the YouTube videos he added were stored temporarily in an array in memory. When he refreshed the browser, the array returned to its original state without his additional links in the list. Chad wasn't happy about this. Fortunately, we had anticipated this problem and had begun work on a true backend API that would store the added video links in a database. The next time Chad added a hundred videos to Brushfire (oops!), they'd still be there when he refreshed his browser. Let's see how we added this functionality to Brushfire.

In chapter 3, we created our initial frontend using Google's Angular web framework. You learned how to deliver static assets using the Sails asset pipeline. Finally, we prototyped a backend using the (previously mentioned) array to simulate a model and database response. We're now ready to refocus our efforts from the frontend to the backend and replace the fake or simulated backend with a fully operational API. To do this, we'll use another core component of Sails called *blueprints*. Blueprint routes and actions, combined with model methods, provide automatic CRUD endpoints around a given resource.

> **DEFINITION**   Recall that CRUD stands for create, read, update, and delete. These are the most common operations performed on stored data in an application.

This means is that, with a single command from the terminal window that generates a Sails API, you can start making AJAX requests to CRUD endpoints. These endpoints can create, update, and/or delete data in a model, as well as retrieve data from a model. It's so easy to create a JSON CRUD API around a resource that you don't even need to simulate a response from the backend. Instead, you can now instantly create the real thing.

4.1 *Prototyping with blueprints*

Figure 4.1 illustrates what you know about a backend API so far.

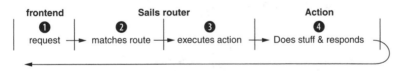

Figure 4.1   The backend API endpoint is triggered by a request from the frontend ❶. The Sails router attempts to match the route ❷, and if it finds a match, executes an action ❸. The action does stuff and responds to the frontend ❹.

Routes are triggered by requests. When a request is made, the Sails router looks for a matching route. If it finds one, the router executes a JavaScript function called an *action*. The action fulfills the requirements of the request by doing stuff added to the action and responds to the device that made the original request. The request, route, router, and action form the building blocks of the API. Instead of manually creating the routes and actions necessary for common CRUD tasks around a resource, you can generate them automatically using blueprints. But enough theory, let's get started building your API.

4.1.1 Designing an API around a user interface

In chapter 3, you identified two frontend requests on the video page of your interactive mockup: a request to list videos and a request to add videos, as shown in figure 4.2. You transformed this interactive mockup into the markup in assets/videos/index.html, and the requests were fulfilled by simulated responses. In this chapter, you'll fulfill those requests with a real backend based on blueprints.

In chapter 1, you learned the importance of also documenting the requirements of each request. The requirements for your requests can be found as a link in the

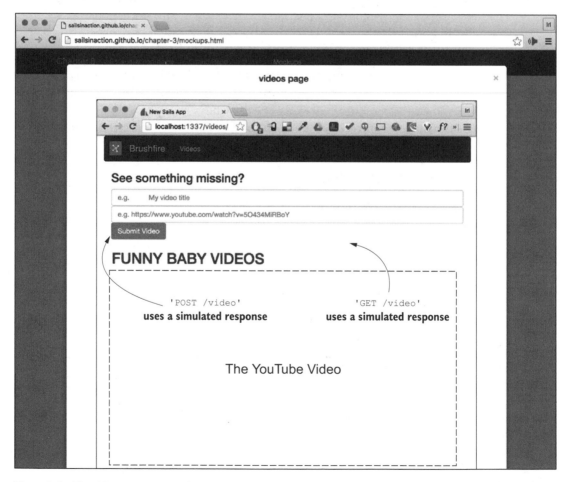

Figure 4.2   The video page can send two requests: one to post new video submissions and the other to get the initial videos of the page.

chapter 4 hub, located at http://sailsinaction.github.io/chapter-4/. The requirement of the list videos action is that Sails find all video records in the database and then respond with a JSON-formatted list of those videos. The requirement of the add videos action is that Sails take two parameters—title and src—as the basis of new records in the video model. Because these two requests are related, you'll group their routes together in one API resource named /video.

4.1.2 Obtaining the example materials for this chapter

To speed up your progress, you'll begin the next section with a fully baked frontend. We've added a few necessary changes to the frontend that you started back in chapter 3. These changes allow you to access your soon-to-be-created backend JSON CRUD API. Clone the chapter 4 repository https://github.com/sailsinaction/brushfire-ch4-start and install its Node module dependencies via npm install.

4.1.3 Generating an API in Sails

Generating a JSON CRUD API in Sails is easy. Head over to the terminal window and type

```
~/brushfire $ sails generate api video
info: Created a new api!
```

That's it. You now have a video JSON CRUD API.

> **NOTE** Recall that you already used the generate command in chapter 3 when you replaced the default server-rendered homepage with a static home-page. In this case, you ran this command to generate the necessary files and folders for a working API.

What did you create? Opening the project in Sublime reveals two new files in the brushfire/api/ folder: /controllers/VideoController.js and /models/Video.js. But the following two listings reveal that both the controller and model files are empty.

Listing 4.1 The initial contents of VideoController.js

```
module.exports = {

};
```

Listing 4.2 The initial contents of Video.js

```
module.exports = {

};
```

Unless disabled, Sails uses the mere existence of these two files to build the blueprint routes and actions in table 4.1 each time the Sails server is started via sails lift.

Therefore, unlike explicit routes, which are created and configured in brushfire/config/routes.js, blueprint shadow routes are created within the Sails core.

Table 4.1   An overview of the blueprint API generated for the `video` resource

CRUD operation	Shortcut blueprint routes			RESTful blueprint routes		
	Route address		Target	Route address		Target
	Verb	Path	Blueprint action	Verb	Path	Blueprint action
Read	GET	/video/find	find	GET	/video	find
Read	GET	/video/find/:id	find	GET	/video/:id	find
Create	GET	/video/create	create	POST	/video	create
Update	GET	/video/update/:id	update	PUT	/video/:id	update
Delete	GET	/video/destroy/:id	destroy	DELETE	/video/:id	destroy

DEFINITION   The *Sails core*, in the context of this section, means the source code of the Sails module. Recall that each Sails project has the `sails` module installed in brushfire/node_modules/sails.

You could override blueprint routes or actions by creating an explicit route or action with the same name, but for now you'll use the `blueprint` API as is.

4.1.4   *First look at Sails auto-migrations*

Sails created a `Video` model when it generated the `video` CRUD API, so it will prompt you for some information about model migrations when you next start the server. Go back to the terminal window and start Sails and your application from the command line by typing

```
~ $ sails lift
info: Starting app…
```

After a few seconds, you should see terminal output similar to figure 4.3.

Let's talk about data auto-migrations, which are quite fascinating. You'll select the `alter` option, and later in chapter 6 we'll come back to the topic. Also, in lieu of being prompted with this dialog each time you start Sails, open brushfire/config/models.js in Sublime and uncomment the `migrate` parameter, which has a default value of `alter`. When Sails is restarted using `sails lift`, auto-migrations will be set to `alter` automatically.

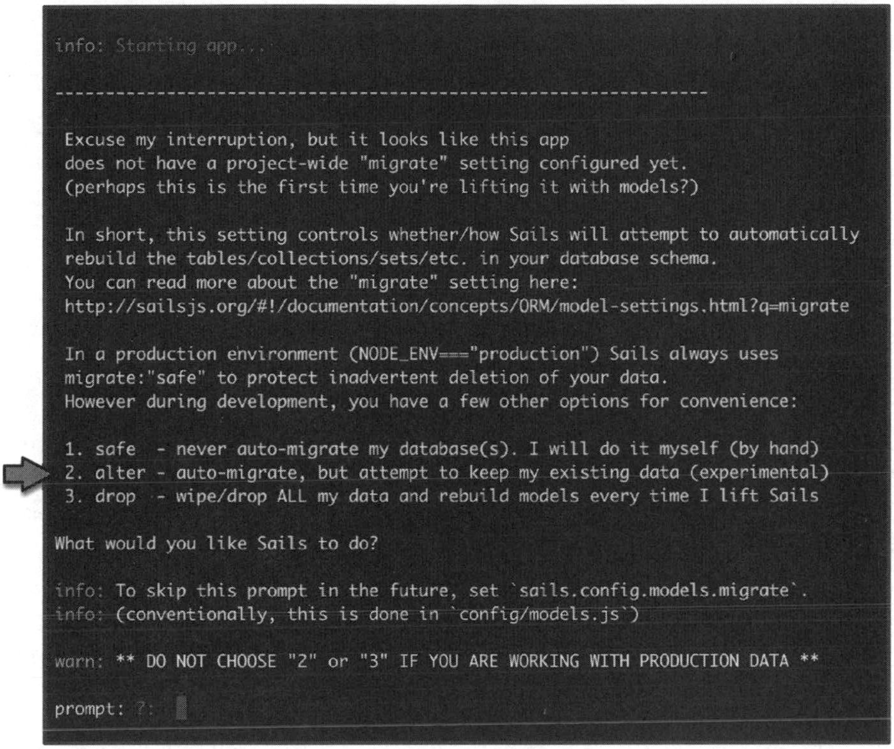

```
info: Starting app...

------------------------------------------------------------

Excuse my interruption, but it looks like this app
does not have a project-wide "migrate" setting configured yet.
(perhaps this is the first time you're lifting it with models?)

In short, this setting controls whether/how Sails will attempt to automatically
rebuild the tables/collections/sets/etc. in your database schema.
You can read more about the "migrate" setting here:
http://sailsjs.org/#!/documentation/concepts/ORM/model-settings.html?q=migrate

In a production environment (NODE_ENV==="production") Sails always uses
migrate:"safe" to protect inadvertent deletion of your data.
However during development, you have a few other options for convenience:

1. safe  - never auto-migrate my database(s). I will do it myself (by hand)
2. alter - auto-migrate, but attempt to keep my existing data (experimental)
3. drop  - wipe/drop ALL my data and rebuild models every time I lift Sails

What would you like Sails to do?

info: To skip this prompt in the future, set `sails.config.models.migrate`.
info: (conventionally, this is done in `config/models.js`)

warn: ** DO NOT CHOOSE "2" or "3" IF YOU ARE WORKING WITH PRODUCTION DATA **

prompt: ?:
```

Figure 4.3   Choosing between `safe`, `alter`, **or** `drop` **auto-migration in Sails**

4.2   *Shortcut blueprint routes*

Shortcut blueprint routes allow you to interact directly with the underlying database via the browser's URL bar. Why would you want to do that? Exploring the contents of one or more databases as you develop an API usually requires switching between different database viewers. Having a quick way to access information from a browser across multiple databases can greatly improve the speed of your workflow. When you generated the JSON CRUD API for the `video` resource, five shortcut blueprint routes were also exposed and made available. These routes, which correspond to common CRUD operations, enable you to find, create, update, and delete/destroy records from the browser. A list of the shortcut blueprint routes is shown in table 4.2.

Table 4.2   Blueprint shortcuts routes and blueprint actions

Route address		Target
Verb	Path	Blueprint action
GET	/video/find	find
GET	/video/find/:id	find

Table 4.2   Blueprint shortcuts routes and blueprint actions *(continued)*

Route address		Target
Verb	Path	Blueprint action
GET	/video/create	create
GET	/video/update/:id	update
GET	/video/destroy/:id	destroy

We pointed out in chapter 1 that the first thing you might notice about shortcut blueprints are that the route address uses the same verb, GET, for each route. Wouldn't that violate the convention that UPDATE, POST, and DELETE should produce no side effects? Yes, it would violate the convention, which is why you should never use shortcut blueprint routes in a production application. But during development, they're insanely useful. Later, when you transition to production, we'll show that they're very easy to disable.

4.2.1   Creating records with blueprint shortcut routes

Your current task is perfectly suited to shortcut blueprint routes. Recall from chapter 3 that the videos array contained three records with two attributes: the title of the YouTube video and the src URL of the video. You want to start development with some initial YouTube video records in the video model. Shortcut blueprint routes make it easy to re-create the catchy yet annoying "GANGNAM STYLE" YouTube video as a record in the video model. Make sure Sails is running via sails lift and navigate your browser to http://localhost:1337/video/create?title=FUNNY BABY VIDEOS &src=https://www.youtube.com/embed/_FvTVWjLiHM. Your browser should display a video record similar to figure 4.4.

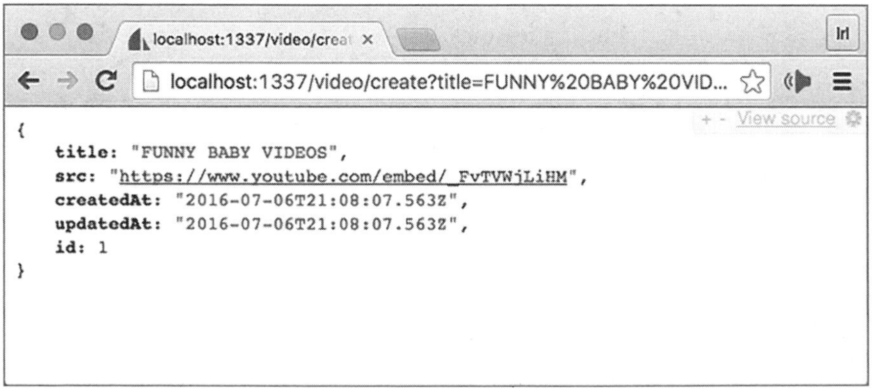

Figure 4.4   The shortcut blueprint route triggered the create blueprint action, which created a new video record in the video model and responded with the record's contents as JSON.

NOTE If you're a JSON geek, like us, you may notice in figure 4.4 that there aren't any quotes on the keys returned in the browser. That's because we're using a Chrome extension that uses JSON.parse to beautify the JSON.

How was this video record created? Let's go through the steps executed by this route illustrated in figure 4.5.

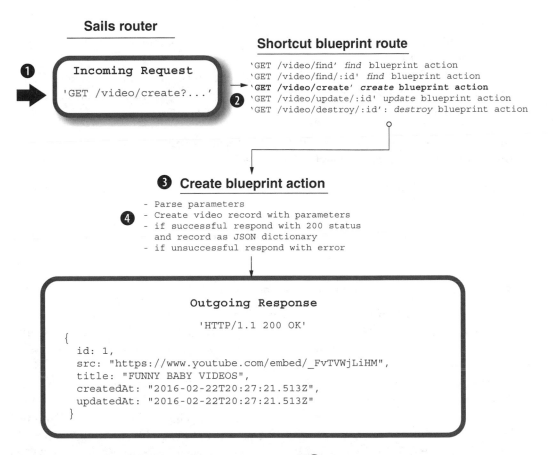

Figure 4.5 The Sails router listens for an incoming request ❶ and tries to match it to an explicit route. Not finding a match with an explicit route, it next tries to match it to a shortcut blueprint route ❷. In this example it finds a match, executes the `create` blueprint action ❸, and ❹ responds with a `200` status code and the newly created video record as JSON.

The GET request ❶ to /video/create matched a shortcut blueprint route, 'GET /video/create' ❷. The path also contained a *query string*. Recall from chapter 1 that a query string is part of the route address, as illustrated in figure 4.6.

The matched route triggered the `create` blueprint action ❸, which parsed the `title` and `src` parameters, created the record, and responded with JSON and status

Figure 4.6   The start of the query string uses a question mark (?) followed by field/value pairs where each pair is separated by an equals sign (=) and the field/value pairs are separated by an ampersand (&).

code 200 ❹. With Sails you can create, find, update, and delete records directly from your browser's URL bar.

Using the same steps, now create two additional records to the `video` model for the "Justin Bieber" and "Charlie bit my finger" YouTube videos. You can copy and paste the following URLs into your browser's URL bar:

http://localhost:1337/video/create?title=Justin Bieber – Baby ft. Ludacris&src=https://www.youtube.com/embed/kffacxfA7G4

http://localhost:1337/video/create?title= Charlie bit my finger – again !&src=https://www.youtube.com/embed/_OBlgSz8sSM

Let's expand our exploration of shortcut blueprint routes to include routes to find, update, and delete video records.

4.2.2   *Accessing the database from the URL bar*

We'll first examine how to find records with shortcut blueprint routes. To obtain a list of all video records, make sure Sails is running using `sails lift`, and navigate your browser to localhost:1337/video/find. Your browser should look similar to the browser in figure 4.7.

The path `/video/find` gets all of the `video` records. If you want to find a particular record, you'll use the `:id` parameter at the end of the path: `/video/find/:id`. In figure 4.7, notice how each video record has a unique `id`. This `id` is typically assigned by the database when the record is created. Let's use the shortcut blueprint route to find a particular video record. Open your browser and navigate to http://localhost:1337/video/find/3. Your browser should look similar to figure 4.8.

Here, the route returned the record with the `id` of 3 to the browser. Without the `:id` parameter, the `find` blueprint would have returned all video records.

Next, let's update the `title` parameter of a video record. You can do that by passing in the `id` of the record you want to update. The `id` becomes the *find criteria*.

> **DEFINITION**   *Criteria* is simply a dictionary that Sails uses to select one or more records from the database.

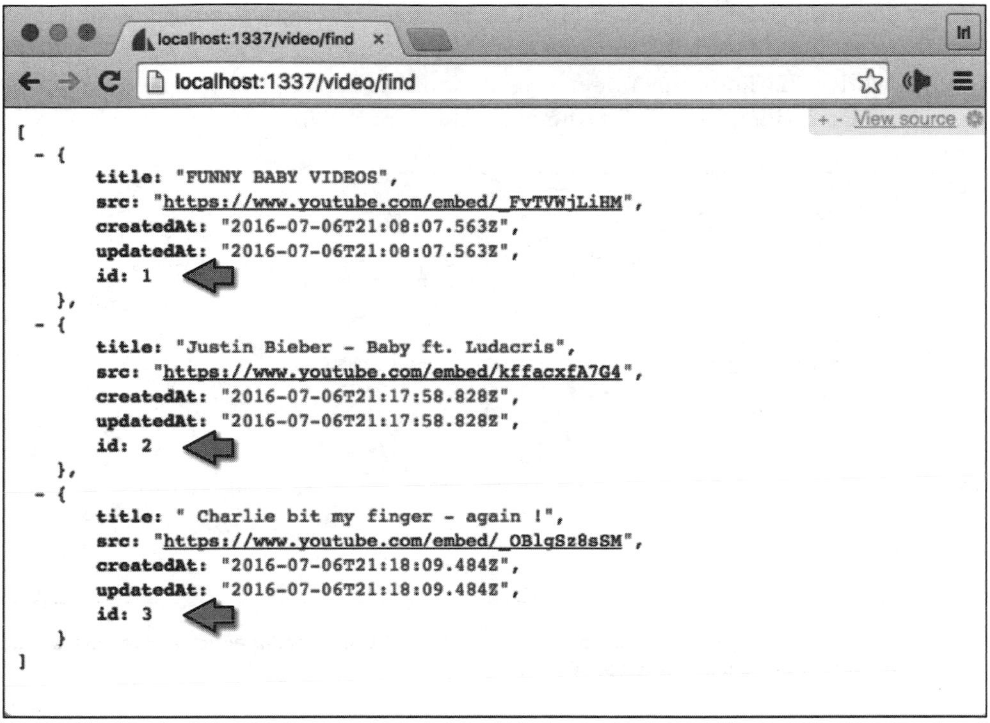

Figure 4.7 The shortcut blueprint route uses the `find` blueprint action and responds with a list of records from the `video` model.

Figure 4.8 When you add an `:id` parameter to the URL, in this case `/3`, the response is a single record from the `video` model.

The find criteria is followed by the parameter you want to update in the query string, in this case the `title`. Navigate your browser to http://localhost:1337/video/update/3?title=Charlie bit my finger – again and it HURT!!. Your browser should return the updated video record with the new `title`, as in figure 4.9.

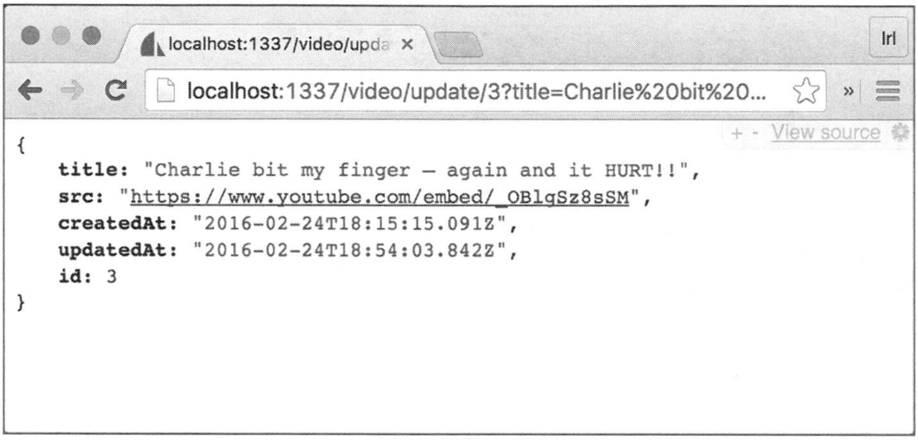
localhost:1337/video/upda
localhost:1337/video/update/3?title=Charlie%20bit%20...
View source
{
title: "Charlie bit my finger – again and it HURT!!",
src: "https://www.youtube.com/embed/_OBlgSz8sSM",
createdAt: "2016-02-24T18:15:15.091Z",
updatedAt: "2016-02-24T18:54:03.842Z",
id: 3
}

Figure 4.9 The shortcut blueprint route uses the `update` blueprint action and responds with the record containing the updated `title`.

By using the path `video/update/3` followed by the new title as a query string, the route updated the video record. Finally, let's delete a record using a shortcut blueprint route with the `destroy` blueprint action. Navigate your browser to localhost:1337/video/destroy/3. Your browser should look similar to figure 4.10.

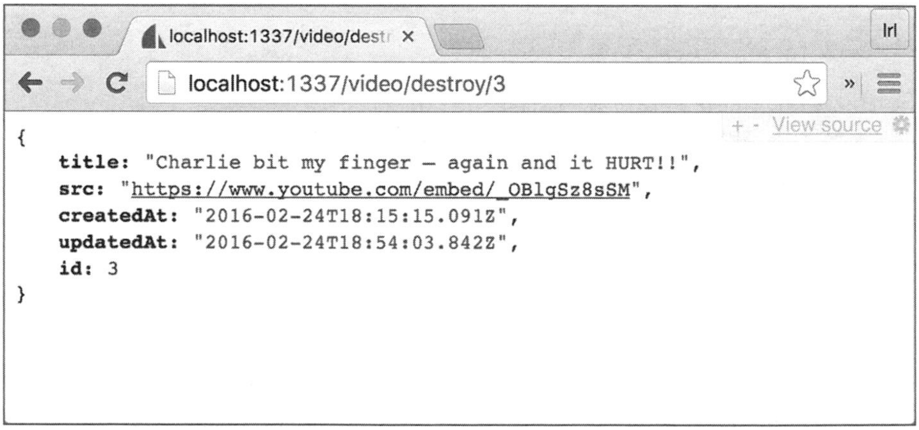
localhost:1337/video/destr
localhost:1337/video/destroy/3
View source
{
title: "Charlie bit my finger – again and it HURT!!",
src: "https://www.youtube.com/embed/_OBlgSz8sSM",
createdAt: "2016-02-24T18:15:15.091Z",
updatedAt: "2016-02-24T18:54:03.842Z",
id: 3
}

Figure 4.10 The shortcut blueprint route uses the `destroy` blueprint action and responds with the deleted video record.

You pass in the id of the record you want to delete, and the destroy blueprint action returns the destroyed video record. The shortcut blueprint routes are a useful tool in your development workflow, and their utility will become more and more apparent throughout the book.

4.3　*Connecting the frontend to your new API*

Now that you have a JSON CRUD API around the video resource, you can connect the frontend to it and satisfy the required functionality of your page's requests. Table 4.3 illustrates the RESTful blueprint routes that are exposed when the Sails server starts.

Table 4.3　RESTful blueprint routes and blueprint actions

Route address		Target
Verb	**Path**	**Blueprint action**
GET	/video/	find
GET	/video/:id	find
POST	/video	create
PUT	/video/:id	update
DELETE	/video/:id	destroy

In chapter 3, you simulated a backend request via a combination of the $timeout method and the use of an array. You'll now replace that code with the Angular $http service to make requests to your API. Specifically, you'll use $http.get() and $http.post() to make AJAX requests to find and create records in the video model. You could just as easily use jQuery, but you'll use Angular for consistency.

4.3.1　*Finding records with AJAX*

When the videos page initially loads, it expects to receive all records from the video model as an array. You can obtain the video records for that array via REST blueprints and the find blueprint action. But first take a look at the Angular AJAX GET request in brushfire/assets/js/video-page.js.

Listing 4.3　The Angular AJAX GET request to /video

The AJAX GET request triggers the RESTful blueprint route and the find blueprint action.

On error, the error is logged to the console.

On success, the find blueprint responds with a 200 status code and an array of video dictionaries.

```
...
$http.get('/video')
    .then(function onSuccess(sailsResponse) {
        $scope.videos = sailsResponse.data;
    })
    .catch(function onError(sailsResponse) {
        console.log("An unexpected error occurred: " +
        sailsResponse.data.statusText);
```

```
  })
  .finally(function eitherWay() {
    $scope.videosLoading = false;
  });
...
```

After making the request, the `find` blueprint action returns all the records in the `video` model as dictionaries in an array. Figure 4.11 shows how this process works within the API.

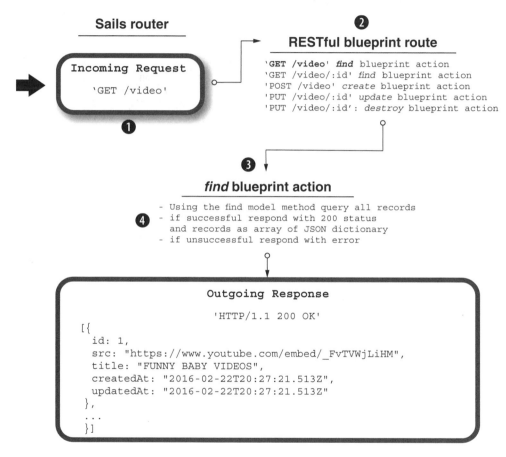

Figure 4.11   The steps in a RESTful blueprint route include recognition of the incoming request by the Sails router ❶, matching the request to a route ❷, and executing the `find` blueprint action ❸, which queries all video records ❹ and responds with an array of video record dictionaries.

The GET request to /video matched a RESTful blueprint route 'GET /video'. This triggered the `find` blueprint action, which queried all the records of the `video` model and responded with them in an array of JSON dictionaries. The important distinction here is that you're now retrieving the videos from an actual backend API instead of a static array.

4.3.2   *Creating a record with AJAX*

Now you need to send the Add Videos request when the Submit Videos button is clicked. You'll use a blueprint API again this time to create a new video record. Take a look at the Angular AJAX POST request in brushfire/assets/js/video-page.js in the next listing.

Listing 4.4   The Angular AJAX POST request to `/video`

```
...
$http.post('/video', {                          The AJAX POST request
    title: _newVideo.title,                     triggers the blueprint RESTful
    src: _newVideo.src                          route and the create action.
  })
  .then(function onSuccess(sailsResponse) {      On success, the create
                                                 action responds with a 200
    // add video to the array videos in the scope    status code and the new
    $scope.videos.unshift(_newVideo);            video record as a dictionary.
  })
  .catch(function onError(sailsResponse) {
    console.log("An unexpected error occurred: " +   On error, the
    ➥ sailsResponse.data.statusText);            error is logged.
  })
  .finally(function eitherWay() {
    $scope.busySubmittingVideo = false;
    $scope.newVideoTitle = '';
    $scope.newVideoSrc = '';
  });
...
```

Recall that in chapter 3 you wired up the Submit button of your form to push the new video onto an array on the $scope. You've now refactored the code to trigger an Angular AJAX POST request to /video instead. Let's see this in action. Make sure Sails is running via sails lift and navigate your browser to http://localhost:1337/videos/, which should look similar to figure 4.12.

Fill out the form and add a new record with the parameters in table 4.4.

Table 4.4   The parameters to create a new YouTube video record

Parameter	Value
title	The North Face: Alex Honnold in Yosemite
src	https://www.youtube.com/watch?vICBrXUuwvgg

**Figure 4.12   The page triggers the RESTful blueprint route and the
`find` blueprint action and then responds with all records in the `video`
model.**

Your browser should now look similar to figure 4.13.

You can see how this process works within the API in figure 4.14.

The POST request to /video ❶ matched a RESTful blueprint route, 'POST
/video' ❷. This triggered the create blueprint action ❸, which parsed the title
and src parameters, created the record, and responded with JSON and status code
200 ❹. Once again, you're creating a video from an actual backend API instead of an

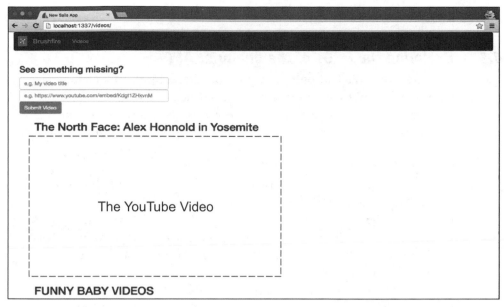

Figure 4.13   The RESTful route and a `create` action were triggered by the Angular AJAX `POST` request, and the action responded with the newly created record of the video.

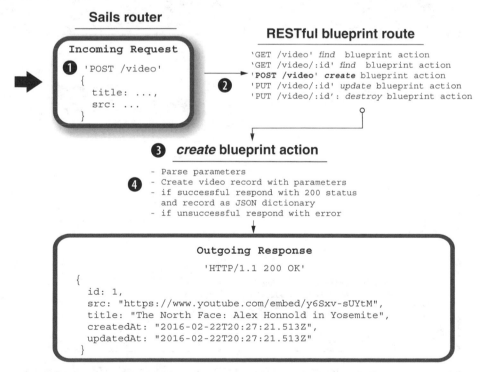

Figure 4.14   The RESTful blueprint route and a `create` action created a new video record based on a `POST` request to `/video`.

array. Next, let's explore the remaining RESTful blueprint routes: find, update, and destroy.

4.4   *Exploring the REST of the blueprint API*

Let's take the RESTful blueprint find, update, and destroy routes for a quick spin. Oftentimes, you'll want to test a route, but because of the complexity of the query parameters, using blueprint shortcut routes can become problematic. Enter Postman, the indispensable way to access and test an API. You installed Postman in chapter 1.

4.4.1   *Locating a particular record with AJAX*

Two RESTful blueprint routes use the `find` action. RESTful blueprint routes differentiate between obtaining a list of all records in a model and a single record in a model by using an `:id` parameter at the end of the path. If you make a GET request to `/video/:id` where the `:id` is the `id` of the record you want to find, Sails will return a single record. Let's see this in action. From within Postman make a GET request to `/video/2`, similar to figure 4.15.

After making the request, Sails returns the record with an `id` of 2 as a JSON dictionary in Postman.

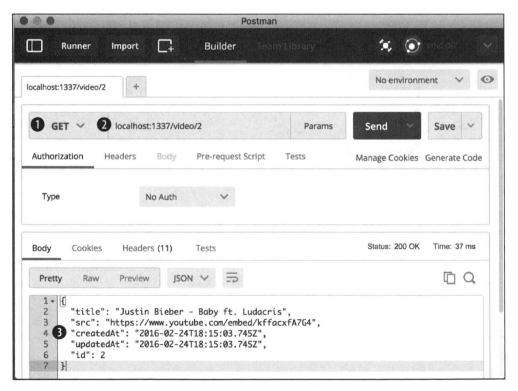

Figure 4.15   Here, you use Postman to make a GET request ❶ to the `/video/2` path ❷. The API responds with a JSON dictionary of the particular `video` record ❸.

4.4.2 Updating a record with AJAX

Suppose you're not satisfied with the title of a YouTube video. You want to change the title of Justin Bieber - Baby ft. Ludacris to just Ludacris.

Figure 4.16 demonstrates how to make the PUT request in Postman.

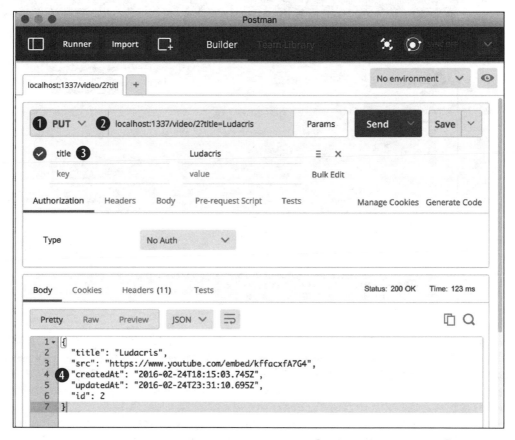

Figure 4.16 Here, you use Postman to make a PUT request ❶ to the path /video/2 ❷ with the URL parameter title=Ludacris ❸. The API responds with a JSON dictionary of the updated video record ❹.

Postman made the request on your behalf, updated the record, and returned the updated video record as JSON dictionary.

4.4.3 Deleting a record with AJAX

The Justin Bieber video has over a billion views and we're probably responsible for at least a thousand. Enough! We'll now show you how to delete the Justin Bieber record from the video model and in the process demonstrate another useful endpoint in the blueprint API. Figure 4.17 demonstrates how to delete a record by making a request in Postman.

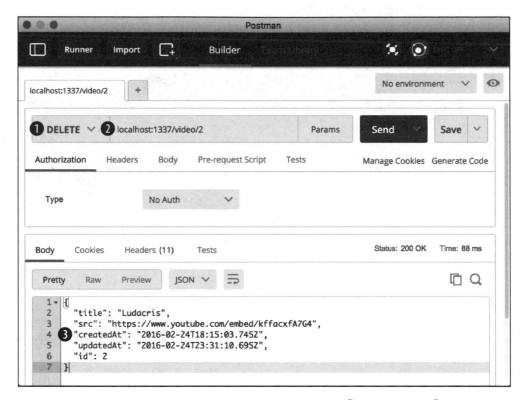

Figure 4.17   Here, you use Postman to make a a DELETE request ❶ to /video/2 ❷ that contains the record id that you want to delete. The API responds with the JSON video record that was deleted ❸.

Postman made the request, deleted the record, and returned the deleted record as a JSON dictionary. We've now reviewed shortcut blueprint routes, RESTful blueprint routes, and blueprint actions. You'll get your first taste of realtime programming in the next section using WebSockets.

4.5   *Upgrading to WebSockets*

After showing Chad the latest version of Brushfire using our prototyped API, he told us that he wants Brushfire to be realtime. We weren't exactly sure what he meant by this. After a few minutes of probing, we deduced that Chad wants Brushfire to update all browsers currently connected to the site at a particular moment with new YouTube videos as they're added. Luckily, we can quickly accomplish this by replacing our Angular AJAX methods with Sails WebSockets methods.

Chapter 14 explains in detail how to configure and use WebSockets in Sails. The Hypertext Transfer Protocol requires that a user-agent make a request to the server before the server can send a response to the client. WebSockets *upgrades* HTTP so that, once a connection is established, a server can send messages and data to the client at will. This mechanism is what Chad refers to as realtime. Let's take our first look at how WebSockets and realtime programming work.

4.5.1 Replacing $http.get() with io.socket.get()

Chad wants some way to update all browsers currently on the Brushfire website without a manual page refresh and after another user creates a new YouTube video link. You'll use WebSockets with some Sails components, pictured in figure 4.18, on the frontend and backend to satisfy this requirement.

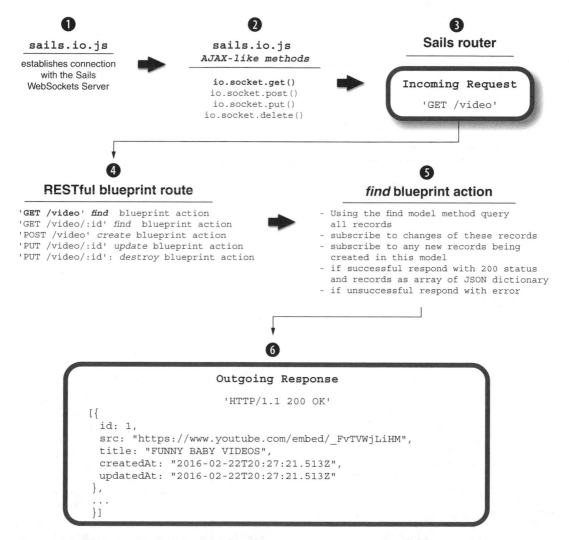

Figure 4.18 Replacing the AJAX GET request with the Sails WebSockets GET enhances the functionality of the find action.

Every new Sails application has a sails.io.js file, located in the brushfire/assets/js/
dependencies folder. By adding this file to the page in a script tag, Sails automatically
connects the browser to the Sails WebSockets server ❶.

You can also equate this file to the way adding jQuery gives you access to jQuery
AJAX methods. Sails provides similar AJAX-like methods ❷ to make requests, but
instead of using HTTP, Sails uses WebSockets. Table 4.5 compares Angular AJAX
methods with their Sails WebSockets equivalents.

Table 4.5 Angular AJAX requests vs. Sails socket requests

Angular AJAX requests	Sails socket requests
`$http.get()`	`io.socket.get()`
`$http.post()`	`io.socket.post()`
`$http.put()`	`io.socket.put()`
`$http.delete()`	`io.socket.delete()`

You'll use `io.socket.get()` instead of `$http.get()` ❷ to make the GET request to
/video. The Sails router will again listen for an incoming request ❸ and match the
request ❹ with the blueprint RESTful `find` route that triggers the blueprint `find`
action. The blueprint `find` action then tries to find all the records of the video
model. What's new is that the blueprint `find` action has some additional functionality
when triggered with Sails' WebSockets GET method. The action is now aware that this
is a socket request and automatically places the requesting browser on a list ❺ to be
notified if there are any changes to the video records found by the action. The blueprint `find` action places the requesting browser on another list to be notified if any
new records are created in the video model. Finally, the blueprint `find` action
responds ❻ with an array of the found video records as an array of JSON dictionaries.
Let's see this in action by replacing the Angular AJAX GET request with the Sails socket
equivalent. Open brushfire/assets/js/video-page.js in Sublime and make the changes
outlined here.

Listing 4.5 Replacing Angular AJAX GET request with `io.socket.get`

```
...
io.socket.get('/video', function whenServerResponds(data, JWR) {        ⤆
  $scope.videosLoading = false;

  if (JWR.statusCode >= 400) {        ⟵
    $scope.submitVideosError = true;
    console.log('something bad happened');
    return;
  }
  $scope.videos = data;

  $scope.$apply();        ⟵
```

On success,
returns video
records to
$scope.videos

If there's an
error, log it to
the console.

Replaces
$http.get() with
io.socket.get(),
passing /video
as an argument

Calls $scope.$apply() to update
the DOM because WebSockets
is not part of Angular

```
io.socket.on('video',
functionwhenAVideoIsCreatedUpdatedOrDestroyed(event) {

    $scope.videos.unshift({
        title: event.data.title,
        src: event.data.src,
    });

    $scope.$apply();
    });
});
...
```

① Event handler listens for changes to the video model (create, update, and destroy)

② Updates $scope.videos with the updated attributes

③ Triggers the digest cycle

The `io.socket.get()` method requires a URL path as a first argument, an optional data dictionary, and a callback. The callback will have two arguments, a `resData` dictionary that contains the body of the response and a JSON WebSockets response (`jwres`) that contains the entire response, including headers, body, and status code.

You might wonder why you add the `io.socket.on()` method **①**. Earlier, we explained that when `io.socket.get('/video')` triggered the blueprint `find` action, that action added the requesting browser's socket to a list. Whenever a video record is changed or a new video record is created, that list is notified of the event. The `io.socket.on()` method listens for the event and, if triggered, updates the `video` array on `$scope` **②**. Because Sails socket requests are not part of Angular, you need to use `$scope.apply()` **③** in order for the digest cycle to kick in and update the DOM. You're now equipped to listen for changes to the `video` model and update the DOM accordingly. To complete the process, you need to update the Add Video request to Sails WebSockets.

4.5.2   *Replacing $http.post() with io.socket.post()*

You now want to replace the Angular AJAX POST method with a method that uses WebSockets. The goal is that when a user submits a new YouTube video to Brushfire, an event will be triggered that lets any other user on the video page know that a new video was added. It will update the videos list with the new video without users having to refresh their browsers. Let's replace the Angular AJAX POST request with the Sails WebSockets equivalent. Open brushfire/assets/js/video-page.js in Sublime and make the changes outlined in the following listing.

Listing 4.6   Replacing Angular AJAX POST request with `io.socket.post`

```
...
io.socket.post('/video', {
  title: _newVideo.title,
  src: _newVideo.src
}, function whenServerResponds(data, JWR) {
    $scope.videosLoading = false;
    if (JWR.statusCode >= 400) {
      console.log('something bad happened');
```

Replaces $http.post() with io.socket.post(), passing the title and src attributes as arguments

If there's an error, logs it to the console

```
        return;
    }
    $scope.videos.unshift(_newVideo);
    $scope.busySubmittingVideo = false;

    $scope.newVideoTitle = '';
    $scope.newVideoSrc = '';
    $scope.$apply();
  });
  ...
```

◁── **On success, adds the new record via $scope.videos.unshift(_newVideo)**

◁── **Calls $scope.$apply() to update the DOM because WebSockets is not part of Angular**

Let's look at this in action. Make sure Sails is running via `sails lift` from the command line. Open a browser and navigate to localhost:1337/videos. Open a second browser window and navigate to localhost:1337/videos. This will simulate two different users accessing Brushfire. From either window, create a new YouTube video with the parameters in table 4.6.

Table 4.6   The parameters of a new YouTube video record

Parameter	Value
Title	The North Face: Alex Honnold in Yosemite
YouTube URL	https://www.youtube.com/watch?v=ICBrXUuwvgg

Your browser should look like figure 4.19.

The other window should automatically update with the new YouTube video.

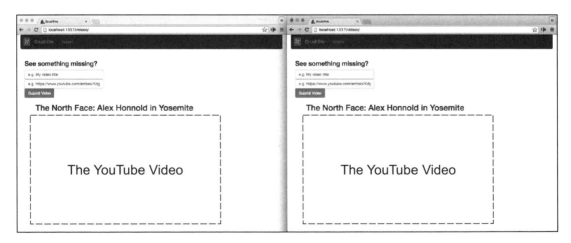

Figure 4.19   When the `io.socket.post()` method made a `POST` request to /video, the `create` action added the new video record that emitted a video event. This event was received by the previously added event handler, which triggered an update to the DOM with the new video record.

4.6   *Summary*

- Sails blueprints automatically generate the routes and actions necessary to produce JSON CRUD APIs around a resource.
- You can use blueprint shortcuts routes to find, add, update, and delete video records.
- Sails' WebSockets support allows the backend to send events to frontend user-agents at will.

Custom backend code

This chapter covers

- Setting up the initial state of your application
- Introduction to custom asynchronous code in Sails
- Counting the number of records in your database
- Creating a new record in your database
- Accessing a third-party API

Almost every commercial web application requires some way to run custom code "on lift," *before* it begins listening for requests. This usually involves creating seed data, like admin user accounts. As we introduce custom backend code in this chapter, we'll show how to use the config/bootstrap.js file to set up the data your application needs at startup.

Next, we'll provide an introduction to communicating with third-party APIs. Specifically, we'll show how to install open source packages from npm, and then take advantage of that preexisting code in your app (without having to write it yourself by hand!). In this chapter, we'll demonstrate how to use Node machines—reusable helper functions with standardized arguments, errors, and return values—but the concepts you learn here apply for any open source package on npm.

Finally, in the process, we'll explore some of the patterns (and anti-patterns) to look out for when writing custom logic for your Sails application, particularly as they relate to marshaling data and handling errors in synchronous versus asynchronous code.

5.1 Chad has a new investor

We just finished a phone meeting with Chad. He told us how he took what we built so far, called it a prototype, and spent a few weeks showing it to some investors. And, luckily, he found one individual who believed in his vision *so much* that she was willing to invest. She was on the call, actually, and introduced herself as Barbara. In just a few short minutes, before Chad could say another word, she'd already won us over. Besides being a very intelligent woman and sharing our love for technology, Barbara is Chad's mother. She keeps Chad on his toes, and it's clear that she knows how to get results.

So when our new investor told us that she believes cat videos are the next social media frontier and insisted that the application devote itself to user-curated cat videos, we nodded and took notes:

- Cat videos: the final frontier.
- Cats: content producers? Or content consumers?
- No one (person or cat) is going to use a video app without any cat videos.

Barbara brought up some important concerns about our lack of content. As it stands, all of Brushfire's videos have to be entered by hand. Barbara called this the common "chicken versus egg" problem with new applications. Brushfire needs users to create content, but it also needs content to attract users. To overcome this issue, we must find a way to seed the database with content—in this case, with cat videos.

5.1.1 Converting requirements into development tasks

Inspired by Barbara's advice, we met with Chad and worked out some requirements. Table 5.1 is the result of our discussion.

Table 5.1 Translating new requirements into actionable solutions

Requirement	Solution
Get cat videos into the system somehow without requiring users to enter them by hand.	Write some code in the config/bootstrap.js file that will be executed every time the Sails server lifts (via `sails lift`).
Check if there are any videos in the Brushfire database.	Use the `Video.count()` model method to determine how many records exist in the `video` model.
Search YouTube for popular cat videos and use those to seed the list of videos displayed on Brushfire.	Install an npm package called `machinepack-youtube` and use one of its methods (a.k.a. machines) to communicate with the YouTube API and search for cat videos. Then, use another model method, `Video.create()`, to create a new record in the database for each one of the results from YouTube. We might need to mess with the data a bit.

Now that we have our requirements and a plan for implementing them, let's get started.

5.2   *Running code on lift*

In chapter 4, you ran backend code by sending requests to your backend, which matched built-in blueprint routes and triggered blueprint actions. Because you were using blueprint actions, you didn't have to write this code yourself, but you could have. Whether blueprint or custom, controller actions run when an incoming request is received. In other words, the execution context, or *habitat*, of any controller action is the request. But in this chapter, you'll explore a slightly different habitat: raw Sails. The code you write in this chapter won't have access to a request, but it will still have access to other features of Sails, like model methods. And instead of running code whenever a particular type of HTTP or socket request is received, you'll trigger the execution of custom code when starting Sails via `sails lift`. To do this, you'll modify a special function in Sails' configuration called the *bootstrap*.

> **CAUTION**   Be careful not to confuse the Sails bootstrap function with the popular Bootstrap CSS framework. The Bootstrap CSS framework is a set of conventions and reusable stylesheets. The bootstrap function in Sails is where you can put custom code if you want it to run when the Sails server lifts.

So far, you've relied on built-in features in Sails, such as blueprint actions, for backend functionality. You haven't needed to write any custom backend JavaScript code yet. But that's all about to change. You'll still use many existing helpers and utilities provided by Sails, npm, and Node.js itself, but from here on out, it will be up to you to create your own custom code to fulfill tasks. As an implementer and not simply a user of code, you'll have the added responsibility of maintaining execution flow. Because Node.js is asynchronous, that can sometimes feel a bit different than in other languages like PHP or Java. Luckily, because Node.js uses JavaScript, you already have a big head start.

5.2.1   *Using bootstrap.js*

To better understand how the bootstrap function works, let's add some code to the bootstrap.js file and take it for a spin. Open config/boostrap.js in Sublime and add the following code.

> **Listing 5.1   A first look at the bootstrap function**

```
module.exports.bootstrap = function(cb) {

  console.log('Hello World!');                    ◁─┐  Logs "Hello World!"
                                                     │  to the console
  return cb();
};
```

Now, start your app using `sails lift`, and after a second or two, you should see the message `Hello World!` appear in the terminal window. What did you just do here? Figure 5.1 illustrates what happened when you started the Sails server.

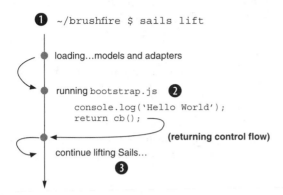

Figure 5.1 **After you started the Sails server, the bootstrap.js file was executed, in which your code logged** `Hello World!` **to the terminal. Then, you passed control back to Sails by calling** `cb()`. **At that point, Sails went about its business, completing the process of lifting the server.**

After you ran `sails lift` ❶ but before Sails started listening for incoming requests, Sails loaded the bootstrap.js file ❷ and executed your custom code. This bit worked just like JavaScript in the browser, except `console.log()` wrote a message to the terminal because this is backend code. In a blocking language like PHP or Java, that would be it! But because Node.js is nonblocking, many library functions are asynchronous. Because of this, the bootstrap function is *itself* asynchronous—which means that it provides a callback. Instead of returning from the bootstrap function, you invoke the callback function, `cb()`, to return control to Sails ❸.

> **NOTE** Whenever you implement an asynchronous function, it's critical that you explicitly call the provided callback, also known as an *outlet*. Otherwise, you'll never pass control back to whatever called your asynchronous function in the first place! In the case of the function defined in bootstrap.js, if you forgot to call the callback, then the Sails server would never start. Instead, it would hang until it eventually timed out and produced an error, telling you "The bootstrap function is taking too long."

Now that you've dipped your toe into implementing an asynchronous function, you're ready to write some more-meaningful backend code for the bootstrap function. You'll start off by using model methods to look up information from the database.

5.3 *A deeper understanding of model methods*

After looking at the requirements we put together at the beginning of the chapter, you see that your next task is to determine whether any existing records exist in the `video` model. To do this you'll use a model method: `.count()`. Because you're interested in counting the number of videos, as opposed to partridges, golden rings, or any other nouns that might be represented by tables in your database, you'll access `.count()` as a method of the `video` model, by calling `Video.count()`.

Remember back in chapter 4, when you ran `sails generate video` from the command line? You saw how this created a model definition file in brushfire/api/models/, and you witnessed the effect that it had on the blueprint API. But there was another handy side effect: when you lift your app, Sails builds a JavaScript dictionary called `Video` and exposes it as a global variable.

This gives you automatic access to `Video` from anywhere in your app, including the bootstrap.js file. So let's use it!

> **NOTE**   Besides `Video.count()`, the `Video` dictionary provides a smorgasbord of other methods for fetching, analyzing, and manipulating the videos stored in your database. We'll look at another one of those, `Video.create()`, later in this chapter.

5.3.1   *Using the Video.count() model method*

Unsurprisingly, the `Video.count()` method returns the number of records in the video model. You need to figure out whether there are *any* videos already in the database, so you can just count the records. If the number is greater than zero, then you know you already have at least one video. So let's take that for a spin. Open brushfire/config/bootstrap.js in Sublime and add the following code.

Listing 5.2   Count the records in the video model

When Video.count() finishes, it runs this callback. It receives either an error
or the number of videos. If an error occurs, bail out through your outlet,
cb(). This is the asynchronous equivalent of throwing an exception.

```
module.exports.bootstrap = function(cb) {

  Video.count().exec(function(err, numVideos) {
    if (err) {
      return cb(err);
    }

    if (numVideos > 0) {
      console.log('Number of video records: ', numVideos);
      return cb();
    }
    // TODO: Seed the database with videos from YouTube.
    console.log('There are no video records.');
    return cb();
  });
};
```

Executes Video.count().
This is asynchronous,
like setTimeout().

Otherwise, check numVideos
to see whether there are any
videos in the database yet.

If you made it here,
there are no existing
records, so you need
to seed the database.

But for now, just log a
message to the console.

Finally, execute the
bootstrap function's
callback, passing
control back to Sails.

If so, execute cb() to pass
control back to Sails. No
seeding today.

Stop Sails using Ctrl-C and restart it using `sails lift`. If you have existing records in the `video` model, your custom code in the bootstrap will execute and log the number of existing video records. Otherwise, if no existing video records exist, it will log a message saying so. Either way, it returns control to Sails so it can finish the lifting process, as shown in figure 5.2.

Existing records in `video` model.

No existing records in `video` model.

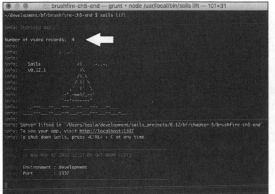
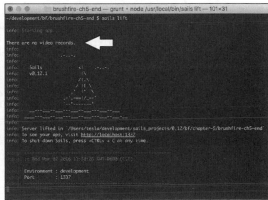

Figure 5.2 The `.count()` method calculates the number of records in the `video` model, and then, depending on the result, your code logs the appropriate message. Either way, you pass control back to Sails and it finishes lifting your app.

Now that you know how to check whether the `video` model contains any records, you can move on to the next requirement: programmatically searching YouTube for cat videos.

5.4 Introducing machinepacks

In chapter 1, you learned about npm packages as a way to take advantage of reusable open source code. This works well, but there's an even easier way. For many years, when you wanted to access a third-party API from Sails, you had the following choices:

- If the third-party API was hosted, you could look up the documentation and access it using an HTTP library like www.npmjs.com/package/request.
- You could copy and paste some code from a tutorial.
- You could search for an existing npm package and learn how to use it from its README file. Then, if you trusted it enough and understood the documentation, you could make it a dependency of your project and access it via `require`.

All these strategies are viable, but they can be problematic. For one thing, there are unavoidable differences in the way that various third-party APIs work. But what causes more confusion for many developers is that even among different npm packages for the same API, usage can vary dramatically. Machinepacks and the machine specification were designed specifically to overcome these inconsistencies.

The *machine specification* is a set of conventions for writing JavaScript functions, with a particular emphasis on open source distribution. These standardized JavaScript functions, called machines, are designed to make it easier to write code in Node.js.

Every machine provides a terse verb phrase (fewer than 140 characters) that describes its purpose—whether it's sending an email, translating a text file, or fetching a web page. It declares inputs, which tell you what arguments you need to pass in. And it declares exits, which serve two major purposes: to tell you what (if any) type of return value you can expect and to give you an easy way to handle certain exceptions or edge cases that might possibly arise.

> **NOTE** The *declarative* nature of machines makes them self-documenting, easy to understand, and, most important, consistent and easy to use, no matter the use case.

Machines are packaged together in *machinepacks,* which are a way of packaging up and publishing related machines. You'll start by using a package called `machinepack-youtube`, which will allow you to interact with the YouTube API.

5.4.1   Finding a package to work with the YouTube API

You know you need to access the YouTube API to search for cat videos. But where should you start? Like most things in life, you can Google it. Search for "youtube machinepack" or just navigate your browser to http://node-machine.org/machinepacks.

Node-Machine.org is a documentation site maintained by the Sails.js team. Any time a new open source machinepack (or a new version of an existing pack) is published to the npm registry, Node-Machine.org updates the documentation page for each of the methods (a.k.a. machines) in that pack. Each page includes metadata about what a particular machine does, the inputs it expects, the exit callbacks it knows how to handle, and sample code you can copy and paste into your app.

Here, you'll find a list of available machinepacks. Use Cmd-F, or scroll down until you find *YouTube,* as shown in figure 5.3.

Reviewing the list of machines, you'll see one that looks particularly promising: `.searchVideos()`. This machine claims to list YouTube videos that match a specified search query. That sounds pretty good, particularly if you were to send in a search query like "cats." Get more details by selecting `.searchVideos()` from the Machines list.

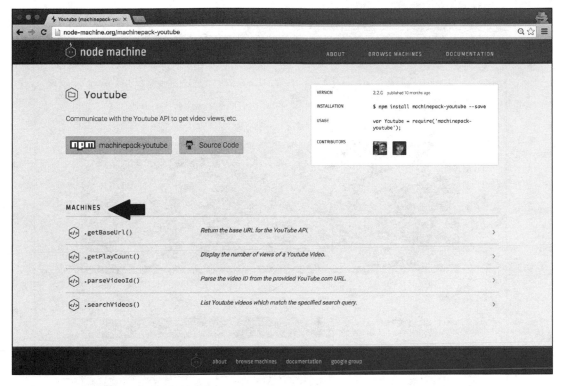

Figure 5.3 The page for `machinepack-youtube` provides a list of methods, called machines. In this case, all the machines are related to the YouTube API.

The main page for `.searchVideos()` on Node-Machine.org, shown in figure 5.4, provides an extensive description of the machine including example code **1**, available, required, and optional inputs and their types **2**, and what to expect as a result of executing the machine, also known as exits **3**. Before you can use `.searchVideos()` or `machinepack-youtube`, you need to install it into your project.

5.4.2 Installing a machinepack

The `machinepack-youtube` package is installed exactly as you installed the `sails-generate-static` package in chapter 3. From the terminal window, type

```
~/brushfire $ npm install machinepack-youtube --save
```

> **NOTE** The instructions in this section will install `machinepack-youtube` into your project's local dependencies in brushfire/node_modules/ (as opposed to installing it as a global dependency as you initially did with Sails).

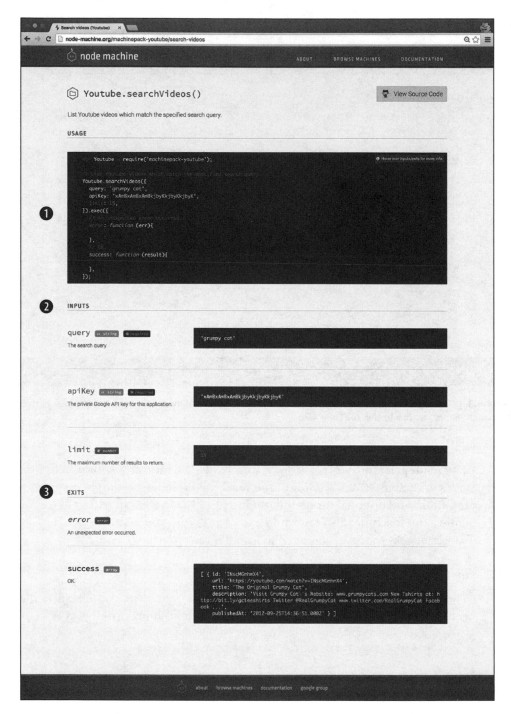

Figure 5.4   The `.searchVideos()` **machine page includes example code that you can copy and paste into your own project, the inputs expected by the machine, including their data types and whether they're required or optional, and what you can expect when the machine exits.**

By running npm install machinepack-youtube, you tell the local npm command-line tool to download source files for this package and install them as a local dependency in /brushfire/node_modules/. And because you added the -- flag, the dependency is also recorded in /brushfire/package.json. This is so that the next time you run npm install by itself to install *all dependencies* of your project, the proper version of machinepack-youtube will be installed automatically. But where do the source files for machinepack-youtube come from? The files are published and stored in the npm registry, as visualized by http://npmjs.com. Let's take a quick look at the npm registry.

5.4.3 Exploring npm

The npmjs registry contains literally hundreds of thousands of modules. Navigate your browser to www.npmjs.com/package/machinepack-youtube. You should see the main page for machinepack-youtube, similar to figure 5.5.

What's the difference between node-machine.org and npmjs.com? The npm registry is where you get the actual machinepack-youtube source files, whereas nodemachine .org is the place for documentation on how to use them.

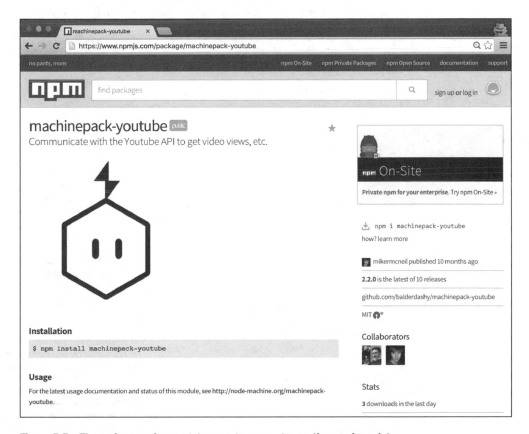

Figure 5.5   The main page for machinepack-youtube on the npmjs registry

NOTE   In this book, we'll be users (not implementers) of npm packages. For information about how to build your own npm package, visit http://node-machine.org.

Now that you understand the mechanics, let's take the `.searchVideos()` machine for a spin.

5.4.4   *Using machines*

You'll recall that your plan is to seed the `video` model with cat videos from YouTube. Now that you've installed a dependency that will allow you to do that easily, you're ready to use it in your code. Importing a machinepack is no different than using `require()` to import any other Node module.

In listing 5.3, you open brushfire/config/bootstrap.js in Sublime and paste the example code from node-machine.org into the callback from the `.count()` method.

NOTE   In subsequent examples, you'll pull the `require()` call up at the very top of the file, instead of calling it inline. This isn't strictly necessary for performance reasons, because Node.js caches the result from `require()` calls, but it does make it much easier to see what dependencies a particular file is using.

Listing 5.3   Using `.searchVideos()` in the bootstrap function

```
module.exports.bootstrap = function(cb) {

  Video.count().exec(function(err, numVideos) {
    if (err) {
      return cb(err);
    }

    if (numVideos > 0) {
      console.log('Existing video records: ', numVideos)
      return cb();
    }
    var Youtube = require('machinepack-youtube');          ❶ Imports (a.k.a.
                                                              requires) the
                                                              machinepack

    // List Youtube videos which match the specified search query.
    Youtube.searchVideos({                                 ❷ Executes the .searchVideos()
      query: 'grumpy cat',                                   machine to search YouTube
      apiKey: 'PLACE YOUR GOOGLE API KEY HERE',              for "grumpy cat" videos
      limit: 15,
    }).exec({
      // An unexpected error occurred.
      error: function(err) {
        console.log('an error: ', err);                    ❸ If anything goes wrong, this
                                                              error callback will be triggered
      },                                                      with details about the error.
      // OK.
      success: function(result) {
        console.log('the result: ', result);              ❹ Otherwise, the success callback
                                                             will be triggered with the result.
      },
    });
```

```
    return cb();
  });
};
```

> **Incorrect usage of the outlet callback. (This is called before you hear back from YouTube!)**

By assigning the result of calling `require()` in a variable (`YouTube`) ❶, you have access to all the methods (machines) of `machinepack-youtube` from any of your code in this file. When your app lifts and runs the bootstrap, your `.searchVideos()` ❷ instruction will run. Under the covers, it calls out to the YouTube API and waits for a result. When it finishes, one of your two different callbacks will run. You'll either log errors ❸ or log your output ❹.

But there's a bug in your code! Restart Sails via `sails lift`. Depending on whether records in your `video` model exist, the terminal window will display either the number of records that exist or an error similar to figure 5.6.

Existing video records →

No existing video records →

Figure 5.6 The terminal window might display the number of existing records in the `video` model. But if no records exist, you'll see this error because of a bug in the example code.

You'll come back to fix this bug a bit later in the chapter. But first, let's make sure you can consistently reproduce the error.

If you've created a few videos using blueprints, then you might have existing records in your `video` model. To reproduce this error, you need a way to remove all of these existing records. In chapter 4, we showed how to use shortcut blueprints to destroy records individually from the URL bar. But if you have a lot of records, that can get annoying. Fortunately, there are a couple of easier ways to do this: in the Sails REPL (`sails console`), or simply by wiping the database altogether. For now, because you're still using the default disk database, you'll wipe all of the data that's been created so far. Pop over to the terminal, and from the root of your project, type

```
~/brushfire $ rm -rf .tmp/localDiskDb.db
```

That's it! Any data that has been created so far is gone. And thanks to Sails' auto-migrations, the next time you lift Sails, an empty database will be re-created.

> **NOTE**   We'll go into more detail about how Sails interacts with databases in the next chapter. For now, just know that the localDisk.db file is where the data for your default, development-only database resides. And any time you delete it, Sails will just create a new empty localDisk.db file the next time you run `sails lift`.

Now, with no records, when you restart Sails with `sails lift` and the bootstrap function runs, it triggers your `.searchVideos()` instruction. If you're following along, your database should be in the same state as ours, so you should definitely see the error we showed earlier back in figure 5.6.

The problem here is that your `.searchVideos()` instruction (the code that calls the `.searchVideos()` machine) isn't configured properly. Even though machines are standardized, every machine expects a particular set of inputs. As in any code, if the argument for a particular machine input isn't provided correctly, weird things can happen. We'll take a closer look at machine inputs in the next section.

5.4.5   *Understanding machine inputs*

Node-Machine.org provides detailed information about the inputs expected by each machine. This information includes what type of data each input accepts, whether the input is required or optional, and an example.

> **DEFINITION**   The *inputs* of a function or machine are its hypothetical expectations. For example, the searchVideos() machine has an input named `query`. *Arguments* (also known as *input values* or *options*) are the actual values that you pass into an *instruction* (a particular occurrence of a function or machine) in your code. In bootstrap.js, you're currently passing in the string "grumpy cat" as your argument for the `query` input.

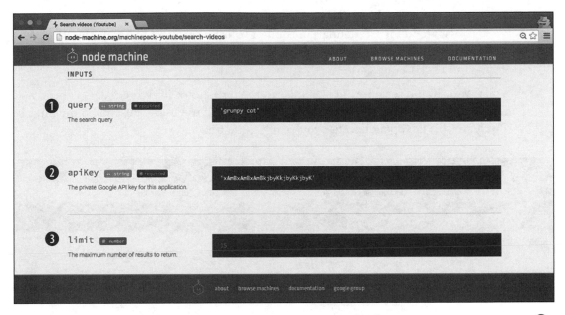

Figure 5.7 The `.searchVideos()` machine takes three inputs: the `query` to use when searching YouTube ❶, a Google developer API key ❷, and an optional `limit` on how many videos to return ❸.

The `searchVideos()` machine expects you to pass in a search `query` (like "grumpy cat") and a Google `apiKey`, as shown in figure 5.7. You already know that you'll be searching for cat-related videos; that part is easy. You'll have to try a couple of different queries to see what returns the best results. You will, however, need to figure out how to obtain your own Google API key.

Most APIs require some type of authentication to monitor usage, prevent abuse, and enforce rate limits. For example, if you exceed 300 lookups per hour, a Google representative might send you an email to ask you how you like the YouTube API and maybe even ask you to pay them some money. This is called a *soft limit*. But if you exceed 500 lookups in a single hour, you might get shut out entirely for a couple of hours (a *hard limit*). Finally, if you send way too many requests, and you don't get your act together and respond to Google's email, you could eventually be banned from the YouTube API altogether. Be sure to use a current email address when you sign up for developer APIs and check it frequently when you deploy your app in production!

Let's take a look at how to obtain an API key for the YouTube API. Although Google's exact user interface and steps change frequently, the basic principle is always more or less the same. For the sake of demonstration, here's how it works as of August 2016:

1. Create a Google account.
2. Navigate your browser to https://console.developers.google.com/.
3. Create a project.

4   Navigate to enable APIs.

5   Navigate to the Credentials portion of your new project to access the API key.

6   Click Create Credentials. Then, click Server Key, provide a name for the key, and click Create.

Voila! You should see an API key similar to the one shown in figure 5.8. Go ahead and select it and copy it to your clipboard, because you'll use it in your code momentarily. But leave this tab open, because you're not quite finished yet.

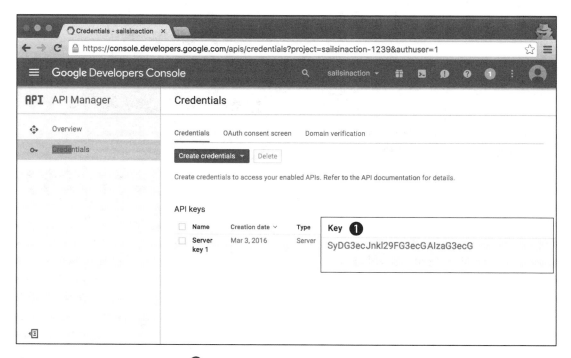

Figure 5.8   Your shiny new API key ❶ is displayed after completing the key-creation process in the Google Developers Console.

You're almost there, but there's one more important step in Google's setup ritual. Even though you now have your Google API key, if you were to try to use it to search for cat videos, Google's servers would simply laugh, slap their knees, and respond with an error. Presumably, this is because Google has so many different products, each with its own developer API, that they track them separately. But whatever the reason, that means you still need to *enable* the YouTube API in Google's dashboard. To do that, navigate to the overview page and click the YouTube Data API link. At the top of the page, you should see a button titled Enable. Take a deep breath, put your feet up, and click this button.

NOTE   The sort of setup flow described here varies between API providers, and it isn't always the most intuitive process. You'll probably encounter different names and styles of API keys. Sometimes they're called tokens, codes, or secrets, and occasionally you'll need to copy and paste two (or even three!) different strings. For some legacy APIs, you might need to call the company and speak to a representative. When in doubt, refer to the information on Node-Machine.org or check out the company's developer documentation.

If you're following along on your computer, congratulations! You just obtained a real Google API key and enabled access to the YouTube API. Now you can use that API key from your code in bootstrap.js, where you'll pass it in to the `.searchVideos()` machine. But just pasting it in there would be kind of messy. So, instead, let's look at a way you can store your new API key and any future credentials in one centralized location in the code base.

5.4.6 *Setting your own custom configuration in local.js*

You could have just pasted your API key inline in the bootstrap.js file. But there's a better way: custom configuration. Sails provides built-in support for creating your own custom, app-specific configuration settings, using the same mechanism that it uses internally.

As you might expect, the files in brushfire/config/ contain settings for various parts of Sails. When Sails starts, these configuration files are merged into one big dictionary called `sails.config`. For the most part, the actual names given to each file don't matter—they're purely organizational.

One notable exception is local.js, a configuration file with special meaning. This file is designed for use in development, and it has two useful properties: First, any configuration you provide in brushfire/config/local.js takes precedence over the rest of the configuration files in your app. Second, this file is explicitly excluded from version control by the default .gitignore file that was created when you first generated your new Sails app. This ensures that only people you explicitly share it with have access to the contents of local.js. If anyone with ill intentions gets access to your Google API key, they can use it to masquerade as you—or even to disrupt your application.

> **DEFINITION** .gitignore is just a hidden file at the top level of your project directory. Its job is to specify a set of paths that Git should ignore, meaning that they're not subject to version control. This is useful as a safeguard, because it prevents you from inadvertently uploading sensitive information to a remote repo like GitHub. It's also handy for making your development tools more efficient for everyone on your team. For example, the default .gitignore file in every new Sails app also ignores the brushfire/.tmp/ folder, because there's no reason to waste your time and bandwidth uploading a bunch of duplicate code every time you run `git push`.

Now, add your Google API key to the local.js file. In Sublime, create brushfire/config/local.js and add the following code. Be sure to paste in your own Google API key.

Listing 5.4   Adding to the local.js file

```
module.exports.google = {
  apiKey: 'PLACE YOUR GOOGLE API KEY HERE'
}
```

Because you exported `google`, you'll be able to access this dictionary as `sails.config.google` from anywhere in your application. Now, you need to change your code in bootstrap.js to grab the configured API key and pass it to `.searchVideos()`.

5.4.7   *Using custom configuration in your code*

Instead of pasting your API key directly into bootstrap.js, you'll set it using Sails' built-in support for custom, app-specific configuration. You configured the API key using the local.js file, but you could have done it any number of other ways: in a command-line option, in an environment variable, or in a different configuration file. But you still haven't seen how to actually *use* that custom configuration setting in your code. Let's begin.

A customized approach to configuration

We've often been asked, "Why not just use environment variables?" And the short answer is "Sure, why not!" You can write code in your Sails app that accesses the Node process's environment variables. But that approach tends to be less maintainable.

If, on the other hand, you build your app to expect custom configuration settings, you'll be able to set them in any of the myriad ways you can set the built-in configuration provided by Sails—including environment variables. Plus, by using Sails' conventional approach, you help everyone on your team know what to expect, even across different apps.

Open brushfire/config/bootstrap.js in Sublime, call `searchVideos()`, and plug in the configured API key shown here.

Listing 5.5   Using custom configuration

```
var Youtube = require('machinepack-youtube');

module.exports.bootstrap = function(cb) {

  Video.count().exec(function(err, numVideos) {
    if (err) {
      return cb(err);
    }

    if (numVideos > 0) {
      console.log('Existing video records: ', numVideos)
```

```
Youtube.searchVideos({
  query: 'grumpy cat',
  apiKey: sails.config.google.apiKey,
  limit: 15,
}).exec({
error: function(err) {
  console.log('an error: ', err);
},
success: function(result) {
  console.log('the result: ', result);
}
});
  }
});
}
```

The API key that was provided as a custom configuration setting

An unexpected error occurred.

Here's an extra-credit question: What would happen if you started the Sails server now? If you're thinking that Sails would refuse to lift because there's a bug in your code, then you're right! Take a close look at the code in listing 5.5. Notice that you don't call your own cb() (the callback from the bootstrap function) in either success or error. Remember, the bootstrap function in Sails is asynchronous, so you *have to* call its callback when you've finished. Now that you're using asynchronous functions (Video.count() and YouTube.searchVideos()), you aren't finished until the last of *their* callbacks fire.

If that doesn't quite make sense yet, don't worry. We'll show more examples of asynchronous flow control again and again throughout the rest of the book. To start with, let's take a closer look at machine exits.

5.4.8 *Understanding machine exits*

Exits are declarations of all of the possible outcomes of executing some code. If you're familiar with a strongly typed language like Java, this might sound familiar. Machines in JavaScript declare exits for the same reasons that methods in Java declare the exceptions they might throw and the type of data they return, if any. The success exit of a machine is the normal scenario—the scenario where everything works and it returns normally. The error exit of a machine is a sort of catchall. It means something went wrong—whether it was the caller passing in invalid data or an unhandled exception in the implementation of the machine.

Every machine has a success exit and an error exit, and in many cases, these are the *only* exits that a machine exposes. As you can see in figure 5.9, the .searchVideos() machine has only these two exits: success and error.

On closer examination, you can see that the success exit provides an example of the data you'll get back from the machine. In this case, you'll get an array of dictionaries, each of which contains five properties: id, url, title, description, and publishedAt.

Figure 5.9   Node-Machine.org provides details about the exits of each machine in every open source machinepack on npm.

NOTE   Machines use a special syntax called *RTTC exemplar notation* to represent data types. This ensures that every input and exit provides some sort of example, instead of just stating the expected or guaranteed data type. In most cases, reading exemplar notation is obvious. But if you encounter syntax you're not sure about, see http://github.com/node-machine/rttc for details.

Now that you know the potential exits for the .searchVideos() machine and you're aware of what data you can expect, you can apply that knowledge in your code.

5.4.9   Using callbacks

You'll first want to handle the error exit. Most of the time, this involves passing through the error to your outlet (the bootstrap function's callback, cb()). To handle the success exit, you'll log the result to the console and then pass control back to Sails by calling your outlet with no arguments. Open brushfire/config/bootstrap.js in Sublime and add the following to the machine exit.

Listing 5.6   Handling the exits for the .searchVideos machine

```
var Youtube = require('machinepack-youtube');

module.exports.bootstrap = function(cb) {

    ...
```

```
  Youtube.searchVideos({
    query: 'grumpy cat',
    apiKey: 'PLACE YOUR GOOGLE API KEY HERE',
    limit: 15,
  }).exec({
    error: function(err) {
      console.log('an error: ', err);
      return cb(err);
    },
    success: function(foundVideos) {

      console.log('the foundVideos: ', foundVideos);
      return cb();
    },
  });
  });
};
```

Passes err as an argument to the callback

Changes the default result to the more descriptive foundVideos

Logs the foundVideos and then passes control back via the callback

Next, restart Sails using `sails lift`. If `Video.count()` doesn't find any existing records, then the `.searchVideos()` machine will run and return a list of videos from the YouTube API. Head over to the terminal window, and you should see that it logged an array of 15 YouTube cat videos similar to the next listing.

Listing 5.7 The `foundVideos` from the `.searchVideos()` machine

```
[
  {
    id: 'INscMGmhmX4',
    url: 'https://youtube.com/watch?v=INscMGmhmX4',
    title: 'The Original Grumpy Cat!',
    description: 'http://grumpycats.com http://twitter.com/realgrumpycat
    ➡ http://facebook.com/theofficialgrumpycat
    ➡ http://instagram.com/realgrumpycat ...',
    publishedAt: '2012-09-25T14:36:51.000Z'
  },
  {
    id: 'qc5PgtdcUBU',
    url: 'https://youtube.com/watch?v=qc5PgtdcUBU',
    title: 'Happiness Finds Grumpy Cat',
    description: 'Grumpy Cat will do anything to avoid Happiness. Friskies
    ➡ Grumpy Cat Variety Pack, available at PetSmart stores. Go get it!
    ➡ Subscribe to the Friskies YouTube ...',
    publishedAt: '2015-08-04T18:00:19.000Z'
  }
},
...
```

You could save this fresh video data in your model right now. But the format of the data doesn't quite match what your frontend is expecting. The frontend expects an array of dictionaries with `src` and `title` properties. But YouTube uses `url` instead of `src`—plus, there are a bunch of extra properties that you don't need right now. You'll fix that by marshaling the data in the next section.

5.4.10 Marshaling data

Figure 5.10 compares the data received from running the `.searchVideos()` machine compared to the format the frontend is expecting.

```
[{
   id: 'INscMGmhmX4',
   url: 'https://youtube.com/watch?v=INscMGmhmX4',
   title: 'The Original Grumpy Cat!',
 ❶ description: 'http://grumpycats.com http://twitter.com/realgrumpycat
http://facebook.com/theofficialgrumpycat http://instagram.com/
realgrumpycat ...',
   publishedAt: '2012-09-25T14:36:51.000Z'
}, ...
                                              from the YouTube API


[{
 ❷  "title": "The Original Grumpy Cat",
    "src": https://www.youtube.com/embed/INscMGmhmX4
}, ...
                                              from the frontend
```

Figure 5.10   The data returned by the YouTube API ❶ is not in the format that the frontend requires ❷.

The differences are minor, but unless the data is exactly the same, your frontend won't work. Luckily, Sails and Node.js use JavaScript, a language you're already familiar with. You can write code to transform the data from YouTube into the exact format your frontend is expecting. This way, your frontend doesn't need to change.

   You already used the Lodash library on the frontend in chapter 3. The methods in Lodash are so useful that, by default, Sails exposes the library as a global variable automatically.

> **TIP**   Like all global variables exposed by Sails, the library can be disabled. This usually only comes up if you want to use a specific version of Lodash different from the one used by Sails.

Let's use Lodash to marshal the data from YouTube. From Sublime, open brush-fire/config/bootstrap.js, and add the following code within the `success` callback of the `.searchVideos()` machine.

Listing 5.8   Marshaling the returned data from the `.searchVideos()` machine

```
...
success: function(foundVideos) {

  _.each(foundVideos, function(video) {          ◁—  Iterates over each
    video.src = 'https://www.youtube.com/embed/' + video.id;   ◁—
                                                               video using _.each()
```

For each video, modifies the src so that
it uses an appropriately formatted URL

```
        delete video.description;
        delete video.publishedAt;          Deletes the
        delete video.id;                    properties you
        delete video.url;                   don't need
      });

      console.log(foundVideos);            ◁──┐  Logs the newly marshaled
      return cb();                    ◁─┐        videos to the terminal
    },
  });                          Executes the bootstrap's
  });                          callback, returning
};                            control to Sails
```

The `title` property can remain as is because it conforms to what the frontend expects. Next, you'll add the `src` property, combining a base URL with the `id`. You'll then remove `description`, `publishedAt`, `id`, and `url`. Once again, make sure you don't have any records in the `video` model. Restart Sails using `sails lift`. Returning to the terminal window, you should see the transformed records displayed in the console. An example of one of the transformed records is included in the following listing.

Listing 5.9   The transformed `foundVideo` records

```
[
  {
    title: 'The Original Grumpy Cat!',
    src: 'https://www.youtube.com/embed/INscMGmhmX4' },
  {
    title: 'Happiness Finds Grumpy Cat',
    src: 'https://www.youtube.com/embed/qc5PgtdcUBU' },
  ...
]
```

You can see that marshaling code has transformed the data from the raw format returned from the YouTube API into a format your frontend expects and can digest. You can now move to the final requirement: creating records in the `video` model using the newly transformed data.

5.5   *Creating multiple records*

Now that you have the data from YouTube transformed into the correct format for your application, adding it to the database through the model is trivial. Open brush-fire/config/bootstrap.js file in Sublime and add the following code.

Listing 5.10   Creating multiple records in the database

```
success: function(foundVideos) {          ◁── In bootstrap.js...
  ...
  Video.create(foundVideos).exec(function(err, videoRecordsCreated) {   ◁─┐
```
                                        ...run Video.create() and pass in the
                                        foundVideos array as an argument.

```
    if (err) {
      return cb(err);
    }
```
◁ **When you hear back, if an error occurred, pass it into your outlet and bail. This tells Sails to abort the lifting process.**

```
    console.log(videoRecordsCreated);
    return cb();
  });
}
```
◁ **Logs the array returned by Video.create()**

◁ **Calls your outlet to return control to Sails**

The `Video.create()` model method is asynchronous, just like `Video.count()`. You pass the transformed `foundVideos` array as its argument, and then, like the `Video.count()` method, you pass an anonymous function to `.exec()`, which binds it as a callback to the `Video.create()` method. The callback will be triggered when `Video.create()` has completed its attempt to create the records. If it's unsuccessful, you'll return an error as an argument via `err` to the callback and return control to Sails. If it's successful, you'll log the results and return control to Sails.

For the final time, make sure there are no records in the `video` model. Restart Sails using `sails lift`, and you should see the records that were created logged to the console. A couple of the `video` model records are displayed here.

Listing 5.11   The newly created video records

```
[
  {
    title: 'The Original Grumpy Cat!',
    src: 'https://www.youtube.com/embed/INscMGmhmX4',
    createdAt: '2016-03-04T01:13:49.417Z',
    updatedAt: '2016-03-04T01:13:49.417Z',
    id: 1 },
  { title: 'Happiness Finds Grumpy Cat',
    src: 'https://www.youtube.com/embed/qc5PgtdcUBU',
    createdAt: '2016-03-04T01:13:49.418Z',
    updatedAt: '2016-03-04T01:13:49.418Z',
    id: 2 },
  ...
]
```

You can see your newly created records in action via your frontend. Navigate your browser to localhost:1337/videos, and your browser should look similar to figure 5.11.

Figure 5.11   The transformed data from YouTube, now safely stored as new video records and displayed by the frontend

5.6   Summary

- Writing custom backend code in Sails.js isn't all that different from the JavaScript you're used to. But because you call *and* implement asynchronous functions more often than you might be used to, you have some new rules to remember.
  - If you're *implementing* an asynchronous function, then instead of returning or throwing an error, you trigger your callback, for example, cb().
  - If you're *calling* an asynchronous function within some other code, instead of expecting the asynchronous instruction to return data or wrapping it in a try/catch block, you attach callback function(s) to receive either the result or the error.
- Sails allows you to configure a bootstrap function that executes every time you lift your app, specifically, just before the Sails server starts up. This is particularly useful for seeding initial records in your database.
- You can require() and use any Node module in your Sails app, including any of the more than 350,000 open source packages available on npm. But because npm packages often vary widely in their usage, it's helpful to rely on

machinepacks whenever possible. Machinepacks are standardized npm packages that provide a systematic, reliable way to organize and use Node.js modules. Like the other conventions we've looked at so far, machinepacks are another way to save time and avoid technical debt by enforcing consistency across your code base.

- A special file in your app's config/ folder, called local.js, allows you to set custom configuration without checking it in to version control. This is particularly useful for plugging in sensitive credentials, like API keys.
- By default, model methods are automatically exposed on global variables that correspond with the names of each of your models. This allows you to fetch, analyze, and manipulate records in your database from custom code anywhere in your application.

Using models

Chad dropped by today. It seems he received a panicked call from the investor last night. She was using Brushfire and to her horror found hundreds of dog videos littering the site. Chad said she insisted in the strongest possible terms, "This will not stand." We explained to Chad that although we couldn't prevent dog videos from being added to Brushfire, we could require users to be logged in to be able to add videos. That way, if a user violated the Terms of Service (ToS), his mom/investor could ban the user's account with extreme prejudice. To accomplish this requirement, we'll need the user to establish their identity and prove that they're the person who created that identity. We can then personalize the frontend and control access to the backend (based on that proven identity). With few exceptions, applications we've built for clients inevitably involve this sort of requirement and the features displayed in figure 6.1.

Identity, authorization, and access control system

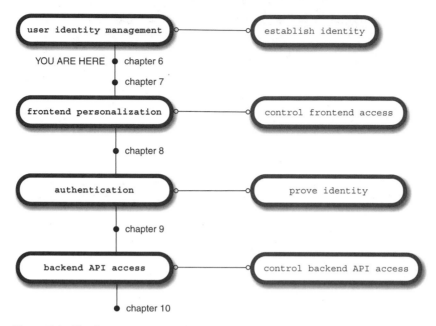

Figure 6.1   **The four components of an identity, authentication, personalization, and access control system**

We'll use this figure as a recurring map for chapters 6 through 10 to show where we are in the process of building out each component. We divided the implementation of user identity, authentication, personalization, and access control into four basic components in table 6.1.

Table 6.1   **Components of user identity, authentication, personalization, and access control**

Component	Description
User identity management	In chapters 6 and 7, you'll create user identity management that enables a user to claim and manage an identity. This component will also enable a super user, referred to as administrator, to manage all identities. The subcomponents of user identity management will be implemented in two parts. The first part is setting up the model, whereas the second part is using the model to fulfill requirements of the backend API.
Frontend personalization	Once you can determine whether a person is logged in or logged out, you'll want to use that state to control what's displayed on the frontend, also known as personalization. In chapter 7, you'll communicate the authenticated state to the frontend, controlling which assets are displayed. In chapter 8, you'll bootstrap the user's authenticated state on the page using server-rendered views. You'll then control what's displayed on the frontend using a combination of server-rendered views and client-side JavaScript.

Table 6.1 Components of user identity, authentication, personalization, and access control *(continued)*

Component	Description
Authentication	In chapter 9, you'll create the authentication component. The authentication component provides a way to challenge the authenticity of a user's claim to a specific identity and determine whether it's genuine on the backend. You'll store the results of the challenge (the authenticated state) between requests using sessions on the backend. Finally, using controller actions, you'll route requests between pages on the backend, which takes the authenticated state from the session and bootstraps that state onto server-rendered views that can be used by the frontend.
Backend API access control	Once a user is authenticated, you'll turn to what they have access to in terms of the backend API. For example, only a user who is authenticated and is the owner of a profile may restore it.

If some of these concepts are unclear, don't despair. By the time you've completed each chapter, you'll have a thorough understanding of not only the concepts but the practical application of using them in real-world examples.

Your first requirement is understanding and implementing user identity management. This involves creating and using a model of a user. We'll make sure you have a firm understanding of the model itself. You'll then concentrate on determining the requirements of the user model and (based on those requirements) implementing the model for identity management. Having an actual model also gives you an opportunity to examine more closely the databases where model records are stored. You'll then transition Brushfire from using the default sails-disk database to a PostgreSQL database. Finally, you'll get to know the main model methods via examples we'll use throughout the book.

6.1   *Understanding Sails models*

You now need a reliable way to create, store, and manage information about a user in Brushfire. But how do you create a new user record and where will it be stored? What will the user record contain and how can you control what's in it? The answers to these questions and more can be found in a *model.*

We first discussed models in chapter 1. If you skipped over that section and are unfamiliar with the concepts of models and databases, now would be a good time to go back and check it out before moving on. Let's start with the highest-level abstraction of a model definition. In Sails, a model is defined by a JavaScript dictionary. For review, figure 6.2 provides a high-level overview of the properties and methods in a model definition.

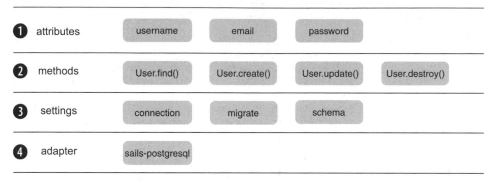

Figure 6.2   Model definitions consist of attributes, methods, and settings. In addition, every model is connected with a particular adapter.

Here are the takeaways of figure 6.2:

1   *Model attributes* are the properties of a user like the `username`, `email` address, and `password`.

2   *Model methods* are functions you use to find and manipulate database records.

3   *Model settings* are configuration settings for the model.

4   *Adapters* are npm packages that you can install in your project to add support for a particular database. Behind the scenes, the adapter is what allows Sails to provide a unified way of configuring, accessing, and managing a model. Sails takes care of translating this unified approach to the specific requirements of each database system.

Let's transition from talking about the model to identifying the attributes you'll use in it for user identity management.

6.2   *Managing user data*

How do you keep track of users? User identity management generally involves the creation, display, update, and removal of information about a specific user's identity. That identity is then used to distinguish the user within the broader application. To make this work, you need to create the subcomponents listed in table 6.2.

Table 6.2 User identity management components

Component	Description
Creating a profile with a signup process	The signup component allows a user to create an identity. Identity is based on one or more unique pieces of information. In your user identity management, you'll prompt the user for a unique email address and unique username. Either of these pieces of information can be used to identify a particular user. The signup process will also prompt the user to create a password. This password will later be used as proof of a claim to a particular identity.
Displaying a user profile	The user profile component displays information about the user via the `user` record. The user also has the ability to edit, delete, and later restore their profile.
Editing a user profile	Editing a user profile allows the user to edit various aspects of their `user` record.
Restoring a user profile	After a user authenticates successfully, this component allows them to restore their deleted user profile.
Administering a user profile	This component allows a designated admin user to perform administrative duties such as adding admin privileges to other users as well as banning users from accessing the system.

Now that you know the general requirements of your frontend, you need to transition those requirements into interactive mockups. Because this book is primarily about the backend and not building a frontend, we've provided the mockups for you in a GitHub repo.

6.2.1 Obtaining the example materials for this chapter

To prevent this book from becoming a multivolume set, you'll start with a fully baked frontend. That is, instead of describing the creation of the frontend, you'll concentrate on the backend and obtain the frontend assets via a GitHub repo. Navigate your browser to https://github.com/sailsinaction/brushfire-ch6-start, and you should see something similar to figure 6.3.

Copy the clone URL from the repo page. From the terminal window, type the following command:

```
~/brushfire $ git clone https://github.com/sailsinaction/brushfire-ch6-start
```

Change into the brushfire-ch6-start folder:

```
~/brushfire $ cd brushfire-ch6-start
```

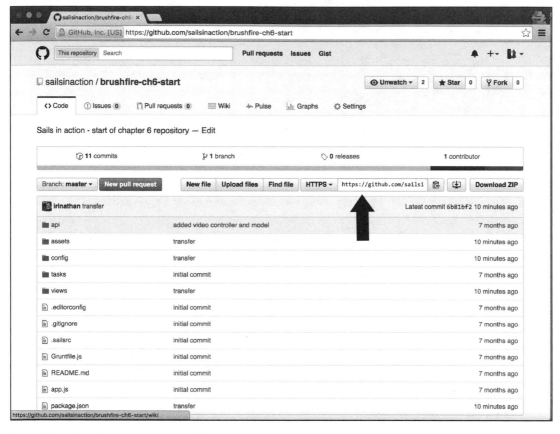

Figure 6.3   Clone the repo using the URL from the main repo page for the start of chapter 6.

Next, you'll install the Node modules listed in the brushfire-ch6-start/package.json file. From the terminal window, type

```
~/brushfire-chp6-start $ npm install
```

Finally, in chapter 5 you used the bootstrap function in Sails to add YouTube videos via `machinepack-youtube`, which requires a Google API key. In Sublime, copy the brushfire/config/local.js file you created in chapter 5. If you haven't completed chapter 5, you'll need to add a brushfire/config/local.js file and add the API key you created in chapter 5. Once you add in the API key, you're all set.

6.2.2   *A frontend-first approach to data modeling*

We'll again turn to our frontend-first approach for guidance on gathering model requirements. This will involve reviewing each interactive mockup to identify user model attributes and any validation or transformation requirements. You'll find a list of model requirements as a link from the chapter 6 hub, http://sailsinaction .github.io/chapter-6/, or directly from http://mng.bz/5yzx.

Validations check the value of a particular model attribute before it's stored in a record. You can specify that a value must exist for a `username` and, if it doesn't, produce an error when attempting to store it.

> **NOTE** As you'll see later in this chapter, because requests can be made outside the browser, any validation that you perform on the frontend will also be implemented on the backend to assure compliance.

A *transformation* changes the format of a model attribute to comply with some requirement. For example, when a user signs up, you'll use the user's email to create a Gravatar URL on the backend.

You want to take a systematic approach to reviewing the frontend mockups. To get an overview of what you need to review, take a look at the current organization of Brushfire's mockup pages illustrated in figure 6.4.

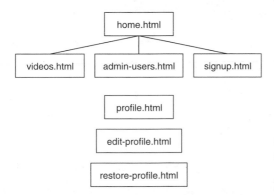

Figure 6.4 **Current organization of the interactive mockups. The profile, edit-profile, and restore-profile pages haven't yet been connected via links.**

This site map and interactive mockups can be found via link from the main chapter 6 hub page, http://sailsinaction.github.io/chapter-6/index.htmlor, or directly here: http://sailsinaction.github.io/chapter-6/mockups.html. The first mockup we'll review is the signup page.

6.2.3 Building a signup page

The signup page will establish a user's initial identity, as shown in figure 6.5.

EMAIL

To achieve identity, you need a minimum of two pieces of information, or *attributes*, in your model: a *unique identifier* and a *password*. For the unique identifier, a user's `email` address is a logical choice because it can serve multiple purposes. In addition to identity, the `email` address will be essential for tasks like notification when there's a

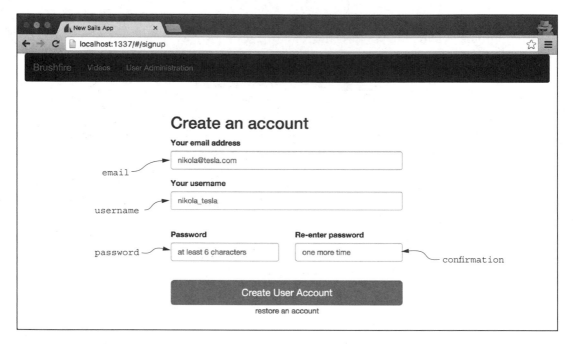

Figure 6.5   The signup page contains four `user` **model attributes:** `email`, `username`, `password`, **and** `confirmation`.

forgotten password, which you'll implement in chapter 11. You'll want to validate that the `email` address has the proper syntax and require it to create a `user` record.

USERNAME

You also have a requirement to display a Brushfire user profile to other users of Brushfire. Displaying an `email` address in such a profile would violate a user's privacy. Therefore, you'll prompt the user to create a unique `username` during the signup process that will display in the profile. The `username` will be required to create a `user` record and it must contain at least six characters. Finally, you want to restrict the `username` to using Aa–Zz and 0–9 only.

PASSWORD

You've set a minimum length of six characters for a user's `password`. You won't be storing passwords as clear text in the `user` model. Instead, you'll encrypt the user's `password` and label the resulting value of the encryption process as an attribute named `encryptedPassword`.

ENCRYPTEDPASSWORD

The `encryptedPassword` will be a required attribute to create a `user` record. The `confirmation` input field won't be stored in the database. Our review of the signup mockup page has produced the model requirements outlined in table 6.3.

Table 6.3 The signup page's model requirements

Input field	Attribute name	Req?	Type	Frontend and backend validations	Transformations
username	username	Yes	string	Must be unique. The attribute is required to create a record. The username can contain only Aa–Zz and 0–9.	None.
email	email	Yes	string	Must be unique. Must be a valid email address. The attribute is required to create a record.	None.
password	encryptedPassword	Yes	string	Password must be at least six characters. The attribute is required to create a record.	Password should be encrypted.

6.2.4 Building a user profile page

The profile page contains information about the user, as shown figure 6.6.

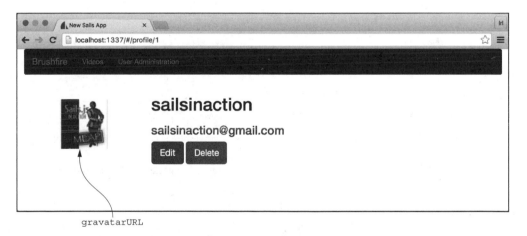

gravatarURL

Figure 6.6 The profile page contains an additional user model attribute we've named gravatarURL. This attribute will store the URL linking the Gravatar image.

The profile page adds the gravatarURL attribute to your user model. The investor wants each user to have a nice picture to represent them on the profile page. You'll use WordPress's ubiquitous Gravatar system for these profile pictures. Gravatar images are accessed via a generated URL based on the user's email address. You'll use the `email` to create and store a transformed URL in an attribute named `gravatarURL`. Table 6.4 contains the profile page's model requirements.

Table 6.4   The profile page's additional model requirements

Input field	Attribute name	Req?	Type	Backend validations	Transformation
`email`	`gravatarURL`	No	`string`	None	Create Gravatar URL from the email address.

6.2.5   *Building an admin interface*

This *administration* page allows a designated admin user to perform administrative duties such as add admin privileges to other users as well as ban users from accessing Brushfire, as shown in figure 6.7.

Figure 6.7   The User Administration page adds two `user` model attributes: `admin` and `banned`.

BANNED

When a user has been restricted from using the site for a violation of the site's Terms of Service agreement, you need a way to store the state of that user's access to Brushfire. You'll use an attribute named `banned` to store whether a user has restricted access.

ADMIN

You also want to limit the right to ban a user to only those users with administrator privileges. To accomplish this, you'll store whether a `user` has administrator privileges in an attribute named `admin`.

After reviewing the administration page, you have the model requirements listed in table 6.5.

Table 6.5 The administration page's additional model requirements

Input field	Attribute name	Req?	Type	Backend validations	Transformations
`banned`	`banned`	No	`boolean`	When a record is created, the field should be set to `false`.	None
`admin`	`admin`	No	`boolean`	When a record is created, the field should be set to `false`.	None

6.2.6 *Recovering data after a soft delete*

Your app includes a restore-profile page, which allows a user to undelete their profile. Let's examine the Restore a Profile page shown in figure 6.8.

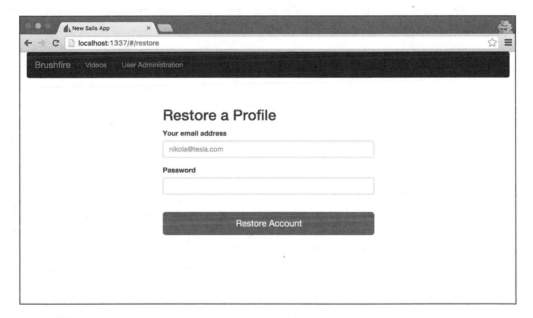

Figure 6.8 The restore-profile page allows a user to remove the deleted state of their profile. This will necessitate adding a `deleted` attribute to the `user` model.

Although the restore-profile page doesn't add any additional fields in the UI, you know you'll need a `deleted` attribute to hold the soft-deleted state of a `user` record.

NOTE We'll examine what a soft delete system entails in chapter 7.

Finally, you'll skip the edit-profile page because it doesn't add any additional model requirements. Now that you have your requirements, let's set about implementing them in an actual model.

6.3   *Creating a new model*

The first step in implementing the model is to generate a default model configuration file. In chapter 4, you created a `video` API that generated empty model and controller files. This enabled you to start using blueprint routes and actions to create and update `video` records. After the `user` API is generated, you'll create a `user` record with the supplied signup page that uses the blueprint RESTful `create` route and action. In chapter 7, you'll transform your blueprint routes and blueprint actions into explicit routes and custom controller actions.

6.3.1   *Running the generator*

Because you know you'll want both a `user` model and some way to manage it via controller actions, let's generate an API. Head over to the terminal window, and from the command line, type

```
~/brushfire-chp6-start $ sails generate api user
info: Created a new api!
```

Sails generates an empty controller and model similar to what it generated in chapter 4. Let's use the blueprint `create` route and action to generate your first `user` record.

6.3.2   *Creating your first record*

Now that you have a `user` API, let's use the knowledge you gained in chapter 4 to create a `user` record with blueprints. Figure 6.9 illustrates the request the Angular controller will execute when the user clicks the Create User Account button.

Not surprisingly, the purpose of this page is to collect the necessary information to create a record using attributes and methods in the `user` model. The form within the page contains four input fields: `email`, `username`, `password`, and `confirmation`.

The Angular controller will execute an AJAX `POST` request to `/user` and include three input fields as parameters when the Create User Account button is clicked.

NOTE   The `confirmation` input field won't be sent in the `POST` request.

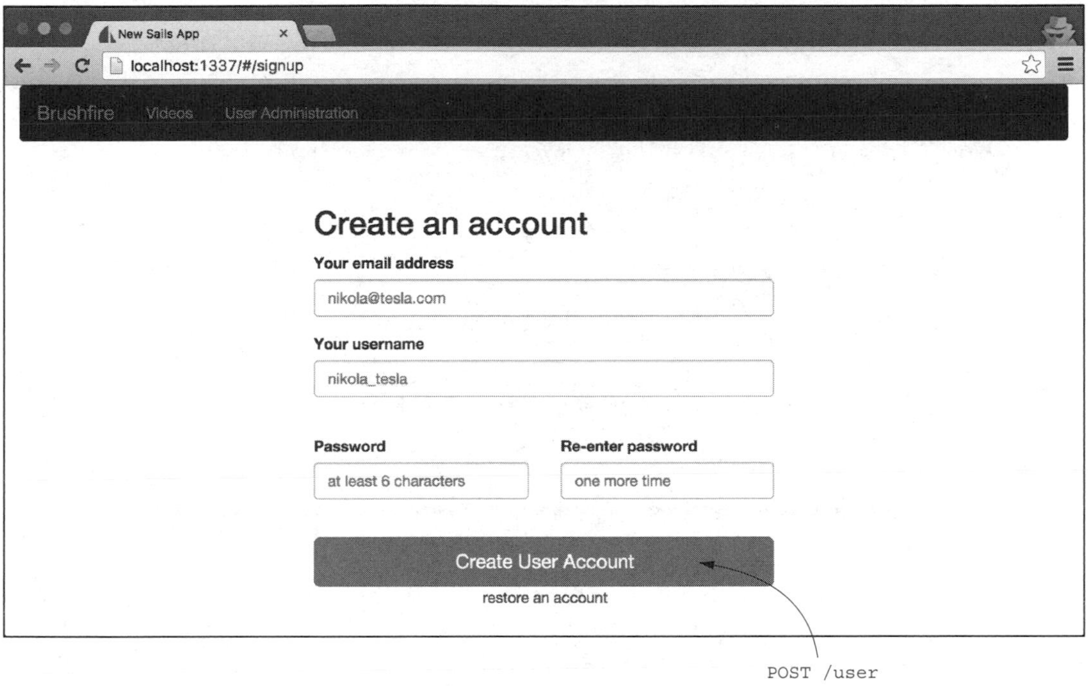

Figure 6.9 Clicking this button sends a POST request to /user.

In figure 6.10, the request **❶** will match the blueprint RESTful create route **❷** that will in turn trigger the blueprint create **❸** action that uses the User.create() model method to create a record **❹**. Let's see this in action. Restart Sails using sails lift and navigate your browser to localhost:1337/#/signup.

NOTE Why use the hash symbol in the path of your signup browser request? HTTP will ignore anything after the hash symbol (#). This allows other frameworks like Angular to come up with their own routing strategy. So, the /signup path of /#/signup is actually being processed by Angular's router and not by the backend Sails router. The Angular router then determines which template file to display. In this case, it's your brushfire/assets/templates/ signup.html file.

Next, sign up a user with an email address of sailsinaction@gmail.com, a username of sailsinaction, and a password of abc123. After clicking the Create User Account button, you should see something similar to figure 6.11 in your browser.

A user record was created using the three input fields from the signup form **❶**. Three other attributes were added to the record **❷**, including id, createdAt, and updatedAt. Where did these other attributes come from? The additional attributes are

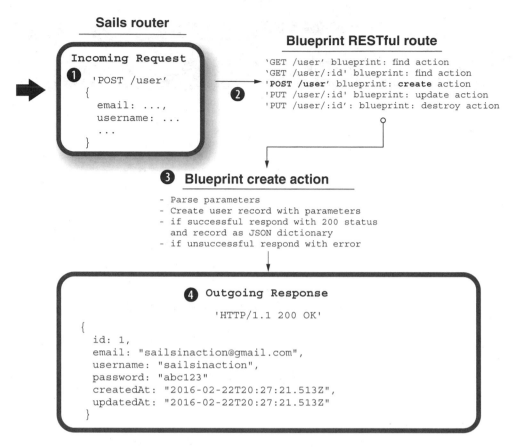

Figure 6.10   The Sails router listens for an incoming request, matches it to a RESTful blueprint route, executes the `create` blueprint action, and responds with a `200` status code and the newly created `user` record as JSON.

Figure 6.11   This is the result of the blueprint `POST` request to `/user` and the redirect to localhost:1337/user/1. In addition to the input fields that were added to the record, `createdAt`, `updatedAt`, and `id` were also added.

created by default with each new record in the database. We'll take a closer look at these three additional attributes in the next section.

You might be wondering how email, username, and password were added to the user record without being defined first as attributes in the user model. By default, Sails uses sails-disk for the database in a new project. The sails-disk database doesn't require a predefined set of attributes to save records using those attributes. This type of database is also referred to as a *schemaless* database.

> **DEFINITION** A *database schema* is a description of the database's structure: how data is organized and how it's constructed. In the case of a relational database, part of its structure is how it's divided into tables and columns. Because SQL databases require a schema, defining attributes provides the added benefit of enabling a model to be SQL compatible.

Let's next take a closer look at databases and the records they store on your behalf.

6.4 Demystifying databases

In chapter 1, we introduced a database as simply an application that stores an organized collection of data into records. The power of Sails models is that they abstract away many of the details you'd normally have to understand when it comes to creating, finding, updating, and destroying records in a database. It's helpful, however, to "follow the turtles all the way down" to the database level at least once. So let's go on a short turtle safari.

6.4.1 Models, connections, and adapters

Figure 6.12 illustrates the relationships between a model and its connection to a database through an adapter.

Each layer in figure 6.12 consists of three columns: the component, the location of the file that configures that component, and an example of a configuration. To determine which database a model will use to store records, Sails first looks in the model definition (for example, brushfire/api/models/User.js) for a connection property. The following listing shows an empty model definition.

Listing 6.1 An empty model definition

```
module.exports.models = {

  attributes: {

  }

};
```

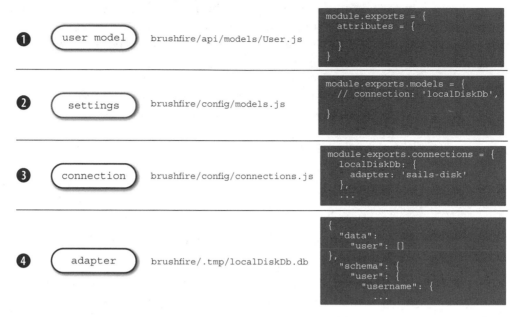

Figure 6.12   Sails looks for the database connection it will use to store and manipulate records for a particular model in brushfire/api/models/User.js ❶. If it doesn't find a connection, it then looks to model settings ❷. If no connection exists, Sails looks to the internal core default connection, `localDiskDb` ❸. The default connection uses the `sails-disk` adapter ❹ to access the `sails-disk` database.

This `connection` property is also referred to as the model's datastore. We'll use *connection* and *datastore* interchangeably in the book. The user model is currently empty and doesn't contain a `connection` property. So Sails will search for a `connection` property in the top-level model settings, which are typically defined by a configuration file located at brushfire/config/models.js. The next listing shows the global settings for all models.

Listing 6.2   The global settings for all models

```
module.exports.models = {

  // connection: 'localDiskDb',
  migrate: 'alter'

};
```
⟵ **Because there's no connection, the default localDiskDb connection is used.**

When Sails generated your project, one of the files it generated was brushfire/config/models.js with the `connection` property commented out.

> **TIP**   Many of the default configuration settings in Sails have corresponding commented parameters for convenience. This makes it easier to recognize the availability of a setting that can be overridden within a file.

Because your models.js file doesn't contain a connection property, Sails will instead rely on a default core connection named localDiskDb.

> **NOTE** We say that localDiskDb is a *core* connection because the property isn't currently defined outside of Sails' core code base.

But what does the connection point to? The connection property is a key name lookup for dictionaries located in brushfire/config/connections.js. These dictionaries contain the connection instructions Sails uses to access a desired database. The connections.js file provides a central location for all potential database connections you'll use for a project. One of the connection dictionaries is localDiskDb. Open brushfire/config/connections.js in Sublime and take a look at the default connection dictionaries, including the localDiskDb connection in the next listing.

Listing 6.3 The default connection settings

```
module.exports.connections = {

localDiskDb: {                          localDiskDb is set to
    adapter: 'sails-disk'               use the sails-disk
  },                                    adapter.
  ...


};
```

Typically, the connection dictionary will contain information including the host, the database access credentials username and password, the name of the database, and the Sails adapter to use.

> **NOTE** The database name we refer to here isn't the actual name of a database system like PostgreSQL, MySQL, or MongoDB. It's whatever arbitrary name you provide for your database like brushfire, mydatabase, and the like.

Here, the localDiskDb property is a dictionary that contains the adapter Sails will use to connect to the database. In this case, the adapter and database are set to sails-disk. Recall that Sails uses adapters to abstract away the complexity of using different syntax to access and manage each database.

> **DEFINITION** An *adapter* is a bit of code that maps model methods like find() and create() to a lower-level syntax like SELECT * FROM and INSERT INTO. The Sails core team maintains open source adapters for a handful of the most popular databases, and a wealth of community adapters is also available at http://mng.bz/67lJ.

sails-disk is an adapter that talks directly to the sails-disk database. It's unfortunate that the adapter and the database have the same names, but you can handle it. You've come this far, so you might as well look at the last turtle—the database itself; see figure 6.13. sails-disk is a simple database that stores data as JSON. It's unique in that it stores the data as a text file you can access located in brushfire/.tmp/local-DiskDb.db. Opening this file reveals the first user record you added as well as the video records added in the bootstrap.

```
{
  "data": {
    "user": [
      {
        "email": "sailsinaction@gmail.com",
        "username": "sails-in-action",
❶       "password": "abc123",
        "createdAt": "2016-03-07T18:28:26.203Z",
        "updatedAt": "2016-03-07T18:28:26.203Z",
        "id": 1
      }
    ],
    "video": [
      {
        "title": "The Original Grumpy Cat!",
        "src": "https://www.youtube.com/embed/INscMGmhmX4",
❷       "createdAt": "2016-03-05T04:26:09.510Z",
        "updatedAt": "2016-03-05T04:26:09.510Z",
        "id": 1
      },
      ...
  },
  "schema": {...},
    "video": {...},
    ...
  }
}
```

Figure 6.13   The sails-disk database located in brushfire/.tmp/local-DiskDb.db reveals the first user record ❶ and the first video record ❷.

Each record must have some way of uniquely identifying itself, typically through a unique id. Sails adapters automatically add this id as a primary key or unique key of the database. The id is autoincremented (meaning that Sails will take care of making sure it's unique). The details of the primary key vary between adapters. For example, PostgreSQL uses an autoincrementing integer primary key, whereas MongoDB uses a randomized string UUID. The adapter also adds attributes when the record is created—createdAt—and updated—updatedAt—to the model attributes.

Other databases might be more sophisticated than sails-disk, but the principles remain the same. A database can store data on disk or in memory and has an API you can use to talk to it. Sails provides a higher-level, easier-to-understand, consistent layer on top of that API that's called a model.

You've made it relatively unscathed, exploring all the steps of how models connect to actual databases. Although Sails is your trusted intermediary and shields you from many tasks, it remains your responsibility to convey which databases you want to employ. This includes providing configuration information like username, password, host, and database name, as well as the appropriate Sails adapter to use before the database can communicate with your models and vice versa.

6.4.2 *Configuring a database*

So far, you've been using models without configuring any information about model attributes, like the `email`, `username`, and `password` properties of the records you've added. In addition, the `video` model and `user` model haven't configured a connection. Therefore, all models are using the default `sails-disk` database. `sails-disk` is a NoSQL or schemaless database and therefore doesn't require defined attributes to store records. This is extremely useful in keeping you nimble during the design phase of your application. For example, you were able to start creating `user` records immediately after generating the API with Sails blueprints.

There are times, however, when you want to use an SQL database. For the `user` model, you'll store records in a PostgreSQL database. PostgreSQL is a popular, open source SQL database that runs on a variety of different platforms and can be downloaded at http://www.postgresql.org/download/. For our OS X environment, we use an all-in-one installation solution called Postgress.app, found at http://postgresapp.com/.

> **NOTE** For now, you'll run the database locally, but in later chapters when you go to production you'll use a hosted version of PostgreSQL.

After you've installed PostgreSQL, launch the Postgres application. OS X users should see an elephant—yes, I said *elephant*—in the upper-right navbar. Click it and open `psql`, which is the PostgreSQL terminal. Next, create a database named `brushfire` by typing

```
CREATE DATABASE brushfire;
```

You learned that Sails uses adapters to abstract away the complexity of using different syntax to access and manage each database. To start the transition, you need to install the PostgreSQL adapter. Head over to the terminal window, not the PostgreSQL terminal, and type

```
~/brushfire-chp6-start $ npm install sails-postgresql --save
```

Installing a module via `npm install` installs the module in the brushfire-chp6-start/node_modules folder. In Sublime, open brushfire-chp6-start/package.json and take a look at the `dependencies` property, shown in the next listing.

> **Listing 6.4 The dependencies property of a package.json file**

```
{
  "name": "brushfire",
  "private": true,
  "version": "0.0.0",
  "description": "a Sails application",
  "keywords": [],
  "dependencies": {
    ...
```

```
  "sails-generate-static": "^0.11.3",
  "sails-postgresql": "^0.11.3"                    ◁─┐   Add the PostgreSQL
},                                                    │   adapter as a dependency.
...
```

A *module dependency* is just a fancy name for a key/value pair in a module's package.json file that identifies the module name and a version npm uses to find and install the module. This becomes essential when you start deploying Brushfire. For example, when you push a Sails application to a hosted service like Heroku, you're sending the applications files and folders without the node_modules folder. Heroku then completes the installation of your app like any other Node module using npm install. If the dependency isn't in the package.json file, npm won't install the necessary modules.

Now that you have the adapter installed, you need to let Sails know that you want your user model to store records using it. In Sublime, open the user model located in brushfire-ch6-start/api/models/User.js. Add a connection property as shown here.

> **Listing 6.5   Adding a connection property to the `user` model**

```
module.exports = {

  connection: 'myPostgresqlServer',              ◁─┐   Add a PostgreSQL
                                                    │   connection to the
  attributes: {                                     │   user model.

  }
};
```

The connection property contains an arbitrary name you've given to the connection that points to some configuration information about your PostgreSQL database in /brushfire-chp6-start/config/connections.js. In Sublime, open /brushfire-chp6-start/config/connections.js and add the following configuration information to myPostgresqlServer.

> **Listing 6.6   Adding a connection to the connections.js file**

```
...
myPostgresqlServer: {
    adapter: 'sails-postgresql',
    host: 'localhost',
    database: 'brushfire'
  },
...
```

Your myPostgresqlServer connection contains a dictionary of configuration information, including the adapter, host, and database name.

> **NOTE**   We could have provided a username and password, but during development we chose not to do so.

Because PostgreSQL is an SQL database, you must provide defined attributes before you can create records using them in your model. That's not a problem because you established what attributes you need earlier in the chapter.

6.4.3 Defining attributes

Let's add attribute definitions to the user model, also known as a *database schema*, based on the requirements created earlier in the chapter. From Sublime, open brush-fire-chp6-start/api/models/User.js and add the following model attributes.

Listing 6.7 Defining `user` attributes in the model

```
module.exports = {

  connection: 'myPostgresqlServer',

  attributes: {

    email: {
      type: 'string',
    },

    username: {
      type: 'string',
    },

    encryptedPassword: {
      type: 'string'
    },

    gravatarURL: {
      type: 'string'
    },

    deleted: {
      type: 'boolean'
    },

    admin: {
      type: 'boolean'
    },

    banned: {
      type: 'boolean'
    }
  }
}
```

Sails bundles support for automatic validations of your models' attributes. Any time a record is updated or a new record is created, the data for each attribute will be checked against all your predefined validation rules. This provides a convenient fail-safe to ensure that invalid entries don't make their way into your app's database(s). Every attribute definition must have a built-in data type (or typeclass) specified. For example, you'll use the string data type for the email, username, encryptedPassword, and `gravatarURL` attributes. For the `deleted`, `admin`, and `banned` attributes, you'll use the `boolean` data type.

Except for `unique` (which is implemented as a database-level constraint), all validations are implemented in JavaScript and run in the same Node.js server process as Sails. Validations can be a huge timesaver, preventing you from writing many hundreds of lines of repetitive code. But keep in mind that model validations are run for every create or update in your application. Before using a validation rule in one of your attribute definitions, make sure you're okay with it being applied every time your application calls `.create()` or `.update()` to specify a new value for that attribute. For example, let's say that your Sails app allows users to sign up for an account either by entering an email address and password and then confirming that email address or by signing up with LinkedIn. Now, let's say your `user` model has one attribute called `linkedInEmail` and another attribute called `manuallyEnteredEmail`. Even though one of those email address attributes is required, which one is required depends on how a user signed up. In that case, your `user` model can't use the `required: true` validation; instead, you'll need to validate that one email or the other was provided and is valid by manually checking these values before the relevant `.create()` and `.update()` methods are executed. In other cases, enforcing the validation on each `.create()` and `.update()` call is advantageous. For example, you can set an `email` validation that enforces the use of valid email syntax. In that case, there's never an instance when you want to allow an improperly formatted email address. Therefore, applying that restriction as an attribute validation makes sense. So, you'll use some of the attribute validations to enforce restrictions in the model, and enforce others directly in a controller action in later chapters.

6.4.4   *Attribute validation*

Your first attribute validation is a requirement for both the `email` and `username` attributes to be `unique`. That means no record can contain an identical `email` or `username` in the database. If an attempt is made to create or update a record using a model method with an identical attribute, the method will produce an error. The unique validation is different than other validations. Imagine you have one million `user` records in your database. If `unique` was implemented like other validations, every time a new user signed up for your app, Sails would need to search through one million existing records to ensure that no one else was already using the email address provided by the new user. Not only would that be slow, but by the time it finished searching through all those records, someone else could have signed up!

Fortunately, this type of uniqueness check is perhaps the most universal feature of any database. To take advantage of that, Sails relies on the database adapter to implement support for the `unique` validation—specifically by adding a uniqueness constraint to the relevant field/column/attribute in the database itself during auto-migration.

NOTE You first encountered auto-migrations in chapter 4 when you set the mode to `alter`. As you'll see in the next section, Sails will automatically generate tables/collections in the underlying database with uniqueness constraints built right in. Once you switch to `migrate:'safe'` in chapter 15, updating your database constraints will be up to you.

You'll also add an `email` validation to the `email` attribute, which validates incoming values to a valid `email address` syntax before the email address can be stored or updated as part of a record. Open brushfire-chp6-start/api/models/User.js in Sublime and add the following attribute options.

Listing 6.8 Adding attribute validations to the `user` model

```
module.exports = {

  attributes: {

    email: {
      type: 'string',
      email: 'true',          Validates whether
      unique: 'true'          incoming value is a
    },                        valid email address

    username: {               Requires each
      type: 'string',         attribute value
      unique: 'true'          to be unique
    },

    encryptedPassword: {
      type: 'string'
    },

    gravatarURL: {
      type: 'string'
    },

    deleted: {
      type: 'boolean'
    },

    admin: {
      type: 'boolean'
    },

    banned: {
      type: 'boolean'
    }
  }
}
```

Let's see this in action. Restart Sails using `sails lift` and navigate back to the signup page. Once again, sign up with an email address of `sailsinaction@gmail.com`, a username of `sailsinaction`, and a password of `abc123`. After clicking Create User Account, your browser should look similar to figure 6.14.

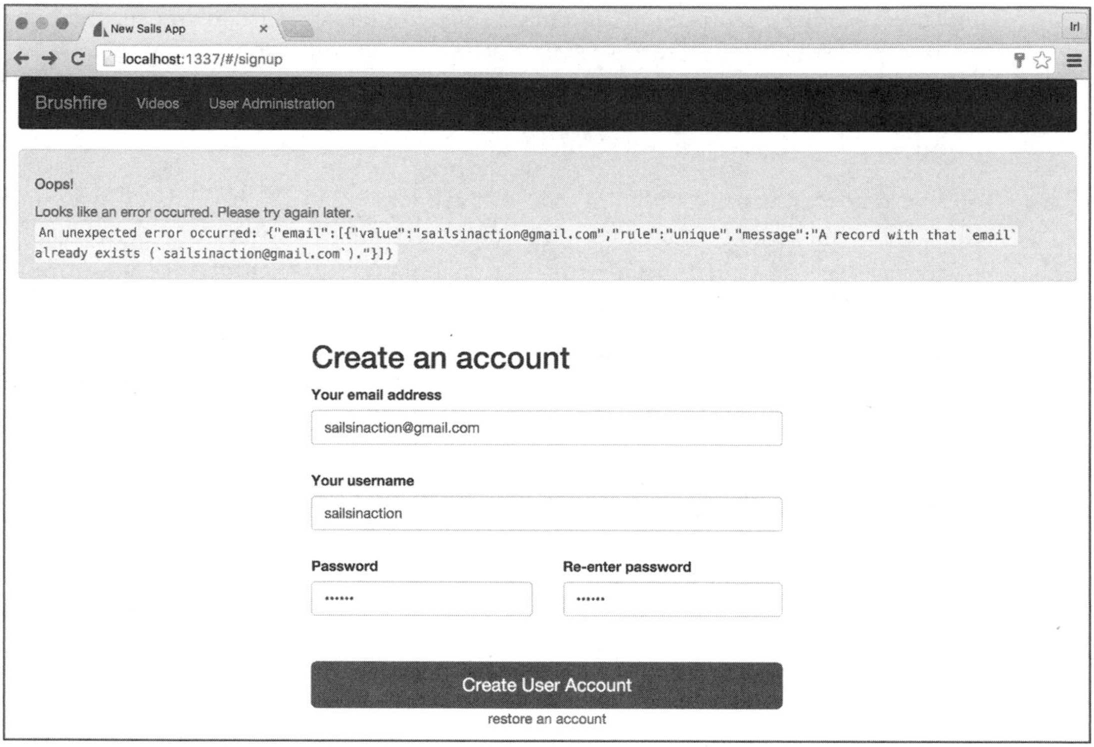

Figure 6.14   When you attempt to create a user, a record with an identical email address exists in the database and therefore produces a validation error.

Your new `unique` validation for the `email` attribute produces an error when you try to add a `user` with an email address equal to an existing `user` record. You could create another user with a different email address, but while you're developing you really need a way for your database to reset to an empty state each time you restart the Sails server. You can do that by changing the model auto-migration setting.

6.4.5   *Handling existing data with Sails auto-migrations*

In chapter 4, you had your first encounter with Sails auto-migrations. Each time you start Brushfire, Sails needs to know whether to attempt to rebuild the database and, if records exist, what to do with them. If you set auto-migrations to `safe`, Sails doesn't do anything other than create a connection to the database and run queries. It's the default environment for production and should be used whenever you're working with production data or any records you don't want to risk losing.

If you set auto-migrations to `drop`, instead of trying to migrate the data, this mode drops the database and creates brand-new tables or collections, essentially giving you a fresh start. If you have a bootstrap file that resets your data each time the Sails server starts and you don't care about existing records, then `drop` auto-migration is a good way to go when your models are constantly changing in the early stages of development.

If you set migrations to `alter`, Sails attempts to store all the records in memory before it drops the database. When the table or collection has been re-created, Sails attempts to reinsert the stored records into the new data structure. The `alter` mode is useful if you have a very small dataset and are making trivial changes to model attributes. You'll ultimately be using `safe` mode because it will ensure data integrity when you go into production, but during the design phase of the app you'll be using `drop` mode.

So far, you've set the global `migrate` property for all models to `alter` in brushfire-chp6-start/config/models.js. For the next chapter, it will be important to start with new data for your `user` model each time the Sails server starts. Using the `alter` mode keeps your `user` records between server restarts. Therefore, you'll change the `migrate` property to `drop`. But instead of setting this property globally in brushfire-chp6-start/config/models.js, you'll add the property specifically to the `user` model. In Sublime, open brushfire-chp6-start/api/models/User.js and change the `migrate` property to `drop`, similar to the following listing.

Listing 6.9 Adding the `migrate` property to `drop` for a specific model

```
...
migrate: 'drop',          ◁──┐  The database will drop
                              │  existing tables on each
attributes: {                 │  server restart.
  email: {
    type: 'string',
    email: 'true',
    unique: 'true'
  },
...
```

Restart the Sails server using `sails lift` and sign up a user with an email address of sailsinaction@gmail.com, a username of `sailsinaction`, and a password of `abc123`. After you click the Create User Account button, your browser will display the new user record. There's no violation of the `unique` validation because the database was reset and no `user` records exist when the Sails server is restarted. The `user` record created, however, contains properties that you don't want returned to the frontend. You'll fix that in the next section.

6.4.6 *Filtering data returned by blueprints*

As you can see from figure 6.15, the blueprint `create` action returned all the stored parameters to the requesting frontend, including the `encryptedPassword`.

You also may have noticed that the password was not returned. Earlier the password was returned by the blueprint `create` action because you were using sails-disk, which didn't require that an attribute be defined before it could be used. Now

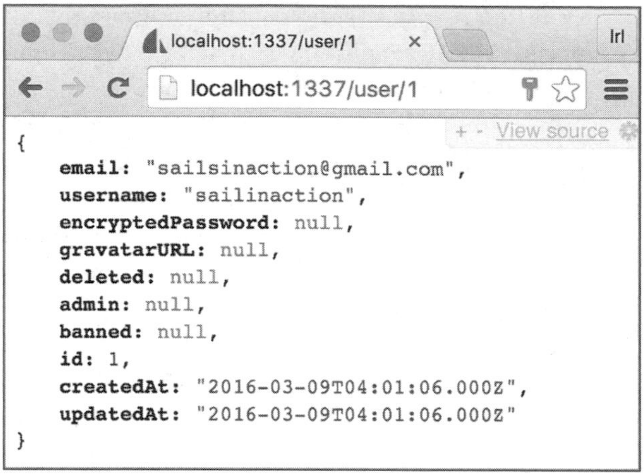

Figure 6.15   Using the blueprint actions, all parameters are returned to the frontend.

that you're using PostgreSQL, any parameter not defined as an attribute won't be stored in the user record. You can limit the attributes defined in the model and returned by a blueprint action by overriding the .toJSON() method in the model. Open brushfire-chp6-start/api/models/User.js in Sublime and add the following toJSON method.

Listing 6.10   Preventing certain attributes from being returned to the client

```
...
banned: {
      type: 'boolean'
    },
                                          Prevents attributes
                                          from being returned
                                          in blueprint actions
toJSON: function() {
  var modelAttributes = this.toObject();
  delete modelAttributes.password;
  delete modelAttributes.confirmation;
  delete modelAttributes.encryptedPassword;
  return modelAttributes;
  }
 }
}
...
```

After overriding the toJSON() method, the blueprint create action will no longer return the password, confirmation, or encryptedPassword parameters to the frontend.

6.5   *Understanding model methods*

In chapter 4, you used the create() and find() methods indirectly to list and create video records via the blueprint create action and blueprint find action. In chapter 5, you used the Video.create() and Video.count() methods directly. Let's now look at the model methods you'll use most in Brushfire, listed in table 6.6.

Table 6.6   Model methods

Method	Description
.create()	Creates a new record in the database
.find()	Finds and returns all records that match a certain criteria
.findOne()	Attempts to find a particular record in your database that matches the given criteria
.update()	Updates existing records in the database that match the specified criteria
.destroy()	Destroys records in your database that match the given criteria
.count()	Returns the number of records in your database that meet the given search criteria

Not surprisingly, all but one of these are part of the ubiquitous create, read, update, and delete (CRUD) operations you learned about in chapter 1. Typically, you'll use model methods in a custom controller action. But in this section you'll use them in the Sails console. The Sails console is a way to start the Sails server in a project and then interact with it in the Node read-eval-print loop (REPL).

> **DEFINITION**   The REPL is an interactive tool that allows you to interact with a programming environment, in this case Node and Sails.

This means you can access and use all of your models to try out various queries during development without having to add them in a controller action and restart the Sails server each time. If your Sails server is currently running, close it by pressing Ctrl-C (twice). To start the Sails console, open a terminal window, and from the root of your project type

```
~/brushfire-chp6-start $ sails console
info: Starting app in interactive mode...

info: Welcome to the Sails console.
info: ( to exit, type <CTRL>+<C> )

sails>
```

Let's use the Sails console to explore some model methods.

6.5.1   *Anatomy of a Sails model method*

First, we'll look at the essential syntax of a Sails model method, as illustrated in figure 6.16.

Methods like .find, .create, .update, and .destroy are the initial methods to start a database query that finds and/or manipulates a record in a database. We use

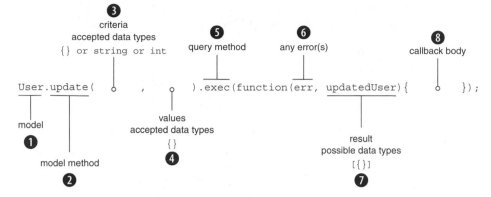

Figure 6.16   The generic syntax of a model method includes the model name ❶, model method ❷, criteria ❸, values ❹, the query method ❺, the callback method with error ❻ and result arguments ❼, and the callback body ❽.

the .update() method as an overall example because it uses both criteria and values as arguments. To use the .update() method, start with the name of the model dictionary, user. Next, add the model method name, update. Most model methods use a criteria, which contains values the query uses to find existing records. The second argument is the values that will be updated. We'll also look at query methods that can be chained on these initial methods to help configure the query with the .exec() method being the last in this chain. So, .exec() passes all the instructions for the query to the adapter, which executes the query and returns results. When the query is completed, Sails will respond using a familiar pattern of returning any errors as the first argument, and a result as the second argument of the callback.

6.5.2   The .create() model method

The create model method doesn't require a criteria, as illustrated in figure 6.17.

Let's create a few records you can use to explore your model methods. Make sure the Sails console is running, and type or copy each query in listing 6.11.

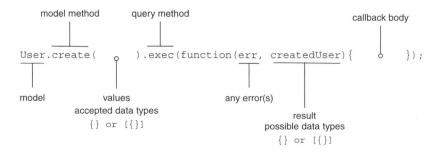

Figure 6.17   The create model method uses a syntax similar to the find, update, and destroy methods, but without criteria.

Listing 6.11 Using the `create` method to create `user` records

First query

```
User.create({email: 'sailsinaction@gmail.com',username:'sailsinaction',
    deleted: false,banned: false,admin: false}).exec(function(err,
    foundRecords){ if (err) console.log(err); console.log(foundRecords);});

User.create({email: 'nikolateslaidol@gmail.com',username:'nikolateslaidol',
    deleted: false,banned: false,admin: false}).exec(function(err,
    foundRecords){ if (err) console.log(err); console.log(foundRecords);});

User.create({email: 'franksinatra@myWay.com',username:' franksinatra',
    deleted: true,banned: false,admin: false}).exec(function(err,
    foundRecords){ if (err) console.log(err); console.log(foundRecords);});
```

Second query

Third query

6.5.3 *The .find() model method*

The `find` method returns all records that meet the criteria passed as the first argument of the method. The criteria can be a dictionary, a string, or a number of the `id` you're trying to find. If no criteria argument is given, all records will be returned. Give this a try. Make sure the Sails console is running, and then type or copy and paste the query shown here.

Listing 6.12 Returning all `user` records using the `find` method with no arguments

```
User.find().exec(function(err, foundRecords){
  if (err) console.log(err);

  console.log('The user records: ', foundRecords);

});
```

The terminal window should return results similar to the following listing.

Listing 6.13 Results from the `find` query

```
[ { email: 'sailsinaction@gmail.com',
    username: 'sailsinaction',
    encryptedPassword: null,
    gravatarURL: null,
    deleted: false,
    admin: false,
    banned: false,
    id: 1,
    createdAt: '2016-03-10T04:25:29.000Z',
    updatedAt: '2016-03-10T04:25:29.000Z' },
  { email: 'nikolateslaidol@gmail.com',
    username: 'nikolateslaidol',
    encryptedPassword: null,
```

```
      gravatarURL: null,
      deleted: false,
      admin: false,
      banned: false,
      id: 2,
      createdAt: '2016-03-10T04:25:39.000Z',
      updatedAt: '2016-03-10T04:25:39.000Z' },
   { email: 'franksinatra@myWay.com',
      username: ' franksinatra',
      encryptedPassword: null,
      gravatarURL: null,
      deleted: true,
      admin: false,
      banned: false,
      id: 3,
      createdAt: '2016-03-10T04:25:45.000Z',
      updatedAt: '2016-03-10T04:25:45.000Z' } ]
```

The find method returns an array of dictionary user records.

NOTE Even if there's a single record returned, that dictionary will be within an array.

Next, let's find a particular user record by passing in a criteria dictionary as the first argument: {username: ['sailsinaction', 'nikolateslaidol']}. Copy and paste the query shown here into the Sails console.

Listing 6.14 Using an IN query

```
User.findOne({username: ['sailsinaction',
'nikolateslaidol']}).exec(function(err, foundRecords){if (err)
console.log(err); console.log(foundRecords); });
```

The console should return results similar to this.

Listing 6.15 Results from the IN query

```
[ { email: 'sailsinaction@gmail.com',
    username: 'sailsinaction',
    encryptedPassword: null,
    gravatarURL: null,
    deleted: false,
    admin: false,
    banned: false,
    id: 1,
    createdAt: '2016-03-10T04:25:29.000Z',
    updatedAt: '2016-03-10T04:25:29.000Z' },
  { email: 'nikolateslaidol@gmail.com',
    username: 'nikolateslaidol',
    encryptedPassword: null,
    gravatarURL: null,
    deleted: false,
    admin: false,
```

```
banned: false,
id: 2,
createdAt: '2016-03-10T04:25:39.000Z',
updatedAt: '2016-03-10T04:25:39.000Z' }]
```

This query is also referred to as an *IN query*, where each value in the array is treated as or, so `sailsinaction` *or* `nikolateslaidol`. Because you have 15 `video` records available to query, you'll use the `video` model for this next example.

NOTE The videos you return in your project may be different than those in the example. The contents of YouTube are constantly changing and, therefore, the search results from the .`searchVideos` machine in bootstrap.js may vary from those shown in the book.

Let's say you want to query on a value that's a fragment of what's contained within a record attribute. That is, you want to find records that contain the value `The` in the `title` attribute of the `video` model. With the Sails console running, type or (copy and paste) the query in the next listing into the Sails console.

Listing 6.16 Using `contains` in a query

```
Video.find({title: {'contains': 'The'}}).exec(function(err, found) {if (err)
console.log(err);console.log(found);});
```

The console should return results similar to the following.

Listing 6.17 Results from the `contains` query

```
[ { title: 'The Original Grumpy Cat!',
    src: 'https://www.youtube.com/embed/INscMGmhmX4',
    createdAt: '2016-03-10T04:25:24.846Z',
    updatedAt: '2016-03-10T04:25:24.846Z',
    id: 271 },
  { title: 'GRUMPY CAT! | The Subscriber City Challenge | Ep.21',
    src: 'https://www.youtube.com/embed/EW_gDH5IqTA',
    createdAt: '2016-03-10T04:25:24.849Z',
    updatedAt: '2016-03-10T04:25:24.849Z',
    id: 275 },
  { title: 'Oscar the Grouch vs. Grumpy Cat | Mashable',
    src: 'https://www.youtube.com/embed/QDUyazvnLkc',
    createdAt: '2016-03-10T04:25:24.851Z',
    updatedAt: '2016-03-10T04:25:24.851Z',
    id: 279 },
  { title: 'Grumpy Cat In The Sky!?!',
    src: 'https://www.youtube.com/embed/iinQDhsdE9s',
    createdAt: '2016-03-10T04:25:24.852Z',
    updatedAt: '2016-03-10T04:25:24.852Z',
    id: 280 },
  { title: 'Minecraft Modded Mini-Game : FEED THE GRUMPY CAT!',
    src: 'https://www.youtube.com/embed/gxfWnVS3U2M',
    createdAt: '2016-03-10T04:25:24.854Z',
    updatedAt: '2016-03-10T04:25:24.854Z',
```

```
          id: 283 },
      { title: 'Minecraft Mini-Game : PLEASE THE GRUMPY CAT!',
          src: 'https://www.youtube.com/embed/AezV3epQLpE',
          createdAt: '2016-03-10T04:25:24.854Z',
          updatedAt: '2016-03-10T04:25:24.854Z',
          id: 284 } ]
```

You can find a complete guide to criteria language options at http://sailsjs.org/documentation/concepts/models-and-orm/query-language. Finally, let's say you want to find a single record returned as a dictionary instead of a dictionary within an array. For that, you can use the `findOne` model method. With the Sails console running, type or copy and paste the following query into the Sails console.

Listing 6.18   Finding a single record with `findOne`

```
User.find({email: 'sailsinaction@gmail.com'}).exec(function(err, found) {if
(err) console.log(err);console.log(found);});
```

The console should return results similar to the following listing.

Listing 6.19   Results from the `findOne` query

```
{ email: 'sailsinaction@gmail.com',
  username: 'sailsinaction',
  encryptedPassword: null,
  gravatarURL: null,
  deleted: false,
  admin: false,
  banned: false,
  id: 1,
  createdAt: '2016-03-10T04:25:29.000Z',
  updatedAt: '2016-03-10T04:25:29.000Z' }
```

As expected, the `findOne` method responds with a single record dictionary.

6.5.4   *The .update() model method*

You already explored the syntax of the `update` model method at the beginning of this section. Now let's see it in action. For example, you'll make the user record with the username `sailsinaction` an administrator by updating the `admin` property to `true`. With the Sails console running, type or copy and paste the following query into the Sails console.

Listing 6.20   Updating a `user` record with the `update` model method

```
User.update({username: 'sailsinaction'}, {admin: true}).exec(function(err,
➥ updatedRecord){if (err) console.log(err);console.log(updatedRecord);
});
```

The console should return results similar to these.

Listing 6.21   Results from the `update` query

```
[ { email: 'sailsinaction@gmail.com',
    username: 'sailsinaction',
    encryptedPassword: null,
    gravatarURL: null,
    deleted: false,
    admin: true,
    banned: false,
    id: 1,
    createdAt: '2016-03-10T04:25:29.000Z',
    updatedAt: '2016-03-10T05:30:24.000Z' } ]
```

The `update` model method returns an array with the dictionary of the record you updated as expected.

6.5.5   *The .destroy() model method*

As its name implies, the `destroy` model method can delete one or more existing records in the model based on the criteria provided as the first argument. The criteria can be a dictionary or an array of dictionaries. The criteria can also be a string or number of the `id` you're trying to destroy. Let's say you want to delete any records that have their `deleted` property set to `true`. Ensure that the Sails console is running, and then type or copy and paste the following query into the Sails console.

Listing 6.22   Deleting a `user` record with the `destroy` model method

```
User.destroy({deleted: true}).exec(function(err, deletedRecord){
if (err) console.log(err); console.log(deletedRecord);});
```

Your terminal window should look similar to this.

Listing 6.23   Results from the `destroy` query

```
[ { email: 'franksinatra@myWay.com',
    username: 'franksinatra',
    encryptedPassword: null,
    gravatarURL: null,
    deleted: true,
    admin: false,
    banned: false,
    id: 1,
    createdAt: Wed Mar 09 2016 23:51:04 GMT-0600 (CST),
    updatedAt: Wed Mar 09 2016 23:51:04 GMT-0600 (CST) } ]
```

The `destroy` model method returns an array with the dictionary of the record that was destroyed as expected.

6.5.6   *The .count() model method*

The count model method returns the number of records in a particular model. Ensure that the Sails console is running, and then type or copy and paste the following query into the Sails console.

Listing 6.24   Counting the records in a model with the `.count()` method

```
Video.count().exec(function(err, count){if (err) console.log(err);
➥  console.log(count);});
```

Your terminal window should display the number 15, which is the number of records in the video model.

6.6   *Summary*

- Sails models contain attributes, methods, settings, and an adapter named around a common resource.
- Model requirements consist of attributes, validations, and transformations.
- Model requirements are identified using the frontend-first approach by reviewing interactive mockups.
- Models connect to a database using a connection that points to an adapter, which translates a common query interface into the specific syntax of the underlying database.

Custom actions

This chapter covers

- Demystifying controllers, actions, and routes
- Developing custom action implementation requirements from requests
- Transitioning blueprint actions into custom actions
- Using the `req` and `res` dictionaries in actions
- Completing a working user identity management system

Recall that our clients have asked us to build functionality that allows them to control access to Brushfire and, more specifically, to indirectly control the content of the site. In a nutshell, we're attempting to enable 24/7 ubiquitous cat content! In chapter 6, you completed the first part of user identity management, which involved creating and configuring a `user` model that will hold attributes to identify a user. In this chapter, you'll connect frontend mockup requests to custom controller actions that use model methods to allow a user to create, modify, and view their identity. Recall that the components of user identity management correlate to the frontend mockups outlined in table 7.1.

171

Table 7.1   User identity management components and mockup pages

Component	Mockup	Description
Creating a profile with a signup process	signup.html	The signup component allows a user to create an identity. Identity is based on one or more unique pieces of information. In our user identity management system, we'll prompt the user for a unique email address and unique username. Either of these pieces of information can be used to identify a particular user. The signup process will also prompt the user to create a password. This password will later be used as proof of a claim to a particular identity.
Displaying a user profile	profile.html	The user profile component displays information about the user via the `user` record. The user also has the ability to edit, delete, and later restore their profile.
Editing a user profile	edit-profile.html	Editing a user profile allows the user to edit various aspects of their `user` record.
Restoring a user profile	restore-profile.html	After a user authenticates successfully, this component allows a user to restore their deleted user profile.
Administering a user profile	admin-users.html	This component allows a designated admin user to perform administrative duties such as add admin privileges to other users as well as ban users from accessing the system.

To keep your eye on the big picture, remember that user identity management is part of the identity, authorization, personalization, and access control system you're building over chapters 6–10 and illustrated in figure 7.1.

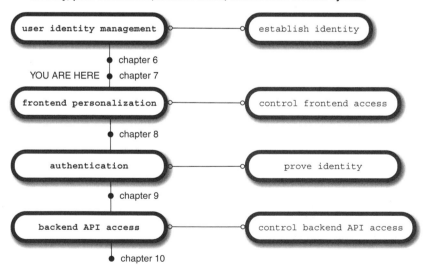

Figure 7.1   The four components of an identity, authentication, personalization, and access control system

In chapter 6, you installed the frontend assets of user identity management. These interactive mockups were created based on a set of requirements derived from the client's initial demands. You then used the mockups to identify model requirements before implementing the actual user model.

In this chapter, we'll again look to the frontend assets for guidance on the requirements of requests to our backend API. As you'll see shortly, the requirements of the API will go beyond the functionality of the blueprint actions we used in chapter 4 for finding, creating, updating, and deleting records on the video model. We'll introduce custom actions that open up infinite possibilities for fulfilling the needs of frontend requests. Before we look at the mockups and start identifying the requirements of each request, let's make sure you have a firm understanding of routes, controllers, and actions.

7.1 Demystifying routes and actions

We introduced routes, controllers, and actions in chapter 1. Combined, they can represent an endpoint within an API. Recall that the route is implemented in JavaScript as a dictionary.

The key in the route dictionary is the request or route address, consisting of the HTTP method and path. The value is another dictionary called the target that consists of a controller and action; see figure 7.2. When a request is made, the router looks for a matching route address and then executes the corresponding controller action.

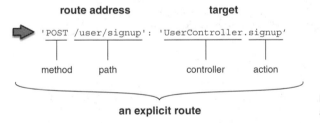

Figure 7.2 An explicit route contains a route address and a target.

The controller is a name you give the dictionary that aggregates *actions* under a common resource. Here, we named the controller user because the actions will all concern a user. You define custom actions in controller files located in the brushfire/api/controllers/ folder. In Sublime, open brushfire/api/controllers/UserController.js, which is similar to the following code.

Listing 7.1 The UserController file

```
module.exports = {};
```

This is the controller that was generated when you created the user API in chapter 6 via sails generate api user. We've already demonstrated what you can do with an empty controller and empty model through blueprint routes and actions. Now, let's add a custom action where you dictate what will occur instead of relying on the fixed set of features in a blueprint action. Head back to Sublime, and add a new custom action named `hello` to brushfire/api/controllers/UserController.js.

Listing 7.2   A custom `hello` action in the `user` controller

```
module.exports = {
  hello: function(req, res) {          An action is a function with
    console.log('Hello World!');       the arguments req and res.

  }                                    The body of the action does
};                                     your bidding; in this case, it
                                       logs some text to the console.
```

Your new custom `hello` action will log "Hello World!" to the console. Let's see this action.

> **TIP**   If you've been following along from chapter 6, you're good to go. If, however, you want to begin your Brushfire journey from here, head to section 7.2.1 for instructions on obtaining the necessary assets to begin this chapter.

Restart the Sails server via `sails lift`. In Postman, make a `GET` request to `/user/hello` similar to figure 7.3.

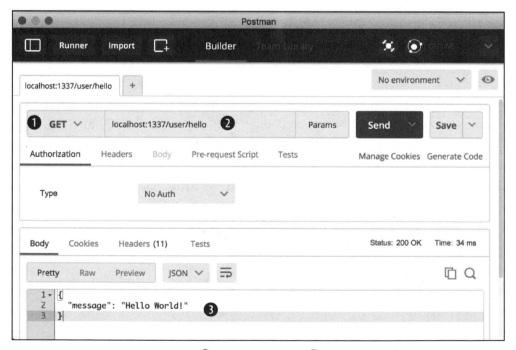

Figure 7.3   You made a `GET` request ❶ to `/user/hello` ❷, but there's something wrong with the action because the loading message ❸ displays and then times out.

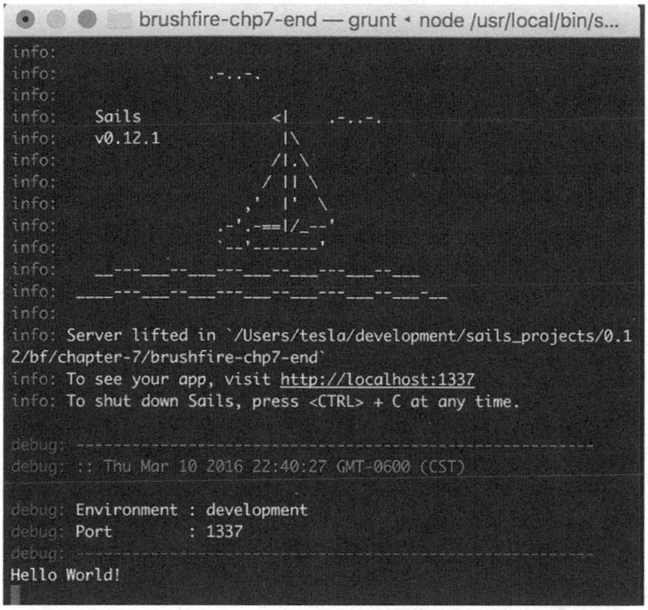

Figure 7.4   The message from the custom action is logged to the console.

Your "Hello World!" message is logged to the console in figure 7.4.

But there's an issue with the request. Postman continues to display a loading message until it gets tired of waiting and tells you that the request didn't get a response. Recall from chapter 1 that web applications use the HTTP request/response protocol to communicate. You made a request, but your action didn't complete the transaction with a response. Let's fix that.

7.1.1   Introducing res.json()

You need a way to respond to a request in the `hello` action. As it turns out, there are many ways to respond to a request. You'll use the `.json()` method of the `res` dictionary to respond to the request. The `res.json()` method responds with a `200` status code and whatever you provide as an argument to the method, formatted as JSON to the user-agent that made the request. In Sublime, add the following response to brushfire/api/controllers/UserController.js.

Listing 7.3   Adding a response to the `hello` action in the `user` controller

```
module.exports = {
  hello: function(req, res) {
    return res.json('Hello World!');          ⟵┤  Execute a method from
  }                                               the res dictionary to
};                                                respond to the request.
```

Restart Sails using `sails lift` and make the same GET request to /user/hello in Postman, as shown in figure 7.5.

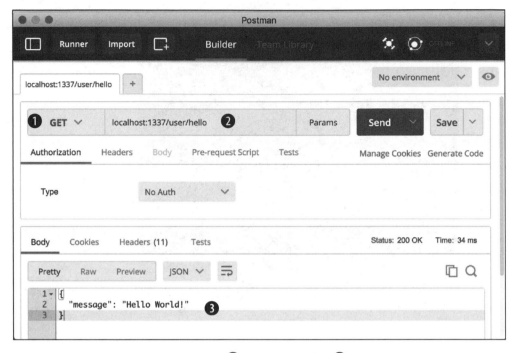

Figure 7.5   Again, you make a GET request ❶ to /user/hello ❷. Now that you've added a response in the action, Postman receives the response and displays it ❸.

Now, when the request triggers the `hello` action, a response is sent back with your Hello World! message completing the request/response transaction. Notice that you also added `return` before `res.json`. This makes `res.json()` a terminal method.

> **DEFINITION**   A *terminal method* is generally the last line of code an action will execute for a given request. You use `return` as an indicator that nothing else will execute with respect to the request after this line of code.

You might be wondering how you got the `.json()` method from the `res` argument in the first place. The `req` and `res` arguments in your `hello` action are JavaScript dictionaries provided by Sails. The details of how they're created aren't important. Instead, it's important to understand that, like all JavaScript dictionaries, they can have methods (functions) and properties. These methods and properties are tied to the request and response. For example, not surprisingly, in a GET request to /user/hello, the `req` dictionary provides access to details about the request like the type of HTTP method used via `req.method`. In this case, the `req.method` property would return GET.

We have one more bit of unfinished business to cover. How was your custom `hello` action triggered without an explicit route? The answer lies in a third type of blueprint route called *blueprint action routes*.

7.1.2　*Automatic routing for custom actions*

Action blueprint routes, a.k.a. *blueprint action routes,* are shadow routes derived from custom actions found in controllers. When the server starts via `sails lift`, Sails examines each controller for custom actions. For each one it finds, Sails binds a shadow route, which it determines by combining the controller name and the action name. Like other blueprint routes, action blueprint routes are considered shadow routes because they don't exist explicitly in the brushfire/config/routes.js file.

> **DEFINITION**　The naming here can be confusing. Just remember that *blueprint actions* are built-in controller actions that you don't have to write yourself. And *blueprint routes* are built-in implicit routes that you don't have to include in your routes.js file. Terms like *action blueprints, shortcut blueprints,* and *RESTful blueprints* just relate to different categories of blueprint routes that are enabled by default in Sails.

Instead, they're available unless overridden using the same path in the routes.js file or disabled in brushfire/config/blueprints.js. So, for your `hello` action, the shadow routes in table 7.2 are created each time the Sails server starts.

Table 7.2　Action blueprint routes for the `hello` action

Method	Path	Action
GET	/user/hello/:id?	hello
POST	/user/hello/:id?	hello
PUT	/user/hello/:id?	hello
DELETE	/user/hello/:id?	hello

These routes speed up initial development by deferring the need to create an explicit route for each action.

> **TIP**　What's up with the `:id?` at the end of each path? We'll cover this extensively in chapter 8, but for now just remember that `:id?` lets Sails know that if there's a value after `/user/hello`, treat it as a variable named `id`.

Ultimately, you'll want to consolidate all routes explicitly in brushfire/config/routes.js. But for now, you can defer that task to chapter 8 and use the automation of blueprints instead.

Let's review. You know an action is simply a handler function that's bound to a particular request via a route. You also know that you have access to properties and methods of the request and response in an action through the `req` and `res` dictionary arguments. Finally, you know that each request needs a corresponding response. Now that you have a solid foundation of understanding how controller actions work, let's start identifying the custom actions you'll need to fulfill the frontend mockup requests and requirements for user identity management.

7.2   *Identifying the requirements for your custom actions*

We'll again use frontend mockups to guide the design of your backend. Instead of simply looking for model requirements, we'll examine the requests on each page to identify the custom actions necessary to satisfy the requirements of each frontend request. An overview of Brushfire's mockup pages is displayed in figure 7.6.

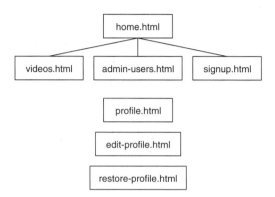

Figure 7.6   **You can use these mockups to identify the requests on each page as well as the requirements and expectations of each endpoint.**

You can see the result of identifying the requirements by clicking the API Reference link on the chapter 7 hub here http://sailsinaction.github.io/chapter-7/ or directly at http://mng.bz/8uy9.

7.2.1   *Obtaining the example materials for this chapter*

You have two options with regard to setting up your Brushfire assets for this chapter. If you've completed chapter 6, you're all set and can simply use your existing project here. If you haven't completed chapter 6, you can clone the end of chapter 6 GitHub repo at https://github.com/sailsinaction/brushfire-ch6-end.git and start from there. Remember to use npm install in the terminal window from the root of the project after you clone the repo.

> **WARNING**   If you do choose the cloning option, don't forget to add the brushfire/config/local.js file with your Google API key from chapter 5 (section 5.4.6) as well as start your local PostgreSQL brushfire database from chapter 6 (section 6.4.2).

7.3   *Handling a signup form*

The first page we'll review is the signup page, which is responsible for creating a user's initial identity. For each mockup, we'll identify the following:

- All the requests on the page including the request that initiated the display of the page itself

- The inputs that will be sent with a request
- The requirements and expectations of the response to the frontend

Figure 7.7 shows three requests that are part of the signup page.

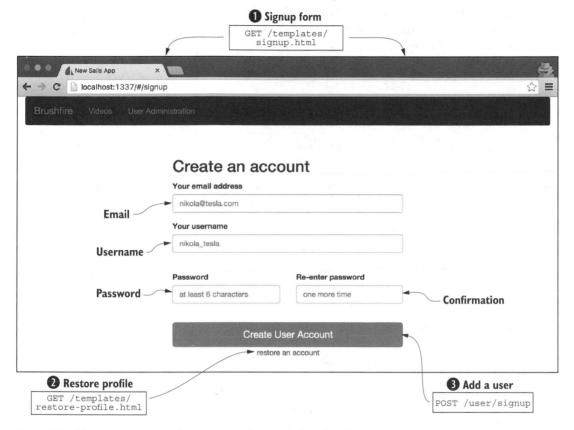

Figure 7.7   The signup page mockup contains three endpoints. The first request initiates the display of the signup page, which is handled by an asset route. The second request is a link to the restore-profile page that's handled by an asset route, and the third is a POST request to /user/signup that will be handled by a custom controller action.

Let's review the requests we've identified in the API Reference. The first request is for the delivery of the signup page itself. Although not technically a request on the signup page, it makes sense to list the request and the backend component that responds with the page. In this case, the Sails asset router responds to the Angular AJAX GET request to /templates/signup.html ❶.

The second request starts as an Angular frontend request to /#/restore-profile that triggers a backend GET request to /templates/restore-profile.html ❷. Sails handles this request with the asset router.

The third request is a POST request to /user/signup ❸. This will trigger a custom signup action. Let's review the requirements for this action by heading back to the

API Reference. The first tab consists of your model requirements. A new column has been added for backend validation and transformation requirements. You'll implement the validations and transformations in a new custom action: `signup`. The second tab contains your endpoint summary. We've altered the requirements of the Add a user endpoint. In chapter 6, you used the blueprint `create` action to create a user based on incoming form parameters. Your requirements, however, have expanded to include the following:

- Backend validation of parameters with appropriate error responses
- Creating a Gravatar image
- Encrypting the user's password
- Creating a `user` record that consists of the `username`, `email`, `encryptedPassword`, `gravatarURL`, `deleted`, `admin`, and `banned` attributes
- Responding with an appropriate error or `200` status code and `username` as JSON

In chapter 6, you used the blueprint `create` action via a blueprint RESTful route to create a new `user` record, as shown in figure 7.8.

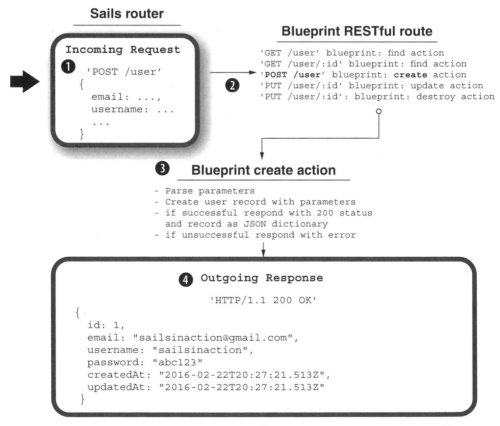

Figure 7.8   The incoming POST request to /user ❶ matched a blueprint RESTful route ❷ that triggered a blueprint create action ❸ that ultimately created the user record ❹.

A simple CRUD action will no longer satisfy the requirements of the request and will necessitate a custom action.

7.3.1 Naming custom actions

Naming things is the most daunting recurring problem in programming. We have an almost unlimited number of choices when deciding on a name for the action. We could use the traditional CRUD operation labels, in this case naming the action *create*. This would, however, overwrite the blueprint `create` action. With all of that said, we think it's more accurate to be descriptive in naming the action and will therefore use the name `signup`.

7.3.2 Creating an action

To create the `signup` action, open brushfire/api/controllers/UserController.js in Sublime and add the following code.

Listing 7.4   The signup action

```
module.exports = {
  signup: function(req, res) {
    return res.json({
      email: req.param('email')
    });
  }
};
```

> **NOTE**   What happened to the `hello` action we created previously? We deleted it, and so should you.

Let's check out the new action. Make sure Sails is running via `sails lift`, and in Postman make a `POST` request to /user/signup configured similarly to figure 7.9.

The `signup` action responds with the `email` as JSON and a `200` status code. Next, let's look at the backend validation requirements.

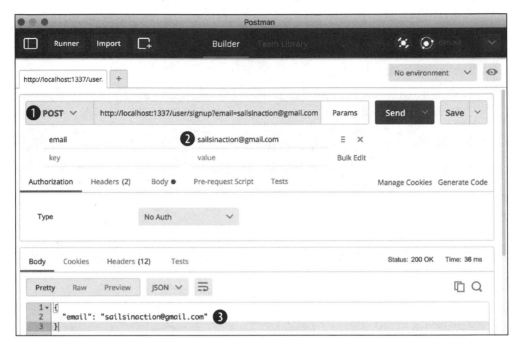

Figure 7.9 Using Postman, create a new user with the custom `signup` action. This will be a POST request to localhost:1337/user/signup ❶ with an `email` parameter set to `sailsinaction@gmail` `.com` ❷.The `signup` action responds with the email address as JSON and a 200 status code ❸.

7.3.3 *Introducing req.param()*

Reviewing the API Reference, specifically the Model Requirements tab, you'll find the backend validation requirements listed in table 7.3.

Table 7.3 Backend validation requirements for the `user` model

Attribute name	Backend validation
username	Must be at least six characters. The attribute is required. Only Aa–Zz and 0–9.
email	Must be a valid email address. The attribute is required.
password	Must be at least six characters. The attribute is required.

Recall that even though you validate user input on the frontend, you must also validate on the backend to protect against requests made outside the browser. Head back to brushfire/api/controllers/UserController.js in Sublime and add the following validation code.

Listing 7.5 Validating the existence of parameters in the `signup` action

```
module.exports = {                                    Uses a Lodash isUndefined()
                                                      method to determine whether a
  signup: function(req, res) {                        request parameter is undefined

    if (_.isUndefined(req.param('email'))) {    ◄─────
      return res.badRequest('An email address is required!');
    }

    if (_.isUndefined(req.param('password'))) {
      return res.badRequest('A password is required!');
    }                                                         Checks the
                                                              value length
    if (req.param('password').length < 6) {    ◄────────
      return res.badRequest('Password must be at least 6 characters!');
    }

    if (_.isUndefined(req.param('username'))) {
      return res.badRequest('A username is required!');
    }

    if (req.param('username').length < 6) {
      return res.badRequest('Username must be at least 6 characters!');
    }

    if (!_.isString(req.param('username')) ||
      req.param('username').match(/[^a-z0-9]/i)) {
        return res.badRequest('Invalid username: must consist of numbers and
        letters only.');
    }                                                  Builds up a user dictionary
    var options = {                       ◄──────────  that contains the parameters
      email: req.param('email'),
      username: req.param('username'),
      password: req.param('password')
    };                                                 Responds with the dictionary
                                                       formatted as JSON
    return res.json(options);             ◄────────
  }
};
```

If a request parameter is undefined, returns a status code 400 Bad Request with a message

Uses a regular expression to ensure only letters and numbers are used in the username

You use the Lodash `_.isUndefined()` method to check for the existence of form fields, now parameters.

NOTE Lodash describes itself as a modern JavaScript utility library. The library is accessible via the global underscore (_) symbol. As its name suggests, it checks to see if a value is `undefined`.

You also introduce another useful method, `req.param()`.

NOTE `req.param()` searches the URL path, query string, and body of the request for a specified parameter provided as an argument. For example, if a form field named `username` is sent in the request, `req.param('username')` will return the value of the `username` field.

Also, you may have noticed that if a value fails a validation test, you respond with `res .badRequest()`.

NOTE   The `res.badRequest()` method is a default response that sends a `400` status code, which by convention means the request has some malformed syntax. You also pass a message that's added to the error as an argument.

You also check the length of the username and password to assure they have a minimum number of characters. Finally, you use a JavaScript regular expression to ensure that the `username` contains only letters and numbers.

Next, you need to ensure the value for the email attribute has the proper syntax, and you'll use the `validate` machine to check the value.

7.3.4   *Validating email addresses*

So far, you've been creating the necessary validations from scratch. Alternatively, you could search the npm registry for an existing Node module to check the validity of the `email` attribute and fulfill the requirement in your custom action. In chapter 5, we introduced a third alternative we call Node machines. Recall that a machine is a single, clear-purpose function that performs a particular task, and machines are aggregated in machinepacks. Navigate your browser to http://node-machine.org/machinepack-emailaddresses/validate, and you should see a page similar to figure 7.10.

Figure 7.10   The `Emailaddresses.validate()` machine page provides example usage.

The `Emailaddresses.validate()` machine takes a string as input and determines whether that string uses valid email address syntax. If it does, the machine will execute the `success` exit; if it's invalid, the `invalid` exit will be executed; and if there's an error, the `error` exit will be executed. Add the example code and then your own code to handle each exit. In Sublime, open brushfire/api/controllers/UserController.js and add the machine and custom handler code to the `signup` action of the `user` controller, similar to the following listing.

Listing 7.6 Using a machine to validate email addresses in the `signup` action

```
var Emailaddresses = require('machinepack-emailaddresses');        ◁─┐  Requires the
                                                                        machinepack
module.exports = {                                                      and assigns it
                                                                        to the variable
  signup: function(req, res) {                                          Emailaddresses
    ...
    return res.badRequest('Invalid username: must consist of numbers and
    ➥ letters only.');
    }
                                                    Adds the email
    Emailaddresses.validate({                       address as input via
      string: req.param('email')            ◁─┘     req.param('email')
    }).exec({
      error: function(err) {                        Returns any errors
        return res.serverError(err);        ◁─┘     via res.serverError()
      },
      invalid: function() {
        return res.badRequest('Doesn\'t look like an email address to me!');  ◁─┐
      },
      success: function() {                                         Upon success,
        var options = {                                             responds with
          email: req.param('email'),                                res.json returning
          username: req.param('username'),                          the user dictionary
          password: req.param('password')
        };

        return res.json(options);          ◁─┐  Returns the options as
      },                                         JSON via res.json(options)
    });
  }
};
```

Next, you need to add the machinepack to the project. Head over to the terminal window and type

```
~/brushfire $ npm install machinepack-emailaddresses --save
```

Let's see this in action. Restart Sails via `sails lift`, and from within Postman make another POST request to /user/signup, similar to figure 7.11.

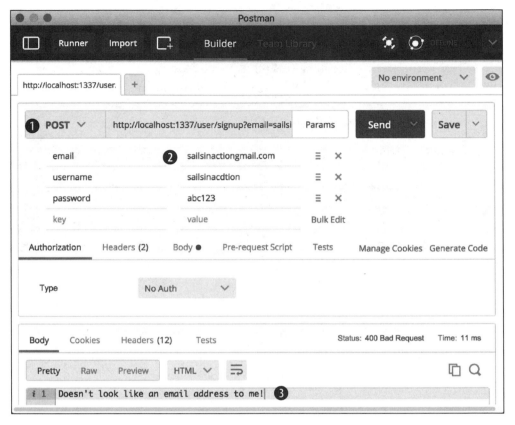

Figure 7.11   Using Postman, check the validity of the email attribute in the custom `signup` action. Generate a `POST` request to `/user/signup` ❶ with an invalid email parameter ❷, with the username and password parameters also provided. The signup action executes the invalid exit and responds with a `400` code and message ❸.

The `validate` machine recognized that the email parameter used improper syntax and responded with an error message. With the email validation requirement fulfilled, let's look at a transformation requirement: encrypting the password (and yes, you have a machine for that).

7.3.5 *Encrypting passwords*

You don't want to store passwords unencrypted. Therefore, you'll use another machine from nodemachine.org to encrypt passwords for you. Navigate your browser to http://node-machine.org/machinepack-passwords/encrypt-password, which should display the `machinepack-passwords.encryptPassword()` page, similar to figure 7.12.

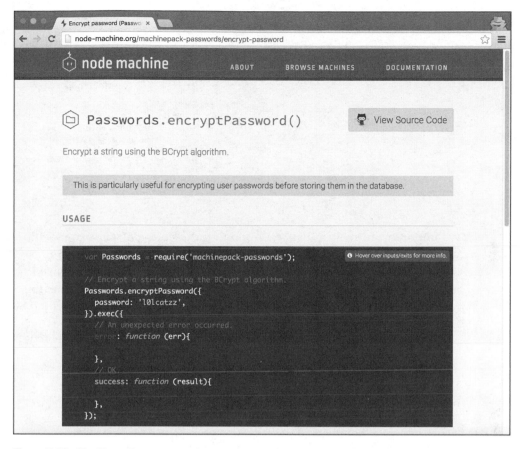

Figure 7.12 You'll use the `Passwords.encryptPassword()` machine to encrypt a user's password before it's stored in the `user` record.

The `Passwords.encryptPassword()` machine takes a string as input and transforms it into an encrypted password. If successful, the machine will execute the `success` exit, or if there's an error, the `error` exit will be executed. Add the example code with some custom handler code by opening brushfire/api/controllers/UserController.js in Sublime and adding the following.

Listing 7.7 Adding the `encryptPassword` machine to the `signup` action

```
var Emailaddresses = require('machinepack-emailaddresses');
var Passwords = require('machinepack-passwords');      ◁— Adds the require
                                                           for Passwords
module.exports = {
  signup: function(req, res) {
    ...
```

```
        success: function() {
          Passwords.encryptPassword({          ◄─┤  Nests the encryptPasswords()
            password: req.param('password'),   ◄─┐    machine with the success exit
          }).exec({                                     of the validate() machine
            error: function(err) {
                return res.serverError(err);       Passes the password
            },                                     parameter via req.param()
            success: function(result) {
              return res.json(result);         ◄─┐
            },                                        Responds with
          });                                         the result as JSON
        },
      });
    }
};
```

It's important to realize that you're nesting the `encryptPassword` machine with the `validate` machine. You do this because the machines are asynchronous. That is, if they're executed independently, you have no way of knowing the order in which each machine will be executed. By nesting the machines, you know that the `validate` machine will complete execution before the `encryptPassword()` machine begins.

NOTE   In later chapters, we'll demonstrate another way to ensure the sequence of asynchronous functions, using a module named `async`.

Before you can see this in action, you need to install `machinepack-passwords`. Head over to the terminal window and type

```
~/brushfire $ npm install machinepack-passwords --save
```

Restart Sails using `sails lift` and make a `POST` request to `/user/signup`, similar to figure 7.13.

Now that you've encrypted the password, you'll use the email address to fulfill the next requirement for a nice profile picture using the Gravatar machine.

7.3.6   *Profile images with Gravatar*

A *Gravatar* is a globally recognized avatar maintained by the folks who produce Word-Press. You can create an account using your email address, and then upload an image that will be associated with that email. Different sites can then use an API to generate a URL that points to the associated image. Navigate your browser to http://node-machine.org/machinepack-gravatar/get-image-url. You'll use a Node machine to generate the URL. The `Gravatar.getImageUrl()` machine has a single input, the email address. Open brushfire/api/controllers/UserController.js in Sublime, and copy the usage example with some custom code, similar to listing 7.8.

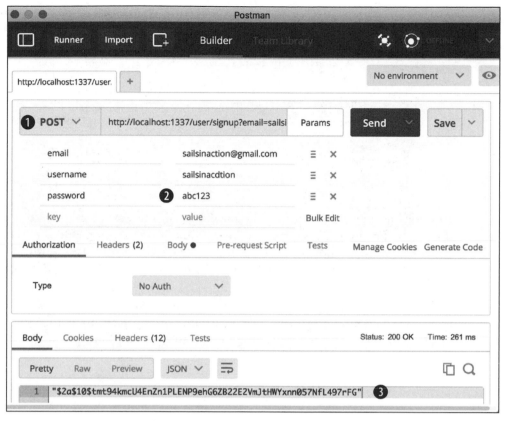

Figure 7.13 Using Postman, make a POST request to /user/signup ❶ and pass the password parameter to the action ❷, which will respond with the encrypted password ❸.

Listing 7.8 Adding the Gravatar.getImageUrl synchronous machine

```
var Emailaddresses = require('machinepack-emailaddresses');
var Passwords = require('machinepack-passwords');
var Gravatar = require('machinepack-gravatar');          ◁─── Adds the require
                                                              for Gravatar
module.exports = {
  signup: function(req, res) {
    ...
        success: function(result) {                          Returns the results
          try {                                              of the machine to
            var gravatarURL = Gravatar.getImageUrl({         gravatarURL
              emailAddress: req.param('email'),
            }).execSync();                                ◁─── Uses the machine
          } catch(err) {                                       synchronously
            return res.serverError(err);
          }
```

Nests the machine within the success of the encrypt-Password() machine

```
            var options = {                        ◁──┐  Builds up the options
              email: req.param('email'),              │  dictionary with attributes
              username: req.param('username'),
              encryptedPassword: result,
              gravatarURL: gravatarURL
            };

            return res.json(options);           ◁──┐  Responds with
          }                                         │  options as JSON
        });
      }
    });
  }
};
```

You may have also noticed that the machine is using `.execSync()` as the last function in the machine. This gives you the option of using a synchronous usage pattern, so let's take this opportunity to configure it to execute synchronously. The usage pattern has two distinct differences in the synchronous usage of a machine. The first is that there's no callback that passes an error and any result of the machine—you need to provide a variable that will be assigned the value of a successfully returned result. The second difference is you're wrapping the machine in a `try/catch`. This will handle any errors without crashing the application. Before you can see this in action, you need to install `machinepack-gravatar`. Head over to the terminal window and type

```
~/brushfire $ npm install machinepack-gravatar --save
```

Restart Sails using `sails lift`, and make a `POST` request to `/user/signup`, similar to figure 7.14.

Let's take a moment to reinforce why you used a `try/catch`. Go back into the UserController.js file and rename the `Gravatar.getImageUrl` to something like `Grvatar.getImageUrl`. In Postman, make a `POST` request to `/user/signup`. Take a look at the console, and you should see an error saying `Gravatar is not defined`, but you didn't crash the server. Next, remove the `try/catch`, restart Sails, and make the same request. Without the `try/catch`, you'd not only have an error, but Brushfire would crash, bringing the server down. So, on those occasions when you use a synchronous function, it's important to wrap it in a `try/catch`.

Now, you've validated your inputs, encrypted the password, and created a Gravatar URL. You're ready to create a record for your user model.

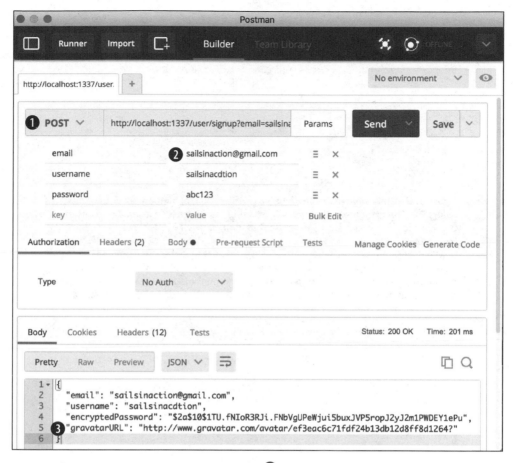

Figure 7.14   Using Postman, make a `POST` request ❶ to /user/signup and pass the email parameter to the action ❷, which will respond with the `gravatarURL` ❸.

7.3.7   Creating user records

It's now time to take the work you've done validating and preparing your attributes and create a user record with the `User.create()` model method. The `.create()` method, shown in figure 7.15, uses the now-familiar asynchronous usage pattern.

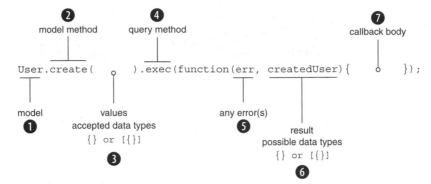

Figure 7.15 This is an example of the `.create()` model method ❷ of the `user` model ❶. The attributes of the record to be created are passed as an argument to the method as a dictionary `{}` or an array of dictionaries `[{}]` ❸. The `.exec()` method ❹ is also referred to as a deferred function. Using `.exec()` will give you the flexibility to chain modifier methods together and to make the usage easier to read. For now, you'll use `.exec()` with an anonymous function as the callback. Within this callback, you'll pass any errors as the first argument ❺ and the resulting data from the method ❻. You can then use the body of the callback ❼ to respond, or continue with another task.

Add the `options` dictionary to the `create` method, as shown here.

Listing 7.9 Using the `create` model method to generate a new `user` record

```
...
module.exports = {
  signup: function(req, res) {
    ...
          var options = {
            email: req.param('email'),
            username: req.param('username'),
            encryptedPassword: result,
            gravatarURL: gravatarURL
          };

          User.create(options).exec(function(err, createdUser) {
            if (err) {
              return res.negotiate(err);
            }
            return res.json(createdUser);
          });
        }
      });
    }
  });
  }
};
```

Passes the options dictionary to the `User.create()` method

Handles the error with `res.negotiate(err)`

Returns the created record as JSON

You passed the options dictionary into the User.create() method as an argument and responded to the request with the created record via res.json(createdUser). Let's take a look at this in action. Restart Sails using sails lift and make a POST request to /user/signup, similar to figure 7.16.

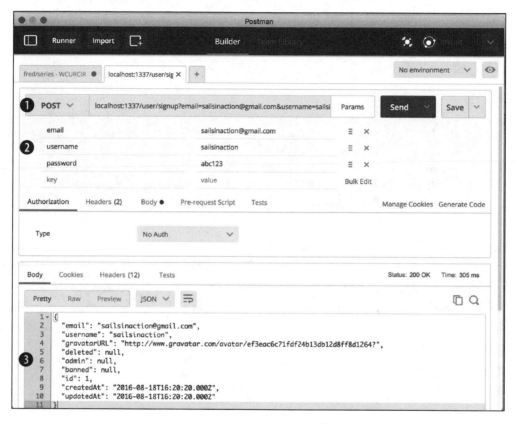

Figure 7.16   The POST request to localhost:1337/user/signup ❶ passes in the email, username, and password parameters ❷, and the action responds with the created record ❸.

You've almost completed the signup portion of user identity management. The last issue to resolve is handling duplicate users.

7.3.8   Preventing duplicate accounts

When you started this chapter, the signup page assets made a POST request to /user whenever a user clicked the Create User Account button. This path triggered the blue-print RESTful create route. You now need to change that request's path in the Angular controller to /user/signup to take advantage of your new custom controller action. In Sublime, open brushfire/assets/js/controllers/signupPageController.js and change the path in the Angular AJAX request to what's shown in the following listing.

Listing 7.10   Changing the AJAX path to use the new controller action

```
...
$scope.submitSignupForm = function(){

    $scope.signupForm.loading = true;

    $http.post('/user/signup', {
      email: $scope.signupForm.email,
      username: $scope.signupForm.username,
      password: $scope.signupForm.password
    })
...
```

Changes the path from
/user to /user/signup

Let's see this in action, now that you've attached your frontend signup page assets with the backend `signup` controller action. Restart Sails via `sails lift` and navigate your browser to localhost:1337/#/signup. From the signup page, create a user with an `email` attribute of sailsinaction@gmail.com, a username of `sailsinaction`, and a password of `abc123`. Click the back button on your browser and create a user with the same credentials you just created. Your browser should display an error message similar to figure 7.17.

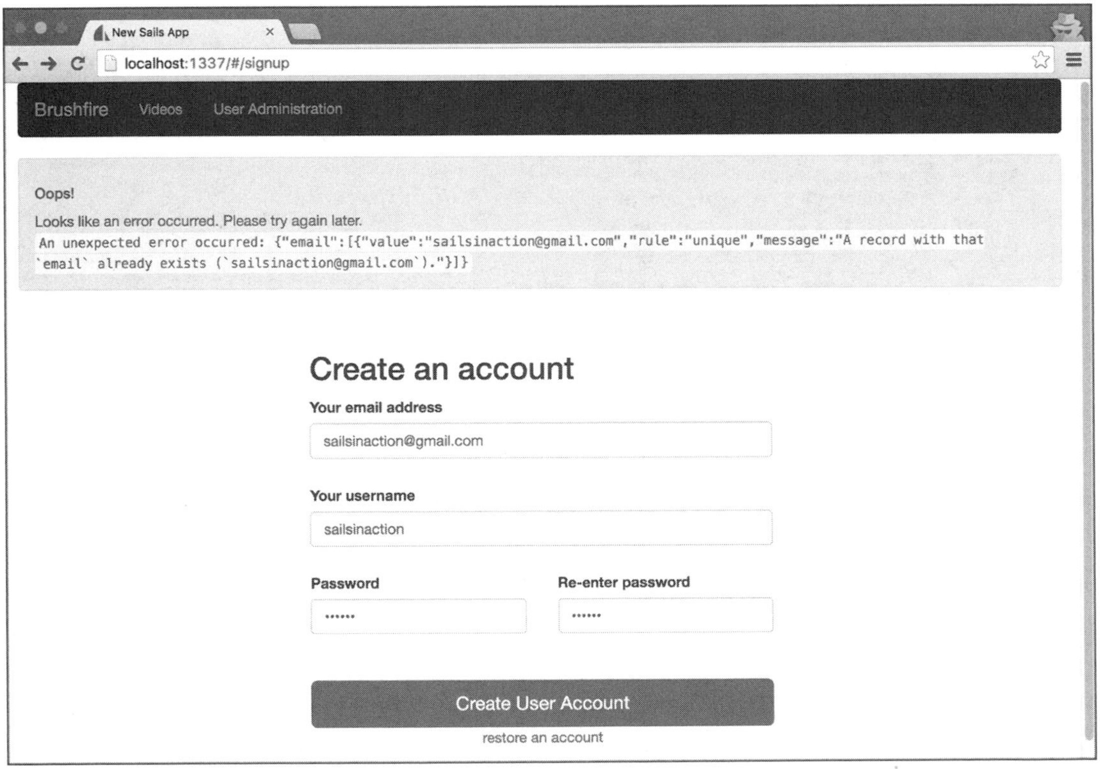

Figure 7.17   The frontend displays an error dictionary returned by the `User.create()` model method that indicates that one of the unique validations has been violated.

The `User.create()` model method returned an error dictionary similar to the following.

Listing 7.11 The duplicate error message from the `signup` action

```
{"email":
  [{
    "value":"sailsinaction@gmail.com",
    "rule":"unique",
    "message":"A record with that `email` already exists
      (`sailsinaction@gmail.com`)."
  }]
}
```

That dictionary gives you a great deal of information. You know the error has to do with the `email` attribute. You know its original value and that the error is a violation of the `unique` attribute validation, and you have a message explaining the error. If you look at brushfire/assets/js/controllers/signupPageController.js, you'll see that your frontend expects a duplicate email address error dictionary to have a `status` property with a value of `409` and a `data` property with an appropriate error message string. In Sublime, open brushfire/api/controllers/UserController.js and add the following responses to the `User.create()` model method in the `signup` action.

Listing 7.12 Handling duplicate `email` and `username` attribute errors

```
    ...
    var options = {
      email: req.param('email'),
      username: req.param('username'),
      encryptedPassword: result,
      gravatarURL: gravatarURL
    };

    User.create(options).exec(function(err, createdUser) {
      if (err) {

        if (err.invalidAttributes && err.invalidAttributes.email &&
        ➥ err.invalidAttributes.email[0] &&
        ➥ err.invalidAttributes.email[0].rule === 'unique') {

          return res.send(409, 'Email address is already taken by
          ➥ another user, please try again.');
        }

        if (err.invalidAttributes && err.invalidAttributes.username
        ➥ && err.invalidAttributes.username[0] &&
        ➥ err.invalidAttributes.username[0].rule === 'unique') {
```

```
            return res.send(409, 'Username is already taken by another
        ➥ user, please try again.');
          }

          return res.negotiate(err);
        }

        return res.json(createdUser);
      });
    }
  });
  }
 });
  }
};
```

Now, if there's a violation of the unique validation option, you'll respond with `res`
`.send()`, passing the status code and a message you want the frontend to display. Let's
comment out the uglier frontend message so the user will see only the `toastr` message. In Sublime, open brushfire/assets/js/controllers/signupPageController.js and
comment out the following.

Listing 7.13   Removing the general error message for unique violations

```
...
if (sailsResponse.status == 409) {
  toastr.error(sailsResponse.data);
  // $scope.signupForm.errorMsg = 'An unexpected error occurred:
  ➥ ' + (sailsResponse.data || sailsResponse.status);        ◁─┐   Adds comment tags to
  return;                                                         remove the general
}                                                                 error message
...
```

Let's see this in action. Restart Sails via `sails lift` and navigate your browser to local-
host:1337/#/signup. Create a user with the familiar credentials `email` of `sailsin-
action@gmail.com`, a `username` of `sailsinaction`, and a `password` of `abc123`. Again,
click the back button and create the same user. You should now see a `toastr` message
similar to figure 7.18.

Let's do one more bit of refactoring that will also introduce custom responses.

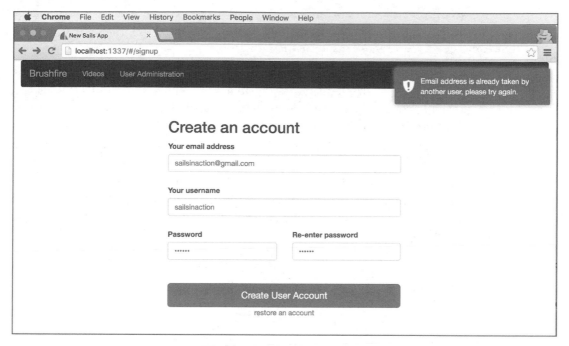

Figure 7.18 The `signup` page now reflects the appropriate error messages when a duplicate `email` or `username` attribute is attempted.

7.3.9 Understanding response methods

So far, you've used a few methods from `res` to respond to requests. Some of these response methods can't be overridden or modified. You've already used two of these response methods:

- `res.json()`—The `res.json()` method encodes the provided data as JSON and sends it in the response. If a number is passed in as the first argument, it will be interpreted as the status code to send, and the second argument will be sent as data (if it is present.) Otherwise, Sails will interpret the first argument as data to encode and send in the response, and it will default to using a status code of `200`.

- `res.send()`—The `res.send()` method is an all-purpose, low-level response method. It works almost exactly like `res.json()`, except that it only JSON-encodes dictionaries and arrays. If a string is provided, it's sent verbatim in the response. This is useful for working with more-traditional data formats like XML or CSV.

There are also configurable responses. We say *configurable* because you can change their implementation by modifying the files in brushfire/api/responses/. You've already used a few of these response methods, too:

- `res.badRequest()`—The `res.badRequest()` method is used to send a 400 response to the frontend indicating that the request is invalid. This usually means it contained invalid parameters or tried to do something impossible based on your application logic.
- `res.serverError()`—The `res.serverError()` method sends a 500 response to the frontend indicating that some kind of server error occurred.
- `res.negotiate()`—The `res.negotiate()` method examines the incoming status message of an error and routes it to the appropriate response. So, instead of determining the status message yourself in a controller action and executing the appropriate response, `res.negotiate()` will do this for you. Note that if the error doesn't contain a `status` property, `res.negotiate()` will default to res .serverError(). The remaining default responses can be found in table 7.4.

Table 7.4 Sails' response methods

Response	Description
`res.forbidden()`	This method is used to send a 403 response to the frontend indicating that the request isn't allowed. This usually means the user-agent tried to do something it wasn't allowed to do, like change the password of another user.
`res.notFound()`	This method is used to send a 404 response using either `res.json()` or `res.view()`. It's called automatically when Sails receives a request that doesn't match any of its explicit routes or route blueprints. When called manually from your app code, this method is normally used to indicate that the user-agent tried to find, update, or delete something that doesn't exist.
`res.ok()`	This method is used to send a 200 response to the frontend.

You can also create your own custom responses to refactor some of the code out of the signup controller action. Create a new file in Sublime named brushfire/api/responses/ alreadyInUse.js and add the following code.

Listing 7.14 Adding a new custom response

```
module.exports = function alreadyInUse (err){

  // Get access to `res`
  // (since the arguments are up to us)        Gets access to the
  var res = this.res;                          correct instance of res

  if (err.invalidAttributes.email) {
    return res.send(409, 'Email address is already taken by another user,
```

```
➥ please try again.');
  }

  if (err.invalidAttributes.username) {
    return res.send(409, 'Username is already taken by another user, please
  ➥ try again.');
  }

  return res.send(500);
};
```

Provides the status code
and custom error message
for duplicate usernames

Provides the status
code and custom error
message for duplicate
email addresses

This new response will determine whether the invalid attribute is an `email` or a user-name attribute and send the `409` response your frontend requires. Let's use this new response in the `signup` action. In Sublime, open brushfire/api/controllers/UserController.js and replace the existing responses in the `User.create()` method of the `signup` action with your new custom response (similar to the next listing).

Listing 7.15 Using the new custom response in the `signup` action

```
...
User.create(options).exec(function(err, createdUser) {

  if (err) {

    if (err.invalidAttributes && err.invalidAttributes.email &&
    ➥ err.invalidAttributes.email[0] && err.invalidAttributes.email[0].rule
    ➥ === 'unique') {

      return res.alreadyInUse(err);
  }

  if (err.invalidAttributes && err.invalidAttributes.username &&
  ➥ err.invalidAttributes.username[0] &&
  ➥ err.invalidAttributes.username[0].rule === 'unique') {

      return res.alreadyInUse(err);
  }
...
```

Let's take this new response for a spin via `sails lift`. Navigate your browser to local-host:1337/#/signup and create the infamous user with an `email` of `sailsinaction @gmail.com`, a username of `sailsinaction`, and a `password` of `abc123`. Again, click the back button and create the same user. Your browser should display the identical `toastr` message from figure 7.18.

That concludes the requirements for the `signup` page. You're probably getting tired of creating a test user each time you restart the Sails server, so let's add a test user in the bootstrap file.

7.3.10 *Quick diversion: adding a dummy user in bootstrap.js*

In chapter 5, you looked at using brushfire/config/bootstrap.js to set up the initial state of Brushfire. You're currently seeding the `video` model with cat videos from

YouTube. Let's add a test user to the bootstrap. Head back to Sublime, and open brushfire/config/bootstrap.js. The source code for the bootstrap.js file can be found in Gist here: https://gist.github.com/sailsinaction/22601ba11f523acccd67. The create-TestUsers() function is almost identical to the signup action in the user controller. The main difference is we stripped out all the references to the res and req dictionaries because they're not available when bootstrap.js is executed.

Recall that the bootstrap originally determined whether any records existed in the video model. If records existed, the bootstrap returned control to Sails via the callback cb function to complete the startup process. Now if records exist for the video model, instead of giving back control to Sails, you'll execute the createTestUsers() function. And if no records exist in the video model, you'll execute the createTest-Users() function after the video records are created. Once the user is created, control passes back to Sails. In either event, you have a test user! You can now move to building out the requirements for the profile page.

7.4   *Providing data for a user profile page*

After you add the profile action, the profile page displays the user's email address, username, and Gravatar image, as shown in figure 7.19.

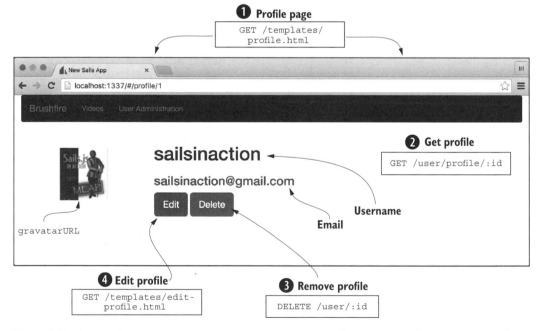

Figure 7.19   The profile page mockup contains four endpoints. The first request initiates the display of the profile page and is handled by an asset route. The second request is a GET request to /user/profile/:id for the initial profile information on the page. The third request is triggered by the Edit button to GET the edit-profile page and is handled by another asset route. The final request is a DELETE request to /user/:id and is handled by a custom controller.

Let's review the requests we've identified in the API Reference. The first request is for the delivery of the profile page itself. The Sails asset router responds to the Angular AJAX GET request to /templates/profile.html ❶. The second request is triggered when the profile page initially loads and an Angular AJAX GET request is made to /user/profile/:id ❷. Sails handles this request with a custom profile action. The third request starts as an Angular frontend request to /#/profile, which triggers a GET request to /templates/edit-profile.html ❸. Sails handles this request with the asset router. The fourth request is a DELETE request to /user/:id ❹. This will trigger a custom delete action that will remove the user record from the database. You'll transition this request from a hard delete into a soft delete, where the user has the option of later restoring the record. Let's start the implementation with the get-profile endpoint.

7.4.1 Retrieving user profile information

To create the profile action, open brushfire/api/controllers/UserController.js in Sublime, and add the following code snippet.

Listing 7.16 Adding the profile action

```
...
  },                        ◁————  Each action is
                                   separated by a comma.

  profile: function(req, res) {

    User.findOne(req.param('id')).exec(function foundUser(err, user) {   ◁——

      if (err) return res.negotiate(err);   ◁——

      if (!user) return res.notFound();   ◁——

      var options = {   ◁——
        email: user.email,
        username: user.username,
        gravatarURL: user.gravatarURL,
        deleted: user.deleted,
        admin: user.admin,
        banned: user.banned,
        id: user.id
      };

      return res.json(user);   ◁——
    });
  }
};
```

The .findOne() model method searches for a particular record based on the id attribute.

Handles errors with res.negotiate(), passing the error as an argument

Uses res.notFound() if no user record is found

Builds up the user to respond

Returns the user record as JSON

You use the User.findOne() model method to retrieve a single user record. This model uses criteria to find a particular user record, as illustrated in figure 7.20.

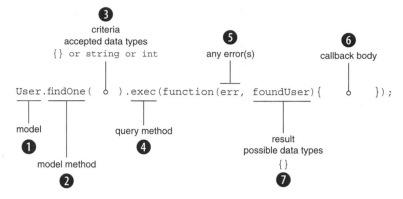

Figure 7.20   The `findOne` model method consists of the model name ❶, the model method ❷, criteria ❸, the query method ❹, the callback method with error ❺, the callback body ❻, and result arguments ❼.

In this case, the criteria is the id of the record you want to find. Let's give this new action a try. Restart Sails using `sails lift`. You know you have at least one test user generated on every `sails lift` that has an id of 1. Navigate your browser to http://localhost:1337/#/profile/1. This triggers an internal Angular route that loads the brushfire/assets/templates/profile.html page.

> **NOTE**   Why use the # symbol in the path of your browser request? HTTP will ignore anything after the hash symbol (#). This allows other frameworks like Angular to come up with their own routing strategy. So the path #/profile/1 is actually being processed by Angular's router.

Now that you have a proper profile page, you need to change the Angular signup-PageController.js so that a user is redirected to the profile instead of the blueprint RESTful `find` route after `signup`. Open brushfire/assets/js/controllers/signupPage-Controller.js in Sublime and make the change shown in the following listing.

Listing 7.17   Changing the redirect to the profile page after signup

```
...
.then(function onSuccess(sailsResponse) {
  window.location = '#/profile/' + sailsResponse.data.id;      ⟵  Changes the
...                                                                redirect to the
                                                                   profile page
```

Next, we'll look the remove-profile endpoint.

7.4.2   Permanently deleting a user

When it comes to deleting records, our experience shows that clients prefer soft deletes versus hard deletes of data. With a soft delete, you can restore the data within an app by toggling an attribute of a record in the database. With a hard delete, that data is gone forever.

> **NOTE** We're relying on you to practice transparency in conveying to your users how their data is treated with respect to removal from your application.

We'll illustrate both ways of performing a delete, but we'll use soft deletes moving forward in Brushfire. You could use blueprint routes to do a permanent delete, but let's see how to do this in a custom action. Open brushfire/api/controllers/UserController.js in Sublime, and add the following code.

Listing 7.18 Adding a delete action to the user controller

```
...
profile: function(req, res) {
  ...
  });
},
delete: function(req, res) {
  if (!req.param('id')){                        ← Validates the id attribute
    return res.badRequest('id is a required parameter.');
  }
  User.destroy({                                ← Uses the .destroy() model
    id: req.param('id')                           method, passing in an id
  }).exec(function (err, usersDestroyed){
    if (err) return res.negotiate(err);         ← Handles any errors
    if (usersDestroyed.length === 0) {          ← with .serverError()
      return res.notFound();
    }
    return res.ok();          ← On success,       Checks for the existence
  });                           responds with a   of a record by checking
}                               200 status        array length
};
```

The `User.destroy()` model method takes criteria, in this case the `id` of the user you want to delete. You've handled any errors as well, such as if the `id` isn't found. The frontend assets are initially configured to trigger a `DELETE` request to /user/delete/:id via the function `$scope.deleteProfile()`. So restart Sails using `sails lift` and navigate your browser to localhost:1337/#profile/1. Next, click the Delete button. The user record is deleted and the browser redirects to the `signup` page. But what if the user wants to restore their user account? If you used a hard delete, they're out of luck. But you're going to implement a soft delete system that will allow a user to easily restore their user profile.

7.4.3   Soft-deleting a user record

Your goal is to provide a way for a user to delete their profile, removing access to it from Brushfire but not from the database. The user can then restore access if they provide an appropriate email/password combination. Implementing a soft delete system requires that an attribute exist in the model that can store the user's deleted state. In chapter 6, you implemented this attribute as a `boolean` and named it `deleted`. To trigger this request, you need to make a small change to the frontend. Open assets/templates/profile.html in Sublime, and change the `ng-click` directive value from `deleteProfile()` to `removeProfile()`, as shown in the following listing.

> **Listing 7.19   Changing the frontend to initiate a soft delete**

```
...
    <a href="#/profile/edit/{{userProfile.properties.id}}" class="btn btn-
    ➥ lg btn-primary">Edit</a>
    <a ng-click="removeProfile()" class="btn btn-lg btn-primary btn-
    ➥ danger">Delete</a>                      ◁── Inserts removeProfile() in
   </div>                                            place of deleteProfile()
  </div>
</div>
```

Next, you'll create a `removeProfile` custom action that will toggle the `deleted` attribute to `true` when the Delete button is clicked on the profile page. Open brushfire/api/controllers/UserController.js in Sublime, and add the following code.

> **Listing 7.20   Adding the `removeProfile` action to the `user` controller**

```
  ...
delete: function(req, res) {
  ...
    return res.ok();
  });
},

removeProfile: function(req, res) {                        Validates the
                                                           id attribute
  if (!req.param('id')){                          ◁──┘
    return res.badRequest('id is a required parameter.');
  }

  User.update({              ◁──  Uses the .update() model
    id: req.param('id')           method, passing in an id
  },{
    deleted: true             ◁──  Toggles the deleted
  }, function(err, removedUser){      attribute to true

    if (err) return res.negotiate(err);     ◁──  Handles any errors
    if (removedUser.length === 0) {              with res.negotiate()
      return res.notFound();
    }
```

```
        return res.ok();
    });
  }
};
```
⊲─── **On success, responds with a 200 status**

The User.update() method accepts criteria, in this case the id of the record you want to update. The second argument of the method is the information you want to update—deleted: true. Now clicking the Delete button will invoke the soft delete method and the page will be redirected to the signup page.

> **NOTE** The profile page is already equipped to handle a user who has been deleted. The profile controller will issue an error if there's an attempt to display a record with the deleted attribute set to true.

Now, what if a user wants to restore their deleted user profile? For that you'll implement the restore-profile page.

7.5 Restoring user accounts

The restore-profile page displays a form for restoring a user profile, given a correct username and password, as displayed in figure 7.21.

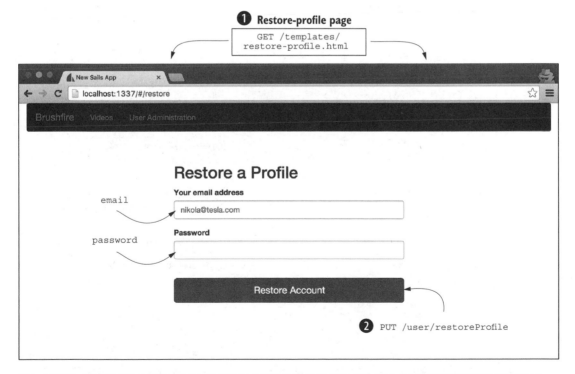

Figure 7.21 The restore-profile page mockup contains two endpoints. The first request initiates the display of the restore-profile page and is handled by an asset route. The second request is a PUT request to /user/restoreProfile and is handled by a custom action.

The restore-profile page is loaded when a user clicks the restore-account link from the signup page. In this case, the Sails asset router responds to the Angular AJAX GET request to /templates/restore-profile.html ❶. The second request is a PUT request to /user/restoreProfile ❷, passing the email and password parameters in an attempt to restore a user account.

7.5.1   *Building an action to restore a user profile*

To create the restoreProfile action, open brushfire/api/controllers/UserController.js in Sublime, and add the following code.

> **Listing 7.21   Adding the `restoreProfile` action to the `user` controller**

```
...
  removeProfile: function(req, res) {
    ...
      return res.ok();
    });
  },
  ...

  restoreProfile: function(req, res) {          Uses the .findOne() model method,
    User.findOne({                              passing in the id of the user to find
      email: req.param('email')
    }, function foundUser(err, user) {
      if (err) return res.negotiate(err);       Handles any errors
      if (!user) return res.notFound();

      Passwords.checkPassword({                 Uses the .checkPassword()
        passwordAttempt: req.param('password'), machine to compare passwords
        encryptedPassword: user.encryptedPassword
      }).exec({

        error: function(err) {                  Handles any errors
          return res.negotiate(err);            with res.negotiate()
        },

        incorrect: function() {                 Handles an incorrect password
          return res.notFound();                with the res.notFound() response
        },

        success: function() {                   On success, updates the
          User.update({                         user and toggles the
            id: user.id                         deleted attribute to false
          }, {
            deleted: false
          }).exec(function(err, updatedUser) {

            return res.json(updatedUser);       Returns the
          });                                   updatedUser as JSON
        }
      });
    });
  }
};
```

The request passes `email` and `password` parameters for the profile to be restored. You first search for a user matching the email address with the `User.findOne` model method. If a matching email address is found, you pass the associated `encryptedPassword` and the `password` parameter to the `.checkPassword()` machine. The machine is part of `machinepack-passwords`, which you already installed and required in the `user` controller. This machine encrypts the provided `password` parameter and compares it to the `encryptedPassword` attribute found by your `User.findOne()` query. If it's a successful match, you'll update the `user` record, setting the `deleted` attribute to `false` using the `User.update()` model method, and respond with the updated record as JSON. The frontend will then redirect the user back to their profile. Known errors are handled by `res.notFound(err)`, and unexpected errors are handled by `res.negotiate(err)`.

7.6 Editing user profiles

The edit-profile page allows users to edit their Gravatar URL, restore their Gravatar URL, and change their password, as displayed in figure 7.22.

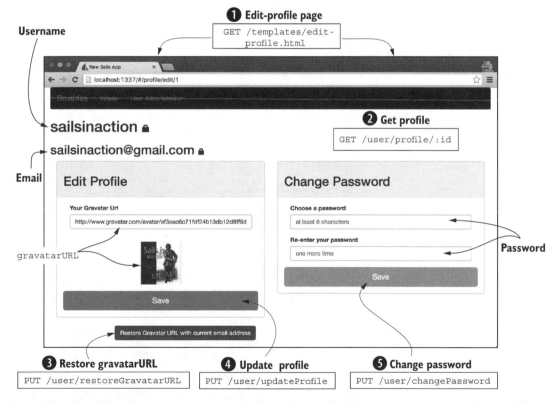

Figure 7.22 The edit-profile page mockup contains five endpoints. The first request initiates the display of the edit-profile page and is handled by an asset route. The second request is a GET request to `/user/profile/:id` for the initial profile information on the page. The third request is triggered by the Restore Gravatar URL With Current Email Address button and is a PUT request to `/user/restoreGravatarURL`, which is handled by a custom action. The fourth request is a PUT request to `/user/updateProfile` and is also handled by a custom action. The final request is a PUT request to `/user/changePassword` and is handled by a custom action.

Let's review the requests we've identified in the API Reference. The first request is for the delivery of the edit-profile page itself. The Sails asset router responds to the Angular AJAX GET request to /templates/edit-profile.html ❶. The second request is triggered when the profile page initially loads and an Angular AJAX GET request is made to /user/profile/:id ❷. The third request occurs when the user wants to restore their Gravatar image to their current email address via a PUT request to /user/restoreGravatarURL ❸. The fourth request occurs when the user wants to update their profile information via a PUT request to /user/updateProfile/:id ❹, which updates the user's gravatarURL attribute. The final request updates the user's password via a PUT request to /user/changePassword ❺. Let's implement the APIs that will satisfy each request.

7.6.1 *Retrieving the record for a particular user*

The GET request to /user/findOne/:id expects a response of a particular user's profile information formatted as JSON. You've already created the profile custom action for the initial loading information of the profile page—you'll use the same endpoint for the edit-profile page.

7.6.2 *Retrieving a user's Gravatar URL*

To create the restoreGravatarURL action, open brushfire/api/controllers/UserController.js in Sublime, and add the following code.

> **Listing 7.22 Adding the `restoreGravatarURL` action to the `user controller`**

```
...
  restoreProfile: function(req, res) {
    ...
          return res.json(updatedUser);
        });
      }
    });
  });
},

  restoreGravatarURL: function(req, res) {        ← Wraps a synchronous machine in a try/catch

    try {

      var restoredGravatarURL = gravatarURL = Gravatar.getImageUrl({    ←  Passes the email as an input to the machine
        emailAddress: req.param('email')
      }).execSync();

      return res.json(restoredGravatarURL);       ← Returns the Gravatar URL as JSON

    } catch (err) {
      return res.serverError(err);                ← Handles any errors with .serverError()
    }
  }
};
```

The request passes the current user's email address via the `email` parameter. You again use the `.getImageUrl()` machine to generate the Gravatar URL using the `email` parameter as the sole input. Because you're using the synchronous version of the `.getImageUrl()` machine, you'll wrap it in a `try/catch` to guard against Brushfire crashing if you get an error. Last, you'll respond with `res.json()` returning the generated URL to the frontend.

7.6.3 Saving updated profile information

To create the `updateProfile` action, open brushfire/api/controllers/UserController.js in Sublime, and add the following code.

Listing 7.23 Adding the `updateProfile` action to the `user` controller

```
var Emailaddresses = require('machinepack-emailaddresses');
var Passwords = require('machinepack-passwords');
var Gravatar = require('machinepack-gravatar');

module.exports = {

  restoreGravatarURL: function(req, res) {
    ...
      return res.serverError(err);
    }
  },

  updateProfile: function(req, res) {          Passes the id of the user
                                                as argument to the
    User.update({                              .update() model method
      id: req.param('id')
    }, {                                        Passes the gravatarURL
      gravatarURL: req.param('gravatarURL')     as the second argument
    }, function(err, updatedUser) {

      if (err) return res.negotiate(err);      Handles any errors
                                                with .serverError()
      return res.json(updatedUser);

    });                                         Returns the updated
  }                                             record as JSON
};
```

The request passes the user's `id` and `gravatarURL` as parameters. You use the `User` `.update()` model method to update the `user` record, passing the `id` parameter as criteria for the first argument and the `gravatarURL` parameter to `update` as the second argument. Finally, you respond with the updated user record to the frontend via `res.json()`.

7.6.4 Updating a user's password

To create the `changePassword` action, open brushfire/api/controllers/UserController.js in Sublime, and add the code in the next listing.

Listing 7.24   Adding a `changePassword` action to the `user` controller

```
...
  signup: function(req, res) {
    ...
  },
  ...
  changePassword: function(req, res) {

    if (_.isUndefined(req.param('password'))) {
      return res.badRequest('A password is required!');
    }

    if (req.param('password').length < 6) {
      return res.badRequest('Password must be at least 6 characters!');
    }

    Passwords.encryptPassword({
      password: req.param('password'),
    }).exec({
      error: function(err) {
        return res.serverError(err);
      },
      success: function(result) {

        User.update({
          id: req.param('id')
        }, {
          encryptedPassword: result
        }).exec(function(err, updatedUser) {
          if (err) {
            return res.negotiate(err);
          }
          return res.json(updatedUser);
        });
      }
    });
  }
};
```

Validates the incoming password attribute

Uses the .encryptPassword() machine, using the password as an input

Handles any errors with .serverError()

Uses the .update() model method to update the user record

Returns the updated user record as JSON

This action is similar to the `signup` action. First, you verify the existence and length of the `password` parameter. Then, you update the `user` record by encrypting the password using the `.encryptPassword()` machine and pass the results to the `User.update()` model method. Finally, you respond with `updatedUser` via `res.json()`. The last part of user identity management is implementing the administration page.

7.7   *Administrative actions*

The administration page allows administrators to grant other users administrator privileges, ban users, and soft-delete users from Brushfire, as displayed in figure 7.23.

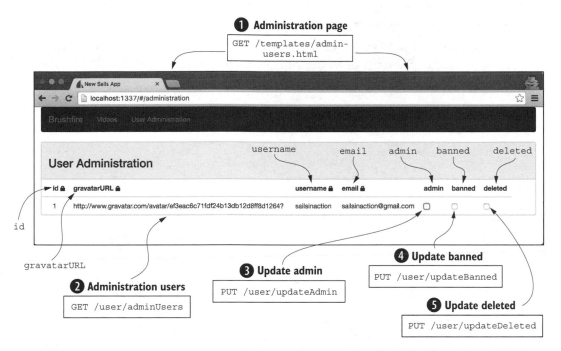

Figure 7.23 **The administration page mockup contains five endpoints. The first request initiates the display of the administration page and is handled by an asset route. The second request is a GET request to /user/adminUsers for the profile information of all users. The third request is a toggle to the admin attribute that triggers a PUT request to /user/updateAdmin, which is handled by a custom action. The fourth request is a PUT request to /user/updateBanned and is also handled by a custom action. The final request is a PUT request to /user/updateDeleted and is handled by a custom action.**

Let's review the requests we've identified in the API Reference. The first request is for the delivery of the administration page itself. The Sails asset router responds to the Angular AJAX GET request to /templates/administration.html ❶. The second request is triggered when the administration page initially loads and an Angular AJAX GET request is made to /user/adminUsers ❷. The third request occurs when an administrator wants to change a user's administrative state via a PUT request to /user/updateAdmin ❸. The fourth request happens when the user wants to update a user's banned status via a PUT request to /user/updateBanned ❹. The final request updates the user's soft-delete status via a PUT request to /user/updateDeleted ❺. Let's implement the APIs that will satisfy each request. Obviously, you'll want to limit access to the administration page to only those users who have the admin attribute set to true. That means controlling what's displayed on the frontend based on the user's authenticated or logged-in state as well as controlling backend access to API endpoints based on the same authenticated state. We'll address that in chapters 8, 9, and 10. For now, let's create the APIs that will satisfy each of the remaining requests.

7.7.1   Listing all the users in the database

The GET request to /user/adminUsers expects a response of an array of user record dictionaries. In Sublime, open brushfire/api/controllers/UserController.js, and add the adminUsers action shown here.

Listing 7.25   Adding an adminUsers action to the user controller

```
...
  changePassword: function(req, res) {
    ...
        return res.json(updatedUser);
      });
    }
  });
},
  adminUsers: function(req, res) {                          Gets all user records via
                                                           the find model method
    User.find().exec(function(err, users){
                                                           Returns any errors using
      if (err) return res.negotiate(err);                  res.negotiate()

      return res.json(users);            If successful, responds
                                         with the users array
    });                                  via res.json()
  }
};
```

You use the User.find() model method to retrieve all user records. Unlike the User.findOne() method, this method responds with an array of all user record dictionaries as JSON. This array is then displayed as a table in Angular on the frontend.

7.7.2   Updating administrative flags

There are three similar PUT requests to actions that update the state of the admin, banned, and deleted attributes. In Sublime, open brushfire/api/controllers/User-Controller.js, and add the updateAdmin, updateBanned, and updateDeleted actions shown here.

Listing 7.26   Adding the updateAdmin, updateBanned, and updateDeleted actions

```
...
  adminUsers: function(req, res) {                  Updates the user record
    ...                                             using the id parameter
      return res.json(users);                       for the find criteria
    });
  },

  updateAdmin: function(req, res) {                 Updates the admin
    User.update(req.param('id'), {                  attribute via the passed-in
      admin: req.param('admin')                     admin parameter
    }).exec(function(err, update){
```

```
      if (err) return res.negotiate(err);        ◁───┐  Handles any errors
                                                       │  with res.negotiate()
      res.ok();                         ◁──────────┐
    });                                            │
  },                                               │  On success, returns a
  updateBanned: function(req, res) {               │  200 status with res.ok()
    User.update(req.param('id'), {
      banned: req.param('banned')
    }).exec(function(err, update){
     if (err) return res.negotiate(err);
      res.ok();
    });
  },
  updateDeleted: function(req, res) {
    User.update(req.param('id'), {
      deleted: req.param('deleted')
    }).exec(function(err, update){
     if (err) return res.negotiate(err);
      res.ok();
    });
  }
};
...
```

Each request passes the user's id and `attribute` to the `User.update()` method as parameters. You respond with a 200 response if successful. The frontend then displays a message to the user notifying them of a successful update or an error.

7.8   Summary

- An API consists of a route, a controller, and an action that combine to fulfill the requirement of a request.
- Blueprint action routes automatically create routes for your custom actions.
- Blueprint routes and actions can be transitioned to custom actions to fulfill requests that go beyond basic CRUD operations.
- Frontend mockups can be used to identify the requirements of the request and fulfill the request with custom actions.

Server-rendered views 8

This chapter covers

- Introducing server-rendered views
- Using server-rendered views in an authentication scheme
- Setting up the layout page and using partials
- Using `locals` to make backend data accessible to views
- Bootstrapping data directly into views with EJS tags

It's now a well-known fact that we're building the greatest virtual edifice to cat videos on the planet Earth, better known as Brushfire. In chapter 6, we embarked on the design and implementation of an identity, authentication, personalization, and access control system, and we established identity with a user model. In chapter 7, we connected that model to frontend elements that enabled a user to create a user record and manage it. Now that a user can create an identity, our next step is deciding how that identity will affect the frontend assets available to the user once they've proven they are who they say they are—a process known as authentication.

214

DEFINITION   When we use the terms *authentication* or *authenticated state*, we're referring to whether a user's claim, on behalf of a user-agent, is genuine. This is typically referred to as a user being logged in or logged out of an application.

For example, as figure 8.1 shows, if a user is authenticated, we'll display the user's Gravatar image and email address in the navigation bar. If the user is not authenticated, we want to display the *login* form instead.

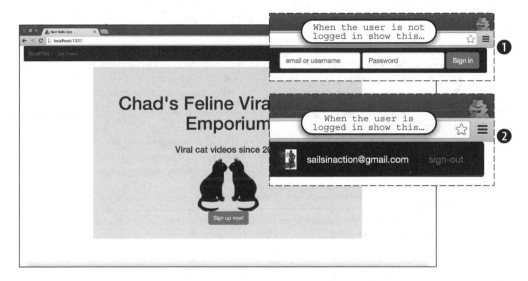

Figure 8.1   You want to show different assets based on the user authenticated state. Here, if the user is not logged in, you'll display the log-in form ❶. If the user is logged in, you'll display their Gravatar image, their email address, and a sign-out button ❷.

The actual mechanics of how a user is authenticated will be implemented in chapter 9, as shown in figure 8.2.

In this chapter, we'll make an assumption that you have access to the user's stored, authenticated state on the backend in the form of a dictionary. This dictionary, named me, will contain an id property whose value is the authenticated user's record id in the database. If the me dictionary exists, you'll assume that the user is authenticated. This will let you concentrate on how to communicate the authenticated state to the front-end in a secure and efficient way. The remainder of the chapter will show you how to communicate the authenticated state of the user using the hybrid approach to page navigation in Brushfire.

8.1   Page navigation

Over countless projects, we've tried various ways of communicating the authenticated state of a user to the frontend. Ultimately, we found the hybrid approach to

Identity, personalization, authorization, and access control system

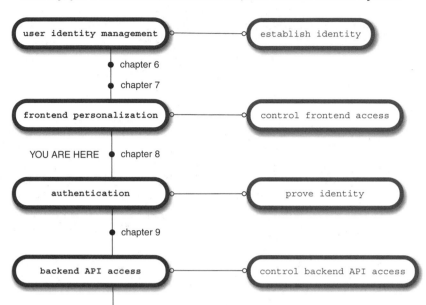

Figure 8.2   **The four components of an identity, authentication, personalization and access control system**

page navigation (first mentioned in chapter 1) to be superior when dealing with user authentication, not just because of its SEO advantages, but also because it combines the benefits of server-rendered views with the flexibility of client-side JavaScript frameworks like Angular. Let's first explore how our current approach to routing and page navigation differs from the hybrid approach.

8.1.1   Client-side vs. server-side routing

So far, the frontend of Brushfire consists of static assets delivered to the browser user-agent and controlled using the Angular framework. We first looked at this approach in chapter 1 using the illustration in figure 8.3.

Using the SPA approach, Sails ❶ delivers the initial HTML view, JavaScript, and CSS as static assets ❷, and then the JavaScript on the frontend is responsible for making intermediate changes to the view via AJAX requests ❸ to the backend API ❹. Wholesale page navigation is controlled by a client-side Angular router ❺. As a user navigates to a different page, client-side routing is used to navigate between pages of Brushfire. These routes are identified by the use of a hashbang (#), and the routes are intercepted by the Angular router. The router then loads templates based on the route into the entry HTML page, as illustrated in figure 8.4.

Single page app (SPA)

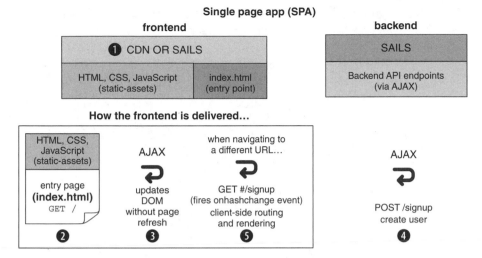

Figure 8.3 Delivering assets and endpoints to a single-page application

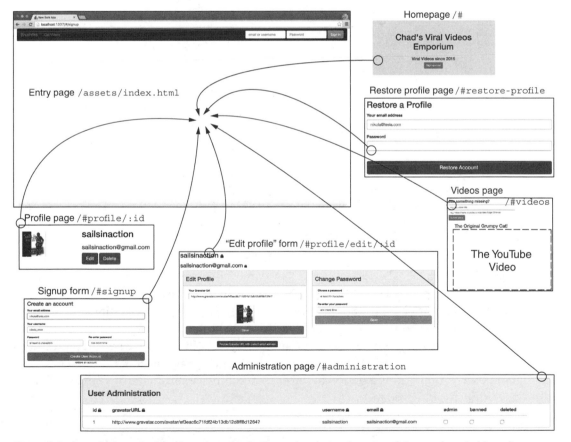

Figure 8.4 In a single-page app, the entry page is the anchor page where templates are inserted based on frontend routes and the Angular router.

The hybrid approach uses a combination of client-side and server-side rendering of pages controlled by backend Sails routes, as depicted in figure 8.5.

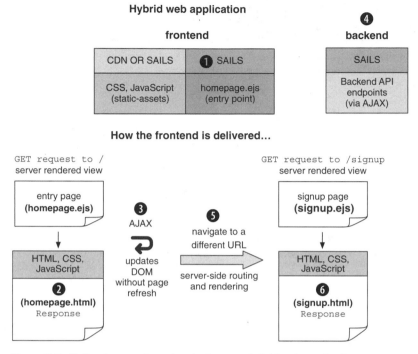

Figure 8.5   Delivering assets and endpoints to a hybrid web application

Using this approach, Sails ❶ provides the initial server-rendered view ❷. From this view, client-side JavaScript can update the DOM by making AJAX calls ❸ to the Sails backend API ❹. Any wholesale page navigation, however, is handled via server-side routes and routing ❺. Therefore, when a user navigates to a different page, a new server-rendered view is sent as a response ❻. In sum, the overall pages in Brushfire remain the same. The difference is that you'll now use explicit routes and backend Sails routing to manage changes between the pages, as illustrated in figure 8.6.

Now that you understand the differences between client-side routing and backend routing, how does this affect your ability to get the information contained in the me dictionary to the frontend? The advantage of combining this type of routing with server-rendered views is that you can control the personalization of the page based on the user's authenticated state. Therefore, you can place the contents of the me dictionary directly in the view.

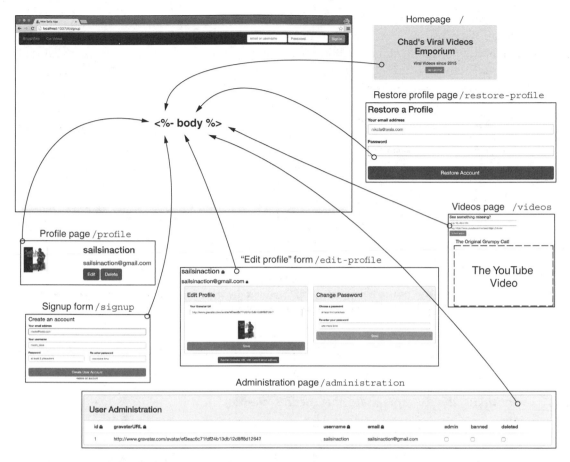

Figure 8.6 Using custom routes and backend Sails routing to manage page navigation in Brushfire

8.1.2   What is a server-rendered view?

Server-rendered views are the result of Sails merging one or more markup templates from the brushfire/views/ folder. The result, illustrated in figure 8.7, is transformed into HTML before being sent to the browser to be displayed.

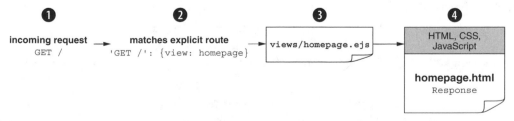

Figure 8.7   An incoming GET request to / ❶ matches an explicit route ❷ that triggers a view named homepage.ejs ❸ to be rendered into homepage.html ❹ and sent as a response to the requesting user-agent.

The real power of server-rendered views is their ability, using special inserted tags, to merge data from the backend into the view. Coupled with Sails' ability to make data available to a view from an explicit route, you now have a way to securely inject values or other templates into a view on the backend before they're sent to the browser for display (as illustrated in figure 8.8).

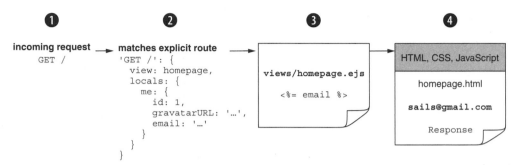

Figure 8.8   An incoming GET request to / ❶ matches an explicit route and passes a locals dictionary ❷ to a view named homepage.ejs ❸. The view contains a special tag that, when rendered, inserts a value from the locals dictionary as a response ❹ to the requesting user-agent.

It's always easier to understand the process when working through an actual example. So, let's get started implementing this hybrid approach.

8.1.3   *Obtaining the example materials for this chapter*

Once again, in an effort to cut down on the number of pages dedicated to source code, we've created a GitHub repo with new assets. You can navigate directly to the repo here, https://github.com/sailsinaction/brushfire-ch8-start, or via a link from the chapter 8 hub at http://sailsinaction.github.io/chapter-8/. After cloning the repo, install the Node module dependencies via npm install.

> **TIP**   If you do choose the cloning option, don't forget to add the brushfire/config/local.js file with your Google API key from chapter 5 (section 5.4.6) as well as to start your local PostgreSQL brushfire database from chapter 6 (section 6.4.2).

8.2   *Personalizing web pages*

Now that you have a better understanding of server-rendered views and the hybrid approach, let's see how you can use them to personalize HTML with data about a logged-in user. To do this, you'll take several steps that include the following:

- Get a better understanding of explicit custom routes.
- Create a custom route that triggers the homepage view.
- Explore how to combine various server-rendered views using the Embedded JavaScript (EJS) template engine, layouts, and tags.

- Simulate bootstrapping of the me dictionary on a browser's window dictionary using markup in the layout template.
- Add EJS tags to the layout template to make the me dictionary contents dynamic.
- Pass the me dictionary values in your custom route to the markup in the layout template.

8.2.1   *A review of explicit routes*

So far, in Brushfire you've relied on Sails asset routes and blueprint routes to trigger the required endpoints and responses from your requests. You learned in chapter 1 that the Sails server listens for incoming requests and, in addition to blueprint routes and asset routes, looks for a matching explicit route in brushfire/config/routes.js, similar to figure 8.9.

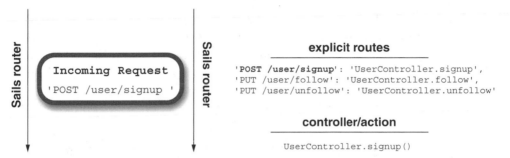

Figure 8.9   How the Sails router matches the incoming request with routes to trigger an action

You also learned that the route itself is implemented in JavaScript as a dictionary, depicted in figure 8.10.

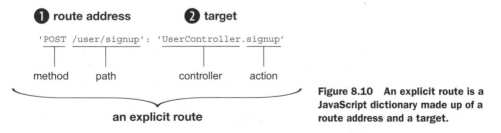

Figure 8.10   An explicit route is a JavaScript dictionary made up of a route address and a target.

The key of the dictionary is the request or route address **①**, consisting of the HTTP method and path, and the value is another dictionary called the target **②**, that consists of a controller, UserController, and an action, signup.

> **NOTE**   Shortly, you'll see that the target can also be a call to execute a server-rendered view.

The Sails router listens for incoming requests and first tries to match the request with an explicit route. If it finds one, the router has done its job and listens for another request. If it's unable to find an explicit route, it tries to match the request with one of the blueprint routes. If it's unable to find a blueprint route, it tries to match the request with an asset route. Finally, if no route is found, Sails will display the 404 Not Found status.

> **NOTE**   The router will also look to see whether the request matches the CSRF token path, but we'll address this potential security issue in chapter 15.

8.2.2 Defining an explicit route

In chapter 3, you used a generator to remove the custom default route to the home-page and to create an index.html file in brushfire/assets/index.html. From that point on, when a browser user-agent made a GET request to / (slash), Sails first looked for a custom route in brushfire/config/routes.js, and, not finding one, it next looked in brushfire/assets/ for an index.html file. This index.html file became the entry page of your application. You're now going to use a hybrid approach where Sails will return to a server-rendered entry page on the backend, with Angular controlling the contents of the page on the frontend. So, you'll override brushfire/assets/index.html by adding a custom route with the same route address. Open /brushfire/config/routes.js, and add the following code.

Listing 8.1   Triggering the homepage via a custom route

```
module.exports.routes = {
  'GET /': {
    view: 'homepage'          ◁⎯┐  A GET request to / will
  },                             │  respond with the view in
                                 │  brushfire/views/homepage.ejs.
  'GET /videos': {
    ...
}
```

You'll notice that the route doesn't trigger a controller action but instead contains a dictionary that identifies the view that should be rendered when the route is triggered. Therefore, custom routes can trigger both controller actions and views. In your custom route, a GET request to / will now trigger the display of a homepage template located in the brushfire/views/homepage.ejs folder. Why are you using the .ejs file extension? EJS is one of many view engines you can use with Sails.

> **DEFINITION**   *View engines*, also called *template engines*, are what combine the templates and data to produce HTML. By default, Sails uses the EJS template engine.

Views are defined by EJS templates located in brushfire/views/. When called on, the view engine combines the templates, which results in HTML. Now that you can trigger the homepage view with a request via a custom route, let's take a closer look at the view itself.

8.2.3 Using EJS views

In Sublime, open brushfire/views/homepage.ejs, and you should see something similar to the following listing.

Listing 8.2 The homepage EJS template

```
<div ng-controller="homePageController" class=" col-md-8 col-md-offset-2">
  <div class="jumbotron">
    <h1 class="jumboHeading">Chad's Feline Viral Videos Emporium</h1>
    <h2 class="jumboSubHeading">Viral cat videos since 2015</h2>
    <div><img src="./images/cat_logo.png" /></div>
    <a ng-hide="me.id || false" href="/signup" class="btn btn-lg btn-
    ➥ success">Sign up now!</a>
  </div>
</div>
```

The first thing that's immediately apparent is that this isn't a complete HTML page. This is only a part of what will make up the homepage view. EJS templates can use a base layout template that merges other templates to form a single page. Let's look at the layout template next.

8.2.4 Using partials and layout.ejs

When building an application with many different pages, it can be helpful to extrapolate markup shared by several HTML files into a layout. This reduces the total amount of code in your project and helps you avoid making the same changes in multiple files down the road. For example, in chapter 3, you learned to use special tags like `<!--STYLES-->` `<!—STYLES END-->` in brushfire/assets/index.html as placeholders for links inserted automatically when Sails starts via `sails lift`. Sails replaced these tags with links to files in the brushfire/assets/ folders. Let's review the tags in table 8.1.

Table 8.1 Automated linking to external CSS and JavaScript files via tags

Tag	Folder	Example
`<!--STYLES-->` `<!—STYLES END-->`	brushfire/assets/styles/ bootstrap.min.css	`<link rel="stylesheet"` `href="/styles/bootstrap.min.css">`
`<!--SCRIPTS-->` `<!--SCRIPTS END-->`	brushfire/assets/js/app.js	`<script` `src="/js/app.js"></script>`

Instead of including the tags directly in each view, we've placed them in a `layout` view provided with the chapter 8 GitHub repo. In Sublime, open the layout in brushfire/views/layout.ejs, and you'll see something similar to the next listing.

Listing 8.3   The layout file for Brushfire

```
<!DOCTYPE html>
<html>
  <head>
    <title>New Sails App</title>
    <!-- Viewport mobile tag for sensible mobile support -->
    <meta name="viewport" content="width=device-width, initial-scale=1,
    ➥ maximum-scale=1">

    <!--STYLES-->
    <!--STYLES END-->
  </head>
  <body ng-app="brushfire">
    <%- partial('./partials/navigation.ejs') %>        ◁———  EJS tags to include
    <%- body %>                              ◁———             a partial template
    <!--TEMPLATES-->
    <!--TEMPLATES END-->                      EJS tags to include
    <!--SCRIPTS-->                            a body template
    <!--SCRIPTS END-->
  </div>
</body>
</html>
```

The layout file also contains a variable named body that's surrounded by yet another
type of EJS tag syntax.

> **TIP**   Don't confuse these tags with the previously mentioned Sails link tags
> like `<!--STYLES-->`; the EJS template engine has its own template tags.

There are three types of EJS template tags. It's important to understand the different
ways they render the values between the opening and closing tags. Table 8.2 provides
example usage of each tag as well as the resulting rendered value.

Table 8.2   EJS template tags

EJS tag example	Rendered result
`<%= <script> alert("Howdy")` `</script> %>`	`&lt;script&gt; alert(&quot;Howdy&quot;)` `&lt;/script&gt;`
`<%- "<script> alert('Howdy')` `</script>" %>`	
`(<% if (!loggedIn) { %>` `<a>Logout</a> <% } %>`	If loggedIn is true, `<a>Logout</a>` will be displayed. If not, nothing will be rendered.

Using an opening <%= (equals) template tag with a closing %> tag, HTML escapes whatever is contained between the tags and then includes it as a string.

> **NOTE** HTML escaping replaces certain characters and replaces them with their encoding equivalent, like the less-than (<) sign <. This prevents the browser from interpreting a string as JavaScript but still displays the correct characters.

This is an important protection against cross-site scripting (XSS) attacks.

> **NOTE** XSS attacks occur when a user enters malicious scripts that are then executed by another user. For example, if a user enters a malicious script in a form field and the value is not stripped of script tags, the script will execute when the value is displayed. It's important to know where your values originate. If you don't have control over where the values originate, you'll display them using HTML escaping.

Using an opening <%- (dash) template tag with a closing %> tag includes whatever is contained between the tags as is, without escaping it. If you decide to use this, be very careful because it can make your application vulnerable to XSS attacks. There are situations where this tag will be both useful and safe. In fact, you've already used the tag in listing 8.3 where you inserted the value of body, and when incorporating partials.

> **DEFINITION** *Partials* are template fragments you can incorporate into views. Common examples of partials are headers and footers.

Using an opening <% template tag with a closing %> tag executes any JavaScript between the tags when the template is being compiled. Unlike the other two tags, whatever value is compiled isn't displayed in the markup. This template tag is useful for inserting conditionals like if/else and looping over data using for/each.

So, in listing 8.3, body and partial('./partials/navigation.ejs') are replaced by whatever view template is being rendered within the layout file as well as the template in the partial's path. In your custom route, the homepage template and the partials/navigation template are combined with the layout template to form a view similar to figure 8.11.

Let's see this in action. Restart Sails using sails lift and navigate your browser to localhost:1337; your browser should look similar to figure 8.12.

The layout wrapped the homepage to deliver the server-rendered view in figure 8.12, but you do have an issue. The layout is displaying the markup for both authenticated ❶ and unauthenticated ❷ states. Your intent is to display the sign-in form when the user is not authenticated and therefore not logged in. When the user is authenticated, you want to hide the sign-in form and display the user's authenticated markup: the Gravatar image, email address, and logout link.

```
<!DOCTYPE html>
<html>
  <head>
    <title>New Sails App</tit
    <!-- Viewport mobile tag
    <meta name="viewport"

    <!--STYLES-->
    <!--STYLES END-->
  </head>
  <body ng-app="brushfire">
    <%- partial('./partials/navigation.ejs') %>
    <%- body %>

    <!--TEMPLATES-->
    <script type="text/javascript" src="/jst.js"></scrip
    <!--TEMPLAT

    <!--SCRIPTS
    <!--SCRIPTS
  </div>
</body>
</html>
```

partials/navigation.ejs
```
...
<span class="icon-bar"></span>
    <span class="icon-bar"></span>
    <span class="icon-bar"></span>
    </button>
    <!-- This is the brand on the left-hand side. -->
    <a class="navbar-brand" href="/"> Brushfire</a>
    <div class="collapse navbar-collapse">
        <ul class="nav navbar-nav">
...
```

homepage.ejs
```
...
    <h1 class="jumboHeading">Chad's Feline Viral Videos Emporium</h1>
    <h2 class="jumboSubHeading">Viral cat videos since 2015</h2>
    <div><img src="./images/cat_logo.png" /></div>
    </div>
</div>
```

Figure 8.11   The layout file contains the navigation partial and surrounds the view that's being rendered.

Figure 8.12   The new navigation section contains both the authenticated and unauthenticated markup states.

The navigation template contains Angular directives that control the display of the markup based on the me dictionary, which contains the user's authenticated state. In Sublime, open brushfire/views/partials/navigation.ejs to see the directives in the following listing.

Listing 8.4 The navigation partial

```
...
<form ng-hide="me.id" ng-submit="submitLoginForm()"
➥ class="navbar-form navbar-right">
  ...
</form>

<ul ng-show="me.id" class="nav navbar-nav navbar-right">
  <li class="gravatarSm"><img class="gravatarSm" ng-src="{{me.gravatarURL}}"
➥ height="30" width="30"/></li>
  <li class="activityOverlord active">
    <a href="/profile" class="pointer"> {{me.email}}</a>
  </li>
  <li>
    <a href="/logout">sign-out</a>
  </li>
</ul>
...
```

The ng-hide directive controls the display of the form based on the value of me.id.

The ng-show directive controls the display of the elements based on the value of me.id.

If me.id has a value, the sign-in form will be hidden and the Gravatar image, email address, and logout link will be displayed. If me.id is null, the sign-in form will be displayed and the authenticated markup will be hidden. How can the frontend get access to the values of the me dictionary? First, you'll bootstrap the me dictionary on the browser's window dictionary via the layout view.

8.2.5 Exposing data for use in client-side JavaScript

Let's add the me dictionary to the browser's window dictionary in the layout view. Once again, open brushfire/views/layout.ejs in Sublime, and add the following code.

Listing 8.5 Bootstrapping data in layout.ejs

```
...
<!--STYLES-->
    <link rel="stylesheet" href="/styles/angular-toastr.css">
    <link rel="stylesheet" href="/styles/bootstrap.min.css">
    <link rel="stylesheet" href="/styles/importer.css">
    <!--STYLES END-->
    <script type="text/javascript">
    window.SAILS_LOCALS = {
      me: {
        id: null
      }
    };
    </script>
  </head>
...
```

The script tag adds a me property to the window dictionary, setting its value to null.

For now, you've hardcoded the value of me.id to null. Next, let's look at your Angular controller for the layout view. In Sublime, open brushfire/assets/js/controllers/nav-PageController.js, and examine the $scope.me property in the next listing.

Listing 8.6   Bootstrapping data on view

```
angular.module('brushfire').controller('navPageController', ['$location',
   '$scope', '$http', 'toastr', function($location, $scope, $http, toastr) {

   $scope.me = window.SAILS_LOCALS.me;          ◁─┐ Assign the value of
                                                     window.SAILS_LOCALS.
}]);                                                 me to $scope.me.
```

The Angular controller's main function is to grab the value of the me dictionary from window.SAILS_LOCALS. By hardcoding the value of me.id equal to null, you simulate a logged-out user. The Angular directives will hide the authenticated markup and show the sign-in form. Restart Sails using sails lift, and navigate your browser to localhost:1337, which should display something similar to figure 8.13.

Figure 8.13   The homepage view with the sign-in form displayed in its unauthenticated state

The homepage view is displayed with the sign-in form in the navigation portion of the markup indicating an unauthenticated state. Next, let's use Sails locals to pass a value from the backend to the me.id property in your explicit route.

You've already hardcoded the value of me.id to null, and you saw how the Angular controller could easily grab data from the browser's window dictionary and save it on

$scope.me. Then Angular directives can use that information to display markup based on the values found in me. Now you want to make the values you bootstrap on the page dynamic. You'll use EJS template tags to inject the values of the me dictionary from locals passed in an explicit route.

In Sublime, open brushfire/views/layout.ejs, and use the template tags shown here, so that the locals passed in the route will be compiled on the view.

Listing 8.7 Using EJS template tags to incorporate `locals` from the route

```
...
<!--STYLES-->
    <link rel="stylesheet" href="/styles/angular-toastr.css">
    <link rel="stylesheet" href="/styles/bootstrap.min.css">
    <link rel="stylesheet" href="/styles/importer.css">
    <!--STYLES END-->
    <script type="text/javascript">
      window.SAILS_LOCALS = {
        me: <%- JSON.stringify(me||null) %>
      };
    </script>
  </head>
...
```

> JSON.stringify the me dictionary if there's a value, or assign it to null.

Next, you'll add the locals to the explicit route to pass the authenticated state to the layout view.

8.2.6 *Hardcoding locals in a route*

You've seen how Sails makes data available to views with variables called locals. In chapter 9, you'll transition to setting locals in your controller actions. For now, just so you get to see some action, you'll pass through stub data in your explicit route. In Sublime, open brushfire/config/routes.js, and add the following locals to the GET / route.

Listing 8.8 Adding `locals` to a view in your custom route

```
module.exports.routes = {
  'GET /': {
    view: 'homepage',
    locals: {
      me: {
        id: 1,
        gravatarURL:
        ➥ 'http://www.gravatar.com/avatar/ef3eac6c71fdf24b13db12d8ff8d1264?',
        email: 'sailsinaction@gmail.com'
      }
    }
  },
  ...
}
```

> Passing locals to the view via a custom route

Here, you pass a static dictionary of a simulated user to the view via locals. Figure 8.14 illustrates the compiling process where locals passed in the route are injected into a view to produce your server-rendered view.

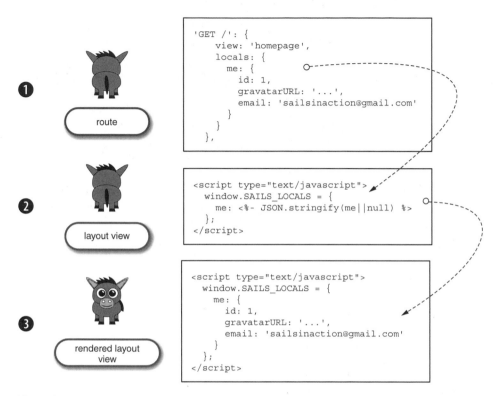

```
'GET /': {
    view: 'homepage',
    locals: {
        me: {
            id: 1,
            gravatarURL: '...',
            email: 'sailsinaction@gmail.com'
        }
    }
},
```

```
<script type="text/javascript">
    window.SAILS_LOCALS = {
        me: <%- JSON.stringify(me||null) %>
    };
</script>
```

```
<script type="text/javascript">
    window.SAILS_LOCALS = {
        me: {
            id: 1,
            gravatarURL: '...',
            email: 'sailsinaction@gmail.com'
        }
    };
</script>
```

route

layout view

rendered layout view

Figure 8.14   Using `locals` **through a custom route to bootstrap data in a server-rendered view**

The route ❶ triggers the view along with locals. You use template tags that will stringify the value of the me dictionary or insert null if the me local is empty ❷. The result of this compile is a server-rendered view that contains the me dictionary ❸. The me dictionary will inform the frontend whether the user who made the request is authenticated or unauthenticated. Let's see this in action. Restart Sails using sails lift, and navigate your browser to localhost:1337. Your browser should look similar to figure 8.15.

Notice that the sign-up button isn't visible because the ng-hide directive hides the sign-up button based on the me dictionary if the user is authenticated. Now that you understand how server-rendered views and frontend frameworks like Angular can be used to control what's displayed on the frontend, let's take a look at the remaining pages of Brushfire.

Figure 8.15   The `homepage` view with the simulated authenticated state displaying the authenticated markup

8.3   *Transitioning from an SPA*

If you're following along in the example repo, you'll notice that we provided views for each of the main frontend pages of Brushfire outlined in figure 8.16.

This allows you to share the same layout, partials, and (to some degree) `locals`, across each of your different views. Currently, your `videos.ejs` view is served by an explicit route that simulates an unauthenticated state of a dummy user. And each of the other views has a corresponding custom route in brushfire/config/routes.js that simulates an authenticated state, similar to the following listing.

> **Listing 8.9   `locals` used to simulate the authenticated state of a user**

```
...
locals: {
    me: {
       id: 1,
       gravatarURL:
       ➥ 'http://www.gravatar.com/avatar/ef3eac6c71fdf24b13db12d8ff8d1264?',
       email: 'sailsinaction@gmail.com'
    }
  }
...
```

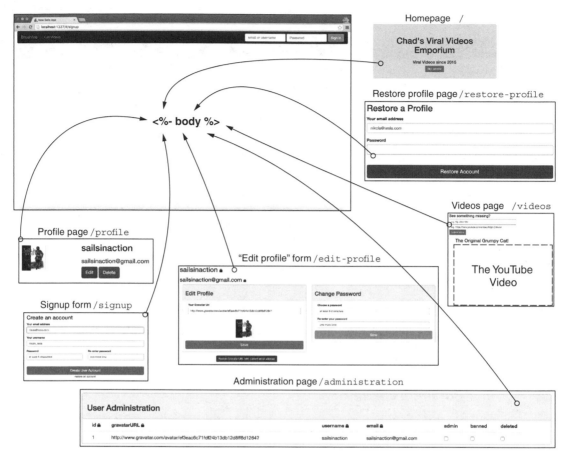

Figure 8.16   The relationship between the `layout` view and the other views of Brushfire

Table 8.3 lists the remaining routes and corresponding views we provided in the GitHub repo. In chapter 9, when we cover authentication, we'll replace this fake data with data about the currently logged-in user.

Table 8.3   Brushfire custom routes and templates

The route	The `view` template
`'GET /videos'`	`brushfire/views/videos.ejs`
`'GET /profile'`	`brushfire/views/profile.ejs`
`'GET /edit-profile'`	`brushfire/views/edit-profile.ejs`
`'GET /signup'`	`brushfire/views/signup.ejs`

Table 8.3   Brushfire custom routes and templates *(continued)*

The route	The `view` template
`'GET /restore-profile'`	`brushfire/views/restore-profile.ejs`
`'GET /administration'`	`brushfire/views/administration.ejs`

Let's see this in action. Restart Sails via `sails lift`, and navigate your browser to localhost:1337/videos. Your browser should look similar to figure 8.17.

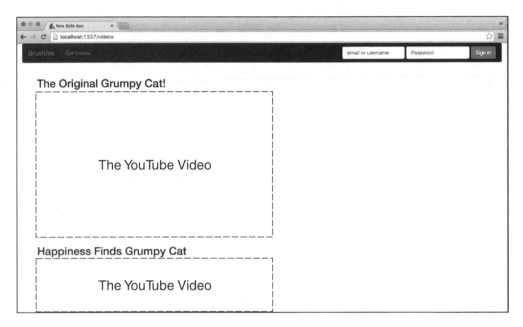

Figure 8.17   This videos page simulates an unauthenticated user and therefore doesn't have the markup to add a video.

You might be wondering whether you could add a `video` with a `POST` request to /videos in an application like Postman even if you weren't authenticated. The answer is yes. It's important to distinguish between controlling what's displayed on the frontend with preventing access to controller actions on the backend. In chapter 10, we'll show you how to lock down access to controller actions with policies based on a user's authenticated state. For now, we're concentrating on managing what's displayed on the frontend, based on the user's authenticated state.

You now have a personalization system for your frontend based on the user's simulated authenticated state. In chapter 9, you'll build out the components of a user authentication system. You'll then transition the frontend that's using a simulated authenticated state to the live authentication system that utilizes what you've built here to personalize the frontend.

8.4   *Summary*

- Sails can be configured to utilize client-side Angular routes or Sails backend routes for page navigation.
- Sails uses the EJS view engine to integrate templates using a `layout` view with EJS tags.
- Custom routes that pass a dictionary can simulate a user authenticated state to the `layout` view.
- EJS tags are used to dynamically inject the user's simulated authenticated state on the view.

Authentication and sessions 9

This chapter covers

- Introducing authentication
- Challenging and determining the authenticity of a user's claim to an identity
- Using sessions to save authentication state between requests
- Creating a way to route between application pages based on authenticated state

We're now well into the implementation of an identity, authorization, personalization, and access control system designed to make the world a safe place for cat videos. A user can now set up and manage their identity. The Brushfire frontend is also personalized based on a user's simulated authenticated status. In this chapter, you'll create the authentication component and replace the simulated state with a user's actual authenticated state. The goal of this authentication, along with the work done in chapters 6–8, is to require a Brushfire user to be authenticated to add

235

video content. That way, if a user violates the content policy and posts a forbidden dog video, our investor can disable the account with extreme prejudice. In chapter 10, we'll wrap up the client's requirements by locking down our backend API based on the user's authenticated state.

9.1 What is authentication?

When we use the term *authentication* or *authenticated state*, we're referring to whether a user's claim, on behalf of a user-agent (in our case, a browser), is genuine or not. To provide authentication, you first needed a user identity. So you added a unique `email` address and a unique `username` to the `user` model as key attributes of a user's identity. You also added a `password` attribute that will later be used as proof of a claim to a particular identity. Thus, your authentication component has three distinct subcomponents:

- The *sign-in process* challenges the authenticity of a user's claim to a specific identity from the frontend via the login page and determines whether the claim is genuine on the backend via a controller action.
- The *session store* stores the results of the challenge, which is the authenticated state, between requests using sessions on the backend.
- The *page controller* routes requests between pages on the backend using a controller action that takes the authenticated state from the session and passes that state via `locals` to views used by the frontend framework, Angular.

In summary, on each request of a view, the page controller checks whether the user is authenticated in the session store. It then passes the `locals` to the view template that gets rendered on the page, thus storing the authenticated state on the page. That authenticated state is either a user's record `id` (if they're authenticated, or logged in) or `null` (if they're unauthenticated, or logged out). You'll spend the remainder of the chapter implementing each of these subcomponents. A summary of where you've been and where you're going can be found in figure 9.1.

9.2 The login process

You first need to challenge the user to authenticate, and then test whether the proof—the `password` provided—is genuine. You know this will consist of some frontend components making requests to your backend API. As we've done throughout the book, let's look at the frontend for guidance on the requirements of your requests, routes, and controller actions.

9.2.1 Obtaining the example materials for the chapter

You have two options with regard to setting up your Brushfire assets for this chapter. If you've completed chapter 8, you're all set and can use your existing project here. If you haven't completed chapter 8, you can clone the end of the chapter 8 GitHub repo

Identity, personalization, authorization, and access control system

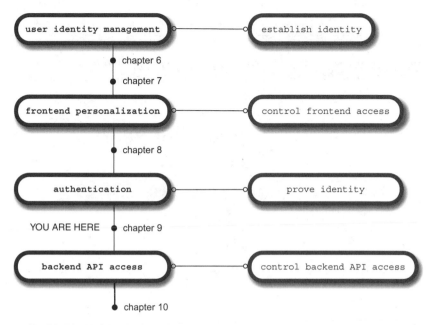

Figure 9.1   The four components of an identity, authentication, personalization, and access control system

located at https://github.com/sailsinaction/brushfire-ch8-end.git and start from there. Remember to use npm install in the terminal window from the root of the project after you clone the repo.

If you do choose the cloning option, don't forget to add the brushfire/config/local.js file with your Google API key from chapter 5 (section 5.4.6) as well as to start your local PostgreSQL brushfire database from chapter 6 (section 6.4.2).

9.2.2 Understanding the backend for a login form

Before you lift Sails, take a look at the requirements for the login action. In figure 9.2, the homepage contains a sign-in form that can trigger a PUT request to /login that passes in either an email address or a username along with a password as parameters.

The backend requirements of the login request are as follows:

- Query the user model for a record using email as a query criteria.
- If a user is not found, send a 404 status as a response.
- If a user record is found, compare the encryptedPassword of that user record with the password provided in the request.
- If the password doesn't match the encryptedPassword, send a 404 status as a response.
- If the password does match, create a session, and send a 200 status as a response.

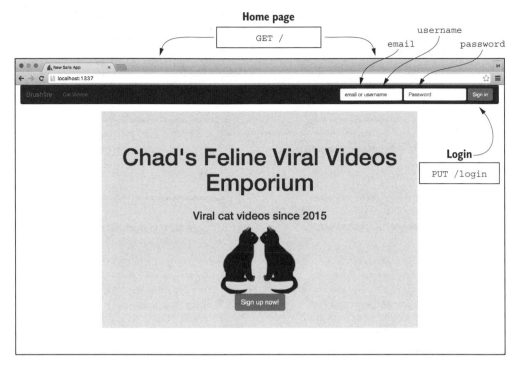

Figure 9.2   The `layout` navigation partial has a sign-in form that executes a `PUT` request to `/login` when the sign-in button is clicked.

Now that you have the requirements of the request, you can create the custom Sails backend route and controller action that will be triggered when the frontend makes the request.

9.2.3   *Creating a /login route*

For your authentication system, you'll create custom routes to trigger each controller action of the system. By doing this, you can have a central place for backend routes to your API. In Sublime, open brushfire/config/routes.js, and add the following route.

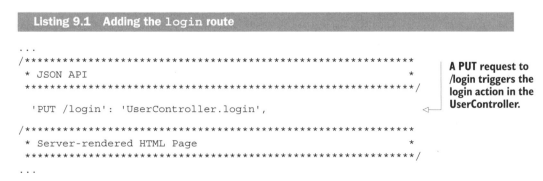

Listing 9.1   Adding the `login` route

```
...
/************************************************************
 * JSON API                                                 *
 ************************************************************/

  'PUT /login': 'UserController.login',

/************************************************************
 * Server-rendered HTML Page                                *
 ************************************************************/
...
```

A PUT request to /login triggers the login action in the UserController.

Now a PUT request to /login will trigger a login action within UserController.js. Next, you'll create the login action that will be triggered when the user clicks the sign-in button.

9.2.4 Handling a login form

When the user clicks the sign-in button, the login action will be triggered. Let's create that action. In Sublime, open brushfire/api/controllers/UserController.js, and add the login action shown in the following listing.

Listing 9.2 Adding the login action

```
...
login: function (req, res) {                    ❶ Looks up the user using
                                                  the submitted email
    User.findOne({                                address or username
        or : [
            { email: req.param('email') },
            { username: req.param('username') }
        ]
    }, function foundUser(err, createdUser) {
        if (err) return res.negotiate(err);
        if (!createdUser) return res.notFound();  ❷ If a user is found,
                                                     compares the submitted
        Passwords.checkPassword({                    password with the stored
            passwordAttempt: req.param('password'),  encryptedPassword
            encryptedPassword: createdUser.encryptedPassword
        }).exec({

            error: function (err){
                return res.negotiate(err);
            },

            incorrect: function (){
                return res.notFound();              ❸ If a user's deleted property
            },                                         is true, returns early with a
                                                       403 Forbidden status and
            success: function (){                      message
                if (createdUser.deleted) {
                    return res.forbidden("'Your account has been deleted. Please visit
                      ➥ http://brushfire.io/restore to restore your account.'");
                }

                if (createdUser.banned) {
                    return res.forbidden("'Your account has been banned, most likely for
                      ➥ adding dog videos in violation of the Terms of Service. Please
                      ➥ contact Chad or his mother.'");
                }                                   If a user's banned
                                                    property is true,
                return res.ok();        ❺ If the passwords    returns early with
            }                             match, returns a     a 403 Forbidden
        });                               200 OK status         status and
    });                                   response              message  ❹
},
```

Your `login` action fulfills the requirements you established earlier by analyzing the frontend request. To summarize, you use the `User.findOne()` model method ❶ to query the user model for a record using the submitted `email` field via `req.param('email')`, or the `username` field via `req.param('username')` as criteria for the query.

> **NOTE** In the past, your query dictionary contained a single parameter and value, for example, `User.findOne({email: req.param('email')})`. This query dictionary uses the `or` property with an array of values to use as criteria. Sails has a powerful query language through Waterline where you can build up sophisticated queries. For a complete overview, see http://mng.bz/qEo9.

The `User.findOne()` model method then returns either an error or a `user` record dictionary of the query results. You handle any errors with `res.negotiate(err)`.

> **NOTE** Recall that `res.negotiate()` is a function that examines the provided error (`err`), determines the appropriate error-handling behavior via the error's `status` property, and routes it to one of the following responses on the `res` dictionary: `res.badRequest()` (400 errors), `res.forbidden()` (403 errors), `res.notFound()` (404 errors), or `res.serverError()` (500 errors).

If a `user` isn't found, you respond with a `404` status and your frontend code displays a message that the `email` address or `username/password` combination is invalid.

In chapters 5 and 6, we introduced the concept of machines and machinepacks. In chapter 7, you used a machine in `machinepack-passwords` to encrypt passwords in your `signup` action. You'll now use another machine in the same machinepack named `.checkPassword()`. The `Passwords.checkPassword()` machine ❷ compares the two incoming parameters as *inputs*—the submitted `password` attribute and the `encrypted-Password` attribute you found in the `user` record. The machine provides three possible exits: an `error` exit, an `incorrect` exit if the passwords don't match, and a `success` exit if the passwords do match.

On success, you first check whether a user has been deleted by checking the `deleted` property of the user dictionary ❸. If the `deleted` property is `true`, you respond with a `403` forbidden status and message. Next, you check whether the user record has been banned by inspecting the `banned` property ❹. If the `banned` property is `true`, you again respond with a `403` forbidden status and message. Finally, if the user isn't deleted or banned, you send a `200` status via `res.ok()` ❺.

To see this in action, you need to change the simulated state of the root route to `null`. In Sublime, open brushfire/config/routes.js, and change the `id` property to `null`, as shown in the next listing.

Listing 9.3 Simulating an unauthenticated state in the root route

```
...

module.exports = {
  'GET /': {
    view: 'homepage',
```

```
locals: {
    me: {
        id: null                        Changes to a simulated
        gravatarURL: '                  unauthenticated state
            http://www.gravatar.com/avatar/ef3eac6c71fdf24b13db12d8ff8d1264?'
        ...
```

Now that you've set up the route that will load the homepage and the backend route that will trigger the `login` action, let's look at your work in action. Restart Sails via `sails lift`, and navigate your browser to localhost:1337. Try to log in using the sign-in form with an email address of `sailsinaction@gmail.com` and a password of `abc123`. Your browser should display a message similar to figure 9.3.

Figure 9.3 A successful challenge to the claim of identity of `sailsinaction@gmail.com`

So far, you've created a sign-in form where a user can present an identity in the form of an email address or username and provided proof, in the form of a password, claiming a particular identity. You also have a custom route and controller action that can test whether the proof is genuine. Because requests are stateless, you need a way to store the result of this test between requests. But what do we mean when we say that requests are stateless?

9.2.5 *What does "stateless" mean?*

Imagine that the Sails web server (and every other web server on the planet) has a lousy memory when it comes to differentiating between requests. For example, a request is made from Nikola Tesla's browser, and Sails routes it to a controller action that checks whether a submitted `password` matches a value stored in a `user` record. The controller action responds to the browser that the values match. In the next instant, another request is made from the same user-agent to the server. Sails has no idea that the previous request involved the successful submission of a matching password. Therefore, the state of that successful submission wasn't stored anywhere, making the request stateless. Moving forward, it would be impractical to ask the user for their password each time they wanted to access something that required authentication. Fortunately, you don't have to. You can use sessions to temporarily save their authenticated state.

9.2.6   *Understanding the Sails session*

Sessions are a way to store information like the authenticated state of a user between HTTP requests or Sails socket requests. The session uses several components to make all this happen. The good news is that sessions are built into Sails and are created and maintained for you with every request. This means that you can set and retrieve values on a property of the `req` dictionary called `session` and know that any values set on the `session` are associated with each request of a particular user-agent. This concept would benefit greatly from an actual example. Open brushfire/api/controllers/User-Controller.js in Sublime, and add the following controller actions.

Listing 9.4   Adding `setSession` and `getSession` actions to better understand sessions

```
...
module.exports = {                              Sets req.session.userId to
                                                the submitted sessionVar
  setSession: function(req, res) {         ◁┘   parameter

    req.session.userId = req.param('sessionVar');

    return res.json(req.session.userId || 'not yet set');

  },                                            Returns the value of
                                                req.session.userId
  getSession: function(req, res) {         ◁┘

    return res.json(req.session.userId || 'not yet set');

  },

...
```

> **NOTE**   Recall that blueprint action routes are enabled, so Sails will generate a route for the `setSession` and `getSession` actions automatically for you.

Restart Sails via `sails lift` and navigate your browser to http://localhost:1337/ user/getSession. Your browser should return `not set yet`. This makes sense, because you haven't assigned any values to `req.session`. Next, navigate your browser to http://localhost:1337/user/setSession?sessionVar=12345. This passes the parameter `sessionVar` to the controller action with a value of `12345`. Your browser should return `12345`. Finally, navigate your browser back to http://localhost:1337/user/getSession and your browser should return `12345`. By storing a value on `req.session.userId`, you've given the request and, more importantly, the user-agent a state, which can be accessed between requests. Therefore, you have a way of storing the state of your password check for each authenticated user-agent.

Let's take a somewhat closer look at the mechanics of the session without getting overwhelmed in how Sails is handling the session behind the scenes. Figure 9.4 illustrates the process at a high level.

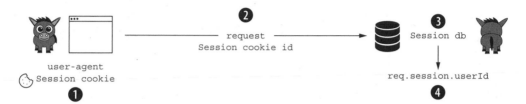

Figure 9.4   The session consists of a session cookie and the user-agent, the session database, and a process for using a value stored on the session cookie to securely identify each request with a particular user-agent.

Each user-agent **1** request **2** to Sails contains a value stored in the session cookie that identifies a particular place in the session database **3** where values are stored on behalf of that user-agent. Sails also provides a way of accessing, adding, or changing values stored in the session database **4** via the `req` dictionary within an action. Storing the authenticated state of a user-agent is as simple as setting the value of a property on `req.session` like in an action.

> **NOTE** But what does the user-agent have to do with it? Because the user-agent for Brushfire is a browser, the browser window is tied to the user's claim of identity through a browser cookie. A user, therefore, can't claim more than one identity from the same user-agent browser because of this relationship with the cookie. Note that a browser window in `incognito` mode extends the browser's ability to identify as an additional user because a different cookie is used for the incognito window.

Now that you have a better understanding of the session, you can put it to use in Brushfire to store a user's authenticated state within the `login`, `logout`, `removeProfile`, `restoreProfile`, and `signup` actions. But before moving on, go back to brushfire/api/controllers/UserController.js, and remove the `setSession` and `getSession` actions.

9.2.7   *Saving the user's logged-in status*

You'll start using the session in the `login` action. Open brushfire/api/controllers/UserController.js in Sublime, and add the `req.session.userId` property to the `login` action, as shown in the following listing.

Listing 9.5   Adding a `userId` property to the session on a successful password check

```
...
login: function (req, res) {

    ...
        if (createdUser.banned) {
            return res.forbidden("'Your our account has been banned, most likely
            ➥ for adding dog videos in violation of the Terms of Service.
            ➥ Please contact Chad or his mother.'");
        }
        req.session.userId = user.id;

        return res.ok();
        }
    });
    });
  },
...
```

Adds the id of the
found user record to
a userId property

Responds with
a 200 status

Now, when a user successfully authenticates via the sign-in form, a userId property is added to the session, which contains the id of the found user record. You now have a way to log in and store this authenticated state, so let's create a way to log out.

9.2.8   *Creating the logout endpoint*

Let's implement the logout route and action and assign the null value to req.session .userId to indicate the user-agent is not authenticated. First, you'll create a custom route that will trigger the logout action. In Sublime, open brushfire/config/routes.js, and add the logout route shown here.

Listing 9.6   Creating the logout route

```
...
'PUT /login': 'UserController.login',
'GET /logout': 'UserController.logout',
...
```

Next, create the logout action in the user controller. In Sublime, open brushfire/ api/controllers/UserController.js, and add the logout action shown in the next listing.

Listing 9.7   Adding the `logout` action in the user controller

Looks up the user via req.session.userId and
uses res.negotiate to handle any errors

If the user is already
logged out, redirects
to the root route

```
    ...
    logout: function (req, res) {
        if (!req.session.userId) return res.redirect('/');

        User.findOne(req.session.userId, function foundUser(err, user) {
            if (err) return res.negotiate(err);
```

```
                   if (!user) {
If a user             sails.log.verbose('Session refers to a user who no longer exists.');
doesn't exist,     }
redirects back
to the root        req.session.userId = null;                      If a user record is found,
route                                                              assigns the session to null

                   return res.redirect('/');                       Redirects the browser
                 });                                               back to the root route
              },
              ...
```

When a GET request to /logout is made, the user's authenticated state is set to null in the session, and the browser is redirected to the root route. You can test whether a user-agent is authenticated by assessing the value of req.session.userId. If it has a value, you know a user is authenticated, and if it's null, you know it's not authenticated. Next, you need to change the authenticated state when a user's account is removed and restored.

9.2.9 Updating the session when a user is deleted or restored

When you soft-delete a user, their authenticated state should be changed. In Sublime, open brushfire/api/controllers/UserController.js, and set the user's authenticated state in the removeProfile controller action, as shown here.

> **Listing 9.8 Changing the user's authenticated state to null when deleted**

```
removeProfile: function(req, res) {
    ...

    User.update({
      id: req.param('id')
    }, {
      deleted: true
    }, function(err, removedUser) {

      if (err) return res.negotiate(err);
      if (removedUser.length === 0) {
        return res.notFound();
      }
                                               Changes the userId
      req.session.userId = null;              property to null
      return res.ok();
    });
  },
...
```

Similarly, when the user is restored, a user's authenticated state should change. In Sublime, open brushfire/api/controllers/UserController.js, and set the user's authenticated state in the restoreProfile controller action as follows.

Listing 9.9   Changing the user's authenticated state to their user `id` when restored

```
restoreProfile: function(req, res) {
    ...
            User.update({
              id: user.id
            }, {
              deleted: false
            }).exec(function(err, updatedUser) {

                req.session.userId = user.id;

                return res.json(updatedUser);
            });
        }
      });
    });
  },
  ...
```

Sets the userId
property to the
user's id

You have one other place to establish the authenticated state: the signup controller
action.

9.2.10 *Authenticating a user after signup*

So far, you've assigned the appropriate session value for the user-agent's authenticated
state for the login, logout, removeProfile, and restoreProfile actions. Finally,
when a user signs up for a user account, you want them to be authenticated if their
user record is successfully created. In Sublime, open brushfire/api/UserController.js,
and add the req.session.userId property to the signup action, as shown here.

Listing 9.10   Adding `req.session.userId` to the `signup` action

```
signup: function(req, res) {
    ...
            User.create(options).exec(function(err, createdUser) {
                ...
                  return res.negotiate(err);
                }

                req.session.userId = createdUser.id;

                return res.json(createdUser);

            });
            ...
```

After the user is created,
authenticates the user using
the session userId property

You've now implemented a process for the user to submit proof of their identity and
for you to test its validity. You also have a way to store the results of that test between
requests. Before moving on, let's look at how to configure the session itself.

9.2.11 Configuring the session store

From the previous section, you know you can add properties to the session. You can change a user's authenticated state by changing the value assigned to `req.session.userId`. But what about the session itself, and how do you control a session's lifecycle? By default, Sails sessions persist until the session database is restarted or the session cookie expires.

The Sails session database is currently configured to reside in memory. So while the session is configured in memory, the session for a request will be reset each time the Sails server starts. You can transition this in-memory store to a database like Redis in brushfire/config.session.js. Once configured, the session will exist independently of Sails so long as the Redis database is running. In fact, you'll be implementing a Redis session store in chapter 15.

By default, Sails doesn't place an expiration date/time on the session cookie, but you can change this in brushfire/config/session.js. In this file, you can create a `maxAge` parameter on the `cookie` property and set it to whatever expiration you desire.

> **TIP** The session cookie can't be copied or altered via JavaScript on the browser. The cookie is also protected against tampering. That is not to say that if someone has access to the computer, the cookie can't be copied directly.

The final step for authentication is to implement a controller, which routes requests between pages and passes the authenticated state via `locals` to the views.

9.3 Personalizing page content for logged-in users

In chapter 8, you made the transition for page navigation from using client-side routes and static assets to Sails custom routes and server-rendered views. With the custom routes, you also added static `locals` that hardcoded a simulated authenticated state of a user in the view. This gave you a chance to understand how custom routes could trigger server-rendered views directly with values via `locals`. Now that you have the user's actual authenticated state, you can move the logic out of the custom route and into an action for each page or view of Brushfire. Figure 9.5 illustrates the progression.

You'll update the route so that instead of directly loading the view, the route will trigger an action. For example, the `homepage` view will have an action named `showHomePage`. In this action, you have greater flexibility to expand the logic than you do in a custom route. You can now determine if the user is authenticated by checking `req.session.userId` and sending `locals` that will trigger the display of the appropriate markup in the `view`. Figure 9.6 illustrates an example of this process.

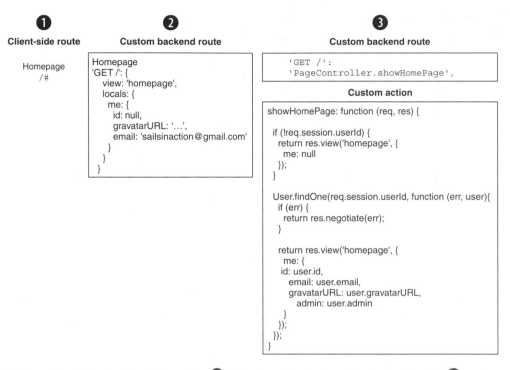

Figure 9.5 You started off using client-side routing ❶ before transitioning to custom backend routes ❷ serving server-rendered views. Now that you have the user's authenticated state, you can move to a combination of custom routes that trigger a custom action ❸ for each view.

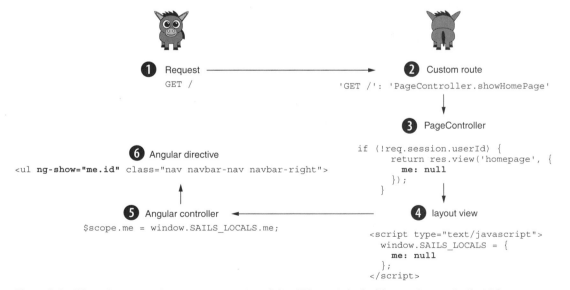

Figure 9.6 When the user makes a `GET` request to `/`, it will be matched with a custom route that triggers an action that determines the user's authenticated state and sends the appropriate `locals` to the `layout` view, which are then added to the frontend via an Angular controller and displayed based on a directive in the view.

When a user-agent makes a GET request to localhost:1337 **❶**, it's matched in a custom route **❷**, which triggers a showHomePage action **❸** in the PageController. The action will determine that req.session.userId is null and render the homepage view **❹** with locals set to null. The frontend (controller) will read the authenticated state from the window dictionary and set an internal $scope.me property **❺**. Finally, an Angular directive will then display the appropriate form **❻** based on the user's authenticated state.

You'll spend the remainder of this chapter adding a custom action for each page in Brushfire that will correspond with your existing custom routes. This action will contain the logic to determine the user's authenticated state and send locals to the view based on that state. Let's start with the root route and the homepage view.

9.3.1 Introducing PageController

Before you start creating custom actions for each page view, you need to create a controller that will contain them. The easiest way to set up a boilerplate controller is via the command line. To create the controller, open a terminal window and type

```
~/brushfire $ sails generate controller page
```

Sails will generate an empty PageController.js file in brushfire/api/controllers. With the controller generated, you can start to transition the homepage view and route.

9.3.2 Using a custom action to serve the homepage

You're now going to move the locals from each route to a custom controller action. First, you need to change the route that triggers an action instead of the view. In Sublime, open brushfire/config/routes.js, and alter the root route, as follows.

> **Listing 9.11 Altering the root route to trigger the showHomePage action**

```
module.exports = {
...
/**********************************************************
* Server Rendered HTML Pages                              *
**********************************************************/

  'GET /': 'PageController.showHomePage',
...
```

Notice that you're no longer passing static locals to the homepage view. Instead, a GET request to the root (for example, /) triggers the showHomePage action of the page controller. So let's create the action. In Sublime, open brushfire/api/controllers/Page-Controller.js, and add the following action.

Listing 9.12   Creating a `showHomePage` action

```
module.exports = {
  showHomePage: function (req, res) {

    if (!req.session.userId) {            ◁──┐  If req.session.userId is null,
      return res.view('homepage', {              returns the homepage view
        me: null                                  with locals set to null
      });
    }
                                          ┌──  Searches for the
    User.findOne(req.session.userId, function (err, user){  ◁──┘  authenticated
      if (err) {                                                   user by id
        return res.negotiate(err);
      }                                   ┌──  If the user isn't found, logs a
                                                message and returns the homepage
      if (!user) {                        ◁──┘  view with locals set to null
        sails.log.verbose('Session refers to a user who no longer exists- did
          ➡ you delete a user, then try to refresh the page with an open tab
          ➡ logged-in as that user?');
        return res.view('homepage', {
          me: null
        });                               ┌──  Using res.view,
      }                                        compiles the homepage
                                               view with locals
      return res.view('homepage', {     ◁──┘
        me: {
          id: user.id,
          email: user.email,
          gravatarURL: user.gravatarURL,
          admin: user.admin             ◁──┐  Adds a new property to
        }                                      locals to control the
      });                                      administration link
    });
  }
};
```

This action responds with a server-rendered `view` using `res.view()`. Table 9.1 contains the two (optional) arguments to `res.view()`.

Table 9.1   The path to the view template in `res.view`

Argument	Type	Details
pathToView	String	The path to the desired view file relative to your views/ folder, without the file extension .ejs and with no trailing slash
locals	Dictionary {}	Data to pass to the view template

Without arguments, Sails will derive the `pathToView` argument as a combination of the *controller name* and the *action name*. You can also provide an explicit path to the view template. Figure 9.7 provides examples of how `pathToView` is resolved.

Use Case	Controller	Action	pathToView
res.view()	UserController.js	login	views/user/login.ejs
res.view()	PageController.js	showHomePage	views/page/showHomepage.ejs
res.view('homepage')	UserController.js	login	views/homepage.ejs
res.view('bar/homepage')	UserController.js	login	views/bar/homepage.ejs

Figure 9.7 Examples of how `pathToView` is resolved based on the configuration used

You want to explicitly provide the path to the `view` as an argument. You also want to pass various `locals` to the `view` template. You can pass `locals` as a dictionary and the second argument of res.view(). So if `req.session.userId` is null, `res.view('home-page')` will render brushfire/views/homepage.ejs. If `req.session.userId` has a value indicating that the user is authenticated, you'll use the user `id` as a criteria object argument in the `User.findOne()` model method. If the `User.findOne()` method returns an error, you'll let `res.negotiate(err)` determine which status code to return. If instead `User.findOne()` doesn't return a `user` record, you'll log a message using `sails.log.verbose`.

> **NOTE** `sails.log` is similar to logging via `console.log`, but you can set the visibility of the message via `config.log.js`. This is useful when you want to display certain messages during development but hide those messages in a production environment. In chapter 15, we'll discuss setting up different environments.

Finally, if the `findOne()` method returns a `user` record, you'll compile a server-rendered view with `res.view()`, passing the `homepage` view with the `locals` including the `id`, `email` address, `Gravatar URL`, and `admin` property of the `user` record.

> **NOTE** The `admin` property was added so the administration link will be displayed only to users with the `admin` property set to `true`.

Instead of displaying the `toastr` message and remaining on the `homepage`, let's redirect to the `videos` page on a successful login. In Sublime, open brushfire/assets/js/controllers/navPageController.js, and make the following changes to the `navPage-Controller`.

Listing 9.13 Redirecting to the `videos` page after successfully logging in

```
$http.put('/login', {
    email: $scope.loginForm.email,
    password: $scope.loginForm.password
})
.then(function onSuccess() {

    window.location = '/videos';          ◁─┐ Replaces the call
})                                            to toastr() with a
                                              redirect to /videos
```

Let's give this new controller a spin. Restart Sails using `sails lift`, and navigate your browser to localhost:1337. Next, sign in to Brushfire using `sailsinaction@gmail.com` as the email address and `abc123` as the password. The browser should redirect to the videos page, similar to figure 9.8.

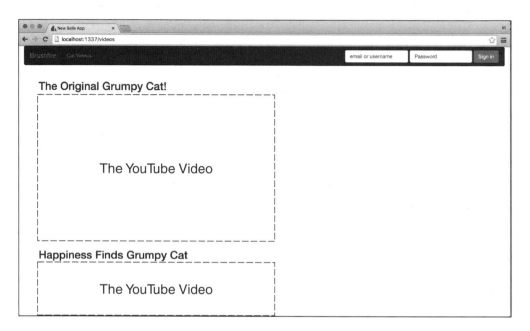

Figure 9.8   The browser was redirected to the `videos` page, but the navigation partial isn't displaying the markup for the authenticated state.

Although the browser redirected to the `videos` page, the navigation partial isn't displaying the authenticated state. That's because you haven't transitioned the custom route and action for the `videos` page. Let's do that next.

9.4   *Implementing the backend application flow*

Now that you have `PageController` as your foundation for managing the frontend user experience, let's transition the remainder of your pages. Figure 9.9 illustrates each mockup page and its associated route.

Let's transition the `videos` page route and add a new action to the page controller.

9.4.1   *Personalizing your list of videos*

In chapter 8, we addressed what should be displayed on the `videos` page based on the authenticated state of the user. Essentially, if the user is authenticated, the submit-videos form is displayed. If the user isn't authenticated, the form isn't displayed and the user can't add videos.

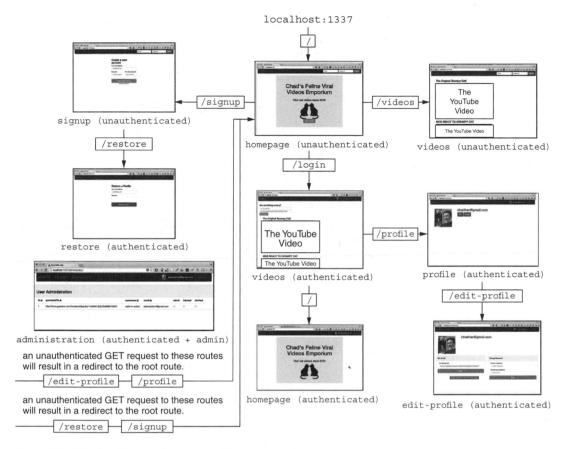

Figure 9.9 The Brushfire mockup pages with custom routes

NOTE In fact, the user can add videos using Postman making a POST request to /videos. In chapter 10, we'll address how to lock down access to controller actions with policies.

Now you want your page controller action to bootstrap the user's authenticated state. First, modify your existing GET request to /videos. In Sublime, open brushfire/config/routes.js, and make the following changes to the route.

Listing 9.14   Adding the /videos route

```
module.exports = {
  'GET /': 'PageController.showHomePage',
  'GET /videos': 'PageController.showVideosPage',
...
```

Notice that you're no longer passing static locals to the homepage view. Instead, a GET request to /videos triggers the showVideosPage action of the page controller. So let's create a showVideosPage action. In Sublime, open brushfire/api/controllers/Page-Controller.js, and add the following action.

Listing 9.15 Creating a `showVideosPage` action

```javascript
module.exports = {
...

  showVideosPage: function (req, res) {

    if (!req.session.userId) {
      return res.view('videos', {
        me: null
      });
    }

    User.findOne(req.session.userId, function (err, user){
      if (err) {
        return res.negotiate(err);
      }

      if (!user) {
        sails.log.verbose('Session refers to a user who no longer exists- did
          you delete a user, then try to refresh the page with an open tab
          logged-in as that user?');
        return res.view('videos', {
          me: null
        });
      }

      return res.view('videos', {
        me: {
          id: user.id,
          email: user.email,
          gravatarURL: user.gravatarURL,
          admin: user.admin
        }
      });
    });
  }
};
```

9.4.2 Securing your administration page

In order for the administration view to be displayed, a user must not only be authenticated but also have the admin attribute in their user record set to true. You currently don't have a user record with the admin property set to true. Let's change that by making your test user an administrator. In Sublime, open brushfire/config/bootstrap.js, and change the admin property to true.

Listing 9.16 Making the test user account an administrator

```javascript
module.exports = {
    ...
      options.email = 'sailsinaction@gmail.com';
```

```
        options.encryptedPassword = result;
        options.username = 'sails-in-action';          Changes the value
        options.deleted = false;                       for admin property
        options.admin = true;                          to true
        options.banned = false;
      User.create(options).exec(function(err, createdUser) {
        ...
```

Now you can set up the administration page. First, create the route that will trigger the showAdminPage action. In Sublime, open brushfire/config/routes.js, and make the following changes to the route.

Listing 9.17 Altering the route to trigger an administration page route

```
module.exports = {                              A GET request to
  'GET /': 'PageController.showHomePage',       /administration triggers
  ...                                           the showAdminPage
  'GET /administration': 'PageController.showAdminPage',    action.
  ...
```

Unlike the other pages in Brushfire, the administration page is displayed only if the admin attribute is set to true. In Sublime, open brushfire/api/controllers/Page-Controller.js, and add the following action.

Listing 9.18 Creating a showAdminPage action

```
...                                               If req.session.userId is null,
  showAdminPage: function (req, res) {            returns the homepage view
    if (!req.session.userId) {                    with locals set to null
      return res.redirect('/');
    }                                                          Searches for the
                                                               authenticated
    User.findOne(req.session.userId, function (err, user){     user by id

      if (err) {
          return res.negotiate(err);            If the user isn't found, logs a
      }                                         message and returns the homepage
      if (!user) {                              view with locals set to null
        sails.log.verbose('Session refers to a user who no longer exists- did
        ➥ you delete a user, then try to refresh the page with an open tab
        ➥ logged-in as that user?');
        return res.view('homepage');
      }

      if (user.admin) {                          If the user's admin property
        return res.view('adminUsers', {          is set to true, renders the
            me: {                                administration page
              id: user.id,
              email: user.email,
              username: user.username,
              gravatarURL: user.gravatarURL,
              admin: user.admin
            }
```

```
      });
    } else {
      return res.view('homepage', {        ◁——  If the user's admin property
        me: {                                     is not set to true, renders
          id: user.id,                            the homepage view
          email: user.email,
          username: user.username,
          gravatarURL: user.gravatarURL,
          admin: user.admin
        }
      });
    }
  });
},
...
```

Now that you have the `administration` page controller completed, let's move on to the profile view.

9.4.3 *Personalizing the user profile page*

The profile page doesn't have an unauthenticated state. Therefore, if the user isn't authenticated and attempts to make a GET request to /profile, you want the browser redirected to the root route or homepage. In Sublime, open brushfire/config/routes.js, and make the following changes to the route.

> **Listing 9.19   Adding the `profile` custom route**

```
module.exports = {
  'GET /': 'PageController.showHomePage',
...
  'GET /profile': 'PageController.showProfilePage',
...
```

Next, let's implement the controller action. In Sublime, open brushfire/api/controllers/PageController.js, and add the following action.

> **Listing 9.20   Creating a `showProfilePage` action**

```
module.exports = {

  showProfilePage: function (req, res) {             Redirects to the root
                                                     route if unauthenticated
    if (!req.session.userId) {              ◁——      request
      return res.redirect('/');
    }

    User.findOne(req.session.userId, function (err, user){
      if (err) {
        console.log('error: ', error);
        return res.negotiate(err);
      }
```

```
      if (!user) {
        sails.log.verbose('Session refers to a user who no longer exists- did
        ➥ you delete a user, then try to refresh the page with an open tab
        ➥ logged-in as that user?');
        return res.view('homepage');
      }

      return res.view('profile', {
        me: {
          id: user.id,
          email: user.email,
          gravatarURL: user.gravatarURL,
          admin: user.admin
        }
      });
    });
  },
...
```

Because you don't have a requirement to display the profile page in an unauthenticated state, if the request is unauthenticated, you'll redirect it to the root route. Now that you've addressed the profile, you can implement the GET requests to /edit-profile.

9.4.4 Securing the edit-profile page

The edit-profile page doesn't have an unauthenticated state. Therefore, if the user is unauthenticated and attempts to make a GET request to /edit-profile, you want the browser redirected to the root route or homepage. In Sublime, open brushfire/config/routes.js, and make the following changes to the route.

Listing 9.21 Altering `edit-profile` to trigger the `showEditProfilePage` action

```
module.exports = {
  'GET /': 'PageController.showHomePage',
  ...
  'GET /edit-profile': 'PageController.showEditProfilePage',
...
```

Next, let's implement the showEditProfilePage controller action. In Sublime, open brushfire/api/controllers/PageController.js, and add the following action.

Listing 9.22 Creating a `showEditProfilePage` action

```
module.exports = {

  showEditProfilePage: function (req, res) {          Redirects to the root route
                                                      if it's an unauthenticated
    if (!req.session.userId) {          ◄──────────   request
      return res.redirect('/');
    }
```

```
User.findOne(req.session.userId, function (err, user){
  if (err) {
    console.log('error: ', error);
    return res.negotiate(err);
  }

  if (!user) {
    sails.log.verbose('Session refers to a user who no longer exists- did
    ➡ you delete a user, then try to refresh the page with an open tab
    ➡ logged-in as that user?');
    return res.view('homepage');
  }

  return res.view('edit-profile', {
    me: {
      id: user.id,
      email: user.email,                    Adds the username
      username: user.username,         ◁⎯⏐ property
      gravatarURL: user.gravatarURL,
      admin: user.admin
    }
  });
});
},
...
```

Because you don't have a requirement to display the profile page in an unauthenticated state, if the request is unauthenticated, you'll redirect it to the root route. You did add the `username` property because it's used on the edit-profile page. Now that you've addressed the edit-profile page, you can implement the `GET` requests to `/restore-profile`.

9.4.5   *Securing other account-related pages*

The restore-profile page doesn't have an authenticated state. Therefore, if the user is authenticated and attempts to make a `GET` request to `/restore-profile`, you want the browser redirected to the root route or homepage. In Sublime, open brushfire/config/routes.js, and make the following changes to the route.

> **Listing 9.23   Altering `restore-profile` to trigger the `showRestorePage` action**

```
module.exports = {
  'GET /': 'PageController.showHomePage',
  ...
  'GET /restore-profile': 'PageController.showRestorePage',
  ...
```

Next, you'll create the `showRestorePage` controller action. In Sublime, open brushfire/api/controllers/PageController.js, and add the following action.

Listing 9.24   Creating a `showRestorePage` action

```
module.exports = {
  showRestorePage: function (req, res) {
    if (req.session.userId) {
      return res.redirect('/');
    }

    return res.view('restore-profile', {
      me: null
    });
  },
  ...
```

If the request is authenticated, redirects to the root route

Returns the restore-profile view with me set to null

The restore-profile page doesn't have an authenticated state; therefore, there's no need to look up a `user` record. This makes the action simple to implement. Next, let's implement the page controller for the signup page.

9.4.6   *Implementing business rules for the signup page*

The signup page doesn't have an authenticated state. Therefore, if the user is authenticated and attempts to make a GET request to /signup, you want the browser redirected to the root route or homepage. In Sublime, open brushfire/config/routes.js, and make the following changes to the route.

Listing 9.25   Altering the `signup` route to trigger the `showSignupPage` action

```
module.exports = {
  'GET /': 'PageController.showHomePage',
  ...
  'GET /signup': 'PageController.showSignupPage',
  ...
```

Notice that you're no longer passing static `locals` to the `homepage` view and instead routing the request directly to the `showSignupPage` action. In Sublime, open brushfire/api/controllers/PageController.js, and add the following action.

Listing 9.26   Creating a `showSignupPage` action

```
module.exports = {
  showSignupPage: function (req, res) {
    if (req.session.userId) {
      return res.redirect('/');
    }
    return res.view('signup', {
      me: null
    });
  },
  ...
```

If the request is authenticated, redirects to the root route

Returns the signup view with me set to null

At this point, the frontend of Brushfire responds with an appropriate UI based on the user's authenticated state. In the next chapter, we'll implement access control on the backend, locking down endpoints based on the user's authenticated state.

9.5   *Summary*

- Authentication is the process of allowing the user to prove their identity.
- Requests are considered stateless because nothing is saved inherently between requests.
- A session consists of a data store, middleware, and a session cookie that all combine to allow a user's authenticated state to be saved between requests.
- Creating an action for each frontend page view provides complete flexibility in personalizing the frontend based on the user's identity and authenticated state.

10

Policies and access control

It's hard to believe that the journey we've taken over the last few chapters was initiated by a love of cats and disdain for dogs. Our job is not to judge but instead fulfill the requirements of our client. In chapters 6 and 7, we created the model and controller actions necessary for a user to create and manage their own identity. In chapter 8, we introduced server-rendered views and backend routes as a way to communicate a hardcoded authenticated state of the user to the frontend using the hybrid approach to page navigation. This approach allows personalization of frontend content by passing the user's simulated authenticated state via locals. The frontend uses locals to determine which markup assets are displayed. In chapter 9, we implemented authentication, which allows users to prove their claim to a specific identity. We also introduced Sails sessions, which allow us to save the user's actual authenticated state between requests and then send that state securely to the frontend. All this functionality enables our client to restrict a user's account if they violate the Brushfire terms of service. If a user violates the ToS, our client can ban the user by setting the user's banned attribute to true. The restrictions are currently limited to the frontend. That same user could access Brushfire outside the browser by using Postman, for example, to make a POST request to /videos, which would trigger a backend controller action that adds content regardless of their authenticated state. To prevent such access, we'll use the user's stored authenticated state within a Sails policy to determine whether access should be granted. Policies allow or deny access to controllers down to a fine level of granularity. We'll spend the remainder of this chapter implementing policies to secure the backend of Brushfire.

To secure the backend, we first need to determine the different rights and restrictions a user can have with regard to access in Brushfire. Then we need to identify the controllers and actions whose access will be affected. Finally, we'll implement the actual policies that contain the logic necessary to manage access to the controller actions according to our defined requirements.

10.1   *A farewell to blueprints*

A user-agent can have access to Brushfire controller actions depending on four conditions. The first condition is whether the user-agent is authenticated or not. So a user who's authenticated will have different access rights to a controller and its actions than a user who isn't authenticated. The remaining conditions require that the user-agent first be authenticated and then have at least one of three other properties set to true: admin, banned, and/or deleted. Table 10.1 describes each condition in greater detail.

Table 10.1   User-agent conditions

Condition	Description
unauthenticated	A user-agent is unauthenticated if req.session.userId is equal to null.
authenticated	A user-agent is authenticated if req.session.userId has a value. The value is the id property of a user record.
administrator	A user-agent is considered an administrator if the user record's admin property is equal to true.
deleted	A user-agent is considered *deleted* if the user record's deleted property is equal to true.
banned	A user-agent is considered *banned* if the user record's banned property is equal to true.

Keep each of the four conditions in mind as we review the API's access control requirements to controller/actions.

10.1.1 Obtaining the example materials for this chapter

You have two options to set up your Brushfire assets for this chapter. If you've completed chapter 9, you're all set and can use your existing project here. If you haven't completed chapter 9, you can clone the end of the chapter 9 GitHub repo at https://github.com/sailsinaction/brushfire-ch9-end.git and start from there. Remember to use `npm install` in the terminal window from the root of the project after you clone the repo.

If you choose the cloning option, don't forget to add the brushfire/config/local.js file with your Google API key from chapter 5 (section 5.4.6) and start your local Post-greSQL `brushfire` database from chapter 6 (section 6.4.2).

10.1.2 Designing custom backend endpoints

The decision of when to transition from blueprint routes to explicit custom routes is a matter of personal programming style. Inevitably, using explicit routes in production is considered a best practice in Sails. You're now beyond the early stages of Brushfire. By consolidating your routes in one location, you can centralize the organization of your endpoints.

Figure 10.1 shows all the current Brushfire controller actions and a corresponding explicit route for each action.

Route	Controller	Action
`'GET /video': 'VideoController.find'`	video	Blueprint: find action
`'POST /video': 'VideoController.create'`	video	Blueprint: create action
`'PUT /login': 'UserController.login'`	user	login
`'GET /logout': 'UserController.logout'`	user	logout
`'POST /user/signup': 'UserController.signup'`	user	signup
Now handled by the showProfilePage action	user	profile
Now handled by the removeProfile action	user	delete
`'PUT /user/removeProfile': 'UserController.removeProfile'`	user	removeProfile
`'PUT /user/restoreProfile': 'UserController.restoreProfile'`	user	restoreProfile
`'PUT /user/restoreGravatarURL': 'UserController.restoreGravatarURL'`	user	restoreGravatarURL
`'PUT /user/updateProfile': 'UserController.updateProfile'`	user	updateProfile
`'PUT /user/changePassword': 'UserController.changePassword'`	user	changePassword
`'PUT /user/adminUsers': 'UserController.adminUsers'`	user	adminUsers
`'PUT /user/updateAdmin': 'UserController.updateAdmin'`	user	updateAdmin
`'PUT /user/updateBanned': 'UserController.updateBanned'`	user	updateBanned
`'PUT /user/updateDeleted': 'UserController.updateDeleted'`	user	updateDeleted
`'GET /': 'PageController.showHomePage'`	page	showHomePage
`'GET /videos': 'PageController.showVideosPage'`	page	showVideosPage
`'GET /administration': 'PageController.showAdminPage'`	page	showAdminPage
`'GET /profile': 'PageController.showProfilePage'`	page	showProfilePage
`'GET /edit-profile': 'PageController.showEditProfilePage/:id'`	page	showEditProfilePage
`'GET /restore-profile': 'PageController.showRestorePage/:id'`	page	showRestorePage
`'GET /signup': 'PageController.showSignupPage/:id'`	page	showSignupPage

Figure 10.1   Brushfire controller action list with corresponding custom routes

10.1.3 More explicit routes

Let's now implement the explicit routes that are defined in figure 10.1 for the video and user controllers. Recall that both brushfire/api/controllers/VideoController.js and brushfire/api/controllers/UserController.js are empty. So the actions you'll be triggering with explicit routes will trigger blueprint actions. In Sublime, open brushfire/config/routes.js, and add the following routes.

Listing 10.1 Adding explicit routes for the blueprint actions in the video controller

```
...
'GET /logout': 'UserController.logout',
'GET /video': 'VideoController.find',
'POST /video': 'VideoController.create',
...
```

Will trigger the blueprint find action

Will trigger the blueprint create action

Next, let's add explicit routes that were previously created automatically with blueprint action routes. From the same brushfire/config/routes.js file, add the following routes.

Listing 10.2 Adding explicit routes for the actions in the `UserController`

```
...
'POST /video': 'VideoController.create',

'POST /user/signup': 'UserController.signup',
'PUT /user/removeProfile': 'UserController.removeProfile',
'PUT /user/restoreProfile': 'UserController.restoreProfile',
'PUT /user/restoreGravatarURL': 'UserController.restoreGravatarURL',
'PUT /user/updateProfile/:id': 'UserController.updateProfile',
'PUT /user/changePassword': 'UserController.changePassword',
'GET /user/adminUsers': 'UserController.adminUsers',
'PUT /user/updateAdmin/:id': 'UserController.updateAdmin',
'PUT /user/updateBanned/:id': 'UserController.updateBanned',
'PUT /user/updateDeleted/:id': 'UserController.updateDeleted',
...
```

Now that you've successfully transitioned from blueprint routes to explicit custom routes, let's examine how to disable blueprint routes.

10.1.4 Disabling blueprint routes

Up to this point, blueprint routes have accelerated your development efforts by allowing rapid design of your initial application without thinking about explicit routes. Now that you've transitioned blueprint routes to explicit custom routes in brushfire/config/routes.js, you can learn how to disable blueprint routes. In Sublime, open brushfire/config/blueprints.js, and set the properties for the `actions`, `rest`, and `shortcuts` blueprints in the following listing to `false`.

Listing 10.3   Disabling blueprint routes

```
module.exports.blueprints = {
  actions: false,
  rest: false,
  shortcuts: false,
  ...
```

Action routes will no longer automatically be created.

Shortcut routes will not be generated.

RESTful routes will no longer be generated.

Table 10.2 details the impact of disabling each blueprint route type.

Table 10.2   The impact of disabling blueprint routes

Blueprint route type	Description
Action routes	Each controller action will now require an explicit route in order to be triggered via a request.
RESTful routes	Disabling RESTful routes eliminates the automatic routes associated with CRUD operations.
Shortcut routes	Disabling shortcut routes removes your ability to access the model via the browser.

10.2   Policies

Up to this point, you've provided access control to various frontend elements via your page controller. For example, the showVideosPage action passes the authenticated state via locals to the videos view. Angular then uses the locals to determine whether to display the submit-videos form on the page. Clicking the Submit New Video button triggers an Angular AJAX POST request to /video. So, from the frontend's perspective, access to the AJAX request is restricted by whether the markup is displayed on the page. This doesn't prevent a user from using a program like Postman to circumvent the user interface and instead make a POST request directly to /video. You need a way to restrict access to requests from outside the user interface. You have two choices. You can add code to manage access to a controller action in the action itself. But in your case, you're using blueprint actions and therefore don't have direct access to add to the action. Instead, you can use a policy to manage access to the action for you.

10.2.1   What is a policy?

Policies provide the ability to inject a reusable set of code before a request executes a controller action. Policies' main benefits are that they can be written once and applied to any controller action. Policies can be used like *middleware*, meaning you can do almost anything you can imagine with them.

> **DEFINITION**   *Middleware* is code that can get in the middle of the request/response cycle. For example, the Sails router is middleware. Policies act like middleware and are executed before controller actions, making them ideal for managing access to endpoints.

That said, our experience using Sails to build all sorts of different applications has taught us that policies are best used for one specific purpose: preventing access to actions for certain users (or types of users). Policies are best used like preconditions. You can use policies to take care of edge cases that are possible only by a user trying to cheat the UI. If you could somehow trust the client, then you wouldn't need policies. Anyone can access your application's URL from different user-agents such as a browser, from Postman, from the command line, or even from a smart refrigerator. Policies provide an easy way to protect against these kinds of edge cases without cluttering up the business logic in your actions.

Policies are first defined in the brushfire/api/policies/ folder. Then, you associate that policy with an access control list in brushfire/config/policies.js. This file is used to map policies to your controllers and actions. When a request is made, Sails first checks whether a policy exists before passing the request to the controller action. Let's create a policy and then implement it in your access control list.

10.2.2 Creating a policy

In figure 10.2, the blueprint find action is used to fulfill a request for all the videos in the video model when the page initially loads.

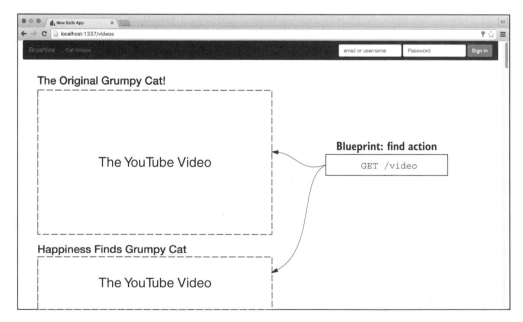

Figure 10.2   The videos page uses the blueprint find action to fulfill a request for all videos in the video model when the page loads.

There's no requirement that the user-agent be authenticated to load videos. That is, there's never a condition where the user-agent is restricted from accessing this particular blueprint action. When the user-agent is authenticated, however, additional UI markup is displayed, as shown in figure 10.3.

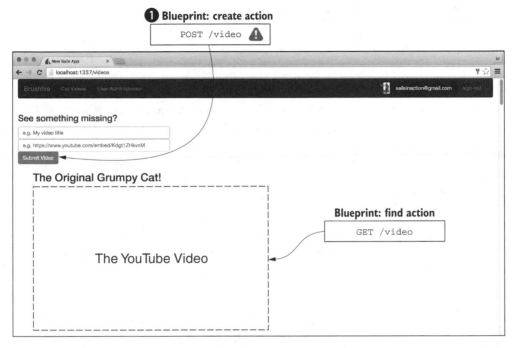

Figure 10.3 When the user-agent is authenticated, the videos page adds the submit-video form ❶, which, when clicked, triggers the blueprint `create` action.

The UI markup for the blueprint `create` action isn't displayed unless the user-agent is authenticated. Therefore, because the action isn't accessible to the UI under those conditions, you'll want to protect this edge case with a policy. Create a policy named `isLoggedIn` that checks whether a user-agent is authenticated and restricts access if it's not authenticated. In Sublime, create a new file named isLoggedIn.js in the brushfire/api/policies folder, and add the code shown in this listing.

Listing 10.4   Creating the `isLoggedIn` policy

```
module.exports = function isLoggedIn(req, res, next) {

  if (req.session.userId) {
    return next();
  }
}
```

If the userId property has a value (that is, authenticated), returns control to the next middleware component

```
    if (req.wantsJSON) {
      return res.forbidden('You are not permitted to perform this action.');
    }

    return res.redirect('/');
};
```

If not, responds with a
redirect to the root route

If the user-agent wants JSON, responds
with a status code and a JSON message

Your policy first checks whether the user-agent is authenticated via a value in `req.session.userId`. If a value is found, the request continues to the controller action. But if the property is `null`, not authenticated, Sails will either respond with JSON or redirect the page, depending on the requirements of the user-agent. But what is `req.wantsJSON`? The `req.wantsJSON` method provides a clean, reusable indication of whether the server should respond with JSON or send back something else like an HTML page or a `302` redirect. Now let's connect the policy to the blueprint `create` action.

10.2.3 Configuring policies

Sails has a built-in access control list (ACL) located in brushfire/config/policies.js. This file is used to map policies to your controllers and actions. The file is declarative, meaning it describes what the permissions for your app should look like, not how they should work. This makes it easier for new developers to jump in and understand what's going on, plus it makes your app more flexible as your requirements change over time. You have an `isLoggedIn` policy, but because it's not mapped to any controller or controller action, it won't get executed. Let's apply your new policy to the blueprint `create` action of the video controller. That way, any time a request wants to execute the action, your policy will be executed first. In Sublime, open brushfire/config/policies.js, and add the following code.

Listing 10.5   Applying `isLoggedIn` policy to `create` action of video controller

```
module.exports.policies = {
  // '*': true,

  VideoController: {
    create: ['isLoggedIn']
  }
}
```

The blueprint create
action is now mapped to
the isLoggedIn policy.

The `isLoggedIn` policy will be applied to an incoming request to the blueprint `create` action of the video controller. Check it out. Start Sails using `sails lift`, and make a `POST` request to `/video` in Postman, similar to figure 10.4.

If the user-agent is authenticated, the blueprint `create` action is executed and the record is created. Because the user-agent was not authenticated, the policy responded with a `403` Forbidden status code. You can also use this policy for other actions in Brushfire. Before moving on to the other pages, requests, and controller/actions, let's look at some best practices surrounding policies.

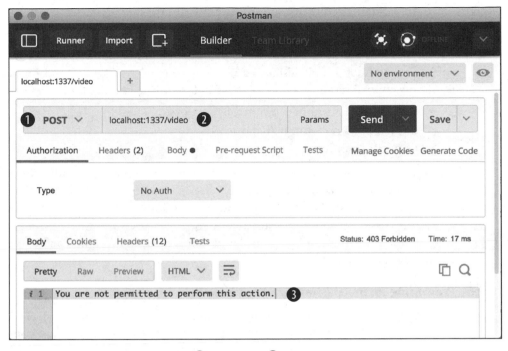

Figure 10.4 Making a POST request **1** to /video **2** with an unauthenticated user-agent returns a 403 forbidden status code and message **3**.

10.2.4 *Best practices*

Working on countless Sails apps has taught us a number of rules of the road that, if followed, will help prevent your application from becoming tangled and confusing:

- *Don't look at parameters.* Truly reusable policies should only look at req.session and the database, *not* at parameters! Relying on parameters makes your policy context-specific and usable only in very specialized circumstances. In that case, why not just put the code in the relevant action(s)?
- *Policies should be nullipotent.* They should not set, write, or, frankly, do anything to state.

TIP In the past, we suggested the strategy of using custom properties of req (specifically req.options) to allow your policies to take on more responsibilities. In practice, we've learned that this ends up causing more pain than it alleviates.

- *Policies shouldn't be a core part of your business logic.* Policies are *not* a good tool for structuring logic in your app. Using them this way makes them just as versatile as raw Express/Connect middleware, and, unfortunately, it also makes them just as dangerous and developer-specific. If you use policies to help with queries or create a complex chain of policies to manage permission systems in your application, you're likely to create a code base that's difficult for you or any other developer to understand.

You've created your first policy and applied it to a controller action. Let's take what you've learned about policies and, guided by your UI, review each controller action for access control requirements. You have at least three choices for access control:

- Manage access within the controller action.
- Implement a policy to manage access.
- Leave the controller action as is.

When is a policy more appropriate than placing the code in a controller action to manage access? The best practice is to use a policy to protect those controller actions that are *not* accessible in the UI. To clarify, that doesn't mean the controller action is never accessible in the UI. Instead, look for instances when the controller action is restricted in the UI by not being displayed, but is open to unwanted access outside the UI with programs like Postman.

10.2.5 *Preventing an inconsistent user experience*

Your initial entry point to Brushfire is a user-agent's unauthenticated access to the homepage, which is managed by the showHomePage action of the page controller in figure 10.5.

Figure 10.5   The homepage when accessed via an authenticated user-agent has two actions that need protection: the showSignupPage action ❶ and the login action ❷.

Does the homepage trigger any requests when loading? No. There are two requests that trigger controller actions that are not available to the UI when the user-agent is authenticated: `showSignupPage` and `login`. You don't want to allow a user-agent to log in or sign up a new user when they're already logged in. Although these endpoints aren't displayed in the frontend, they're vulnerable to direct access via programs like Postman. Therefore, you'll create and apply one or more policies to manage access to them. In Sublime, create a new file named isLoggedOut.js in the brushfire/api/policies folder, and add the code in the following listing.

Listing 10.6   Creating the `isLoggedOut` policy

If the userId property is null (that is, not authenticated), returns control to the next middleware component

If the user-agent wants JSON, responds with a status code and a JSON message

```
module.exports = function isLoggedOut(req, res, next) {
  if (!req.session.userId) {
    return next();
  }

  if (req.wantsJSON) {
    return res.forbidden('You are not permitted to perform this action.');
  }

  return res.redirect('/');
};
```

If not, responds with a redirect to the root route

Your new policy checks whether the user-agent is authenticated via `req.session .userId`. If the `userId` property is `null`, the request continues to the controller action. But if the `userId` property has a value, Sails will either respond with JSON or redirect the page depending on the requirements of the user-agent. Next, you'll apply `isLoggedOut` to the `showSignupPage` and `login` controller actions. In Sublime, open brushfire/config/policies.js, and add the following code.

Listing 10.7   Applying `isLoggedOut` to actions in the user and page controllers

```
module.exports.policies = {
  ...

  VideoController: {
    create: ['isLoggedIn']
  },

  UserController: {
    login: ['isLoggedOut']
  },

  PageController: {
    showSignupPage: ['isLoggedOut']
  }
}
```

The login and showSignupPage actions are now mapped to the isLoggedOut policy.

The `isLoggedOut` policy will be applied to an incoming request to the `login` and `showSignupPage` actions. If the user-agent is not authenticated, control is passed to the action to be executed. If the user-agent is authenticated, a `403` status is returned if JSON is required, or redirected if HTML is required. You can also use this policy for other actions in Brushfire. The homepage also has an authenticated state, as depicted in figure 10.6.

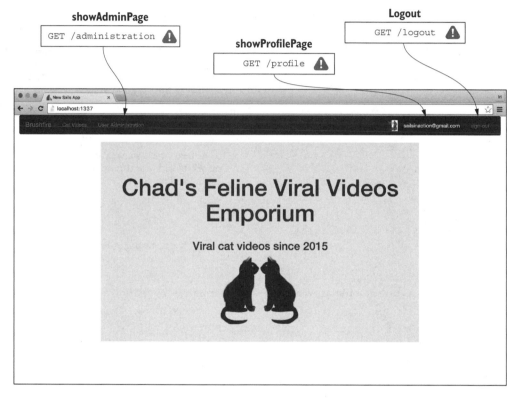

Figure 10.6   The homepage when accessed via an unauthenticated user-agent with endpoints that trigger three different controller actions

There are three endpoints that trigger controller actions that are not available to the UI when the user-agent is not authenticated. You'll manage access to them via the `isLoggedIn` policy. Because you've already created the policy, you simply have to apply it to the three controller actions. In Sublime, open brushfire/config/policies.js, and add the following code.

Listing 10.8   Applying `isLoggedIn` to actions in the user and page controllers

```
module.exports.policies = {
  ...
```

```
UserController: {
  login: ['isLoggedOut'],
  logout: ['isLoggedIn']
},

PageController: {
  showSignupPage: ['isLoggedOut'],
  showAdminPage: ['isLoggedIn'],
  showProfilePage: ['isLoggedIn']
}
}
```

The logout, showAdminPage, and showProfilePage actions are now mapped to the isLoggedIn policy.

The showAdminPage action needs restricted access to only those user-agents that have the admin flag set to true. Should the code be in the controller action or a policy? The showAdminPage isn't available to the UI when a user is not an admin. You'll implement a new isAdmin policy and apply it to the showAdminPage. In Sublime, create a new file named isAdmin.js in the brushfire/api/policies folder, and add the code in the next listing.

Listing 10.9   Creating the isAdmin policy

```
module.exports = function isAdmin(req, res, next) {

  if (!req.session.userId) {               Ensures that user-agent
    if (req.wantsJSON) {                    is authenticated
      return res.forbidden('You are not permitted to perform this action.');
    }
    return res.redirect('/');
  }                                        Looks up user based
                                           on user record id
  User.findOne(req.session.userId).exec(function(err, foundUser) {

    if (err) return res.negotiate(err);

    if (!foundUser) {                      Handles if user
      if (req.wantsJSON) {                 is not found
        return res.forbidden('You are not permitted to perform this action.');
      }
      return res.redirect('/');            If user's admin property
    }                                      is true, goes to the
                                           controller action
    if (foundUser.admin) {
      return next();                       If not, returns
    } else {                               forbidden
      if (req.wantsJSON) {
        return res.forbidden('You are not permitted to perform this action.');
      }
      return res.redirect('/');
    }

  });
};
```

Next, let's apply the `isAdmin` policy to the `showAdminPage` controller action. In Sublime, open brushfire/config/policies.js, and add the following code.

> **Listing 10.10   Applying `isAdmin` to the `showAdminPage` action in the page controller**

```
module.exports.policies = {
  ...

  PageController: {
    showSignupPage: ['isLoggedOut'],
    showAdminPage: ['isLoggedIn', 'isAdmin'],
    ...
```

Adds the isAdmin policy as an element of the ACL array

10.2.6   *Restricting access to account management endpoints*

Take a look at the profile page, and specifically when a user-agent is authenticated, in figure 10.7.

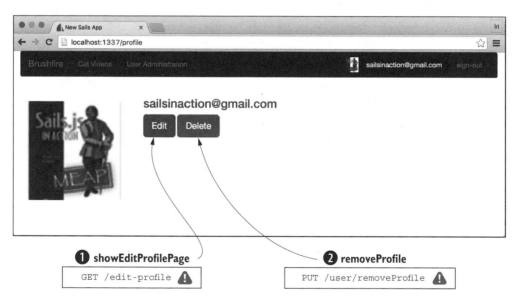

Figure 10.7   The profile page, when accessed via an authenticated user-agent, adds two unprotected actions.

We've already addressed the `showAdminPage`, `showProfilePage`, and `logout` endpoints in earlier sections. There are two endpoints we haven't addressed. These endpoints trigger controller actions that are unavailable to the UI when the user-agent is not authenticated: the `showEditProfilePage` ❶ and `removeProfile` ❷ actions. Access to these controller actions should be restricted unless the user-agent is authenticated. You'll add the `isLoggedIn` policy to each action's ACL. In Sublime, open brushfire/config/policies.js, and add the following code.

```
module.exports.policies = {
  ...

    UserController: {
      ...
      removeProfile: ['isLoggedIn']        <-----  Adds the isLoggedIn policy
    },                                             to the removeProfile and
  PageController: {                                showEditProfilePage actions
    ...
    showEditProfilePage: ['isLoggedIn']    <-----
  }
  ...
```

You also want to ensure that the user-agent who's removing the profile is the same user-agent who's currently authenticated. You could do this within a policy, but an easier way is to refactor the `removeProfile` action to use `req.session.userId` instead of relying on the frontend to send an `id`. In Sublime, open brushfire/apis/UserController.js, and make the following changes.

```
...
module.exports = {
  ...
  removeProfile: function(req, res) {

    // if (!req.param('id')){
    //   return res.badRequest('id is a required parameter.');
    // }

    User.update({
      id: req.session.userId         <-----  Now relying on the
    }, {                                      user ID property of
      deleted: true                          the session instead
    }, function(err, removedUser) {          of a parameter

      if (err) return res.negotiate(err);
      if (removedUser.length === 0) {
        return res.notFound();
      }

      req.session.userId = null;
        return res.ok();
      });
  },
...
```

Notice that you remove the check for if (!req.param('id'). Because you're no longer relying on an `id` parameter from the frontend, you need to change the AJAX PUT request to /user/removeProfile. In Sublime, open brushfire/assets/js/controllers/profilePageController.js, and add the following path.

Listing 10.13   Changing the request path to eliminate the `id` parameter

```
...
$scope.removeProfile = function() {
  $http.put('/user/removeProfile', {
...
```
⊣ Removes the id parameter
  from the request path

10.2.7 *Preventing users from messing with each other's data*

Next, let's examine the edit-profile page shown in figure 10.8.

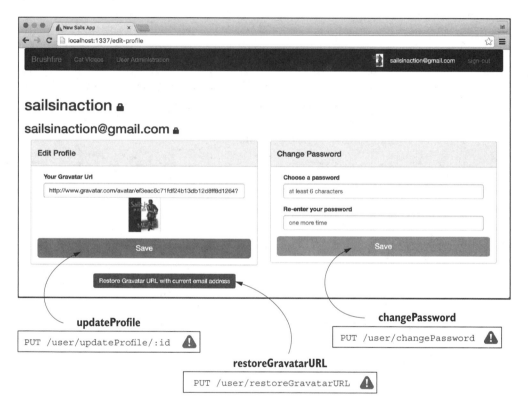

Figure 10.8   The edit-profile page, when accessed via an authenticated user-agent, adds three unprotected actions.

The edit-profile page will be displayed only if the user-agent is authenticated based on the `isLoggedIn` policy applied to the `showEditProfilePage` action. You've already addressed five of the eight controller actions that can be triggered within the page. The three actions that haven't been addressed are `updateProfile`, `restoreGravatar-URL`, and `changePassword`. Each of these controller actions has conditions when they won't be accessible to the UI. Therefore, you'll again use the `isLoggedIn` policy to restrict access to the actions if a user-agent isn't logged in. In Sublime, open brush-fire/config/policies.js, and add the following code.

Listing 10.14 Applying the `isLoggedIn` policy to actions in the user controller

```
module.exports.policies = {
  ...

    UserController: {
      ...
      removeProfile: ['isLoggedIn']
      updateProfile: ['isLoggedIn'],
      restoreGravatarURL: ['isLoggedIn'],
      changePassword: ['isLoggedIn']
    },
  ...
```

> Adds the isLoggedIn policy to the updateProfile, restoreGravatarURL, and changePassword actions

You also want to ensure that the user-agent who's updating the profile or changing the password is the same user-agent who's currently authenticated. You could do this within a policy. An easier way is to refactor the `updateProfile` and `changePassword` actions to use the `req.session.userId` instead of relying on the frontend to send an id. In Sublime, open brushfire/apis/UserController.js, and make the following changes.

Listing 10.15 Refactoring `updateProfile` and `changePassword`

```
...
module.exports = {
  ...
  updateProfile: function(req, res) {
    User.update({
      id: req.session.userId
    }, {
      gravatarURL: req.param('gravatarURL')
    }, function(err, updatedUser) {

      if (err) return res.negotiate(err);

      return res.json(updatedUser);

    });
  },
  changePassword: function(req, res) {
    Passwords.encryptPassword({
      password: req.param('password'),
    }).exec({
      error: function(err) {
        return res.serverError(err);
      },
      success: function(result) {

        User.update({
          // id: req.param('id')
          id: req.session.userId
```

> Now relying on the userId property of the session instead of an id parameter

```
     }, {
       encryptedPassword: result
     }).exec(function(err, updatedUser) {
       if (err) {
         return res.negotiate(err);
       }
       return res.json(updatedUser);
     });
   }
 });
},
...
```

You're no longer relying on an `id` parameter from the frontend for the `update-Profile` action, so you need to change the AJAX `PUT` request to `/user/updateProfile`. In Sublime, open brushfire/assets/js/controllers/editProfilePageController.js, and add the following path.

Listing 10.16   Change request path to eliminate `id` parameter in `updateProfile` action

```
...
$scope.updateProfile = function() {                    Removes the id parameter
  $http.put('/user/updateProfile', {          ⟵┘       from the request path
...
```

You're no longer passing an `id` parameter for the `changePassword` action. In Sublime, open brushfire/assets/js/controllers/editProfilePageController.js, and remove the `id` parameter.

Listing 10.17   Removing the `id` parameter in the request to the `changePassword` action

```
...
$scope.changePassword = function() {
  $http.put('user/changePassword', {               Removes the
    // id: $scope.me.id,                    ⟵┘      id parameter
    password: $scope.editProfile.properties.password
  })
    .then(function onSuccess(sailsResponse) {
      ...
```

10.2.8 *Preventing confusion for signed-in users*

The signup page in figure 10.9 will be displayed only if the user-agent is logged out (for example, not authenticated) based on the applied `isLoggedOut` policy to the `showSignupPage`.

The signup page includes two controller actions we haven't addressed: `showRestorePage` and `signup`. Both these actions are unavailable when the user-agent is not authenticated. Therefore, you'll add the `isLoggedOut` policy to each action's ACL. In Sublime, open brushfire/config/policies.js, and add the the code in listing 10.18.

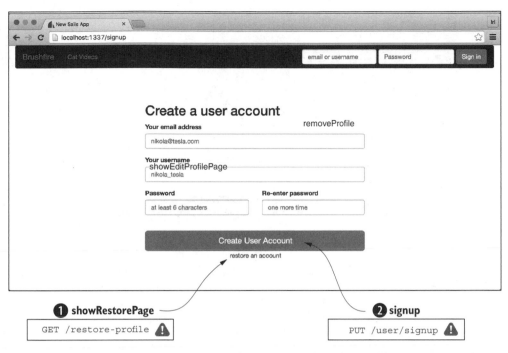

Figure 10.9 The signup page when accessed via an unauthenticated user adds two unprotected actions: `showRestorePage` ❶ and `signup` ❷.

Listing 10.18 Applying `isLoggedOut` to the `showRestorePage` and `signup` actions

```
module.exports.policies = {
  ...

    UserController: {
      ...
      signup: ['isLoggedOut']
    },
  PageController: {
    ...
    showRestorePage: ['isLoggedOut']
  },
  ...
```

> Adds the isLoggedOut policy to the showRestorePage and signup controller actions

The restore-profile page is displayed when a user-agent isn't authenticated, similar to figure 10.10.

The restore profile page contains one endpoint that triggers a controller action we've yet to address: `restoreProfile` ❶. Because the restore-profile page isn't displayed unless the user-agent is logged out, you'll implement access control within the existing `isLoggedOut` policy. In Sublime, open brushfire/config/policies.js, and add the code in listing 10.19.

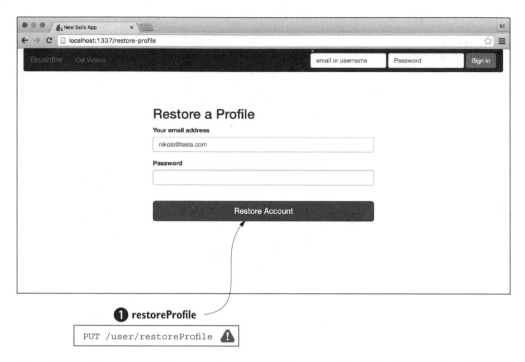

Figure 10.10   The restore-profile page, when accessed via an unauthenticated user-agent, adds one unprotected action.

Listing 10.19   Applying the `isLoggedOut` policy to the `restoreProfile` action

```
module.exports.policies = {
  ...
    UserController: {
      ...
      restoreProfile: ['isLoggedOut']
    },
  ...
```

> Adds the isLoggedOut
> policy to the restoreProfile
> controller action

10.2.9   *Restricting access to administrative actions*

The administrative page, depicted in figure 10.11, is displayed only when the user-agent is authenticated and the `admin` property is set to `true`. The administration page has four controller actions we haven't addressed: `adminUsers`, `updateAdmin`, `update-Banned`, and `updateDeleted`. Because these actions aren't available via the UI when a user-agent is logged out, you'll add two policies to their ACLs: `isLoggedIn` and `isAdmin`. In Sublime, open brushfire/config/policies.js, and add the code in listing 10.20.

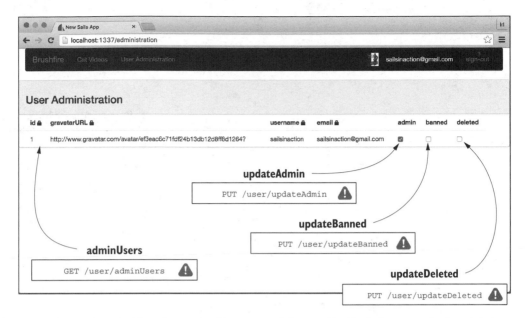

Figure 10.11 **The administration page, when accessed via an authenticated user-agent whose admin property is set to true, adds four unprotected actions.**

Listing 10.20 Applying `isLoggedIn` and `isAdmin` to actions in the user controller

```
module.exports.policies = {
   ...
    UserController: {
      ...
      adminUsers: ['isLoggedIn', 'isAdmin'],
      updateAdmin: ['isLoggedIn', 'isAdmin'],
      updateBanned: ['isLoggedIn', 'isAdmin'],
      updateDeleted: ['isLoggedIn', 'isAdmin']
    },
    ...
```

> **Adds the isLoggedIn and isAdmin policies to the ACL**

10.3 Summary

- Policies provide a highly granular way to control access to controllers and their actions.
- Best practices for policies include not basing policies on parameters but instead relying on session properties and the results from database queries.
- Backend actions can be controlled from within the action itself or through policies.
- Policies have the advantage of being reusable across multiple actions.

11

Refactoring

It's been several months since we delivered the last version of Brushfire to Chad. We thought we'd begin work on the next phase of content management: associating users with the videos they added. But when Chad arrived at our offices, plans had changed. Chad was anxious to give us some good news and some bad news. The bad news was his investor/mom was again shaken by the lack of cat videos on Brushfire. She could not "in good conscience" continue to subsidize the proliferation of "videos without cats." We explained to Chad that although we could associate users with the videos they added, thereby identifying violations of his mom's Terms of Service, we could not manufacture exclusive interest in cats. He understood and added, "None of that mattered when compared to the other exciting development."

Chad's good news was the spectacular growth in traffic generated by do-it-yourself (DIY) videos on Brushfire during our hiatus. Brushfire users were adding their favorite how-to YouTube videos at a phenomenal rate. Bottom line, he said, "The market had spoken," and he would take the last of his mom's investment and pivot once again.

> **DEFINITION** A *pivot* is a change in product direction and features. Chad started this project as a way to aggregate YouTube videos. Based on his mom's influence, Brushfire pivoted to a cat video site. So this was Chad's second pivot of Brushfire.

Chad's last bit of news was that he managed to obtain some new investors who don't share his DNA.

In chapters 6–10, we went on a journey to achieve the design and implementation of an identity, personalization, authorization, and access control system. Along the way you learned a lot about Sails. With this pivot, we'll set out on another journey in chapters 11–15. By the end of the journey, we'll have a fully realized version of Brushfire deployed into the wild. We'll also be exploring many more features of Sails.

In this chapter, we'll differentiate between pivots based on market forces versus a lack of frontend decision making. We'll take a systematic approach to identify requirements based on the needs of the client and how that translates to the needs of the frontend and backend. We'll also cover best practices for refactoring when changes are unavoidable, as well as some tricks you can use to make your applications easier to maintain.

> **DEFINITION** *Code refactoring* is a process in which you take existing code and restructure it. This is done for a variety of reasons including organization, readability, and an overall reduction in the complexity.

Finally, we'll explore Sails custom responses as well as build out an initial requirement of the new Brushfire—*user-initiated password resets.*

Brushfire has an expanded number of models to support the new requirements. In chapter 12, we'll introduce associations, which are a way of organizing and accessing multiple models. In chapter 13, we'll take what you've learned and implement additional core features to Brushfire, including the ability to rate content, follow users, and search and browse tutorials. In chapter 14, we'll add chat to Brushfire, which will allow you to thoroughly explore WebSockets integration with Sails. Finally, in chapter 15, we'll address security and testing and ultimately deploy Brushfire into the wild. You have a lot to learn, so let's get started.

11.1 Maintaining your sanity when requirements change

The client pivot is a very common scenario. But you want to distinguish a pivot based on market feedback versus a pivot based on a lack of frontend decision making. You know you have a pivot based on a lack of frontend decision making when you hear either of these comments:

- *"You know, after looking at this <insert feature> implemented, what I really want is...."* This response is endemic when there's a lack of frontend wireframes that show what a feature will look like.
- *"I didn't know you needed me to respond with the* username. *It's going to take some time to change the backend to make that kind of response."* This response indicates a lack of wireframes to identify requests and the requirements of those requests.

A *market-based* pivot involves user-driven feature changes that aren't always predictable. A pivot based on a lack of frontend decision making, however, is highly predictable and preventable. What do we mean by a lack of frontend decision making? At this point, we can't imagine implementing a backend without first examining the frontend for requests and requirements of those requests. This examination leads to decisions on how to design the backend to meet the requirements of the frontend. It also results in deciding what the application will look like and how it will function before fully implementing the backend. Making these decisions isn't easy because choosing to do one thing means that we're choosing not to do another thing.

Without getting into behavioral psychology, a field we're completely unqualified to address, we've determined that developers (us included) like the infinite possibilities of coding. And given an opportunity, developers will spend eternity examining each of those infinite possibilities because it's easier to do that than to make decisions. Barry Schwartz, author of *The Paradox of Choice*, claims that too many options make it difficult to make any choice at all. And that's why having a clearly defined frontend to guide our choices is so valuable.

Before we can design the frontend, we need to get our client's requirements. So, let's do that next.

11.1.1 *Obtaining and revising requirements*

When Chad was able to calm down from his excitement, he began to explain some of the similar feature requests he received from many Brushfire users. With all due respect to Chad's mom, no one wanted cat videos. They did ask that Brushfire be enhanced so that they could add YouTube videos around a particular subject matter they called *tutorials*. For example, one user wanted to aggregate his individual YouTube videos into a JavaScript closure tutorial. Others wanted to aggregate videos about house-training a puppy, makeup techniques, and even how to distill homemade whiskey. They also wanted the ability to rate and search for tutorials as well as follow their favorite tutorial creators. Finally, they wanted to be able to leave messages about a particular video and chat in real time if someone else was watching the same video. As a complete aside, Chad pleaded with us to add a way for users to reset their own passwords. He said this feature alone would reduce his inbox "by at least 80%." How do we effectively create a plan based on this new information?

11.1.2 Organizing views into five categories

We're already well equipped to handle the pivot. In chapters 3 and 4, we started a process of examining wireframes to guide our backend development we called *a frontend-first approach*.

> **NOTE** We take a very broad view of wireframes. They can include anything from a mockup to working frontend assets. Our personal choices of tools for mockups include combining the contents of Keynote, Google Docs, and Photoshop.

Based on the pivot requirements, we've divided Brushfire views and their wireframes into five categories in table 11.1.

Table 11.1 The five categories of views in Brushfire

Category	Description	Views
Navigation bar	The overall top bar navigation has states that dictate how the markup is displayed.	navigation.ejs signin.ejs signup.ejs signout.ejs
Search, browse, and administration	Brushfire includes a search view, browse view, and our existing administration view.	homepage.ejs browse-tutorials-list.ejs administration.ejs
Profile	The user profile takes on a new level of importance in the way users can find content created by other users.	profile.ejs profile-followers.ejs profile-following.ejs edit-profile.ejs
Tutorial and video	Tutorials aggregate one or more videos.	tutorials-detail.ejs tutorials-detail-new.ejs tutorials-detail-edit.ejs show-video.ejs tutorials-detail-video-new.ejs tutorials-detail-video-edit.ejs
Other	A catchall for all other views.	layout.ejs restore-profile.ejs password-recovery-email.ejs password-recovery-email-send.ejs password-reset.ejs

Some of the views within each of these categories can display different content based on the condition of the user-agent, including

- The authenticated state
- Whether the authenticated user-agent is the designated owner of a tutorial or profile
- Whether the authenticated user-agent is designated as an admin

Let's examine some of the category's wireframes to identify their requests and request requirements, as well as how to manage displaying content based on the condition of the user-agent. Although we'll review only a portion of the wireframes and requirements in this chapter, you can access all of them via the chapter 11 hub here: http://sailsinaction.github.io/chapter-11/.

11.1.3   *Obtaining the example materials for this chapter*

Before we look at the wireframes, you need to get the assets for the remainder of the book. As we said earlier, this pivot will encompass the remaining five chapters of *Sails.js in Action*. Therefore, the repo that contains the starting assets for these remaining chapters is vast. We encourage you to take a tour of the new assets, but don't get overwhelmed. We'll go over every inch of the project in the coming chapters. The chapter repo can be cloned directly here: https://github.com/sailsinaction/brushfire-ch11-start. After cloning the repo, install the Node module dependencies via `npm install`.

First, you added a local.js file in chapter 6 to hold the Google API key you were using in the bootstrap.js file to seed YouTube videos. You no longer need to seed YouTube videos and therefore don't need to configure the API key in the local.js file. But there are several configuration parameters you'll want to aggregate in a local.js file. In Sublime, create brushfire/config/local.js, and add the following code.

> **Listing 11.1   Adding to the local.js file**

```
module.exports.blueprints = {
  shortcuts: true,
  prefix: '/bp',
};

module.exports.connections = {
  myPostgresqlServer: {
    adapter: 'sails-postgresql',
    host: 'localhost',
    database: 'brushfire'
  }
};
```

These settings will override any existing settings.

> **NOTE**   If you're using different credentials for your PostgreSQL database, you can simply copy the database credentials from your brushfire/config/local.js file from your chapter 10 repo.

As it turns out, using blueprint shortcut routes to access the underlying database records can be extremely helpful. So we've decided to bring blueprint shortcut routes back during development. But to protect any of your existing or future routes, we've namespaced the blueprint shortcut routes using the prefix /bp. To use a shortcut, you'll need to preface the URL with /bp.

> **DEFINITION**   *Namespacing* is a technique to avoid collisions of similarly named things, in this case route names. By adding the prefix /bp, you'll avoid colliding with paths of routes with the same name.

We've also modified the way our models connect to PostgreSQL. Up to this point we were using PostgreSQL strictly for the user model by assigning the `connection` property in the user model itself. We've removed the connection from the user model and instead included it in brushfire/config/model.js. This makes the myPostgresqlServer connection the default connection for all models. If we had a requirement for a particular model to use a different connection, then we could specify the connection directly in that model file so that it would override the default connection in brushfire/config/model.js. But we don't have that as a requirement. Let's see this in action. Restart Sails via sails lift and navigate your browser to localhost:1337/ bp/user/find. You should see the two user accounts that are created using the bootstrap.js file.

11.1.4 Refactoring navigation

We now have a requirement to incorporate tutorials into Brushfire. We also have a requirement to allow all users to access user profiles. Finally, we have a requirement to add standalone signup and sign-in pages. These requirements make new demands of the navigation view to display different markup based on the condition of the user–agent, as illustrated in figure 11.1.

Figure 11.1 The navigation markup has five basic states based on the conditions of the user-agent: unauthenticated ❶, authenticated without the add tutorial button displayed ❷, authenticated with the add-tutorial button displayed ❸, authenticated and an admin ❹, and authenticated and an admin with the add tutorial button displayed ❺.

The display of the administration link will remain unchanged. What has changed is the way in which Sign Up and Sign In now function. Based on Chad's requirements, we've created two new wireframes that coincide with standalone views for the sign-in and signup pages. Links to each page are now on the navigation bar when the user-agent is unauthenticated, as depicted in figure 11.2.

Figure 11.2   Sign In and Sign Up now have standalone views.

When the user-agent is authenticated, there's a drop-down to navigate to the user profile or to log out, as illustrated in figure 11.3.

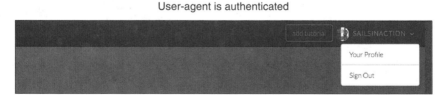

Figure 11.3   The navigation bar adds a drop-down when the user-agent is authenticated to allow access to the user profile and the ability to log out.

We've also added a brushfire/views/logout.ejs view that you'll use later to provide functionality if a `GET` request to `/logout` is made. These changes to the assets are reflected in the frontend markup you cloned earlier. You'll also see a new button on the navigation bar named *add tutorial*. A user must be authenticated to add a tutorial. There are situations where you don't want an authenticated user-agent to be able to add a tutorial. For example, if a user is editing a tutorial, then you want to hide the display of the add-tutorial button from the navigation bar. Therefore, we added some logic to the partial view brushfire/views/navigation.ejs to handle a new local property, showAddTutorialButton, shown in listing 11.2.

Listing 11.2 Handling the display of the add-tutorial button in the navigation bar

```
...
<% if (me) { %>                                          Checks if the user-agent
  <ul class="nav navbar-nav navbar-right">               is authenticated
    <% if (typeof showAddTutorialButton !== 'undefined' &&
    showAddTutorialButton) { %>
      <li style="margin-right:5px"><p class="navbar-btn"><a type="button"
      class="btn btn-primary" href="/tutorials/new">add tutorial</a></p></li>
    <% } %>
...
```

Makes sure the showAddTutorialButton property
is defined and then, if true, displays it

By checking whether the property is defined via the typeof operator, you have the option of passing it via a local or not. If you don't pass the local, then the button won't be displayed. The following listing shows how to change the home action to also pass a value for showAddTutorialButton so that it's displayed when the homepage is rendered.

Listing 11.3 Passing the showAddTutorialButton property via a local in the view

```
...
return res.view('homepage', {
  me: {
    username: user.username,
    gravatarURL: user.gravatarURL,       Setting the showAdd-
    admin: user.admin                    TutorialButton property
  },                                      to display the button
  showAddTutorialButton: true
});
...
```

We've documented all the requests and request requirements for Brushfire in an online API Reference that can be found at http://mng.bz/apXw. Navigate your browser to that link and look at the requirements for the Signup form, which are similar to the display in figure 11.4.

The Brushfire API Reference contains the inputs and exits of each request shown in the wireframes, similar to figure 11.5.

We used the wireframes for each view to create the API Reference documentation and the documentation to create a working frontend with partially implemented end-points. We say *partially implemented* because we won't integrate actions using real data until chapter 12. For now, we'll simulate records using arrays of dictionaries for lists and individual dictionaries for particular records. Speaking of models, the pivot will involve the use of a feature of Waterline we haven't covered yet: *associations*. We'll

Signup form ❶		❻	GET	/signup
Display the signup page and respond with me *set to* null. ❷				
Incoming Params			**Target Action**	**Response Type**
none ❸		❼	PageController.signup ❽	html
View				
signup.ejs ❹			**Front-end Controller**	
Locals:		❾	signupPageController.js	

{
  "me": null ❺
}				

Figure 11.4   The API Reference documents each request's friendly name ❶, description ❷, incoming parameters (if any) ❸, view (if any) ❹, locals ❺, method and URL path ❻, controller and action ❼, response type ❽, and frontend controller (if any) ❾.

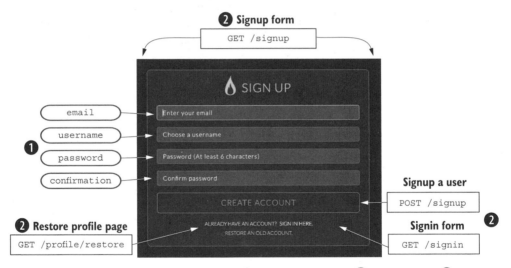

Figure 11.5   The wireframes contain documentation for the attributes ❶ and requests ❷ of each view.

explain associations in detail in chapters 12 and 13. For now, know that associations will provide some helpful functionality to manage the relationships between related models: users, tutorials, videos, and ratings. You may have noticed that the API Reference documentation for the login request also contains a Responses section, as shown in figure 11.6.

This is where you can document requests that have different responses based on different response status codes. Next, let's look at the search, browse, and administration views.

Login			PUT	/login
Params			**Target Action**	**Response Type**
email		sailsinaction@gmail.com	UserController.login	n/a
username		sails-in-action		
password		abc123	**Front-end Controller**	
			n/a	
Responses				
❶ 403 Forbidden	❷	403 Forbidden	❸ 200 OK	
"Your our account has been deleted. Please visit http://brushfire.io/restore to restore your account.'"		"'Your our account has been banned, most likely for adding dog videos in violation of the Terms of Service. Please contact Chad or his mother.'"	create session	

Figure 11.6   The login request has three different response codes if the user-agent is deleted ❶, banned ❷, or successful ❸.

11.1.5   Refactoring views

Users want the ability to search and browse for the tutorials created within Brushfire. So we transformed the homepage into a search page, as shown in figure 11.7.

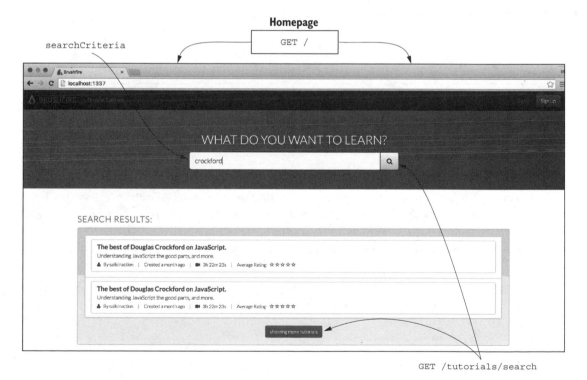

Figure 11.7   The post-pivot home/search page

We'll implement search in chapter 13 where we'll use the home/search page to capture `searchCriteria` to use as criteria for a query of the `tutorial` model. It's important to note that the content of the homepage doesn't change based on the condition of the user-agent. For example, the homepage doesn't change whether the user-agent is authenticated or not. We also have a requirement that users have the ability to browse tutorials. We created a wireframe for the browse-tutorials page shown in figure 11.8.

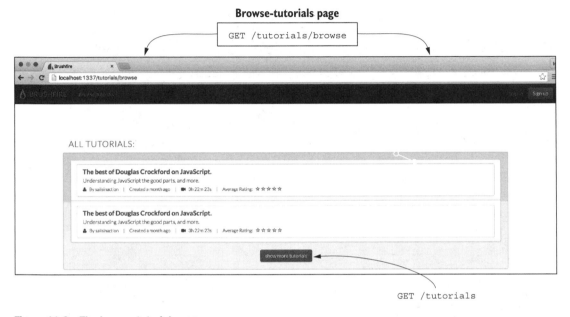

Figure 11.8   The browse-tutorials page

Like the homepage, the browse-tutorials page doesn't display different content based on the condition of the user-agent. Finally, we created a wireframe for the User Administration page in figure 11.9, but the functionality of this page hasn't changed from previous earlier versions of Brushfire.

Now let's move to the profile category of views.

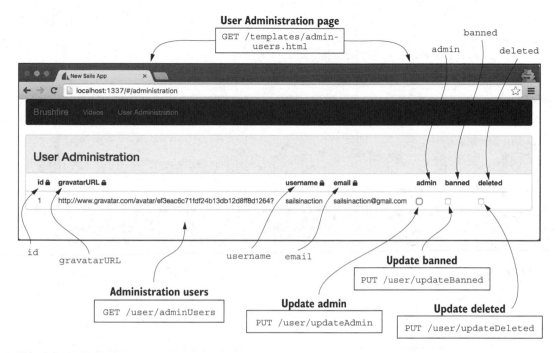

Figure 11.9   The User Administration page

11.2   *Custom routing and error pages*

Before the pivot, a profile could be viewed only if the user was authenticated in Brush-fire. We used req.session.userId as criteria for a query of the user model to find the user record with the email, gravatarURL, and admin attributes to display the profile. Because we were using the req.session.userId property to determine which profile to display, only the profile of the authenticated user could be displayed. Chad's new requirements provide for a profile that can be viewed with or without authentication, including users other than the profile owner. This will enable Brushfire users to explore tutorials created by other Brushfire users via their profile page. Brushfire users also want the ability to follow users they like as well as other followers of the user. The profile page will therefore be expanded to three different views:

- A profile with tutorials view
- A profile with followers view
- A profile with those being followed view

Let's look at each view and its requests and request requirements. The first view is the profile page, shown in figure 11.10.

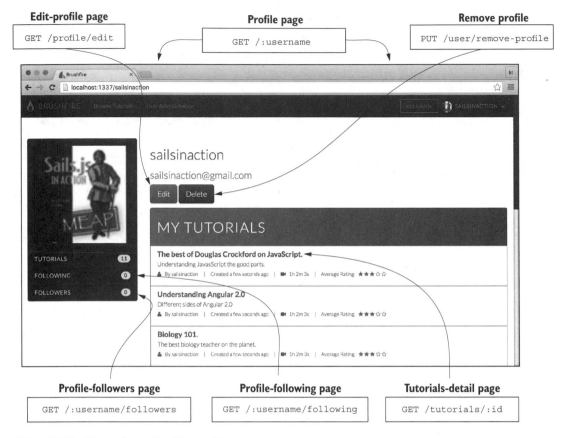

Figure 11.10   The profile page with tutorials

The second view is the profile-following page, shown in figure 11.11. The final view is the profile-followers page, shown in figure 11.12.

The profile link on the navigation bar now displays the username related to the current session's userId property instead of the email address. We did this for both privacy and continuity, because the path of the route that links to the profile in the navigation bar now uses /:username. We'll discuss the impact of using a variable, also referred to as a *slug*, in the next section.

DEFINITION   *Slug* is shorthand for a generated URL that distinguishes between endpoints using a string.

Open brushfire/api/controllers/PageController.js in Sublime and see how to distinguish between profile owners in the profile action, similar to the next listing.

Edit-profile page

`GET /profile/edit`

Profile-following page

`GET /:username/following`

Remove profile

`PUT /user/remove-profile`

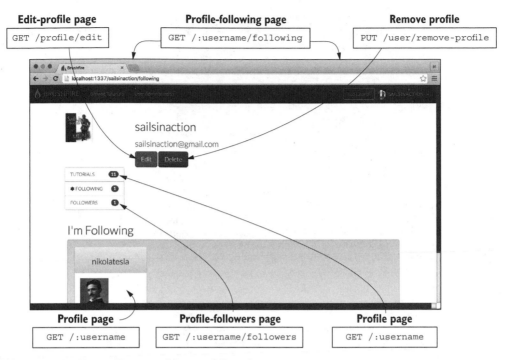

Profile page

`GET /:username`

Profile-followers page

`GET /:username/followers`

Profile page

`GET /:username`

Figure 11.11   The profile page with users followed

Edit-profile page

`GET /profile/edit`

Profile-followers page

`GET /:username/followers`

Remove profile

`PUT /user/remove-profile`

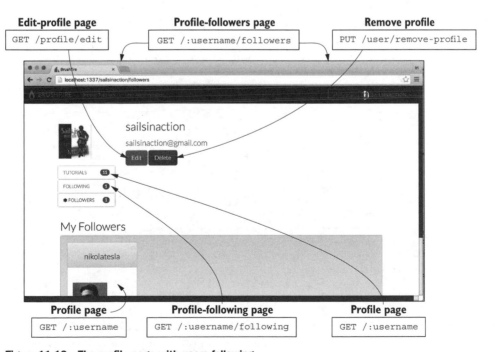

Profile page

`GET /:username`

Profile-following page

`GET /:username/following`

Profile page

`GET /:username`

Figure 11.12   The profile page with users following

```
...
var me = {
  email: loggedInUser.email,
  username: loggedInUser.username,
  gravatarURL: loggedInUser.gravatarURL,
  admin: loggedInUser.admin
};
  if (req.session.userId === foundByUsername.id) {
    me.isMe = true;
  }
return res.view('profile', {
  me: me,
  showAddTutorialButton: true,
  username: foundByUsername.username,
  gravatarURL: foundByUsername.gravatarURL,
  tutorials: tutorials
});
...
```

Builds up a dictionary of information about the user and assigns it to me

isMe is true if the userId of the current session is equal to the foundByUsername id.

Passes the locals to the profile view

You'll either pass the isMe property set to true to the me dictionary, which will enable the user-agent to modify the profile, or pass the locals without it, allowing the user to view but not modify the profile.

11.2.1   *The impact of variables in routes*

The new profile route, and specifically the path /:username (a.k.a. a *slug*) presents an opportunity to address some issues related to the use of variables in a route's path. In Sublime, open brushfire/config/routes.js, which is similar to the following listing.

```
...
 /*************************************************************
  * JSON API Endpoints                                       *
  *************************************************************/

  'PUT /login': 'UserController.login',
  'POST /logout': 'UserController.logout',
  'GET /logout': 'PageController.logout',
  ...
 /*************************************************************
  * Server Rendered HTML Page Endpoints                      *
  *************************************************************/
  ...
  'GET /:username': 'PageController.profile'
}
```

Before we discuss the impact of using /:username, let's look at some overall organization changes we've made to brushfire/config/routes.js. We've aggregated the explicit routes into two general groups: JSON API endpoints and server-rendered HTML page endpoints. For added organization, we've also associated related resources together within each of these groups. For example, routes related to the user resource are placed together. But what's the impact of the order of routes?

From previous chapters, you know that the routes contained in brushfire/config/routes.js are considered explicit or custom routes. The Sails router looks to match an incoming request to explicit routes before trying to match the request to the other types of Sails routes like blueprint routes, asset routes, and the /csrfToken route. Routes are matched by the Sails router in the order in which they're placed in the brushfire/config/routes.js file. If a variable like :username isn't specified in the path of a route, then the order chosen for routes can be purely based on your organizational aesthetic. But if you include a variable like :username in your path, the order becomes important.

For example, the path /:username will be triggered on any combination of characters after the initial slash (/). Therefore, any routes after /:username whose path contains a single segment will never be triggered.

DEFINITION   A *segment* consists of a slash (/) and one or more alphanumeric characters. For example, the following path contains two segments: /tutorials/:id.

When using variables in a route's path, place the route with the variable below any other routes with the same number of segments. Figure 11.13 illustrates how this works.

If you don't place routes with the same number of segments below the route with a variable like :username, those routes will never be matched by the Sails router. There's

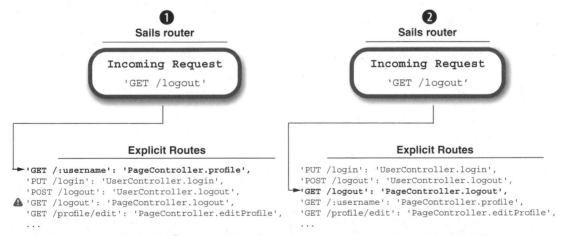

Figure 11.13   The first example ❶ illustrates the impact of the route order on other single-segment routes when using the :username variable. A GET request to /logout would be matched with the GET /:username route, which isn't the intended result. In the second example ❷, we placed the GET /:username route below the route to the GET /logout route. The GET request to /logout was matched with the route that contained the GET /logout path, which is what was intended. Note that the two-segment route to GET /profile/edit was unaffected.

one other issue with /:username. Start Sails via sails lift and navigate your browser to localhost:1337/favicon.ico. Open the browser's console window, and you should see that Sails responded with a 404 Not Found status.

> **NOTE** You get bonus points if you also recognized that the Sails 404 response page wasn't rendered. We'll deal with that issue in the next section.

Sails provides a favicon.ico file in the root of brushfire/assets/ folder. As you learned in chapter 3, the assets folder performs like the *web root* of a web server. Any file in that folder automatically has a built-in asset route. If the file has a recognized type, it will be rendered by the browser. So navigating to localhost:1337/favicon.ico should result in the browser rendering the favicon.ico file. The issue is that localhost:1337/favicon.ico is being superseded by /:username. You can easily fix this by using the skip-Assets property in the route's configuration. Head back to Sublime and open brushfire/config/routes.js, and make the following changes to /:username.

Listing 11.6   Adding the `skipAssets` property to a route

```
...
'GET /:username': {
    controller: 'PageController',
    action: 'profile',
    skipAssets: true
},
...
```

Any files in the root of brushfire/assets won't be superseded by this route.

After adding the skipAssets property to the route configuration, any file in the root of brushfire/assets will no longer be superseded by /:username. Restart Sails using sails lift and navigate your browser to localhost:1337/favicon.ico. You should now see the Sails favicon displayed. But why wasn't the Sails 404 response page displayed earlier when the favicon.ico file couldn't be found? You'll fix that in the next section.

11.2.2 *Customizing Sails' built-in response pages*

Earlier, the Sails 404 response page wasn't displayed when we made a GET request to localhost:1337/favicon.ico. The page didn't get displayed because the me dictionary wasn't sent as a local to the view. When the 404 page was rendered, the layout file added the navigation markup in brushfire/views/partials/navigation.ejs. That navigation view attempted to use a property named me, and because it didn't exist, an error was generated. But where did this error come from? It came from the notFound.js response. Let's back up for a moment. Sails provides a convenient way of handling common response types like Bad Request (400), Forbidden (403), and Not Found (404) with custom code for each response: badRequest.js, forbidden.js, notFound.js, and so on. The source code for these responses can be found in the brushfire/api/responses/ folder. Some of the responses also have corresponding views that are sent as the response if the requesting user-agent doesn't require JSON.

NOTE Each response tries to guess whether the user-agent requires JSON. For example, if the request is an AJAX request, you can assume that the request wants JSON.

For example, forbidden.js uses brushfire/views/403.ejs, notFound.js uses brushfire/views/404.ejs, and serverError.js uses brushfire/views/500.ejs. In our current situation, the code that renders the not-found response in the 404.ejs view is in brushfire/api/responses/notFound.js. Let's again take a look at the 404 response generated but this time using a different example.

Restart Sails using `sails lift` and navigate your browser to localhost:1337/irlIsOld. The Sails router matches a GET request to /irlIsOld with the route containing the path GET /:username and executes the `profile` action of the page controller. The resulting 404 error in the terminal window should look similar to the next listing.

Listing 11.7 A 404 error related to the 404.ejs response

```
warn: res.notFound() :: When attempting to render error page view, an error
➥ occurred (sending JSON instead). Details:   ReferenceError:
➥ /brushfire/views/layout.ejs:36
    34|    </head>
    35|    <body ng-app="brushfire">
 >> 36|      <%- partial('./partials/navigation.ejs') %>
    37|      <%- body %>
    38|
    39|      <!--TEMPLATES-->
/brushfire/views/partials/navigation.ejs:21
    40|        <ul class="nav navbar-nav">
    41|          <li><a style="font-family:verdana;font-size: 18px;"
                 ➥ href="/tutorials/browse">browse</a></li>
 >> 42|          <% if (me && me.admin) { %>
me is not defined
```

It looks like the brushfire/views/partials/navigation.ejs view was looking for a `me` local that doesn't exist. You can confirm that no `locals` were sent by looking at the `profile` action of the page controller that's executing the `res.notFound()` response. In Sublime, open brushfire/api/controllers/PageController.js, and locate `return res.notFound()` in the `profile` action, as shown here.

Listing 11.8 The `notFound` response of the `profile` action

```
...
User.findOne({
  username: req.param('username')
  }).exec(function(err, foundByUsername) {
    if (err) {
      return res.negotiate(err);
    }
  if (!foundByUsername) {
      return res.notFound();          ⟵  If the user isn't
    }                                      found, respond
...                                        with notFound().
```

After the GET request to /irlIsOld is made, the :username parameter irlIsOld is used as criteria by a User.findOne() model method in the profile action to find a user. There's no user record with irlIsOld as a username, so brushfire/api/responses/notFound.js is executed via return res.notFound(). Let's see what happens when res.notFound() is executed, as illustrated in figure 11.14.

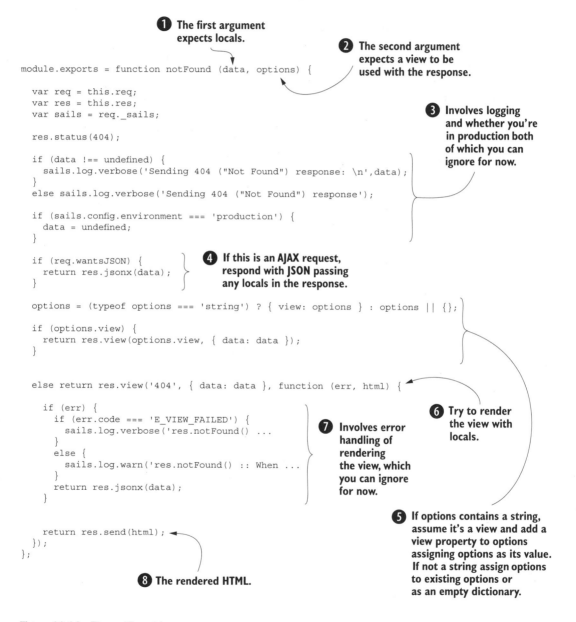

Figure 11.14   The notFound.js response

The notFound.js response method expects `locals` ❶ as the first argument and a view ❷ as the second argument. In this case, you didn't pass any `locals` or a view. The code in ❸ logs errors and prevents `locals` from being sent if you're in a production environment, and it can be ignored for now. If you were making an AJAX request ❹, the response would return early, passing any `locals` as JSON. You're not making an AJAX request in this case. If a second argument was passed as a view, the response would check if the argument is a string ❺. If it is, you'll attempt to add a `view` property to the `options` dictionary and assign its value to the new `options.view` property. Once again, you didn't pass in any view to the response. Here's the important part: the response ❻ will try to render the default view, `404`, with any `locals` sent as the first argument. The response will handle any errors ❼ and then render the view ❽.

When the 404.ejs view is rendered, it tries to render brushfire/views/partials/navigation.ejs because it's part of the layout.ejs view, which expects a `me` property that doesn't exist, and so you get an error. To resolve this, you could pass `me` as an argument to `notFound({me: null})`, but `locals` would now have the signature `data.me` instead of what the view is expecting: `me`. This also wouldn't handle your authenticated state. The best solution is to alter notFound.js to take a detour before it renders the view. You'll check whether the user-agent is authenticated via `req.session.userId`. If the user-agent isn't authenticated, you'll pass a `me` dictionary that's `null`. If the user-agent is authenticated, you'll find that `user` and pass a `me` dictionary that contains the found `email`, `username`, `gravatarURL`, and `admin` properties. Making these changes to the response will also provide an opportunity to demonstrate how to incorporate asynchronous detours in existing source code.

Your first option is to copy all the existing response code for both cases: the unauthenticated state and the authenticated state. This would result in duplicative code and a rather inelegant solution. If you'd like to see the source code for this solution in all its ugliness, check out the gist at http://mng.bz/6nLw. A second approach, found in the next listing, isn't perfect, but it allows you to take your detour without adding duplicative code.

Listing 11.9 Creating an asynchronous detour in the `notFound` response

```
...
  options = (typeof options === 'string') ? { view: options } : options ||
    {};

  function afterwards(err,loggedInUser){        ◁──  Declares a function that will be
    if (err) { return res.serverError(err); }        executed after you determine the
                                                      user-agent's authenticated state
    var me;
    if (!loggedInUser) {
      me = null;              ◁──  If there's no loggedInUser,
    }                              assigns me to null
    else {
      me = {                                    ◁──  If loggedInUser exists, assigns
        email: loggedInUser.email,                   the necessary properties for
                                                     the navigation bar to me
```

```
            gravatarURL: loggedInUser.gravatarURL,
            username: loggedInUser.username,
            admin: loggedInUser.admin
        };
    }

    var locals = {                 ◁─┐    Declares a locals dictionary
      data: data,                    │    with the legacy data dictionary
      me: me                         │    and the new me dictionary
    };
                                            If a view is specified as an
                                            argument, renders it with
    if (options.view) {                     the locals dictionary
      return res.view(options.view, locals);    ◁─┘
    }

    else return res.view('404', locals, function (err, html) {

        if (err) {
          if (err.code === 'E_VIEW_FAILED') {
            sails.log.verbose('res.notFound() :: Could not locate view for
            ➥ error page (sending JSON instead). Details: ',err);
          }
          else {
            sails.log.warn('res.notFound() :: When attempting to render error
            ➥ page view, an error occurred (sending JSON instead). Details: ',
            ➥ err);
          }
          return res.jsonx(data);
        }
        return res.send(html);
    });
    }
                                    If no session exists,
    if (!req.session.userId) {      executes afterwards()
      return afterwards();    ◁─┘
    }

    User.findOne({ id: req.session.userId }).exec(function(err,user){    ◁─┐
      if (err) return afterwards(err);                                     │
      return afterwards(null, user);         Looks up the session's userId │
    });                                      property in the user model and │
};                                           returns the result to afterwards()
```

If no view is specified, renders 404.ejs with the locals dictionary

Here, you move the actual rendering of the 404.ejs view into a function named after-wards(err,loggedInUser). The User.findOne() model method will execute first, and then your afterwards method will execute, passing in the results of your User.findOne() query. This isn't a bad option, but you can do even better.

The next approach may look strange at first, but we promise that after you've gone through it a few times, you'll be transformed into an asynchronous virtuoso.

Listing 11.10 Using an asynchronous IIFE detour in the `notFound` response

```
...
   options = (typeof options === 'string') ? { view: options } : options || {};
(function ifThenFinally (cb){                    Declares the IIFE
   if (!req.session.userId) {
     return cb();                                If no session exists, executes
   }                                             the callback afterwards()

   User.findOne({ id: req.session.userId }).exec(function(err,user){
     if (err) return cb(err);
     return cb(null, user);                      Looks up the session's
   });                                           userId property in the
                                                 user model and returns
}) (function afterwards(err,loggedInUser){       the result to the
   if (err) { return res.serverError(err); }     callback named
                                                 afterwards()
   var me;
   if (!loggedInUser) {
     me = null;
   }
   else {
     me = {
       email: loggedInUser.email,
       gravatarURL: loggedInUser.gravatarURL,
       username: loggedInUser.username,
       admin: loggedInUser.admin
     };
   }

   var locals = {
     data: data,
     me: me
   };

   if (options.view) {
     return res.view(options.view, locals);
   }
   else return res.view('404', locals, function (err, html) {
     if (err) {
       if (err.code === 'E_VIEW_FAILED') {
         sails.log.verbose('res.notFound() :: Could not locate view for
         ➥ error page (sending JSON instead). Details: ',err);
       }
       else {
         sails.log.warn('res.notFound() :: When attempting to render error
         ➥ page view, an error occurred (sending JSON instead). Details: ',
         ➥ err);
       }
       return res.jsonx(data);
     }
     return res.send(html);
   });
 });
};
```

Passes the afterwards() function as the callback

You first declare an immediately invoked function expression (IIFE). This function will check for the authenticated state of the user-agent and execute the `User.find-One()` model method if the user-agent is authenticated. The results of those checks are passed in as arguments to the IIFE. The advantage here is that you accomplish the same result as the last option with what we feel is a much more intuitive flow.

> **DEFINITION**   An IIFE is a function that's both declared and executed at the same time.

What about the other responses that have views, like forbidden.js and serverError.js? These error pages shouldn't show up in the normal course of using the application. Therefore, we've chosen to remove the layout and the navigation partial from server-Error.js and forbidden.js. We removed the layout by passing in the `layout` property and assigning it to `false` in each response of your cloned repository, similar to the following listing.

Listing 11.11   Removing the layout in serverError.js and forbidden.js

```
...                                     If the a view is passed as an argument,
if (options.view) {                     adds a layout property in locals set to false
  return res.view(options.view, { data: data, layout: false });
}
...
else return res.view('403', { data: data, layout: false }, function (err,
    html) {              ◁                If the default view is rendered, adds a
...                                       layout property in locals set to false
```

Let's move on to the `tutorial` and `video` views in the next section.

11.3   *Adjusting access control rules*

By far, the `tutorial` and `video` views are the largest additions to Brushfire functionality. Recall that users want the ability to aggregate YouTube videos into a collection called Tutorials. They want to be able to rate the tutorials, chat with other users who happen to be watching a particular tutorial, and post chat messages. Based on these requirements, we created wireframes that encompass the functionality for each view, including these:

- *tutorials-detail.ejs*—Used as the main page for a tutorial
- *tutorials-detail-new.ejs*—Used when creating a new tutorial
- *tutorials-detail-edit.ejs*—Used when editing an existing tutorial
- *show-video.ejs*—Used when viewing a video
- *tutorials-detail-video-new.ejs*—Used when creating a new video
- *tutorials-detail-video-edit.ejs*—Used when editing an existing video

In addition to creating the wireframes, we documented the requirements for each request in the API reference.

11.3.1 *Customizing a view based on edit permissions*

The tutorials-detail page has three different wireframe states depending on the user-agent's condition:

- Unauthenticated user-agent
- Authenticated user-agent but *not* the owner of the tutorial
- Both an authenticated user-agent and the owner of the tutorial

Figure 11.15 shows the model and attributes for each state of the view.

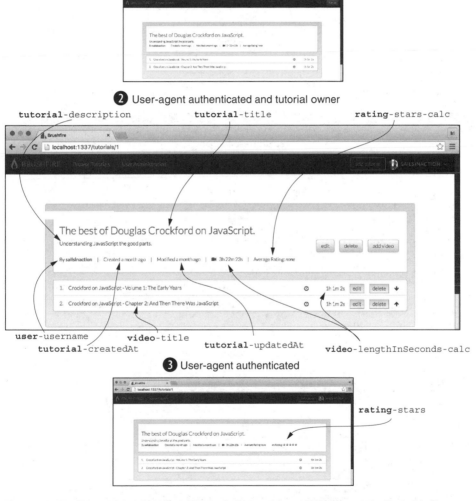

Figure 11.15 The model and attribute for each view are shown if they're not duplicated in the user-agent authenticated and tutorial-owner views ❷. Therefore, all the attributes in the unauthenticated view ❶ are referenced in ❷. Notice that some of the attributes use the term *calc* for "calculated value." The value isn't stored as displayed but instead calculated in an action.

Next, let's look at the requests for each state of the view in figure 11.16.

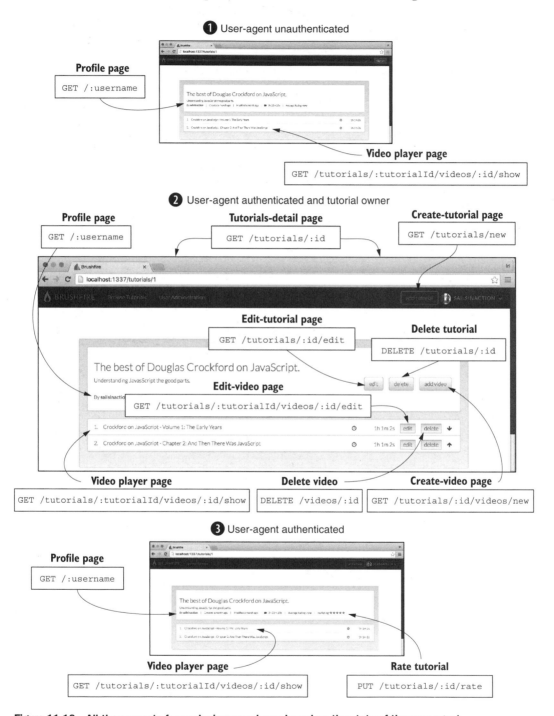

Figure 11.16   All the requests for each view are shown based on the state of the user-agent.

To control the contents of the view based on the user-agent's state, you'll employ a combination of the me dictionary you've been using and a new me.isMe property, which, if true, indicates that the user-agent is authenticated as the creator of the tutorial. As shown in figure 11.16, when a user-agent is not authenticated, a read-only view of the tutorial detail page is displayed ❶. In this state, the page contains two requests. One request links the tutorial back to its owner, and the other request loads a video record into the video player page. ❸ When a user-agent is authenticated but isn't the owner of the tutorial, a read-only version of the page is again displayed but with an added myRating request, similar to figure 11.17.

Figure 11.17   This tutorial was created by the user `sailsinaction`, but it's being viewed by the user `nikolatesla`. Therefore, `nikolatesla` can rate and view the tutorial but not edit it.

Finally, ❷ when a user-agent is both authenticated and the owner of the tutorial, UI elements to edit, delete, and otherwise alter the tutorial and video are displayed, similar to figure 11.18.

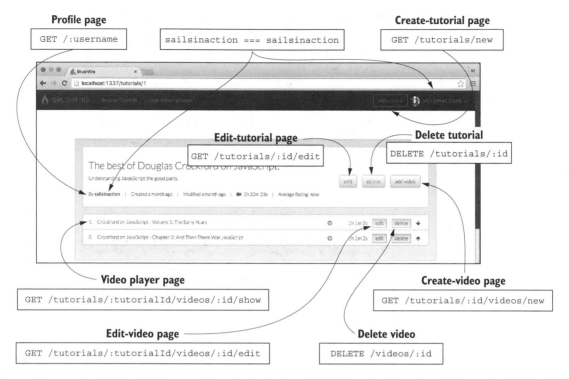

Figure 11.18   A user-agent who is both authenticated and the owner of the tutorial adds an additional request to modify the tutorial and video. Note that an owner of a tutorial can't rate their own tutorial.

So the display of additional requests is controlled via an `isMe` local in the `tutorials-detail` action of brushfire/api/controllers/PageController.js, similar to the following.

Listing 11.12   The `isMe` property in the `tutorials-detail` action of the page controller

```
...
if (user.username === tutorial.owner) {
  me.isMe = true;

  return res.view('tutorials-detail', {
    me: me,
    stars: tutorial.stars,
    tutorial: tutorial
  });
}
...
```

> The isMe property is true if the user-agent's session username is equal to the tutorial's owner.

If the user-agent is authenticated, you look up the user by the session's `userId`. You then compare the returned `username` property of that found user with the `tutorial` record's `owner`. If the two properties are equal, the `isMe` property is set to `true` and passed on as a `local` to the `view`. Markup in the view is displayed depending on the value of `me.isMe`. We'll look at the wireframes for the other views related to the tutorial and video as we implement each feature in coming chapters. If you're curious, you can review the requirements of all the wireframes in the API Reference and see all the wireframes in the chapter 11 hub located here: http://sailsinaction.github.io/chapter-11/.

11.4　Patterns and best practices

Application development is a constantly evolving process of solving problems and then editing and refining the solutions. Certain times, however, are better than others for refining your code. The pivot is one of those opportunities to reflect on the current code base and make changes before embarking on new features. One of the first tasks you should consider is removing code that's no longer used in the project. For example, in chapter 3 we began working on the frontend as a single-page application (SPA) and later transitioned to a hybrid combination of using server-rendered views and a frontend framework like Angular. We were able to remove a lot of unused templates and code. As you review the repo, you'll see that we were able to trim quite a bit of unused source code from the project. In this chapter, we'll also do some actual refactoring of our source.

11.4.1　Refactoring repetitive action names

As your application grows, you'll start to notice things that annoy you. One of these things is your naming choices. For example, when we started Brushfire we wanted to be descriptive in our page controller, so we prefixed each action with the word `show` and added the word `Page` on the end (for example, `showHomePage`, `showProfilePage`). What began as a well-intended naming structure has now become a distraction, making the actions more difficult to read. To remedy this, we removed `show` and `Page` from each action name. This, of course, required us to check our action name changes in explicit routes found in the brushfire/config/routes.js file as well as changes to action names in policies via brushfire/config/policies.js. As you review the new repo, you'll see these and other naming enhancements to the Brushfire project.

11.4.2　Using folders to organize views

Sometimes it makes sense to go back and aggregate views into folders for better organization. Let's look at an example relating to the password-recovery system to aggregate some views. We decided to organize all the views related to password recovery in a views subfolder named password-recovery. The following listing illustrates the way you reference the path to a view in `res.view()`.

> **Listing 11.13　Referencing a path to a view in Sails**

```
...
passwordRecoveryEmail: function(req, res) {
  return res.view('./password-recovery/password-recovery-email', {
    me: null
  });
},
...
```

Now that you know how to access views in subfolders from res.view(), we'll leave it up to you to determine how best to organize other related views based on your future requirements.

11.4.3 *Refactoring EJS views and client-side templates*

We've settled on a hybrid approach to creating frontend views that combines EJS tags with Angular controllers and directives. But how do you know when to use either approach? As a general rule, if the current elements on a page won't change between a page refresh, we'll use EJS. For example, in brushfire/views/partials/navigation.ejs, none of the elements—nav links, gravatarURL, and so on—change between a page refresh, so we refactored using if statements within EJS tags instead of using Angular ng-hide and ng-show directives. But if an element will change between page refreshes, we'll use Angular. As you'll see shortly, the search form on the homepage displays a results list before the page itself is refreshed.

> **NOTE** As always, when we say to use *Angular*, we mean you can use whatever frontend JavaScript framework you prefer.

Another factor that influences the use of EJS tags versus Angular is search engine optimization (SEO). Generally, a page whose content is already rendered versus one that must be rendered on the frontend after the page is loaded will achieve better search engine results. Search engines are improving their ability to derive content from JavaScript, but we've found that if it's important for a page to be incorporated by a search engine, then you should use EJS tags and server-rendered views instead.

Any interaction with the user that involves responding to click events will also require some form of frontend JavaScript such as Angular's ng-click directive. Form validation is also made easier using a frontend JavaScript framework like Angular. The same holds true for form management in general. For example, using a combination of ng-submit and ng-model makes form submission easier to accomplish than harvesting form elements manually. Finally, loading states benefit from frontend JavaScript because of the ease of configuring them.

The biggest consideration when combining these two approaches, however, is how you transfer backend data to the frontend. Recall that there are three ways to get backend data to your frontend in Brushfire:

- You can send locals to an EJS view and use EJS tags to render the locals on the page.
- You can append locals to the browser's window dictionary and make them accessible in an Angular controller via assignment to the $scope dictionary.
- You can make an AJAX request to a backend endpoint and assign the results to the Angular $scope dictionary.

The first two options are necessary when the frontend framework requires access to the data between a page refresh. For example, because the navigation bar doesn't change between a page refresh, you can simply send the me dictionary as a local to the view. This avoids the need to grab the values of me from the window dictionary and place them into a frontend controller and then into the page via Angular. As you review the new Brushfire repo, you'll see that we incorporated all these general principles in our decisions of when to use EJS and Angular in the project.

11.4.4 Using async.each()

Because users aren't bashful about adding videos as part of tutorials, we no longer need to seed YouTube videos in the bootstrap. But in order to do adequate testing, we need to create multiple test users. So we've refactored the bootstrap to use the popular async library. async is an npm module that provides functions for working with asynchronous JavaScript. Here, we use asynchronous methods to build up our test users. We need a way to coalesce the results of each method that won't produce issues because we don't know when each method will return. In Sublime, open brushfire/config/bootstrap.js to see the changes similar to the following listing.

> **Listing 11.14   Refactoring the bootstrap.js file**

```
module.exports.bootstrap = function(cb) {          ⟵  cb is a way to tell Sails
                                                       you're finished with the
  var async = require('async');                        bootstrap and it can
  var Passwords = require('machinepack-passwords');    continue lifting.
  var Gravatar = require('machinepack-gravatar');

  var TEST_USERS = [{
    email: 'sailsinaction@gmail.com',
    username: 'sails-in-action',
    password: 'abc123',
    admin: true
  },
  ...
  }];

  async.each(TEST_USERS, function findOrCreateEachFakeUser(fakeUser, next){  ⟵

    User.findOne({                                         next is a way to tell
      email: fakeUser.email                                async.each() you're
    }).exec(function (err, existingUser){                  finished with an
                                                           iteration.
      if (err) return next(err);

      if (existingUser) {
        return next();
      }

      Passwords.encryptPassword({
        password: fakeUser.password,
      }).exec({
        error: function(err) {
          return next(err);
        },
        success: function(encryptedPassword) {
```

```
        var gravatarURL;
        try {
          gravatarURL = Gravatar.getImageUrl({
            emailAddress: fakeUser.email
          }).execSync();

        } catch (err) {
          return next(err);
        }

        User.create({
          gravatarURL: gravatarURL,
          encryptedPassword: encryptedPassword,
          email: fakeUser.email,
          username: fakeUser.username,
          deleted: false,
          admin: fakeUser.admin,
          banned: false,
        }).exec(function(err, createdUser) {
          if (err) {
            return next(err);
          }
          return next();
        }); //</User.create()>
      }
    }); //</Passwords.encryptPassword>
  }); // </ User.find
}, function afterwards(err){                    ◁──┐  afterwards will call either
  if (err) {                                         cb(err) if there's an error
    return cb(err);                                  or cb() if the iterations
  }                                                  were successful.
  return cb();
  });
};
```

`async.each()` provides a callback named `next` as an added argument to the iterator. This provides a way for you to tell `async` when you've finished with each iteration. After all iterations have been successfully completed or you get an error, the `after-wards` method is executed, either returning bootstrap's `cb`—or callback—with an error, or simply `cb` if the iterations were successful. It's important to distinguish the bootstrap `cb` from `async`'s `next` callback. You can think of both callbacks as a way of telling either `async` or the bootstrap when you've finished. Therefore, you wouldn't use `cb` within the `async.each()` method because that's a different scope and time than the bootstrap method. You can name the callback methods whatever you want. By convention, we use `cb()` for the bootstrap file and `next()` for `async.each()`.

11.4.5 Adding new features

Based on user feedback, Chad asked us to implement ratings on tutorials. He said, "Let users rate tutorials up to five stars." This seems like an innocuous request. But when you don't lock down what *ratings* really means, you can quickly get in a quagmire:

- Can an unauthenticated user rate a tutorial?
- Can an owner of a tutorial rate their own tutorial?
- What does the UI do, if anything, to let a user who has already rated this tutorial know that they've already rated it?
- What does the UI do, if anything, to let a user who has already rated this tutorial know that, after choosing a new rating, they've updated their previous rating?
- How do you differentiate in the UI an average of many users' ratings and a particular user's rating?

As you can see, there's a bit more involved with defining the requirements of the rating feature. After some additional discussions, Chad agreed on the following more-specific requirements:

- There will be two ratings: an overall rating and a myRating. Whether a particular view displays one or both of the ratings will depend on the requirements of that view.
- A user-agent must be authenticated in order to rate a tutorial. Therefore, the myRating won't be displayed if the user-agent isn't authenticated.
- A user-agent can change their vote at will.
- When a user-agent hasn't yet rated a tutorial, the myRating will have empty stars. When a user-agent successfully rates a tutorial, a `toastr` message will be displayed.

Our point here is to never underestimate the need to fully document a feature because even a seemingly simple one can quickly become complex.

11.5 In depth: adding a password-recovery flow

Chad has been inundated with emails from Brushfire users who forgot their passwords. To address this, we'll create a password-recovery flow into Brushfire. This will allow users to reset their passwords.

11.5.1 Understanding how password recovery works

A typical password-recovery system allows the user to request a password reset in the event they can't remember their existing password. The system sends an email to the address used when signing up for an account. We'll use a popular service called Mailgun that allows us to send email programmatically. A reset link is then attached to the email that provides a one-time-use token to reset the password. Figure 11.19 illustrates the flow of the recovery system.

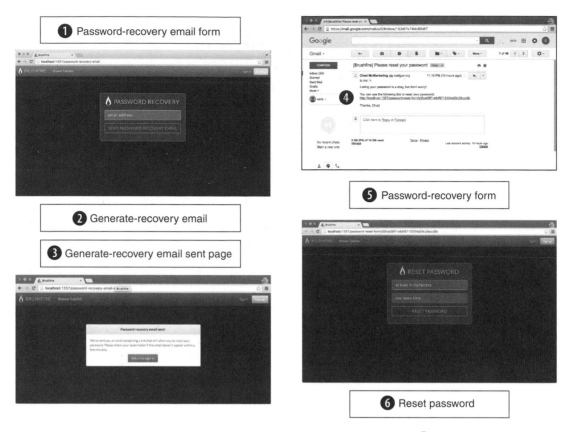

Figure 11.19   A password-recovery system has several components including a form ❶ that captures the email address used when creating the account, an action that generates a one-time token ❷ and the email ❹ and responds with an email-sent form ❸, and the ❺ password-reset form with the reset password action ❻.

The password-recovery system starts with a GET request to /password-recovery-email from the sign-in page. This triggers the passwordRecoveryEmail action, as shown in the next listing, of the page controller that you set up in the repo you cloned at the beginning of the chapter.

Listing 11.15   The `passwordRecoveryEmail` action

```
passwordRecoveryEmail: function(req, res) {
  return res.view('./password-recovery/password-recovery-email', {
    me: null
  });
},
```

The user supplies the email address they provided when originally signing up for Brushfire. Clicking the Send Password Recovery Email button triggers the genera-teRecoveryEmail action of the user controller, similar to this.

Listing 11.16 The `generateRecoveryEmail` action

```
generateRecoveryEmail: function(req, res) {

  if (_.isUndefined(req.param('email'))) {
    return res.badRequest('An email address is required!');
  }
  User.findOne({                                              Finds the user via the
    email: req.param('email')                                 provided email parameter
  }).exec(function foundUser(err, user) {

    if (err) return res.negotiate(err);

    if (!user) return res.notFound();                         Generates a random
                                                              alphanumeric
    try {                                                     string using the
      var randomString = Strings.random({}).execSync();       machinepack-strings
    } catch (err) {                                           random machine
      return res.serverError(err);
    }

    User.update({
      id: user.id
    }, {                                                       Updates the user record's
      passwordRecoveryToken: randomString                      passwordRecoveryToken
    }).exec(function updateUser(err, updatedUser) {
      if (err) return res.negotiate(err);

      var recoverUrl = sails.config.mailgun.baseUrl + '/password-reset-
        form/' + updatedUser[0].passwordRecoveryToken;

      var messageTemplate = 'Losing your password is a drag, but don\'t
        worry! \n' +
          '\n' +
          'You can use the following link to reset your password: \n' +
          recoverUrl + '\n' +
          '\n' +
          'Thanks, Chad';

      Mailgun.sendPlaintextEmail({                             Sends the email
        apiKey: sails.config.mailgun.apiKey,                   template using the
        domain: sails.config.mailgun.domain,                   machinepack-mailgun
        toEmail: updatedUser[0].email,
        subject: '[Brushfire] Please reset your password',
        message: messageTemplate,
        fromEmail: 'sailsinaction@gmail.com',
        fromName: 'Chad McMarketing',
      }).exec({
        error: function(err) {
          return res.negotiate(err);

        },
        success:  function() {

          return res.ok();
        },
      });
```

Annotations in left margin:

Generates the URL to be inserted in the email

Creates the email template

```
    });
  });
},
```

We already reviewed most of the mechanics of how this action works in previous chapters. There are a few new details. For example, we're using two new machines: one to generate a random string—machinepack-strings—and one to send email—machinepack-mailgun.sendPlainTextEmail.

The Mailgun service requires an API key and domain, which you'll obtain and configure in brushfire/config/local.js in the next section. For now, know that the local.js file places the properties on a global Sails dictionary that you access in this action. The result of the generateRecoveryEmail action is that an email is sent to the user's email address with a link that (when clicked) makes a GET request to /password-reset-form/:passwordRecoveryToken, passing the passwordRecoveryToken as a parameter. The frontend passwordRecoveryPageController redirects the user-agent to a password-recovery-email-sent page via a GET request to /password-recovery-email-sent. When the user clicks the link in the email message, a GET request to /password-reset-form/:passwordRecoveryToken is made that triggers the passwordReset action of the page controller, which renders the password-reset view. This view contains a form for the user to provide a new password. When the user clicks the Reset Password button, a PUT request to /user/reset-password is made, which triggers the resetPassword action of the user controller, similar to the following listing.

Listing 11.17 The resetPassword action

```
resetPassword: function(req, res) {

if (!_.isString(req.param('passwordRecoveryToken'))) {         ⟵
  return res.badRequest('A password recovery token is required!');
}
...
    success: function(encryptedPassword) {
      User.update(user.id, {
        encryptedPassword: encryptedPassword,
        passwordRecoveryToken: null
      }).exec(function (err, updatedUsers) {
        if (err) {
          return res.negotiate(err);
        }

        req.session.userId = updatedUsers[0].id;
  ...
```

Using __.isString() checks for a value and if that value is a string.

Remember that User.update() returns an array.

The functionality in this action should look familiar from previous chapters. You use _.isString() for secondary validation instead of _.isDefined(). This gives you the advantage of checking for both a value as well as whether that value is a string in one method. Also recall that the User.update() method of the model returns an array of dictionaries and not a single dictionary. If everything is successful, the frontend redirects the user-agent to the profile page via a GET request to /:username.

11.5.2 Sending emails

Mailgun is a commercial service that provides APIs that allow you to send email programmatically. In order to use the service, you need credentials, and in this section we'll show you how to store and incorporate your credentials using the local.js file. You're not limited to using Mailgun for sending emails. Create a free account by navigating your browser to http://mailgun.com. You'll want to select the free account that allows for up to 10,000 emails per month. Once you've created your account, you'll need to collect two values: your domain and your API key. In Sublime, open brushfire/config/local.js, and add the following code with your credentials.

> **Listing 11.18 Adding `mailgun` credentials to local.js**

```
...
module.exports.mailgun = {
  apiKey: 'ADD YOUR API KEY',
  domain: 'ADD YOUR DOMAIN',
  baseUrl: 'http://localhost:1337'
};
...
```

Your password-recovery system is now ready to start sending emails and resetting passwords.

11.6 Summary

- Proper attention to detail on frontend mockups, requirements, and decision making should limit pivots to those based on market feedback.
- Refactoring is a process in which existing code is restructured to increase organization and readability and produce an overall reduction in complexity.
- Using variables in custom routes requires added emphasis on the route's order in brushfire/config/routes.js.
- Third-party services like Mailgun can send emails on Sails' behalf to fulfill an essential component of a password-recovery system.

Embedded data
and associations

This chapter covers

- Using embedded records and associations to create relationships between models
- Reducing duplicative code by creating a service
- Understanding the differences between one-way and two-way associations

In chapter 11, we examined the new requirements of a market-based pivot that significantly enhanced and extended the features of Brushfire. We applied our frontend-first approach to the requirements. Using this approach compelled us to make design decisions in advance of implementing the backend, thereby reducing the likelihood of second-guessing based on inadequate information. Essentially, we wanted to eliminate questions that begin with "I didn't know that...." Our work in chapter 11 produced a set of documented decision points in the API Reference, wireframes, and a functioning frontend with simulated backend responses.

Up to this point in our application, we haven't had to concentrate on the organization of models and the underlying database of Brushfire. We began the book by creating and storing URLs of YouTube videos in a video model, first using an array on the frontend to simulate a database and then storing the array using Sails'

NoSQL in-memory database. We expanded the initial model/database implementation to include storing information about users in a `user` model, and then stored `user` records in a PostgreSQL database. With our new feature requirements, we now need to take the added models to support those features and relate them to each other. For example, a `user` record will be associated with the `tutorial` records it creates. This chapter will examine our new models, their relationships, and how to fulfill the requirements of requests using Sails associations.

12.1 Obtaining the example materials for this chapter

If you've been following along in chapter 11 with an existing project, you can continue to use that project in this chapter. If you want to start from this chapter and move forward, clone the following repo: https://github.com/sailsinaction/brushfire-ch11-end. After cloning the repo, install the Node module dependencies via `npm install`. You'll also want to add the local.js file you created in chapter 11. In Sublime, create a new file in brushfire/config/local.js, and add the following code to it.

Listing 12.1 Adding to the local.js file

```
module.exports.blueprints = {
  shortcuts: true,
  prefix: '/bp',
};

module.exports.connections = {
  myPostgresqlServer: {
    adapter: 'sails-postgresql',
    host: 'localhost',
    database: 'brushfire'
  }
};

module.exports.mailgun =  {
  apiKey: 'ADD YOUR MAILGUN API KEY HERE',
  domain: 'ADD YOUR MAILGUN DOMAIN HERE',
  baseUrl: 'http://localhost:1337'
};
```

12.2 Understanding relationships between data

We've established that a model is an abstract representation of a noun, like a `User`. You probably recognize figure 12.1 by now.

Each model has details about the types of attributes it contains; the methods used to find, create, update and destroy records; and information related to where and how the records are stored. You use models to organize, access, and modify records whose values are part of the requirements of requests generated from the frontend.

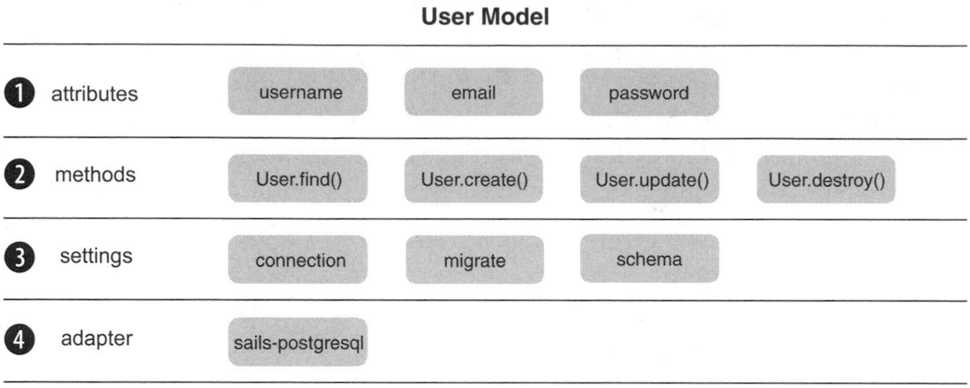

User Model

Figure 12.1   **A model consists of attributes ❶, methods ❷, settings ❸, and an adapter ❹.**

12.2.1   *Brushfire models after the pivot*

After the pivot, the Brushfire repo now contains the following models:

- user—Holds values about a user
- tutorial—Holds values about a tutorial
- video—Holds values about a video
- rating—Holds values about a rating
- chat—Holds values about a chat message (which you'll implement in chapter 14)

You'll explore these models when you use them to implement the remaining Brushfire features. Post-pivot, you also have requests that require records from multiple models. For example, the tutorials-detail page contains attributes from four different models, as shown in figure 12.2.

Let's look at how you can set up relationships to more effectively access and modify the attributes of records across multiple models.

12.2.2   *Relationships between models*

Figure 12.3 illustrates some of the inherent relationships between Brushfire models.

Each of the relationships in figure 12.3 shares two important characteristics—the direction of the reference between models and the number of records referenced:

- *Direction (one-way or two-way reference)*—A relationship has a two-way reference if both models require the ability to find, create, update, or destroy records in each model. For example, between the user and tutorial models, there's a need for a user to find all tutorials created by that user and for the tutorial to find the user who created it. This relationship requires a two-way reference.
- *Quantity (one or many)*—Does the related model have a relationship with one record or multiple records? Between the user and tutorial models, the user can own multiple tutorials, but a tutorial can be owned by only one user.

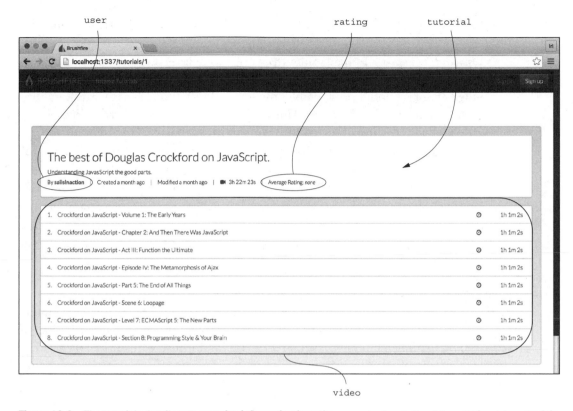

Figure 12.2   The tutorials-detail page contains information from the user, tutorial, video, **and** rating **models.**

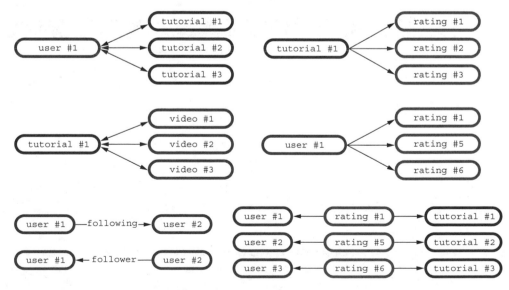

Figure 12.3   Models have relationships that go in different directions, as depicted by the arrows in the figure.

You know that relationships exist, but how are they implemented between models? You have three ways to create relationships in models and their records in Sails:

- *Embedding values*—Embed values from one model's record into another model's record and then maintain each embedded value for each record. For example, the tutorial model could embed the sort order of the video records for a tutorial as an array of dictionaries. This works as long as you don't need to query on the embedded value of the record. We'll expand on this in the next section.
- *One-way association reference*—Use Waterline associations to create a one-way reference association between two models and then maintain each reference.
- *Two-way association reference*—Use Waterline associations to create a two-way referenced association between two models and maintain a single reference for both associations.

You'll implement all three types of relationships in order to fully understand how they work and when to use them.

12.3 *Associating data using embedded JSON*

Remember, *embedding* means you're adding the actual values of one record to another record and then manually syncing those values on both records when they change. You're going to implement the backend requirements for the create-tutorial page to create all three types of relationships. First, look at the wireframe for the view in figure 12.4.

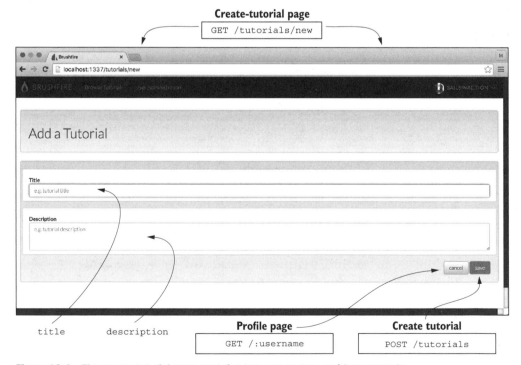

Figure 12.4 The create-tutorial page contains two parameters and two requests.

The create-tutorial request requirements from the API reference are shown in figure 12.5.

Create tutorial		②	POST	/tutorials
Create a new tutorial with the `title` *and* `description` *parameters provided and associate it with the currently authenticated user before responding with the new tutorial id as JSON.* ①				
Back-end Notes ③				
- *Policy:* `isLoggedIn` - *Check to make sure current authenticated* `user` *is* `owner`				
Params ④	**Example**	⑤ **Target Action** ⑥	**Response Type**	
`title`	The best of Douglas Crockford on JavaScript.	TutorialController.create	json	
`description`	*Understanding JavaScript the good parts.*			
		Front-end Controller		
Response ⑦		n/a		
`200 OK`				

`{`
 `  "id": 325`
 `}`				

Figure 12.5 The create-tutorial request reference contains a description ①, the method and path of the request ②, backend notes ③, incoming parameters ④, the target action ⑤, the response type ⑥, and the response ⑦.

The request expects you to take the incoming `title` and `description` parameters and create a new tutorial. You need to associate the new `tutorial` record with the currently authenticated user and then respond with the new tutorial `id` as JSON. So your task on the backend is to create a record in the `tutorial` model that embeds the user who created it, as well as to update a record in the `user` model that embeds the new tutorial.

12.3.1 Setting up an embedded relationship

First, you'll set up the models with attributes that will hold your embedded values. In Sublime, open brushfire/api/models/Tutorial.js and brushfire/api/models/User.js. The models should look similar to figure 12.6.

The `tutorials` attribute in the `user` model will keep track of the tutorials created by the currently authenticated user-agent. This will enable you to query on the `user` model to obtain a list of the tutorials created by that user. The `user` model can contain one or more tutorials to be stored as an array of dictionaries in JSON. The `owner` attribute in the `tutorial` model will keep track of which user created the tutorial.

user model

```
module.exports = {
  ...

  passwordRecoveryToken: {
    type: 'string'
  },

  tutorials: {        (1)
    type: 'json'
  },

  ...
```

tutorial model

```
module.exports = {
  attributes: {
    title: {
      type: 'string'
    },

    description: {
      type: 'string'
    },

    owner: {          (2)
      type: 'json'
    },

    ...
```

Figure 12.6 The `user` model contains a `tutorials` attribute (1) that will hold the embedded array of `tutorial` dictionaries as JSON and an `owner` attribute (2) that will hold the embedded `username` dictionary as JSON.

12.3.2 Creating a record with embedded JSON

You now must implement the backend `createTutorial` action to fulfill the requirements of the create-tutorial request. When a user-agent fills out the form on the create-tutorial page and clicks the Save button, the frontend makes an Angular AJAX `POST` request to `/tutorials`, triggering the `createTutorial` action of the tutorial controller. Let's start adding code to the action. In Sublime, open brushfire/api/controllers/TutorialController.js, and add the code to validate the incoming parameters in the existing `createTutorial` action, as shown in the following listing.

Listing 12.2 The `createTutorial` action—validating incoming parameters

```
createTutorial: function(req, res) {

  if (!_.isString(req.param('title'))) {          <- Validates the title parameter as a string
    return res.badRequest();
  }

  if (!_.isString(req.param('description'))) {    <- Validates the description parameter as a string
    return res.badRequest();
  }
  ...

},
```

You use Lodash's `_.isString()` method to ensure that the incoming parameters are both defined and of the proper type. Next, you must query for the user using the currently authenticated user-agent. In Sublime, add the following to the `createTutorial` action.

Listing 12.3 The `createTutorial` action—find the currently authenticated user

```
...
    User.findOne({
      id: req.session.userId
    }).exec(function(err, foundUser){
      if (err) return res.negotiate;
      if (!foundUser) return res.notFound();
      ...
```

Finds the user using the currently authenticated user-agent and the criteria

Handles any errors

Now you can create the tutorial using the incoming parameters and assign the embedded username attribute with the username found in the user record. In Sublime, add the following code to the createTutorialaction action.

Listing 12.4 The `createTutorial` action—create the tutorial and update `owner`

```
...
    Tutorial.create({
        title: req.param('title'),
        description: req.param('description'),
        owner: { username: foundUser.username },
      }).exec(function(err, createdTutorial){
        if (err) return res.negotate(err);
            ...
```

Creates the tutorial

Adds incoming parameters

Adds the username dictionary from the found user record

Handles any errors

You'll complete the action by updating the user record with the embedded tutorial array of dictionaries, and then you'll return the id of the new tutorial as JSON. In Sublime, add the following code.

Listing 12.5 The `createTutorial` action—update the `tutorials` attribute

```
        foundUser.tutorials = [];
        foundUser.tutorials.push({
          title: req.param('title'),
          description: req.param('description'),
          created: foundUser.createdAt,
          updated: foundUser.updatedAt,
          id: foundUser.id
        });
        User.update({
          id: req.session.userId
        }, {
          tutorials: foundUser.tutorials
        })
        .exec(function(err){
          if (err) return res.negotiate(err);

          return res.json({id: createdTutorial.id});
        });
      });
    });
  },
```

Assigns an empty array to the tutorials property

Pushes the properties of the tutorial record to the dictionary

Updates the user based on the session userId

Updates the user record with the newly created array and dictionary

Handles any errors

Responds with the newly created tutorial id

Notice that you copy the unique record id, createdAt date, and updatedAt date from the tutorial record as elements of your dictionary and embedded array. This combination of a separate tutorial model with an embedded JSON array in the user model is working, but there are pitfalls to this approach.

12.3.3 Populating embedded data

Turn your attention to the edit-tutorial page shown in figure 12.7.

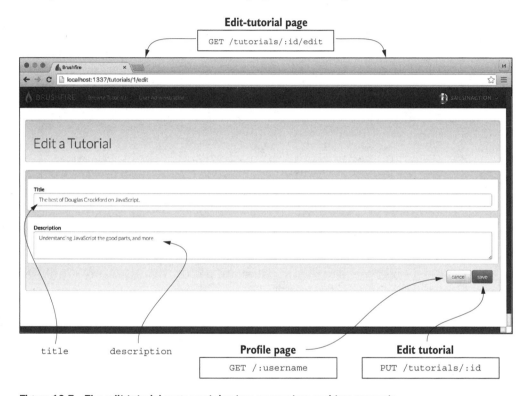

Figure 12.7   The edit-tutorial page contains two parameters and two requests.

Unlike the create-tutorial page, the edit-tutorial page requires that you gather some tutorial attributes for the view. You'll first alter the existing editTutorial action of the PageController to find the tutorial by using the incoming tutorial id parameter, and you'll find the user of the currently authenticated user-agent via the session userId.

> **TIP**   You use the unary operator (+) to coerce the tutorial id into a number. You do this to ensure that the id you provide is a number and not a string.

In Sublime, open brushfire/api/controllers/PageController.js, and replace the fake tutorials dictionary with the Tutorial.findOne() method, similar to the next listing.

Listing 12.6 The editTutorial action—find the tutorial and authenticated user

```
editTutorial: function(req, res) {
  Tutorial.findOne({                                    Finds the tutorial to
    id: +req.param('id')                                edit using incoming
  }).exec(function (err, foundTutorial){                id parameter
    if (err) return res.negotiate(err);
    if (!foundTutorial) return res.notFound();          Finds the current
                                                        user using the
    User.findOne({                                      session userId
      id: +req.session.userId
    }).exec(function (err, foundUser) {                 Handles errors with
      if (err) return res.negotiate(err);               res.negotiate()

      if (!foundUser) {
        sails.log.verbose('Session refers to a user who no longer exists-
        ➥ did you delete a user, then try to refresh the page with an open
        ➥ tab logged-in as that user?');
        return res.redirect('/tutorials');
      }
      ...
```

Handles Not Found with a redirect → (points to `if (!foundUser) {`)

After finding the tutorial and the currently authenticated user-agent, you'll check whether that user is the owner of the tutorial. In Sublime, add the following code.

Listing 12.7 The editTutorial action—check for the owner and display or redirect

```
                                        Checks whether the currently authenticated
                                        user-agent is the owner of the tutorial
    ...
    if (foundUser.username !== foundTutorial.owner.username) {
      return res.redirect('/tutorials/'+foundTutorial.id);         If not,
    }                                                              redirects to
                                                                   the tutorial
    return res.view('tutorials-detail-edit', {      Renders the   page
      me: {                                          edit-tutorial
        gravatarURL: foundUser.gravatarURL,          page with
        username: foundUser.username,                appropriate
        admin: foundUser.admin                       locals
      },
      tutorial: {
        id: foundTutorial.id,
        title: foundTutorial.title,
        description: foundTutorial.description,
      }
    });
  });
});
},
...
```

If the user is the owner, you render the edit-tutorial page with the appropriate `locals`. If not, the browser is redirected back to the tutorial. Next, you implement the edit-tutorial request that actually updates the tutorial.

12.3.4   Updating a record with embedded data

Now that you have the edit-tutorial page displayed with the appropriate tutorial title and description, let's look at the requirements for the edit-tutorial request from the API Reference, as shown in figure 12.8.

Edit tutorial		❷	PUT	/tutorials/:id
❶ Update the `title` and `description` for the `tutorial` of the specified `id`.				
Back-end Notes				
❸ - Assure that the currently logged in user is the owner of the tutorial, if not respond with forbidden().				
❹ **Params**		❺	**Target Action** ❻	**Response Type**
id		2	TutorialController.updateTutorial	json
title	The best of Douglas Crockford on JavaScript.			
description	Understanding JavaScript the good parts, and more.		**Front-end Controller**	
			n/a	
❼ **Response**				
200 OK				

Figure 12.8   The edit-tutorial request reference contains a description ❶, the method and path of the request ❷, the backend notes ❸, incoming parameters ❹, the target action ❺, the response type ❻, and the response ❼.

The request requires you to update the tutorial with the incoming `title` and `description` parameters and then to respond with a `200` status. In Sublime, open brushfire/api/controllers/TutorialController.js, and begin implementing the action by adding the following code to validate the incoming parameters in the existing `createTutorial` action.

Listing 12.8   The `updateTutorial` action—validating incoming parameters

```
...
updateTutorial: function(req, res) {

  if (!_.isString(req.param('title'))) {        ◁┐
    return res.badRequest();                      │ Validates
  }                                               │ the incoming
  if (!_.isString(req.param('description'))) {  ◁┘ parameters
    return res.badRequest();
  }
...
```

Next, you'll find and update the `title` and `description` of the tutorial.

Listing 12.9 The `updateTutorial` action—update the tutorial

```
...
User.findOne({
  id: req.session.userId
}).exec(function (err, foundUser){
  if (err) return res.negotiate(err);
  if (!foundUser) return res.notFound();

  Tutorial.findOne({
    id: +req.param('id')
  })
  .exec(function(err, foundTutorial){
    if (err) return res.negotiate(err);
    if (!foundTutorial) return res.notFound();

    if (foundUser.username != foundTutorial.owner.username) {
      return res.forbidden();
    }
    Tutorial.update({
      id: +req.param('id')
    }, {
      title: req.param('title'),
      description: req.param('description')
    }).exec(function (err) {
      if (err) return res.negotiate(err);
      ...
```

Ensures that the currently authenticated user is the owner of the tutorial

Updates the tutorial using the coerced id parameter

Passes in the title and description parameters to update

Handles any errors

Because the owner of the tutorial doesn't change, you don't need to update the `tutorial.owner` embedded attribute of the `tutorial` model. But because the tutorial has been modified, you need to update the `user.tutorial` attribute on the user record. You'll start the process of updating this embedded `tutorials` array in the following listing.

Listing 12.10 The `updateTutorial` action—update the user's `tutorials` attribute

```
...
User.find().exec(function (err, users) {
  if (err) { return res.negotiate(err); }

  async.each(users, function (user, next){

    var cachedTutorial = _.find(user.tutorials, { id:
      +req.param('id') });

    if (!cachedTutorial) {
      return next();
    }
    cachedTutorial.title = req.param('title');
    cachedTutorial.description = req.param('description');

    User.update({
      id: user.id
    }, {
```

Finds all user records

Iterates over the found users using the async.each method

Uses the Lodash find method to locate the tutorial dictionary that matches the tutorial id parameter

If no tutorial is found, goes to the next user record

If there's a match for the embedded tutorial, updates the title and description

Updates the user using the id of the currently iterated user record

```
                    tutorials: user.tutorials
                })
                .exec(function (err) {
                    if (err) { return next(err); }
                    return next();
                });
            }, function (err) {
                if (err) {return res.negotiate(err);}
                return res.ok();
            });
        });
        });
        });
    },
        ...
```

◁⎤ **Adds the updated tutorials array**

◁⎤ **Goes to the next user**

◁⎤ **After iterating, responds with res.ok()**

This is where things get a bit more verbose. In order to update the embedded user.tutorials array with the updated title and description parameters, you first need to gather all users in memory and search through each user's tutorials attribute for a matching tutorial id. The function that loops through the array of user dictionaries needs to be asynchronous because it also contains User.update(), which is also asynchronous. This prevents User.update() from executing before the loop has a chance to iterate through all the users, as illustrated in figure 12.9.

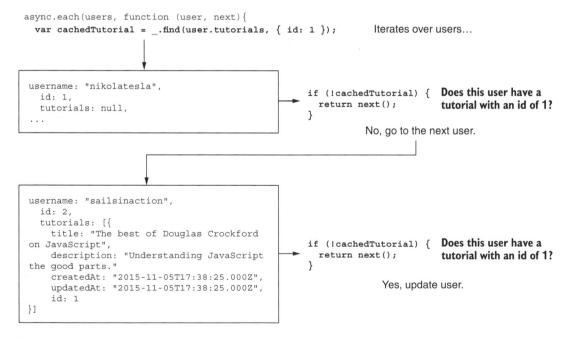

Figure 12.9   Using async.each() allows you to iterate over the users to find the tutorial before executing User.update().

Once you determine the matching tutorial, you can update `user.tutorials` with it. Although this works, it seems like a lot of extra work to maintain both sides (`tutorial` and `user` models) of the embedded attributes. There's also another issue related to server memory. As Brushfire grows more popular, there could be thousands—even millions—of users. Given enough users, server memory could be exhausted by trying to load each user's `tutorials` array. You need another way of handling relationships of large datasets between models. Fortunately, Sails provides another approach through Waterline associations.

> **NOTE** Situations will arise when an embedded attribute is superior to an association. Later in this chapter, you'll use an embedded array to track the sort order of videos. A good candidate for an embedded value is one in which the information you're embedding won't be queried outside the context of the model where it's being embedded.

12.4 Understanding Sails associations

Figure 12.10 illustrates the embedding approach used in the last section by copying a record from a model and embedding it into a record from a different model.

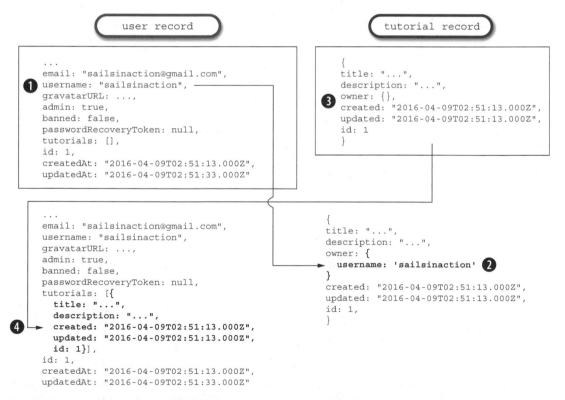

Figure 12.10 An illustration of embedding a record from one model into the record of another model. The `user` record's `username` attribute ❶ is embedded in the `tutorial` record's `owner` attribute ❷. The entire `tutorial` record ❸ is embedded into the `user` record's `tutorials` attribute ❹.

This requires you to maintain information that might change in two different places: in the model and in the embedded location. Associations set up a reference between models instead of copying and embedding parts of a record from another model, as illustrated in figure 12.11.

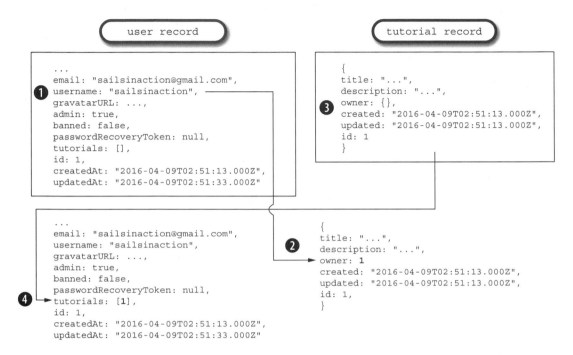

Figure 12.11   An illustration of associating a record from one model into the record of another model. The user record's id value ❶ is now referenced in the tutorial record's owner attribute ❷. The tutorial record's id ❸ is now referenced in the user record's tutorials attribute ❹. Note that the user record's tutorials attribute won't be displayed as an array. To obtain what's in the tutorials attribute, you'll use the populate method later in this chapter.

> **TIP**   An association can be thought of as similar to a shortcut or alias to a file or folder in OS X's Finder or Windows' File Explorer. The shortcut, when clicked, opens a file or folder without having to have a copy of the contents of the file or folder.

But how are the references turned into what is referenced? How do you exchange a reference for the actual values of the record being referenced? We're getting a little ahead of ourselves, but later in this chapter we'll show you how to use the populate method to populate a reference with the actual record values the reference is pointing to. What's important now is to understand that with associations any update to a referenced record's attributes (other than the id that references them) is automatically in sync with the record that's referencing it. If there was ever a need for an illustration for a tongue-twisting concept, this is it! As shown in figure 12.12, if you update

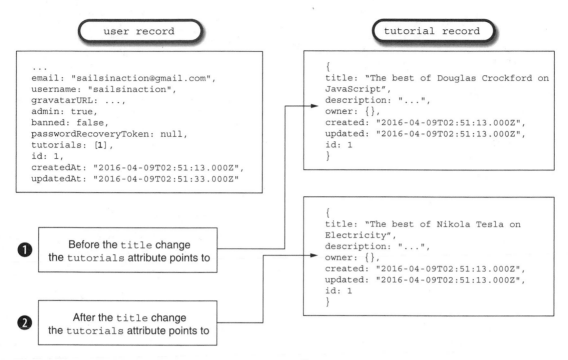

```
                ╭──────────────╮                              ╭────────────────╮
                │ user record  │                              │ tutorial record │
                ╰──────────────╯                              ╰────────────────╯
┌──────────────────────────────────────┐      ┌──────────────────────────────────────────┐
│ ...                                  │      │ {                                          │
│ email: "sailsinaction@gmail.com",    │      │ title: "The best of Douglas Crockford on  │
│ username: "sailsinaction",           │      │ JavaScript",                               │
│ gravatarURL: ...,                    │      │ description: "...",                        │
│ admin: true,                         │──────│ owner: {},                                 │
│ banned: false,                       │      │ created: "2016-04-09T02:51:13.000Z",       │
│ passwordRecoveryToken: null,         │      │ updated: "2016-04-09T02:51:13.000Z",       │
│ tutorials: [1],                      │      │ id: 1                                       │
│ id: 1,                               │      │ }                                          │
│ createdAt: "2016-04-09T02:51:13.000Z", │    └──────────────────────────────────────────┘
│ updatedAt: "2016-04-09T02:51:33.000Z" │
└──────────────────────────────────────┘
```

① Before the `title` change the `tutorials` attribute points to

```
┌──────────────────────────────────────────┐
│ {                                          │
│ title: "The best of Nikola Tesla on      │
│ Electricity",                              │
│ description: "...",                        │
│ owner: {},                                 │
│ created: "2016-04-09T02:51:13.000Z",       │
│ updated: "2016-04-09T02:51:13.000Z",       │
│ id: 1                                       │
│ }                                          │
└──────────────────────────────────────────┘
```

② After the `title` change the `tutorials` attribute points to

Figure 12.12 Before the `title` of the `tutorial` record **①** is changed, if you exchange the `tutorials` attribute reference for the actual `tutorial` record values, you get a title of "The best of Douglas Crockford on JavaScript." After the `title` of the `tutorial` record is changed **②**, exchanging the `tutorials` attribute reference for the actual `tutorial` record values will produce a title of "The best of Nikola Tesla on Electricity." Thus, the reference remains in sync after changes.

the `title` of the `tutorial` record, the `tutorials` reference in the user model remains the same. When you exchange the `tutorials` attribute for `tutorial`, the updated `title` is displayed.

Referencing another record through an association eliminates the requirement to update both records in the relationship. In order to use the association, you need to configure your models to use them. You'll do that in the next section.

12.4.1 *Configuring an association between two models*

Configuring an association is a simple process of adding an attribute to a model that tells Sails the following:

- The model to associate to
- Whether to associate one record, also called a *model association*, or many records, also called a *collection association*
- In the case of a collection, whether it's a one-way or a two-way association

For example, in figure 12.13, let's take a look at the `user` and `tutorial` models, specifically the attributes related to the relationship that's configured.

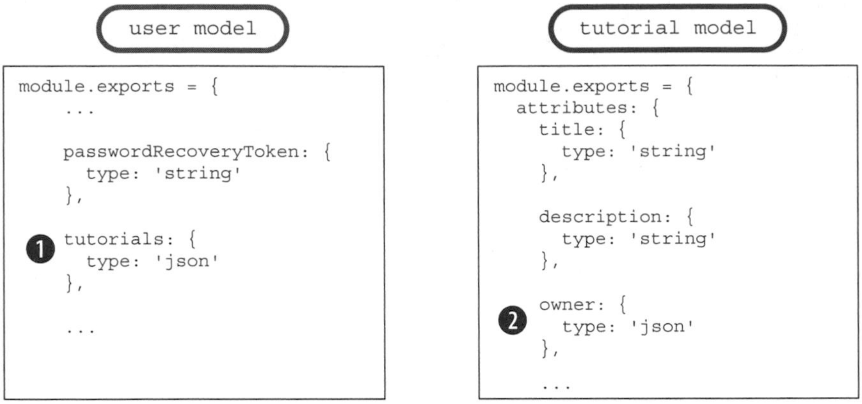

Figure 12.13   The user **model contains a** tutorials **attribute** ❶ **that configures a collection association between the** user **and** tutorial **models. The** tutorial **model contains an** owner **attribute** ❷ **that configures a model association between the** tutorial **and** user **models.**

The user model employs the same attribute name you used with the embedded technique: tutorials. You want to set up an associated reference to all tutorials created by this user. Because this references multiple records, a collection association will be used. Because this is a collection association, you can configure it to be a one-way or two-way reference. We'll explore two-way references later in this section. For now, you'll use a one-way reference that doesn't require any further configuration. In Sublime, open brushfire/api/models/User.js, and add the tutorials association attribute shown in the next listing.

Listing 12.11   The user **model's** tutorials **collection association attribute**

```
...
passwordRecoveryToken: {
  type: 'string'
},                                          The tutorials
                                            attribute
tutorials: {
  collection: 'tutorial',
},                                          Configuring a collection with
...                                         the tutorial model to reference
```

Now let's create the association in the tutorial model. In Sublime, open brushfire/api/models/Tutorial.js, and add the owner association attribute shown here.

Listing 12.12   The tutorial **model's** owner **association attribute**

```
...
description: {
  type: 'string'
},
```

```
owner: {
  model: 'user'
},
...
```

The owner attribute

**Configuring the model
association with the user model**

The `tutorial` model employs the same attribute name you used with the embedded technique: `owner`. You want to set up an associated reference to a single user, so you'll use a model association. At first, this can be confusing. But all this means is that the `owner` attribute, when populated, will produce a single record: a `user` record. Let's head back to the `createTutorial` action in the tutorial controller and start using these associations.

12.4.2 Using .add(), .remove(), and .save()

When a user-agent creates a tutorial, you have two references to keep in sync: one for the `user` model and one for the `tutorial` model. With a collection association, you use `.add()` to add a reference and `.remove()` to remove a reference. With a model association, you add the `id` of the record you want to associate. In Sublime, open brushfire/api/controllers/TutorialController.js, and add the following code to the `createTutorial` action.

Listing 12.13 Refactored `createTutorial` action using associations

```
createTutorial: function(req, res) {
  ...
  User.findOne({
    id: req.session.userId
  }).exec(function(err, foundUser){
    if (err) return res.negotiate;
    if (!foundUser) return res.notFound();

    Tutorial.create({
      title: req.param('title'),
      description: req.param('description'),
        owner: foundUser.id,
      videoOrder: [],
    }).exec(function(err, createdTutorial){
      if (err) return res.negotiate(err);

      foundUser.tutorials.add(createdTutorial.id);

      foundUser.save(function (err) {
        if (err) return res.negotiate(err);

          return res.json({id: createdTutorial.id});
      });
    });
  });
},
```

**Adds the id of the user
who created the tutorial
to add the associated
reference**

**Uses the add() method
to add a reference to the
tutorials attribute of the
user model**

**Uses the save() method
to save the changes to
the user model**

When a user creates a tutorial, you first add the `id` of that user to the `owner` attribute of the currently authenticated user-agent. This provides a reference to the `tutorial` record from the user record. You then use `.add()` to add the id of the newly created tutorial to the user's `tutorials` attribute. This provides a reference to the `user` record from the `tutorial` record. Now that you've set up the references, you can use the `.populate()` method to add a snapshot of the record or records referenced by a particular association at the time of the query. Head back to the `createTutorial` action in Sublime at brushfire/api/controllers/TutorialController.js, and add the following code.

Listing 12.14   Using `.populate()` to transform a referenced link

```
...
createTutorial: function(req, res) {
  ...
      foundUser.save(function (err) {
        if (err) return res.negotiate(err);

        User.findOne({
          id: req.session.userId          Returns a snapshot of
        })                                the user's tutorials
        .populate('tutorials')            attribute
        .exec(function (err, demoUser){
          if (err) return res.negotiate(err);
          console.log('demoUser: ', demoUser);

          Tutorial.findOne({
            id: createdTutorial.id         Returns a snapshot of
          })                               the tutorial's owner
            .populate('owner')             attribute
            .exec(function (err, demoTutorial){
              if (err) return res.negotiate(err);
              console.log('demoTutorial: ', demoTutorial);

              return res.json({id: createdTutorial.id});
            });
        });
      });
    });
  });
},
    ...
```

Now, when a user creates a tutorial, the terminal window will contain a log similar to figure 12.14.

With associations, you have the benefits of the embedded technique without the inherent syncing requirements and memory challenges.

```
      ┌─────────────────┐                                    ┌─────────────────┐
      │   user record   │                                    │ tutorial record │
      └─────────────────┘                                    └─────────────────┘

...                                                    {
email: "sailsinaction@gmail.com",                        title: "...",
username: "sailsinaction",                               description: "...",
gravatarURL: ...,                                        owner: 1,
admin: true,                  before populate            created: "2016-04-09T02:51:13.000Z",
banned: false,                                           updated: "2016-04-09T02:51:13.000Z",
passwordRecoveryToken: null,                             id: 1
tutorials: [1],                                        }
id: 1,
createdAt: "2016-04-09T02:51:13.000Z",
updatedAt: "2016-04-09T02:51:33.000Z"
```

```
...                                                    {
email: "sailsinaction@gmail.com",                        title: "...",
username: "sailsinaction",                               description: "...",
gravatarURL: ...,                                        owner: {
admin: true,                                         ❷    username: 'sailsinaction',
banned: false,                                           }
passwordRecoveryToken: null,                             created: "2016-04-09T02:51:13.000Z",
tutorials: [{                                            updated: "2016-04-09T02:51:13.000Z",
  title: "...",                 after populate            id: 1
  description: "...",                                  }
❶ owner: 1,
  created: "2016-04-09T02:51:13.000Z",
  updated: "2016-04-09T02:51:13.000Z",
  id: 1
}],
id: 1,
createdAt: "2016-04-09T02:51:13.000Z",
updatedAt: "2016-04-09T02:51:33.000Z"
```

Figure 12.14 Before using `.populate()`, the `user` and `tutorial` records contain references whose value is the `id` of the associated record. After using `.populate()`, those references are populated with the `tutorial` record ❶ and the `username` attribute ❷ of the `user` record.

12.4.3 Using via to create a two-way association

Earlier, we discussed the possibility of using a two-way reference with collection associations. When a collection association has a second model that points back to it, you have the option of using the `via` parameter. Using `via` reduces the number of references you need to manage in the association. In our current example, the `user` model has a collection referencing the `tutorial` model, and the `tutorial` model has a reference to the `user` model. If you add the `via` parameter to the user's `collection` model when you update one reference, then the other reference is automatically in sync. In Sublime, open brushfire/api/models/User.js, and add the following parameter to the user model.

Listing 12.15   Using the `via` parameter in the user's `tutorials collection` attribute

```
...
tutorials: {
  collection: 'tutorial',
  via: 'owner'                    ◁─┐  Adds a via parameter
},                                   │  to the collection
...
```

12.4.4 Refactoring an action to use associations

To understand the advantages of `via`, let's refactor the `createTutorial` action to utilize `via` by opening brushfire/api/controllers/TutorialController.js in Sublime, and adding the code in the following listing.

Listing 12.16   Refactoring the `createTutorial` action to take advantage of `via`

```
  ...
User.findOne({
  id: req.session.userId
})
.exec(function(err, foundUser){
  if (err) return res.negotiate;
  if (!foundUser) return res.notFound();

  Tutorial.create({
    title: req.param('title'),                         │  You can add a reference
    description: req.param('description'),             │  once, and both associations
    owner: foundUser.id,                         ◁─┘  will be in sync.
  })
  .exec(function(err, createdTutorial){
    if (err) return res.negotiate(err);

    return res.json({id: createdTutorial.id});
  });
});
},
```

Previously, when a user created a tutorial, you updated the `owner` attribute in the tutorial model and the `tutorials` attribute in the user model. By adding the `via` parameter, you can update either reference and the other reference will be kept in sync automatically. So, in listing 12.16, when you updated the `owner` parameter reference of the tutorial model, there was no need to update the `tutorials` parameter reference in the user model.

12.4.5 Using .populate()

The `editTutorial` action of the page controller determines whether the currently authenticated user-agent is the creator of the tutorial. Within the action, you compare the results of a query from the `user` model to a query from the `tutorial` model. Because you're using associations, the value of `tutorial.owner.username` will be null. This is because the `owner` property is now an association model reference and returns the `id` of a user record and not the entire record. You need to replace the value of `tutorial.owner` from a user record `id` to a snapshot of the record itself. In Sublime, open brushfire/api/controllers/PageController.js, and add the following code to the `editTutorial` action.

Listing 12.17 Refactoring the `editTutorial` action to take advantage of associations

```
...
editTutorial: function(req, res) {

  Tutorial.findOne({
    id: +req.param('id')
  })
  .populate('owner')                      Populates the owner
  .exec(function (err, foundTutorial){     association reference
    if (err) return res.negotiate(err);
```

When you populate the `owner` association reference, the value for `foundTutorial` `.owner` will be replaced with a snapshot of the user record. Your comparison of the currently authenticated user-agent `username` with the `username` of the `tutorial.owner` `.username` will now work as required.

Now you can remove all the code for the `updateTutorial` that involved propagating the changes to the embedded `tutorials` array attribute in the user model. Remember, with the association reference, you simply need to update the record that changes and all references to that record will be in sync. In Sublime, open brushfire/api/controllers/TutorialController.js, and refactor the `updateTutorial` action similar to the next listing.

Listing 12.18 Refactoring `updateTutorial` action to take advantage of the association

```
...
updateTutorial: function(req, res) {

  if (!_.isString(req.param('title'))) {
    return res.badRequest();
  }

  if (!_.isString(req.param('description'))) {
    return res.badRequest();
  }

  Tutorial.update({
    id: +req.param('id')
  },{
    title: req.param('title'),
    description: req.param('description')
  }).exec(function (err) {
    if (err) return res.negotiate(err);

    return res.ok();
  });
},
...
```

Using associations substantially eliminates a lot of the syncing overhead you'd need to do manually. You'll use these techniques to complete more of the backend requirements of Brushfire.

12.4.6   Refactoring bootstrap.js to use associations

Post-pivot, you need to adjust the way you create test records in the bootstrap. Your needs go beyond test users and now include tutorials, videos, and ratings. The techniques used to create the test data are beyond the scope of the book. A link to a mini-tutorial for the bootstrap can be found off the main hub link at http://sailsinaction.github.io/. For now, make the following changes to brushfire/api/config/bootstrap.js in Sublime.

Listing 12.19   Changing the way you create test users in bootstrap.js

```
module.exports.bootstrap = function(cb) {
  var FixtureBootstrapper = require('../fixtures');
  return FixtureBootstrapper(cb);
};
```

Restart Sails using `sails lift` and navigate your browser to localhost:1337/bp/user/find. The blueprint `find` shortcut is executed and three users are displayed. The user `sailsinaction` has tutorials, videos, and ratings. You'll use these test records throughout the next chapters.

12.5   Using services

Much of what you do in page controller actions is transforming data into a format that the frontend expects. The tutorials-detail page is currently using a simulated `tutorial` dictionary that was added when you cloned the project in chapter 11. The simulated dictionary also contains the `tutorial.owner` attribute of the user who created the tutorial. Let's start refactoring the `tutorialDetail` action of the page controller by replacing the simulated dictionary with a query to the `tutorial` model.

12.5.1   Example: using associations for the tutorials-detail page

You want to transition from using a simulated dictionary in the `tutorialDetail` action to an actual query to the `tutorial` model. You'll also need to populate the `owner` association reference to exchange the user `id` with an actual `user` record. In Sublime, open brushfire/controllers/PageController.js, and replace the simulated dictionary in the `tutorialDetail` action with the following code.

Listing 12.20   Replacing the simulated tutorial dictionary

```
...
tutorialDetail: function(req, res) {

  Tutorial.findOne({          ◁─────┐   Replaces the tutorial dictionary
    id: req.param('id')             │   with Tutorial.findOne()
  })
```

```
.populate('owner')
.exec(function(err, foundTutorial){
  if (err) return res.negotiate(err);
  if (!tutorial) return res.notFound();

  foundTutorial.owner = foundTutorial.owner.username;      ⟵ Transforms the
                                                              populated
  if (!req.session.userId) {                                  attribute into
    return res.view('tutorials-detail', {                     what the
      me: null,                                                frontend expects
      stars: foundTutorial.stars,
      tutorial: foundTutorial
    });
  }

  User.findOne(req.session.userId)
  ...
```

Populating the owner association reference will replace the user id with a snapshot of the user record. Because the frontend requires that the owner attribute contain the username of the user who created the tutorial, you'll transform it to contain just the username. Make sure Sails is running via sails lift, and navigate your browser to localhost:1337/tutorials/1, which should look similar to figure 12.15.

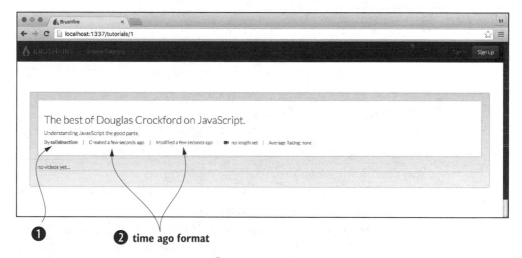

Figure 12.15 The username attribute ❶ is displayed, but the tutorials-detail page expects the createdAt and updatedAt attributes in the time-ago format ❷.

The username is properly displayed, but the createdAt and modifiedAt attributes are not being displayed. Let's fix that next.

12.5.2 *Using a service to consolidate duplicative code*

Again looking at the API Reference, you need to transform the createdAt and modifiedAt attributes from their current JSON timestamp format, 2015-09-27T16: 32:55.000Z, to the popular time-ago format, 2 days ago. At first, it might appear that the best thing to do is declare a function similar to the following.

Listing 12.21   Formatting the createdAt date with machinepack-datetime

```
...
foundTutorial.owner = foundTutorial.owner.username;

var Datetime = require('machinepack-datetime');           Requires the
                                                          machinepack

var getTimeAgo = function (options) {                     Declares a function that
                                                          will transform the date
  var niceTimeAgoString = Datetime.timeFrom({             to time-ago format
    toWhen: Datetime.parse({
      datetime: options.date                              Passes the argument
    }).execSync(),                                        to the machine
      fromWhen: new Date().getTime()
    }).execSync();

  return niceTimeAgoString;                               Returns the
};                                                        formatted date

foundTutorial.created = getTimeAgo({date: foundTutorial.createdAt});    Executes the function
...                                                                     to format the date
```

This works, but it violates one of our internal truisms: *Never declare a function inside another function unless it's a callback or deals with recursion.* Declaring a function within another function (for example, inline) in Sails can lead to issues for these reasons:

- You don't know when the code is going to run.
- You don't know if the code inside the function implementation is relying on closure scope for variables or function calls.
- When reading the code, it completely derails the linear flow of what's supposed to happen. It's as if, in the book, we interrupted ourselves in the middle of a paragraph and went on a tangent for three pages about cats. Even though Chad's mom would certainly approve, that wouldn't make sense.

If you look through the Brushfire API Reference, you'll find that you need to transform various dates into this format in no less than six different Brushfire actions. This violates another internal truism: *If you've repeated code in three or more locations, it's time to think about writing a service.* But what's a service?

A *service* is one or more functions declared within a dictionary that Sails globalizes, making the functions available everywhere. The project you cloned in chapter 11 already contains the new service in brushfire/api/services/DateTimeService.js, similar to the following listing.

```
module.exports = {
  getTimeAgo: function (options) {
    var Datetime = require('machinepack-datetime');

    var niceTimeAgoString = Datetime.timeFrom({
      toWhen: Datetime.parse({
        datetime: options.date
      }).execSync(),
      fromWhen: new Date().getTime()
    }).execSync();

    return niceTimeAgoString;
  }
};
```

The name of the file will become the globalized name of the service. You also add the suffix *Service* to the name to differentiate it from other globalized dictionaries such as models like User.js. Our preferred method signature for services that contain synchronous functions is `function(options) {}`. Our preferred method signature for asynchronous functions is `function (options, cb){}`. In Sublime, open brushfire/controllers/PageController.js, and add the code to transform the `createdAt` and `updatedAt` attributes using the `Datetime` service, as shown here.

```
...
  foundTutorial.owner = foundUser.username;

  foundTutorial.created = DatetimeService.getTimeAgo({date:
    foundTutorial.createdAt});

  foundTutorial.updated = DatetimeService.getTimeAgo({date:
    foundTutorial.updatedAt});
...
```

Using DatetimeService to format createdAt date value to time-ago

Using DatetimeService to format updatedAt date value to time-ago

Restart Sails using `sails lift` and navigate your browser to localhost:1337/tutorials/1, and you should see something similar to figure 12.16.

The `username`, `createdAt`, and `updatedAt` properties are now in the format the frontend expects.

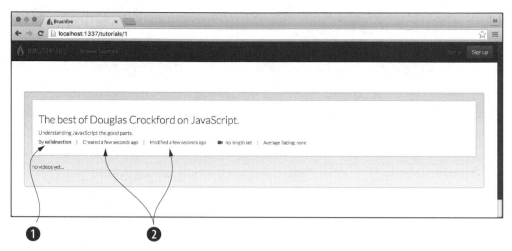

Figure 12.16   The tutorials-detail page with the `username` ❶, `createdAt` ❷, and `updatedAt` ❷ properties formatted properly

12.6   *Summary*

- You can create relationships between models using embedded attributes or association attributes.
- Model relationships have two important characteristics: the direction of the relationship and the quantity of the relationship.
- The Sails ORM uses embedded attributes, models, and collections via associations.
- You should use an embedded relationship only if the attribute embedded won't need to be queried outside the model.

Ratings, followers, and search

13

This chapter covers

- Creating a rating system for tutorials
- Understanding follower/following associations
- Building search into Brushfire
- Incorporating pagination for tutorials and a sorting mechanism for videos

You're now well into your post-pivot journey that started in chapter 11. In chapter 12, you learned how to establish relationships between models using embedded values and Waterline associations. In this chapter, you'll build on that knowledge to implement other requirements of Brushfire, including adding videos, rating content, following users, searching, and more. We'll end with a review of policies and restrictions in actions that manage access to various features. So let's get started.

13.1 Obtaining the example materials for this chapter

If you followed along in chapter 12 with an existing project, you can continue to use that project in this chapter. If, however, you want to start from this chapter and move forward, clone the following repo: https://github.com/sailsinaction/brushfire-ch12-end. After cloning the repo, install the Node module dependencies via npm install. You'll also want to add the local.js file you created in chapter 11. In Sublime, create a new file in brushfire/config/local.js, and add the following code.

> **Listing 13.1   Adding to the local.js file**

```
module.exports.blueprints = {
  shortcuts: true,
  prefix: '/bp',
};

module.exports.connections = {
  myPostgresqlServer: {
    adapter: 'sails-postgresql',
    host: 'localhost',
    database: 'brushfire'
  }
};

module.exports.mailgun =  {
  apiKey: 'ADD YOUR MAILGUN API KEY HERE',
  domain: 'ADD YOUR MAILGUN DOMAIN HERE',
  baseUrl: 'http://localhost:1337'
};
```

13.2   *Incorporating ratings*

Chad impressed on us that early adopters of Brushfire wanted the ability to rate tutorials in order to differentiate between content. Users who are authenticated and are not the owner of a tutorial may rate a tutorial from the tutorials-detail page. The average of the ratings is displayed on that page as well as other pages, including search, browse, profile, and add-video. You've already set up the association configuration among the user, tutorial, and rating models, similar to figure 13.1.

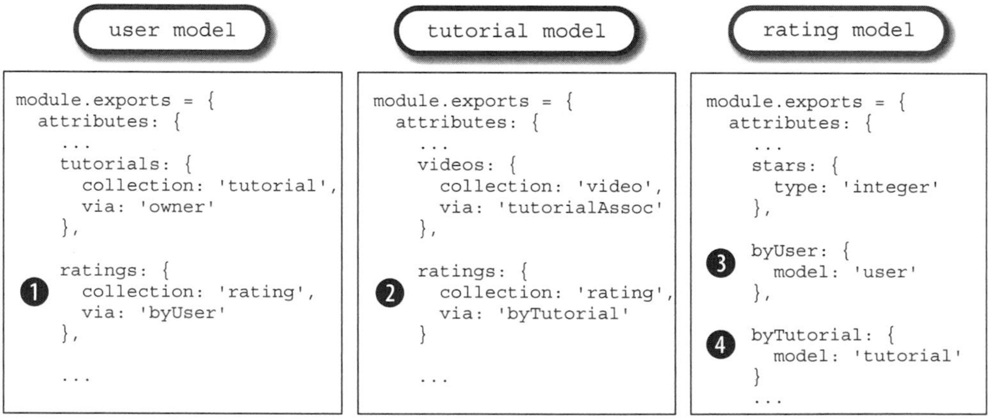

Figure 13.1   The user model has a ratings association attribute ❶ configured as a collection with the rating model that uses via. The tutorial model has a ratings association attribute ❷ configured as a collection with the rating model that uses via. The rating model has a byUser association attribute ❸ configured as a model with the user. The rating model also has a byTutorial association attribute ❹ configured as a model with the tutorial.

A quick look at the tutorials-detail page in the Brushfire API Reference reveals that the frontend is expecting a tutorial dictionary that contains averageRating and myRating attributes. We've chosen to not store these values as attributes in models and instead calculate each value using the stars attribute from the rating model.

13.2.1 Calculating averages

You need to add the necessary code to calculate the average ratings for a found tutorial. In Sublime, open brushfire/api/controllers/PageController.js, and add the following changes to the tutorialDetail action.

Listing 13.2   Adding populate and rating query to the tutorialDetail action

```
...
tutorialDetail: function(req, res) {

  Tutorial.findOne({
    id: req.param('id')
  })
  .populate('owner')
  .populate('videos')
  .populate('ratings')          ◁————  Populates ratings on
  .exec(function(err, foundTutorial){            the tutorial model
    if (err) return res.negotiate(err);
    if (!foundTutorial) return res.notFound();

    Rating.findOne({                      ◁——  Finds the currently
      byUser: req.session.userId               authenticated user's
    }).exec(function(err, foundRating){         rating, if any
      if (err) return res.negotiate(err);
      ...
```

You now have all the ratings for the tutorial that you'll use to calculate the average-Rating. You also have a rating, if any, for the currently authenticated user. You need to check whether the current tutorial being rated has been rated before by this authenticated user-agent. If it has, you'll pass it to the view as myRating through locals. In Sublime, continue adding the following code to the tutorialDetail action.

Listing 13.3   Computing the averageRating value in the tutorialDetail action

```
...                              If there are no ratings for
if (foundRating.length === 0) {  ◁—  currently authenticated user-
  foundTutorial.myRating = null;     agent, assigns myRating to null
} else {

  _.each(foundRating, function(rating){       ◁—  Iterates through each
                                                  rating for a match with
    if (foundTutorial.id === rating.byTutorial) {  the current tutorial
      foundTutorial.myRating = rating.stars;
      return;
    }
  });
}
```

If there's a match, assigns it to myRating

```
if (foundTutorial.ratings.length === 0) {
  foundTutorial.averageRating = null;
} else {

  var sumfoundTutorialRatings = 0;

  _.each(foundTutorial.ratings, function(rating){

    sumfoundTutorialRatings = sumfoundTutorialRatings +
      rating.stars;
  });

  foundTutorial.averageRating = sumfoundTutorialRatings /
    foundTutorial.ratings.length;
}
...
```

If there are no ratings for the tutorial, assigns foundTutorial .averageRating to null

Otherwise, calculates the average of all ratings

Assigns the value of the average to foundTutorial.averageRating

The bootstrap provides you with two test ratings: one from franksinatra (Frank was a bit stingy giving a rating of three stars) and one from nikolatesla, who gave a rating of three stars to the Crockford tutorial. Restart Sails using sails lift, log in as nikolatesla, and navigate your browser to localhost:1337/tutorials/1. You should see something similar to figure 13.2.

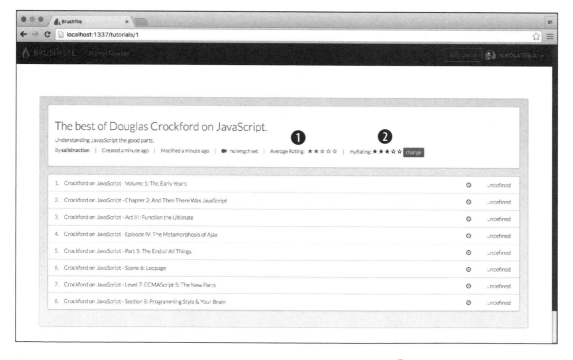

Figure 13.2 The tutorials-detail page now displays the correct average rating ❶ and a rating for the currently authenticated user-agent ❷, if any. In this case, the nikolatesla test user has provided a rating of three stars.

When the user rates the tutorial by clicking the stars next to `myRating` or clicks the Change button if a rating has already been given, the rate-tutorial request is triggered. You'll implement that endpoint in the next section.

13.2.2 Adding a new rating

Let's implement the rate-tutorial request defined in the API Reference as "Create or update rating for a tutorial using the session of the user-agent and respond with the average rating for the tutorial." The rate-tutorial endpoint has two incoming parameters: the `tutorial` id and the number of `stars` provided for the tutorial rating. You'll use both parameters to fulfill the requirements of the endpoint. In Sublime, open brushfire/api/controllers/TutorialController.js, and add the following code to the rateTutorial action.

> **Listing 13.4 Implementing the `rateTutorial` action—the initial queries**

```
rateTutorial: function(req, res) {

  User.findOne({                                      ◁── Finds the currently
    id: req.session.userId                                authenticated user-agent
  })
  .exec(function(err, currentUser){
    if (err) return res.negotiate(err);
    if (!currentUser) return res.notFound();

    Tutorial.findOne({                          ◁──  Finds the tutorial
      id: +req.param('id')                            being rated
    })
    .populate('owner')
    .exec(function(err, foundTutorial){
      if (err) return res.negotiate(err);
      if (!foundTutorial) return res.notFound();
                                                          ◁── Prevents a rating if the
      if (currentUser.id === foundTutorial.owner.id) {        currently authenticated
        return res.forbidden();                              user-agent created the
      }                                                      tutorial

      Rating.findOne({                          ◁──  Finds a rating, if any, of the
        byUser: currentUser.id,                        currently authenticated
        byTutorial: foundTutorial.id                   user-agent
      }).exec(function(err, foundRating){
        if (err) return res.negotiate(err);
```

You'll first query for the currently logged-in user-agent, the tutorial being rated, and any rating by the currently logged-in user-agent for this tutorial. Notice that you don't use the `Rating.find()` model method and then iterate through the array of dictionaries to find a matching rating. Instead, you use an `IN` query that specifies multiple criteria in the query. This eliminates the need for iterating through returned ratings results from the query. If a rating exists, you'll update the existing rating in Sublime with the following code.

Listing 13.5   Implementing the `rateTutorial` action—updating an existing rating

```
...
if (foundRating) {                          Updates the existing
                                            rating with the new
  Rating.update({                           rating
    id: foundRating.id
  }, {
    stars: req.param('stars')
  }).exec(function(err, updatedRating){
    if (err) return res.negotiate(err);
    if (!updatedRating) return res.notFound();

    Tutorial.findOne({                      Queries the current tutorial for
      id: req.param('id')                   all ratings using .populate()
    })
    .populate('ratings')
    .exec(function(err, foundTutorialAfterUpdate){
      if (err) return res.negotiate(err);
      if (!foundTutorialAfterUpdate) return res.notFound();

      var sumTutorialRatings = 0;           Iterates
                                            through
      _.each(foundTutorialAfterUpdate.ratings, function(rating){   each rating

        sumTutorialRatings = sumTutorialRatings + rating.stars;
      });
                                            Adds up all the ratings

      foundTutorialAfterUpdate.averageRating =
        Math.floor(sumTutorialRatings /
        foundTutorialAfterUpdate.ratings.length);   Calculates
                                                     the average

      return res.json({
        averageRating: foundTutorialAfterUpdate.averageRating
      });                                   Responds with
    });                                     the average as
  });                                       JSON
});
...
```

You'll update the individual number of stars in the `rating` model. Because the average number of stars is calculated and not stored, you need to first get all the ratings for the tutorial and then calculate the average by iterating over them. Next, if no rating exists, you'll create a new one in Sublime with the following code.

Listing 13.6   Implementing the `rateTutorial` action—creating a new rating

```
...
} else {                                    Creates the
  Rating.create({                           new rating
    stars: req.param('stars'),
    byUser: currentUser.id,
    byTutorial: foundTutorial.id
  }).exec(function(err, createdRating){
    if (err) return res.negotiate(err);
    if (!createdRating) return res.notFound();
```

```
Tutorial.findOne({                          ← ⌐ Queries for the current tutorial
  id: req.param('id')                          populating the rating's attribute
})
.populate('ratings')
.exec(function(err, foundTutorialAfterUpdate){
  if (err) return res.negotiate(err);
  if (!foundTutorialAfterUpdate) return res.notFound();
                                                              Iterates
  var sumTutorialRatings = 0;                                 through
                                                              each rating
  _.each(foundTutorialAfterUpdate.ratings, function(rating){ ← ⌐

    sumTutorialRatings = sumTutorialRatings + rating.stars;
  });

  foundTutorial.averageRating = sumTutorialRatings /        ⌐ Calculates
  ➡ foundTutorialAfterUpdate.ratings.length;                ← the average

  return res.json({                          ← ⌐ Responds with the
    averageRating: foundTutorial.averageRating    average as JSON
  });
  ...
```

Adds up all the ratings ⌐▷

You've now repeated the calculation of the average rating code in three different places. Let's refactor the averaging code to a service that can be executed from multiple places. In Sublime, create a new file at brushfire/api/services/MathService.js, and add the following code.

Listing 13.7 The `MathService`

```
module.exports = {

  calculateAverage: function (options) {

    var sumTutorialRatings = 0;

    _.each(options.ratings, function(rating){
      sumTutorialRatings = sumTutorialRatings + rating.stars;
    });

    var averageRating = sumTutorialRatings / options.ratings.length;

    return averageRating;
  }
};
```

Refactoring the `rateTutorial` action code to execute the service is simple. In Sublime, open brushfire/api/controllers/TutorialController.js, and replace the code that does the averaging (in two places) with the service in the `rateTutorial` action, similar to the next listing.

Listing 13.8 The refactored `rateTutorial` action

```
...
return res.json({
  averageRating: MathService.calculateAverage({ratings:
```

```
➥ foundTutorialAfterUpdate.ratings})
});
...
```

Let's also update the `tutorialDetail` action of the page controller to take advantage of the service. In Sublime, open brushfire/api/controllers/PageController.js, and exchange the following service for the existing averaging code, similar to this.

> **Listing 13.9**   **The `tutorialDetail` action after refactoring**

```
...
if (foundTutorial.ratings.length === 0) {
  foundTutorial.averageRating = null;
} else {

  foundTutorial.averageRating =
  ➥ MathService.calculateAverage({ratings: foundTutorial.ratings});
}
...
```

13.3   *Implementing videos*

Before you can move on to building features like followers and search, you need to finish the last set of tasks left over from the pivot. Now that you're a master of associations, this will be a breeze!

You still need to implement the video functionality to Brushfire. Recall that a tutorial can contain YouTube video links. Figure 13.3 depicts the association between the

```
         ┌─────────────────┐                    ┌─────────────────┐
         │ tutorial model  │                    │   video model   │
         └─────────────────┘                    └─────────────────┘
┌─────────────────────────────┐      ┌─────────────────────────────┐
│ module.exports = {          │      │ module.exports = {          │
│   attributes: {             │      │   attributes: {             │
│     ...                     │      │     title: {                │
│                             │      │       type: 'string'        │
│     ratings: {              │      │     },                      │
│       collection: 'rating', │      │                             │
│       via: 'byTutorial'     │      │     src: {                  │
│     },                      │      │       type: 'string'        │
│                             │      │     },                      │
│     videos: {               │      │                             │
│  ❶    collection: 'video',  │      │     lengthInSeconds: {      │
│       via: 'tutorialAssoc'  │      │       type: 'integer'       │
│     }                       │      │     },                      │
│                             │      │                             │
│     ...                     │      │     tutorialAssoc: {        │
│                             │      │  ❷    model: 'tutorial'     │
│                             │      │     }                       │
│                             │      │   }                         │
│                             │      │ }                           │
└─────────────────────────────┘      └─────────────────────────────┘
```

Figure 13.3   **The `tutorial` model has a `videos` association attribute ❶ configured as a collection with the `video` model that uses `via`. The `video` model has a `tutorialAssoc` association attribute ❷ configured as a model with the `tutorial` model.**

video and tutorial model associations that are similar to the configuration you set up between the user and tutorial models.

A tutorial record can have multiple videos, and a video record can have one tutorial.

13.3.1 The Create-video form

The create-video page is currently using a simulated dictionary you added when you cloned the project in chapter 11. This simulated dictionary also contains the title, description, owner, id, created, totalTime, and stars attributes in the format the frontend expects. In this section, you'll replace the simulated dictionary with a combination of queries and transformations to achieve the simulated results with real data. Let's look at the wireframe for the attributes you need to retrieve and format for the create-video page in figure 13.4.

Figure 13.4 The create-video page displays attributes from the user, tutorial, and rating models.

Similar to the tutorial-detail page, the create-video page needs attributes from all four models. You'll transform, calculate, and format all the values for dictionary properties similar to figure 13.5.

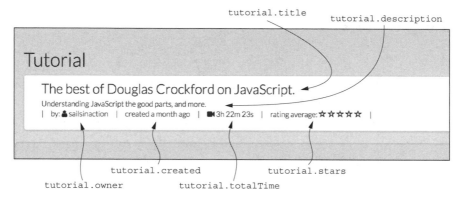

Figure 13.5　The frontend expects these attribute formats in the create-video page.

To get started, open brushfire/api/controllers/PageController.js in Sublime, and add the following code to the newVideo action.

Listing 13.10　The initial queries of the `newVideo` action

```
...
newVideo: function(req, res) {

  Tutorial.findOne({
    id: +req.param('id')
  })
  .populate('owner')         Populates owner,
  .populate('ratings')       ratings, and videos
  .populate('videos')        for the tutorial
  .exec(function (err, foundTutorial){
    if (err) return res.negotiate(err);
    if (!foundTutorial) return res.notFound();

    User.findOne({
      id: req.session.userId
    }).exec(function (err, foundUser) {
      if (err) {
        return res.negotiate(err);
      }

      if (!foundUser) {
        sails.log.verbose('Session refers to a user who no longer
        ➥ exists.');
        return res.redirect('/');
      }
```

Next, you'll use your previously created `MathService` to format the `createdAt` date and calculate the average rating. In Sublime, add the following code.

Listing 13.11 Formatting the `createdAt` date and calculating the average rating

```
...
if (foundUser.username !== foundTutorial.owner.username) {

  return res.redirect('/tutorials/'+foundTutorial.id);
}

foundTutorial.created = DatetimeService.getTimeAgo({date:
➥ foundTutorial.createdAt});

if (foundTutorial.ratings.length === 0) {
  foundTutorial.averageRating = null;
} else {

  foundTutorial.stars = MathService.calculateAverage({ratings:
➥ foundTutorial.ratings});
}
  ...
```

> Notice that you use a stars attribute and not averageRating

Similar to the way you're calculating the average rating, you'll calculate the `totalTime` attribute in the action. The Brushfire API Reference indicates that the `totalTime` attribute is the total length of all videos. There's a variety of ways you could store and calculate this value. You're opting to store the total `lengthInSeconds` of each video as an attribute of the `video` model. You'll then use that attribute to calculate and later format the various video length formatting requirements of the frontend. Because you need to do the calculation and formatting in more than three Brushfire locations, you already added the method `getHoursMinutesSeconds` to the existing `DateTimeService`. Take a look by opening brushfire/api/services/DateTimeService.js in Sublime, which should yield code similar to the following listing.

Listing 13.12 The `getHoursMinutesSeconds` method of the `DateTimeService`

```
...
getHoursMinutesSeconds: function(options) {

  var hours = Math.floor(options.totalSeconds/ 60 / 60);
  var minutes = Math.floor(options.totalSeconds / 60 % 60);
  var seconds = options.totalSeconds % 60;

  var hoursMinutesSeconds = hours + 'h ' + minutes + 'm ' + seconds + 's ';

  return {
    hoursMinutesSeconds: hoursMinutesSeconds,
    hours: hours,
    minutes: minutes,
    seconds: seconds
  };
}
};
```

Annotations:
- Passes totalSeconds via an options dictionary
- Transforms totalSeconds into hours, minutes, and seconds
- Returns formatted hours-Minutes-Seconds
- Formats totalSeconds into 1h 2m 3s format
- Returns hours, minutes, seconds

Now that you have the service, let's use it to complete the `newVideo` action. In Sublime, open brushfire/api/controllers/PageController.js, and add the following code.

Listing 13.13 Using `getHoursMinutesSeconds` to calculate `totalTime`

```
...
var totalSeconds = 0;                                    ◁── Iterates through each
_.each(foundTutorial.videos, function(video){               video in the tutorial

  totalSeconds = totalSeconds + video.lengthInSeconds;   ◁── Keeps a running
                                                             total of the
  foundTutorial.totalTime =                                  lengthInSeconds
  ➥ DatetimeService.getHoursMinutesSeconds({totalSeconds:
  ➥ totalSeconds}).hoursMinutesSeconds;                 ◁──
});                                                          Sends the totalSeconds
return res.view('tutorials-detail-video-new', {             dictionary as an argument
  me: {                                                      to the service to get the
    username: user.username,                                hoursMinutesSeconds
    gravatarURL: user.gravatarURL,                          property
    admin: user.admin
  },
  tutorial: {
    id: foundTutorial.id,
    title: foundTutorial.title,
    description: foundTutorial.description,
    owner: foundTutorial.owner.username,
    created: foundTutorial.created,
    totalTime: foundTutorial.totalTime,
    stars: foundTutorial.stars
  }
  });
  });
  });
},
```

Renders the view with the appropriate locals → `return res.view('tutorials-detail-video-new', {`

You'll also need that same bit of code in the tutorials-detail page. In Sublime, open brushfire/api/controllers/PageController.js, and add the following code to the `tutorialDetail` action.

Listing 13.14 Calculating the tutorial length in the `tutorialDetail` action

```
...
foundTutorial.averageRating =
➥ MathService.calculateAverage({ratings: foundTutorial.ratings})
}

var totalSeconds = 0;
_.each(foundTutorial.videos, function(video){

  totalSeconds = totalSeconds + video.lengthInSeconds;

  video.totalTime =
  ➥ DatetimeService.getHoursMinutesSeconds({totalSeconds:
  ➥ video.lengthInSeconds}).hoursMinutesSeconds;
```

```
foundTutorial.totalTime =
➥ DatetimeService.getHoursMinutesSeconds({totalSeconds:
➥ totalSeconds}).hoursMinutesSeconds;
});
...
```

You might be wondering how the total was calculated when you haven't created any videos yet: bootstrap created tutorials and videos including `lengthInSeconds` as well as a `rating`. Next, let's move to actually adding a video with its attributes.

13.3.2 Review: adding a record to a collection association

Adding a video to the model is easy. First, look at the create-video page attributes in figure 13.6.

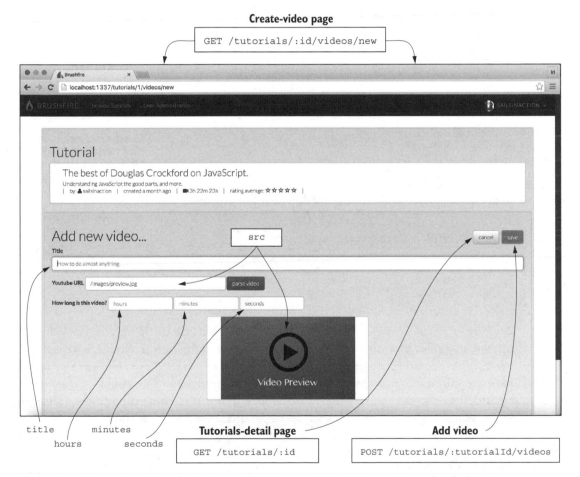

Figure 13.6 The create-video page has some properties you'll store in the `video` model, like `title` and `src`, and some properties that you'll use to calculate the `lengthInSeconds` on the backend, like `hours`, `minutes`, and `seconds`.

In Sublime, open brushfire/api/controllers/TutorialController.js, and add the following code to the `addVideo` action.

Listing 13.15   Creating a `video` record

```
...
addVideo: function(req, res) {

  if (!_.isNumber(req.param('hours')) || !_.isNumber(req.param('minutes')) ||
      !_.isNumber(req.param('seconds'))) {
    return res.badRequest();
  }
  if (!_.isString(req.param('src')) || !_.isString(req.param('title'))) {
    return res.badRequest();
  }

  Tutorial.findOne({
    id: +req.param('tutorialId')
  })
  .populate('owner')
  .exec(function(err, foundTutorial){
    if (err) return res.negotiate(err);
    if (!foundTutorial) return res.notFound();

    if (foundTutorial.owner.id !== req.session.userId) {
      return res.forbidden();
    }

    Video.create({
      tutorialAssoc: foundTutorial.id,
      title: req.param('title'),
      src: req.param('src'),
      lengthInSeconds: req.param('hours') * 60 * 60 +
        req.param('minutes') * 60 + req.param('seconds')
    }).exec(function (err, createdVideo) {
      if (err) return res.negotiate(err);

      return res.ok();
    });
  });
},
```

Validates incoming parameters as a backup to the frontend validation → (points to the two `if` validation blocks)

Finds the tutorial that will contain the video → (points to `Tutorial.findOne`)

Checks if the current user is the owner of the tutorial → (points to the owner check)

Creates the video using the incoming parameters → (points to `Video.create`)

Associates the video to the tutorial by setting the tutorialAssoc attribute to the tutorial id → (points to `tutorialAssoc: foundTutorial.id`)

Converts hours, minutes, and seconds into lengthInSeconds → (points to `lengthInSeconds`)

Because you use a `collection` association with the `via` property, you need only update the reference to the record in one place. The easiest choice is to set the `tutorialAssoc` attribute of the `video` model to the current `tutorial` id. You could have used the `.add()` method within the `tutorial` model, but this would have required an added step to execute `.save()`. Also, notice that you're converting hours, minutes, and seconds of the `video` into total seconds and then assigning the total seconds to `lengthInSeconds`.

13.3.3   *Editing video details*

Updating a video uses very similar code to creating a video. We suggest you review the requirements in the Brushfire API Reference under "Edit video page" and "Edit video metadata." To implement the edit-video page endpoint, open brushfire/api/control-lers/PageController.js in Sublime, and add the code to the editVideo action from this gist: http://mng.bz/m828. To implement the edit-video metadata endpoint, open brushfire/api/controllers/TutorialController.js in Sublime, and add the code to the updateVideo action from this gist: http://mng.bz/tB0B.

13.3.4 Managing the sort order of videos using an embedded array

In chapter 12, we pointed out that although issues exist when embedding records to create relationships between models, there are situations where embedding a value or group of values would be advantageous in a model. In fact, embedded values or groups of values work as long as the embedded value doesn't need to be queried outside the context of the model where it's embedded. Managing the sort order of videos in tutorial records is a good example of using an embedded array in a model. First, you added a videoOrder attribute as JSON to the video model similar to the following listing.

> **Listing 13.16   Configuring the `videoOrder` attribute in the model**

```
...
videoOrder: {
  type: 'json'
},
...
```

You want to be able to add videos to a tutorial and then reorder the videos up and down. The createTutorial, addVideo, tutorialDetail, reorderVideoUp, and reorder-VideoDown endpoints are affected by managing the video sort order. You'll use the embedded array to cache the sort order of video ids. The sorting process will include the tasks in table 13.1.

Table 13.1   Tasks related to the video order

Action	Task
createTutorial	When a tutorial is created, set the videoOrder property to an empty array.
addVideo	When a video is created, push the video id to the videoOrder embedded array.
tutorialDetail	When the tutorials-detail page is rendered, use the videoOrder embedded array to sort the videos.
reorderVideoUp	When the up arrow is clicked, move the video id up one element in the array.
reorderVideoDown	When the down arrow is clicked, move the video id down one element in the array.

Let's implement each of these tasks. First is the createTutorial action of the tutorial controller. In Sublime, open brushfire/api/controllers/TutorialController.js, and set the videoOrder property to an empty array in the createTutorial action, similar to this.

Listing 13.17   Setting the `videoOrder` property in the `createTutorial` action

```
...
Tutorial.create({
  title: req.param('title'),
  description: req.param('description'),     ┐  Sets the videoOrder
  owner: foundUser.id,                       │  property to an
  videoOrder: [],                         ◄──┘  empty array
})
.exec(function(err, createdTutorial){
  if (err) return res.negotiate(err);
        ...
```

Next, you'll add the video id to the tutorial.videoOrder array when a new video is created. Head back to brushfire/api/controllers/TutorialController.js in Sublime, and add the following code.

Listing 13.18   Adding a video `id` to the `tutorial.videoOrder` array

```
...
Video.create({
  tutorialAssoc: foundTutorial.id,
  title: req.param('title'),
  src: req.param('src'),
  lengthInSeconds: req.param('hours') * 60 * 60 +
  ➥ req.param('minutes') * 60 + req.param('seconds')
}).exec(function (err, createdVideo) {
  if (err) return res.negotiate(err);                        Pushes the video id
                                                             to the videoOrder
  foundTutorial.videoOrder.push(createdVideo.id);    ◄───    array

  foundTutorial.save(function (err){
    if (err) return res.negotiate(err);
  ...
```

Now that you've added the video id to the array, you'll use it to calculate the sort order when the tutorial detail page is rendered. In Sublime, open brushfire/api/controllers/PageController.js, and add the following code to the tutorialDetail action.

Listing 13.19   Adding the sorting code to the `tutorialDetail` action

```
                                              Uses _.sortBy to iterate over the videos
                                                   and sort by whatever is returned
...
foundTutorial.videos = _.sortBy(foundTutorial.videos, function
➥ getRank (video) {

  return _.indexOf(foundTutorial.videoOrder,video.id);   ◄──  Returns the index of
});                                                            the video id in the
                                                              videoOrder array
```

Here's how it works. Let's say tutorial.videoOrder has three video ids, [4, 3, 5], and tutorial.videos is [{id: 5}, {id: 4}, {id: 3}]. After iterating through _.sortBy, the tutorial.videos array is transformed into [{id: 4}, {id: 3}, {id: 5}]. Now, let's enable the user to reorder the videos from the tutorials-detail page. When a tutorial contains more than one video, the user can click an up or down arrow to adjust the sort order, similar to figure 13.7.

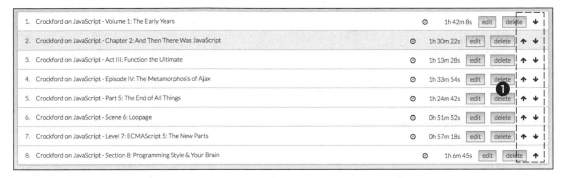

1. Crockford on JavaScript - Volume 1: The Early Years	⊘ 1h 42m 8s	edit delete	↓
2. Crockford on JavaScript - Chapter 2: And Then There Was JavaScript	⊘ 1h 30m 22s	edit delete	↑ ↓
3. Crockford on JavaScript - Act III: Function the Ultimate	⊘ 1h 13m 28s	edit delete	↑ ↓
4. Crockford on JavaScript - Episode IV: The Metamorphosis of Ajax	⊘ 1h 33m 54s	edit delete	↑ ↓
5. Crockford on JavaScript - Part 5: The End of All Things	⊘ 1h 24m 42s	edit delete	↑ ↓
6. Crockford on JavaScript - Scene 6: Loopage	⊘ 0h 51m 52s	edit delete	↑ ↓
7. Crockford on JavaScript - Level 7: ECMAScript 5: The New Parts	⊘ 0h 57m 18s	edit delete	↑ ↓
8. Crockford on JavaScript - Section 8: Programming Style & Your Brain	⊘ 1h 6m 45s	edit delete	↑

Figure 13.7 Users can reorder the videos using the up and down sort order buttons ❶.

Let's enable the up button first. In Sublime, open brushfire/api/controllers/video/VideoController.js, and add the following code to the reorderVideoUp action.

Listing 13.20 Moving a video up in the sort order

```
...
reorderVideoUp: function(req, res) {          ← Finds the video you're sorting

  Video.findOne({
    id: +req.param('id')
  })
  .populate('tutorialAssoc')          ← Populates the tutorial that's associated with the video
  .exec(function(err, video){
    if (err) return res.negotiate(err);
    if (!foundVideo) return res.notFound();

    if (req.session.userId !== foundVideo.tutorialAssoc.owner) {   ← Ensures that the currently authenticated user-agent owns the tutorial
      return res.forbidden();
    }

    var indexOfVideo = _.indexOf(video.tutorialAssoc.videoOrder,   ← Finds the index of the video id in the embedded videoOrder array
      ➥ +req.param('id'));

    if (indexOfVideo === 0) {          ← If the index is 0, it's already at the top of the list.
      return res.badRequest('This video is already at the top of the
        ➥ list.');
    }

    video.tutorialAssoc.videoOrder.splice(indexOfVideo, 1);   ← Removes the video id from the videoOrder array
```

```
    video.tutorialAssoc.videoOrder.splice(indexOfVideo-1, 0,
➥    +req.param('id'));

    video.tutorialAssoc.save(function (err) {
      if (err) return res.negotiate(err);
      return res.ok();
    });
  });
},
...
```

Moves the video id up in order by splicing it into the videoOrder array using indexOfVideo-1

Saves the changes to the tutorial using the tutorialAssoc association

You'll use similar code to move a video down in the sort order. Return to brushfire/api/controllers/video/VideoController.js, and add the following code to the reorderVideoDown action.

Listing 13.21   Moving a video down in the sort order

```
...
reorderVideoDown: function(req, res) {

  Video.findOne({
    id: +req.param('id')
  })
  .populate('tutorialAssoc')
  .exec(function (err, foundVideo){
    if (err) return res.negotiate(err);
    if (!foundVideo) return res.notFound();

    if (req.session.userId !== foundVideo.tutorialAssoc.owner) {
      return res.forbidden();
    }

    var indexOfVideo = _.indexOf(foundVideo.tutorialAssoc.videoOrder,
➥    +req.param('id'));

    var numberOfTutorials = foundVideo.tutorialAssoc.videoOrder.length;

    if (indexOfVideo === numberOfTutorials) {
      return res.badRequest('This video is already at the bottom of the
➥    list.');
    }

    foundVideo.tutorialAssoc.videoOrder.splice(indexOfVideo, 1);

    foundVideo.tutorialAssoc.videoOrder.splice(indexOfVideo+1, 0,
➥    +req.param('id'));

    foundVideo.tutorialAssoc.save(function (err) {
      if (err) return res.negotiate(err);
      return res.ok();
    });
  });
}
...
```

If the current index of the video id is at the end of the videoOrder array, responds with a badRequest()

Assigns the length of the videoOrder array to numberOf-Tutorials

Moves the video id down in order by splicing it into the videoOrder array using indexOfVideo+1

13.3.5 *Integrating a video player*

Each video is displayed in a list on the tutorials-detail page. When the user selects a video, the video player page will be displayed, similar to figure 13.8. Let's implement this.

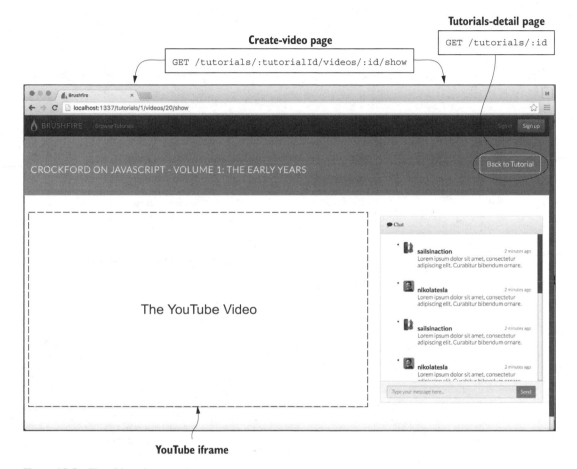

Figure 13.8   The video player page

The video player contains the YouTube video in an iframe, a Back button to the tutorial, and a chat interface that you'll implement in chapter 14. The API Reference reveals the endpoint has two incoming parameters, `tutorialID` and the `id` of the `video` record, as well as an authenticated response and an unauthenticated response. In Sublime, open brushfire/api/controller/PageController.js, and add the following code to the `showVideo` action.

Listing 13.22   Implementing the `showVideo` endpoint

```
...
showVideo: function(req, res) {

  FAKE_CHAT = [{
    username: 'sailsinaction',
    message: 'Lorem ipsum dolor sit amet, consectetur adipiscing elit.
    ➥ Curabitur bibendum ornare.',
    created: '2 minutes ago',
    gravatarURL:
    ➥ 'http://www.gravatar.com/avatar/ef3eac6c71fdf24b13db12d8ff8d1264'
  }]

  Video.findOne({                              ◁────┐   Finds the
    id: +req.param('id')                              │   video to play
  }).exec(function (err, foundVideo){

    if (!req.session.userId) {                 ◁──┐
      return res.view('show-video', {              │
        me: null,                                  │   If the user isn't
        video: foundVideo,                         │   authenticated,
        tutorialId: req.param('tutorialId')        │   returns locals for the
      });                                          │   unauthenticated state
    }                                              │

    User.findOne({                             ◁──┘
      id: +req.session.userId
    }).exec(function (err, foundUser) {
      if (err) {
        return res.negotiate(err);
      }

      if (!foundUser) {
        sails.log.verbose('Session refers to a user who no longer
        ➥ exists');
      }

      return res.view('show-video', {          ◁──┐   Finds the currently
        me: {                                      │   authenticated user and
          username: foundUser.username,            │   return locals for the
          gravatarURL: foundUser.gravatarURL,      │   authenticated state
          admin: foundUser.admin
        },
        video: foundVideo,
        tutorialId: req.param('tutorialId')
      });
    });
  });
}
```

13.3.6 Cascading delete

When a tutorial is deleted, it's important to also remove any associated videos and ratings. In Sublime, open brushfire/api/controllers/TutorialController.js, and add the following code to the `deleteTutorial` action.

Listing 13.23 Deleting a tutorial in the `deleteTutorial` action

```
...
deleteTutorial: function(req, res) {          Finds the currently
  User.findOne({                              authenticated user-agent
    id: req.session.userId
  }).exec(function (err, foundUser){
    if (err) return res.negotiate(err);       Finds the
    if (!foundUser) return res.notFound();    requested
                                              tutorial
    Tutorial.findOne({
      id: +req.param('id')
    })
    .populate('owner')                        Populates the owner,
    .populate ('ratings')                     ratings, and videos
    .populate('videos')                       associations
    .exec(function(err, foundTutorial){
      if (err) return res.negotiate(err);                    Ensures that the
      if (!foundTutorial) return res.notFound();             current user is the
                                                             owner of the tutorial
      if (foundUser.id != foundTutorial.owner.id) {
        return res.forbidden();
      }
      Tutorial.destroy({                      Destroys
        id: req.param('id')                   the tutorial
      }).exec(function(err){
        if (err) return res.negotiate(err);

        Video.destroy({                            Uses _.pluck to build up an
          id: _.pluck(foundTutorial.videos, 'id')  array of videos to destroy
        }).exec(function (err){
          if (err) return res.negotiate(err);

          Rating.destroy({                            Uses _.pluck to build up an
            id: _.pluck(foundTutorial.ratings, 'id')  array of ratings to destroy
          }).exec(function (err){
            if (err) return res.negotiate(err);

            return res.json({username: foundUser.username});
          });
        });
      });
    });
  });
},
```

After retrieving the tutorial and populating the `owner`, `ratings`, and `videos` associations, you'll use the `.pluck()` method to return an array of video and rating `ids`. You'll then use those arrays to destroy the associated records.

13.3.7 *Removing a record from a collection*

You also need to enable the frontend request to delete a video. In Sublime, open brushfire/api/controllers/TutorialController.js, and add the following code to the removeVideo action.

Listing 13.24   Deleting a video in the `removeVideo` action

```
...
removeVideo: function(req, res) {

  Tutorial.findOne({                          Finds the tutorial
    id: +req.param('tutorialId')              that contains the
  })                                          video to delete
  .exec(function (err, foundTutorial){
    if (err) return res.negotiate(err);       Ensures that the currently
    if (!foundTutorial) return res.notFound();  authenticated user is the
                                              tutorial owner
    if (req.session.userId !== foundTutorial.owner) {
      return res.forbidden();
    }                                         Removes the video from
                                              the video's association
    foundTutorial.videos.remove(+req.param('id'));   attribute

    foundTutorial.videoOrder = _.without(foundTutorial.videoOrder,
      +req.param('id'));                      Removes the video id from
                                              the tutorial.video attribute
    foundTutorial.save(function (err){        using the _.without() method
      if (err) return res.negotiate(err);

      Video.destroy({                         Destroys the video
        id: +req.param('id')                  in the video model
      }).exec(function(err){
        if (err) return res.negotiate(err);   Saves the changes to
                                              the foundTutorial
        return res.ok();
      });
    });
  });
},
...
```

13.4   *Implementing support for followers*

Part of the Brushfire post-pivot feature requests was to give users the ability to follow other users and the tutorials they created. Therefore, you need a way to associate users with each other. Sails makes it simple to configure this type of relationship. In the user model, you already created two association attributes, `followers` and `following`, from the repo you originally cloned in chapter 11. Take a look at the model configuration in Sublime by opening brushfire/api/models/User.js, similar to the following listing.

Listing 13.25   Configured followers and following attributes in the `user` model

```
...
// Who is following me?
followers: {
  collection: 'user',
  via: 'following'
},
```

```
// Who am I following?
following: {
  collection: 'user',
  via: 'followers'
},
...
```

That's it. The user model now has attributes that will track followers and following users. The two association attributes point to each other as a collection using the via parameter.

13.4.1 *The follow and unfollow endpoints*

An authenticated user-agent may follow or unfollow a user by clicking the Follow Me or Unfollow Me button, as illustrated in figure 13.9.

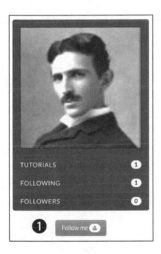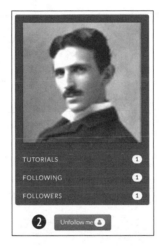

Figure 13.9 The Follow Me ❶ and Unfollow Me ❷ buttons on the user profile toggle whether the user is following another user.

The follow action was added to the assets of the project you cloned back in chapter 11. Let's take a look. In Sublime, open brushfire/api/controllers/UserController.js, and review the follow action code, which is similar to the next listing.

Listing 13.26 Reviewing the follow action of the user controller

```
...
follow: function(req, res) {               Finds the owner
  User.findOne({                            of the profile
    username: req.param('username'),
  })
  .populate('followers')          Populates the user's followers and
  .populate('following')          following association attributes
  .exec(function (err, foundUser){
    if (err) return res.negotiate(err);
    if (!foundUser) return res.notFound();
```

```
        if (foundUser.id === req.session.userId) {
            return res.forbidden();
        }
```
                                                        Ensures that the authenticated
                                                        user is not the current profile

```
        foundUser.followers.add(req.session.userId);
        foundUser.save(function (err, updatedUser){
            if (err) return res.negotiate(err);
            if (!updatedUser) return res.notFound();

            return res.json({
                numOfFollowers: updatedUser.followers.length,
                numOfFollowing: updatedUser.following.length,
                followers: updatedUser.followers,
                following: updatedUser.following
            });
        });
    });
},
```

Saves the changes to the profile owner

Adds the currently authenticated user's id to the profile owner's followers attribute

Responds with the number of followers and following, as well as their arrays of user dictionaries

When an authenticated user clicks the Follow Me button, their user `id` is added to the profile owner's `following` attribute. Later, when you populate the profile owner's `following` attribute, you get an array of dictionaries of users who are following this profile owner. The `unfollow` input is identical except you use the `.remove()` method instead of the `.add()` method.

13.4.2 Displaying a user's followers on their profile

The follower/following relationship is manifest in the three `user` profile page configurations—tutorial, following, and followers—similar to figure 13.10.

Let's first implement the profile page with tutorials. In Sublime, open brushfire/api/controllers/PageController.js, and add the following code to the `profile` action.

> **Listing 13.27   Initial queries for the `user` profile page with tutorials**

```
...
profile: function(req, res) {
    User.findOne({
        username: req.param('username')
    })
    .populate("followers")
    .populate("following")
    .exec(function (err, foundUser){
        if (err) return res.negotiate(err);
        if (!foundUser) return res.notFound();

        Tutorial.find({where: {
            owner: foundUser.id
        }, sort: 'title ASC'})
        .populate('ratings')
        .populate('videos')
        .exec(function (err, foundTutorials){
            if (err) return res.negotiate(err);
            if (!foundTutorials) return res.notFound();
            ...
```

Finds the owner of the profile

Populates the user's following and follow association attributes

Finds all the tutorials for the profile owner and sorts in ascending order

Populates the tutorial's ratings and videos association attributes

authenticated   unauthenticated

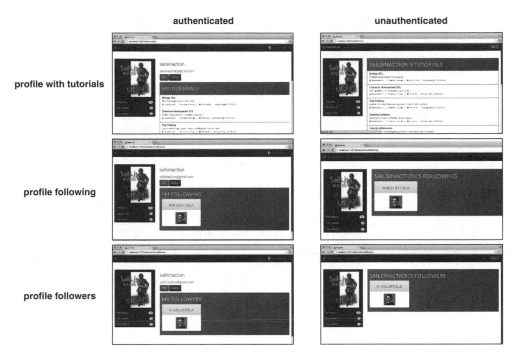

profile with tutorials

profile following

profile followers

Figure 13.10   The three profile page configurations in authenticated and unauthenticated states

NOTE If you're adding the code via the online gist, listings 13.27, 13.28, 13.29, and 13.30 are excerpts of the same gist.

Notice that you're using where and sort in the query criteria. It's a best practice to use the where clause any time you want to also include query options sort, limit, and/or skip. If the where clause is excluded, the entire dictionary is treated as where criteria. After completing the initial queries, you'll iterate through each tutorial, making transformations similar to those you made in previous actions. Head back to Sublime, and add the code in the next listing.

Listing 13.28   Transforming each tutorial's attributes

```
...
_.each(foundTutorials, function(tutorial){          Assigns the user
                                                    dictionary of the profile
  tutorial.owner = foundUser.username;          ◁── owner to tutorial.owner

  tutorial.created = DatetimeService.getTimeAgo({date:    Formats the created date
➥ tutorial.createdAt});                              ◁── using the DatetimeService

  var totalSeconds = 0;                             Iterates over the
  _.each(tutorial.videos, function(video){       ◁── tutorial's videos
```

Iterates over the profile owner's tutorials → `_.each(foundTutorials, function(tutorial){`

```
    totalSeconds = totalSeconds + video.lengthInSeconds;        ◁   Adds up the total
                                                                    number of seconds
    tutorial.totalTime =                                            for all videos
    ➥ DatetimeService.getHoursMinutesSeconds({totalSeconds:
    ➥ totalSeconds}).hoursMinutesSeconds;                 ◁
  });
                                                               Formats the totalTime
                                                               attribute with the
                                                               DatetimeService
  var totalRating = 0;
  _.each(tutorial.ratings, function(rating){              ◁
    totalRating = totalRating + rating.stars;
  });                                                        Iterates over the
                                                             tutorial's ratings

  var averageRating = 0;
  if (tutorial.ratings.length < 1) {      │  If no ratings, assigns
    averageRating = 0;                    │  averageRating equal to 0
  } else {
    averageRating = totalRating / tutorial.ratings.length;   ◁
  }                                                            Calculates the average
                                                               for averageRating

  tutorial.averageRating = averageRating;      ◁   Assigns the average to
});                                                tutorial.averageRating
...
```

If the user isn't authenticated, you'll send back counts for the profile owner's followers, following, and tutorials as well as an array of tutorial dictionaries. From Sublime, add the code in this listing.

Listing 13.29   Responding to the unauthenticated state of the `profile` endpoint

```
...
if (!req.session.userId) {

  return res.view('profile', {
    me: null,
    username: foundUser.username,
    gravatarURL: foundUser.gravatarURL,
    frontEnd: {
      numOfTutorials: foundTutorials.length,
      numOfFollowers: foundUser.followers.length,
      numOfFollowing: foundUser.following.length
    },

    tutorials: foundTutorials
  });
}
...
```

Finally, if the user-agent is authenticated, you'll respond with the owner's followers, following, and tutorials, as well as an array of tutorial dictionaries. In Sublime, add the following code.

Listing 13.30 Responding to the authenticated state of the `profile` endpoint

```
...
User.findOne({                              Finds the currently
  id: req.session.userId              ⟵    authenticated user
})
.exec(function (err, loggedInUser){
  if (err) {
    return res.negotiate(err);
  }

  if (!loggedInUser) {
    return res.serverError('User record from logged in user is
    ➥ missing?');
  }
                                                    Iterates over the profile
  var cachedFollower = _.find(foundUser.followers,  owner's followers to
  ➥ function(follower){                       ⟵    determine whether the
    return follower.id === loggedInUser.id;         current user is a follower
  });

  var followedByLoggedInUser = false;         If the currently authenticated user
  if (cachedFollower) {                   ⟵  is a follower of the profile owner, sets
    followedByLoggedInUser = true;            followedByLoggedInUser equal to true
  }

  var me = {                              ⟵   Provides locals for
    username: loggedInUser.username,          the navigation bar
    email: loggedInUser.email,
    gravatarURL: loggedInUser.gravatarURL,
    admin: loggedInUser.admin
  };

  if (req.session.userId === foundUser.id) {  ⟵   Checks to see if the
    me.isMe = true;                                current user is the
  } else {                                         authenticated owner
    me.isMe = false;
  }

  return res.view('profile', {            ⟵   Responds with the
    me: me,                                     necessary locals
    showAddTutorialButton: true,
    username: foundUser.username,
    gravatarURL: foundUser.gravatarURL,
    frontEnd: {
      numOfTutorials: foundTutorials.length,
      numOfFollowers: foundUser.followers.length,
      numOfFollowing: foundUser.following.length,
      followedByLoggedInUser: followedByLoggedInUser
    },
    tutorials: foundTutorials
  });
}); //</ User.findOne({id: req.session.userId})
  });
});
},
...
```

When the user-agent is authenticated, you'll find their user dictionary, which also contains their `id`. From there we'll look in the owner's followers to determine whether the user-agent is a follower—their user `id` is in the profile owner's follower's array. If it is, you set `followedByLoggedInUser` to `true`. You'll also check whether the user is the profile owner and set the `me.isMe` property accordingly.

There are two other `profile` actions: `profileFollower` and `profileFollowing`. These actions use code similar to the `profile` action, but they don't require the formatting of the tutorials. Replace the current `profileFollower` and `profileFollowing` actions from the following gist: http://mng.bz/94Ms. Once this is implemented, you'll have all three configurations of the profile page.

13.5 *Search*

Advanced search with support for indexing is beyond the scope of this book. But it's not that bad! For example, GitHub uses a special database called Elasticsearch to allow users to search code files, issues, and repos. You can integrate this technology in your own app in a matter of days or even hours. But here we'll show a simpler approach: instead of relying on a third-party tool, you'll simply use the ORM. Specifically, you'll support searching tutorials based on their `title` and/or `description`, similar to figure 13.11.

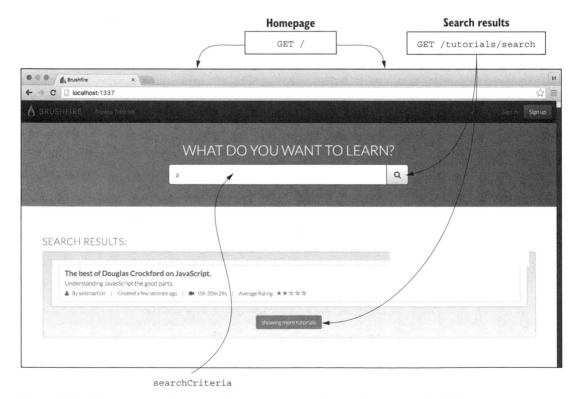

Figure 13.11 The search page has two different requests to the search-result endpoint that uses `searchCriteria` as an incoming parameter.

Both the Search and Search More Tutorials buttons trigger the `searchTutorials` action of the `TutorialController`. The `searchTutorials` action also uses the `limit` and `skip` query options to manage pagination.

13.5.1 Paginating search results

You want the search results to display a maximum of 10 results. Thereafter, you'll paginate in lots of 10 tutorials per page. In Sublime, open brushfire/api/controllers/TutorialController.js and, add the following code to the `searchTutorials` action.

Listing 13.31 Implementing the `searchTutorials` action—the search criteria

```
...
searchTutorials: function(req, res) {
  Tutorial.count().exec(function(err, found){          ⟵ Calculates the number of tutorials
    if (err) return res.negotiate(err);
    if (!found) return res.notFound();

    Tutorial.find({                                     ⟵ Finds all tutorials that contain the text of the searchCriteria in either the title or description attributes
      or : [
        {
          title: {
            'contains': req.param('searchCriteria')
          },
        },
        {
          description: {
            'contains': req.param('searchCriteria')
          }
        }
      ],
      limit: 10,                                         ⟵ Limits the number of responses to 10
      skip: req.param('skip')                            ⟵ Skips based on the incoming skip parameter
    })
    .populate('owner')                                   ⟵ Populates the owner, ratings, and videos association attributes
    .populate('ratings')
    .populate('videos')
    .exec(function(err, tutorials){
    ...
```

NOTE For details about other query options for `.find()`, `.findOne()`, `.create()`, `.update()`, `.destroy()`, `.findOrCreate`, or `.count()`, see http://mng.bz/lrxo.

Next, you'll format the results of the search. In Sublime, add the following code.

Listing 13.32 Implementing the `searchTutorials` action—formatting the search results

```
...
_.each(tutorials, function(tutorial){                   ⟵ Iterates through each tutorial and formats the owner and created attributes
  tutorial.owner = tutorial.owner.username;
  tutorial.created = DatetimeService.getTimeAgo({date:
  ➥ tutorial.createdAt});
```

```
                    // Determine the total seconds for all videos and each video
                    var totalSeconds = 0;
                    _.each(tutorial.videos, function(video){
```

Iterates through each video and calculates the totalTime and individual video length

```
                      // Total the number of seconds for all videos for tutorial
                      total time
                      totalSeconds = totalSeconds + video.lengthInSeconds;

                      tutorial.totalTime =
                      DatetimeService.getHoursMinutesSeconds({totalSeconds:
                      totalSeconds}).hoursMinutesSeconds;

                      // Format average ratings
                      var totalRating = 0;
                      _.each(tutorial.ratings, function(rating){
                        totalRating = totalRating + rating.stars;
                      });
```

Iterates through each rating and calculates the average rating

```
                      var averageRating = 0;
                      if (tutorial.ratings.length < 1) {
                        averageRating = 0;
                      } else {
                        averageRating = totalRating / tutorial.ratings.length;
                      }

                      tutorial.averageRating = averageRating;
                    });
                  });

                  return res.json({
                    options: {
                      totalTutorials: found,
                      updatedTutorials: tutorials
                    }
                  });
                });
              });
            },
```

13.5.2 *General pagination*

When the user clicks the Browse button on the navigation toolbar, you want to display a maximum of 10 tutorials on a page. Thereafter, you'll paginate in 10 tutorials per page. Figure 13.12 illustrates the tutorials for an initial browsing page.

The browseTutorials action is almost identical to the searchTutorials action except for the criteria in the .find() method. We've provided the source code for the browseTutorials action in the following gist: http://mng.bz/tGPS.

Figure 13.12 The browse-tutorial page contains a browse-results endpoint trigger by the Show More Tutorials button.

13.6 *Summary*

- The rating model uses a model association relationship to the user and tutorial models. The user and tutorial models use a collection association relationship with via to the rating model.
- As a general rule, code that's repeated in three different actions should be refactored into a service.
- Use an embedded array attribute to manage the sort order because the array won't be queried outside the tutorial model.
- A following/follower relationship can be created by adding two collection association attributes in the same model with via.

Realtime with WebSockets

14

This chapter covers

- Understanding WebSockets
- Using the Sails WebSocket client
- Implementing a chat system in Brushfire
- Incorporating resourceful pubsub into chat

Brushfire users want to communicate with each other about the videos they're watching. We'll satisfy this requirement by implementing a chat system where each video will have its own persistent chat room. Making the chat persistent, meaning storing the chats, will give users the flexibility to interact synchronously (at the same time) or asynchronously (leaving a question that can be answered later).

In this chapter, we'll differentiate WebSocket events from the HTTP request/response scheme we've used in prior chapters. We'll show Sails virtual request integration that makes WebSockets work like regular ol' requests but with access to the WebSocket via the `req` dictionary. With access to the user-agent's WebSocket, we'll introduce the concept of using rooms to organize those connected to the Sails WebSocket server and currently viewing a particular video. We'll enable user-agents to chat using lower-level methods like `sails.sockets.join()` and `sails.sockets.broadcast()` on the backend and `io.socket.on()` on the frontend. Next, we'll transition to Sails *resourceful pubsub* (RPS) methods, replacing `sails.sockets.join()` with `Video.subscribe()` and `sails.sockets.broadcast()` with `Video.publish-Update()` on the backend. Finally, we'll take a closer look at using resourceful pubsub with blueprint CRUD actions, which have added features regarding WebSockets. If that seems like a lot of material, don't worry. We'll take each topic step by step with examples. Let's get started.

14.1 Obtaining the example materials for this chapter

If you followed along in chapter 13 with an existing project, you can continue to use that project in this chapter. If you want to start from this chapter and move forward, clone the following repo: https://github.com/sailsinaction/brushfire-ch13-end. After cloning the repo, install the Node module dependencies via `npm install`. You'll also want to add the local.js file you created in chapter 11. In Sublime, copy and paste your local.js file you created in chapter 13, or create a new file in brushfire/config/local.js, and add the following code.

Listing 14.1 Adding to the local.js file

```
module.exports.blueprints = {
  shortcuts: true,
  prefix: '/bp',
};

module.exports.connections = {
  myPostgresqlServer: {
    adapter: 'sails-postgresql',
    host: 'localhost',
    database: 'brushfire'
  }
};

module.exports.mailgun =  {
  apiKey: 'ADD YOUR MAILGUN API KEY HERE',
  domain: 'ADD YOUR MAILGUN DOMAIN HERE',
  baseUrl: 'http://localhost:1337'
};
```

14.2 Understanding WebSockets

A WebSocket is an enhancement to HTTP and can run side by side with HTTP.

NOTE By making the process of connecting to a WebSocket server similar to an HTTP request, a WebSocket server can listen for both HTTP requests and WebSocket connection requests on the same port.

Unlike HTTP, once a client connects to the WebSocket server and establishes a WebSocket `id`, the server can send events to listening clients with a matching `id` and vice versa. This is in contrast to HTTP, where the client must first make a request, which briefly opens a connection, before the server can respond and close it. Once the server responds, the connection is closed and the server can no longer initiate communication with the client until another request is received. Figure 14.1 illustrates this important difference between HTTP and WebSockets communication.

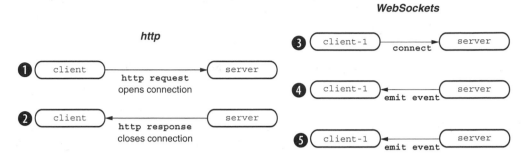

Figure 14.1   An HTTP request is necessary for a server to respond. The request ❶ creates an open connection between the client and server. Once the server ❷ responds, the connection is closed and another request is needed before the server can again respond to the client. With WebSockets, once a client makes a connection ❸, the server can send a message to it ❹, ❺ at any time so long as the connection remains open.

The Sails HTTP/WebSocket server is listening for both HTTP requests and upgraded WebSocket events.

> **DEFINITION**   Often you'll encounter the terms *events*, *messages*, and *notifications* used interchangeably with WebSockets. For clarity, we'll use the term *event* to specify the thing the Sails WebSocket server and client send to each other. Events can have names like `chat`, and their contents are referred to as the `message`.

After establishing a connection with the Sails server, the user-agent is given an `id`. Let's build an example that will demonstrate these concepts.

14.2.1   *Establishing a socket connection*

Overall, Sails uses WebSocket.io for the lower-level WebSocket communication between the client and server.

> **DEFINITION**   Socket.io is a JavaScript library that enables access to WebSockets in Node.

By default, Sails creates a WebSocket server on the backend when the Sails server starts via `sails lift`. The Sails WebSocket client, located in brushfire/assets/js/dependencies/sails.io.js, is a tiny client-side library on the frontend that's bundled by default in new Sails apps.

> **TIP**   You can, of course, choose not to use the library by deleting the file in the assets/ folder.

The Sails WebSocket client is a lightweight wrapper that sits on top of the Web-Socket.io client, whose purpose is to simplify the sending and receiving of events from your Sails backend. You've connected to the WebSocket server via the client throughout the book. For example, restart Sails using `sails lift` and navigate your browser to localhost:1337 with the browser's console window open. You should see a browser console log message indicating that a connection was established, as shown in figure 14.2.

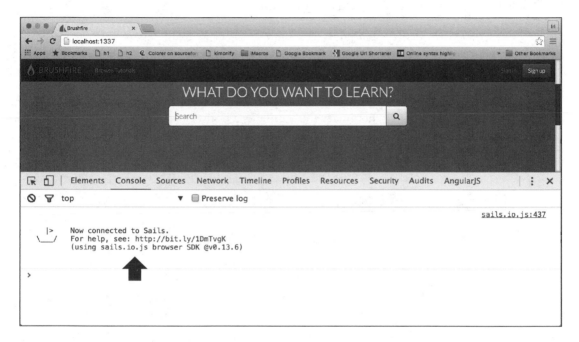

Figure 14.2 Each time Sails responds with a server-rendered view, a new WebSocket connection is created.

This message is coming from the Sails WebSocket client and is automatic as long as you utilize the default sails.io.js. Now that you've established a connection between the client and the Sails WebSocket, you can build requests on the frontend and add methods to controller actions on the backend. This allows you to create and join rooms, send events to connected WebSockets, and more.

14.2.2 *Virtual requests*

Let's quickly create a Sails app to solidify the distinction between an HTTP request and a Sails WebSocket virtual request. From the command line, create a new Sails application named `WebSocketExample`:

```
~ $ sails new WebSocketExample
info: Created a new Sails app `socketExample`!
```

After changing into the WebSocketExample folder, create a controller and name it example:

```
~/socketExample $ sails generate controller example
info: Created a new controller ("example") at
    api/controllers/ExampleController.js!
```

You'll start on the backend by creating an action that can be accessed by both an HTTP request and a WebSocket virtual request.

> **NOTE** We use the qualifier *virtual* request because WebSockets don't make plain HTTP requests. Instead, the Sails WebSocket client, a.k.a. sails.io.js, contains methods that allow you to access HTTP actions as if you were using AJAX. The Sails backend then takes care of transforming the WebSocket event into a virtual request that routes the request to the appropriate controller action with a req dictionary that contains a body, headers, and so on.

In Sublime, open WebSocketExample/api/controllers/ExampleController.js, and add the following `helloWorld` action.

Listing 14.2   Adding an action that will be accessed by both HTTP and WebSockets

```
module.exports = {
  helloWorld: function(req, res) {        An added Sails property to the req dictionary,
                                          isSocket indicates whether the request
    if (req.isSocket) {                 ◁ originated from a WebSocket connection.
      return res.json({
        WebSocketId: sails.sockets.getId(req),   ◁  Gets the id of a
        hello: 'world'                               WebSocket request
      });
    }

    return res.json({
      hello: 'world'
    });
  }
};
```

If you make an HTTP GET request to /example/helloWorld, the backend will respond with a dictionary that contains the key/value pair hello and world. If you use the Sails WebSocket client and make a Sails WebSocket virtual request to helloWorld, the backend will respond with a dictionary that also contains the WebSocket id. So, how do you access the Sails WebSocket client to use the virtual requests?

Sails provides a familiar AJAX-like interface for communicating with the Sails WebSocket server. Through the client you have access to CRUD methods like io.socket .get(), .post(), .put(), and .delete(). Let's look at this in action. Make sure Sails is running via sails lift and make a GET request in Postman to localhost:1337/ example/helloWorld, similar to figure 14.3.

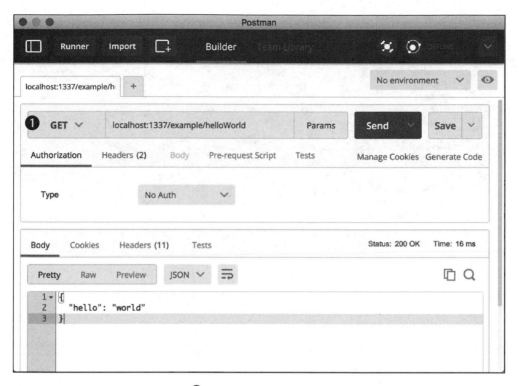

Figure 14.3 Making a `GET` request ❶ to localhost:1337/example/helloWorld returns the dictionary without the `WebSocketId` property and formatted as JSON.

The Postman HTTP request to the `helloWorld` action isn't a WebSocket request and thus doesn't have access to request's `WebSocketId`. It responds solely with the JSON dictionary.

Now, you'll make a WebSocket virtual request using the Sails WebSocket client. Because the homepage view loads the Sails WebSocket client via sails.io.js, you have access to its methods from the browser console. Navigate your browser to localhost:1337 with the console window open. From the browser console window, copy and paste the following code snippet on the command line.

Listing 14.3 Making a WebSocket request using the Sails WebSocket client

```
io.socket.get('/example/helloWorld', function(resData, jwres){
  console.log(resData);
});
```

When the code is executed, the browser console should return something like figure 14.4.

Unlike the HTTP request, the Sails WebSocket virtual request yields the WebSocket `id`. The WebSocket `id` is used to differentiate between requesting clients. Sails

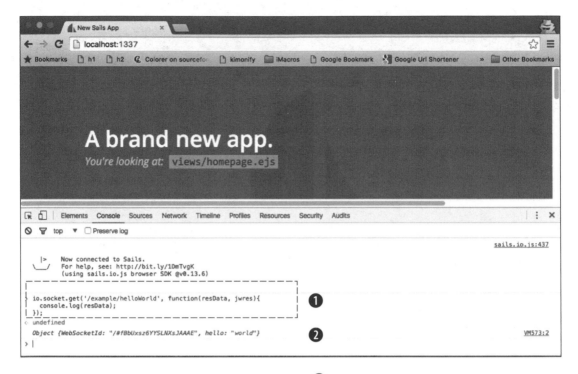

Figure 14.4   Using `io.socket.get()` **to make a request ❶ triggers a WebSocket virtual** `GET` **request that matches a blueprint action route and executes the** `helloWorld` **action that responds with the WebSocket id ❷ via the** `WebSocketId` **property.**

abstracts away the need to worry about the WebSocket id the same way it does with HTTP by making it part of the req dictionary.

Figure 14.5 illustrates that the function signature of the Sails virtual get, post, put, and delete WebSocket methods is similar to an AJAX request.

Figure 14.5   The function signature of the `get` **WebSocket method ❶ should look familiar to anyone who has used an AJAX equivalent method. The function takes the URL as the first argument and the callback as the second argument ❷. Within the callback, you can get access to the response data as JSON ❸ and the JSON WebSocket** `Response` **dictionary ❹.**

The callback to the virtual methods contains two arguments: resData and jwres. The resData argument contains any data passed back from the request as JSON. Optionally, you can get access to the JSON WebSocket response (jwres), which contains a dictionary of response headers, the body, and the status code of the response similar to what you'd get with a standard HTTP request. Depending on the type of application, you can also get a reduction in the latency (elapsed time) between the request and response using WebSockets. But clearly the biggest advantage is you can now create features that allow the server to send events to clients without the client having to make a request. Let's expand what you've learned and implement the chat features of Brushfire.

14.3 Implementing chat

Figure 14.6 illustrates the video player page `locals`, parameters, and endpoints that relate to chat.

The API Reference provides the seven locals that will be sent to the view. Table 14.1 describes each `locals`' attribute.

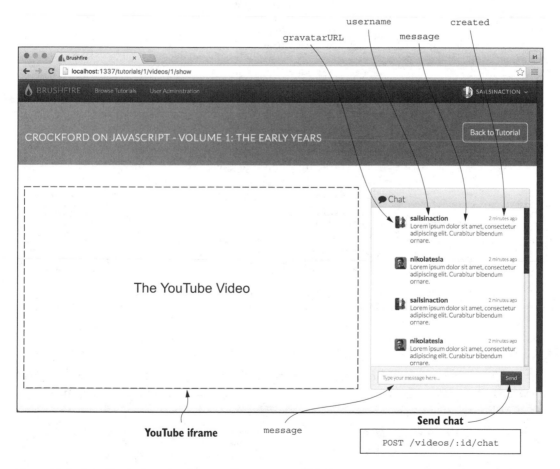

Figure 14.6 Specific to chat, the video player page endpoint will pass seven locals to the view, four of which will be displayed: `gravatarURL` and `username` from the `user` model, `message` and `created` from the `chat` model. The view also contains a single outgoing parameter, `message`, sent within a request, `Send chat`.

Table 14.1   The `locals` dictionary: `chats` for the video player page

`locals` attribute	`chat` model attribute	Description
`message`	`message`	The text of the message a user can send to the `video` room.
`sender`	`sender`	The model association attribute that contains the `id` of the `user` that sent the `chat`.
`video`	`video`	The model association attribute that contains the `id` of the `video` that's related to the `chat`.
`id`	`id`	The `id` of the record in the `chat` model.
`created`	`createdAt`	The date and time the `chat` record was created.
`username`	N/A	The `username` attribute of the user who created the `chat`. The `username` isn't stored in the `chat` model, but through the `sender` model association attribute you can populate `sender` to get the `username`.
`gravatarURL`	N/A	The `gravatarURL` attribute of the user who created the `chat`. The `gravatarURL` isn't stored in the `chat` model, but through the `sender` model association attribute you can populate `sender` to get the `gravatarURL`.

Notice that not all the `locals` will be stored in the `chat` model. Instead, you'll take advantage of Sails' associations to provide the necessary `locals` from other models. Figure 14.7 illustrates the relationships between the `chat`, `user`, and `video` models.

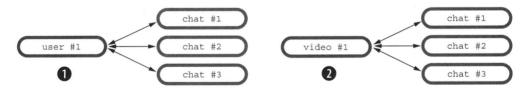

Figure 14.7   A user ❶ can have many chats, but a chat can have only one user. A `video` record ❷ can have many chats, but a chat can have only one video.

14.3.1   *Creating a chat API*

Your first step in implementing chat function in Brushfire is to create an API for the chat resource. From the root of the project on the command line, create a new chat API by typing

```
~ $ sails generate api chat
info: Created a new api!
```

Now, let's configure the attributes of the new `chat` model and other related models. Figure 14.8 illustrates the association relationships you'll need between the `user`, `video`, and `chat` models.

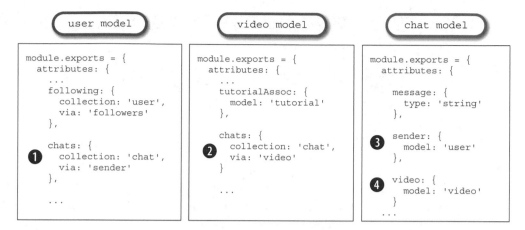

Figure 14.8 **The model associations between the** `user`**,** `video` **and** `chat` **models. The** `user` **model has a** `chats` **association attribute configured as a collection with the** `chat` **model that uses** `via` ❶**. The** `video` **model has a** `chats` **association attribute configured as a collection with the** `chat` **model that uses** `via` ❷**. The** `chat` **model has a** `sender` **association attribute configured as a model with the** `user` ❸**. The** `chat` **model also has a** `video` **association attribute configured as a model with the** `video` ❹**.**

In Sublime, open brushfire/api/models/Chat.js, and add the following attributes.

Listing 14.4 The `chat` **model attributes**

```
...
module.exports = {

  attributes: {

    message: {
      type: 'string'
    },

    sender: {
      model: 'user'
    },

    video: {
      model: 'video'
    }
  }
};
...
```

Next, you'll add the `chats` association attribute to the `user` model. This attribute, when populated, contains all of the `chat` records created by this user. In Sublime, open brushfire/api/models/User.js, and add the following attributes.

Listing 14.5   The `user` model attributes

```
...
following: {
  collection: 'user',
  via: 'followers'
},

chats: {
  collection: 'chat',
  via: 'sender'
},
...
```

Finally, you'll add a `chats` association attribute to the `video` model. This attribute, when populated, contains all of the `chat` records made about the `video` record. In Sublime, open brushfire/api/models/Video.js, and add the following attributes.

Listing 14.6   The `video` model attributes

```
...
tutorialAssoc: {
  model: 'tutorial'
},

chats: {
  collection: 'chat',
  via: 'video'
}
...
```

Now that you have the models configured, let's implement the video player page and, specifically, the `showVideo` action.

14.3.2 Adding chat to an existing page

The `showVideo` action is responsible for displaying the video player page with the appropriately formatted `locals`. You're currently using an array of dictionaries that simulate `chat` records, `FAKE_CHAT`, as well as a dictionary, `video`, to simulate a `video` record. Let's replace the simulated `chat` records with the real thing. In Sublime, open brushfire/api/controllers/PageController.js, and add the following code to the show-Video action to first find the `video` to play.

Listing 14.7   Finding the `video` to play

```
...
Video.findOne({                           Finds the video from
  id: +req.param('id')                    the provided id
})
  .populate('chats')                                   Uses .populate() to add
  .exec(function (err, foundVideo){                    the video's chats array
    if (err) return res.negotiate(err);
```

```
    if (!foundVideo) return res.notFound();
...
```

In addition to finding the particular video, you populate the chats association attribute so that you have access to an array of chat dictionaries related to the video model. Next, you'll iterate through each chat and format its properties based on the requirements in the Brushfire API Reference. In Sublime, add the following code.

Listing 14.8 Iterate through the `chats` array and format each video's `chat` record

```
    ...
    async.each(foundVideo.chats, function(chat, next){        ⟵  Iterates through each
                                                                  of the video's chats
      User.findOne({
        id: chat.sender                                       ⟵
      }).exec(function (err, foundUser){                         Finds the sender of the chat using
        if (err) return next(err);                              the association parameter id

        chat.username = foundUser.username;
        chat.created = DatetimeService.getTimeAgo({date: chat.createdAt});
        chat.gravatarURL = foundUser.gravatarURL;            ⟵
        return next();                                           Adds a gravatarURL
      });                                                        property to the chat

    }, function(err) {
      if (err) return res.negotiate(err);
    ...
```

Adds a username property to the chat

Adds a created property with the formatted time-ago value of createdAt

Finally, you'll respond based on the user's authenticated state. If the user isn't authenticated, respond with the me dictionary set to null, the found video information for the page, the tutorial id, and the chat information. In Sublime, add the response if the user isn't authenticated, similar to the following listing.

Listing 14.9 The response if the user isn't authenticated

```
...
if (!req.session.userId) {                             ⟵
  return res.view('show-video', {                      ⟵   If the user isn't
    me: null,                                               authenticated ...
    video: foundVideo,
    tutorialId: req.param('tutorialId'),                   ... renders the show-video
    chats: foundVideo.chats                                view with the me property
  });                                                      set to null
}
...
```

If the user is authenticated, you'll add the required information about the authenticated user to the me property as well as related chat information. In Sublime, add the response if the user is authenticated, similar to the next listing.

Listing 14.10   The response if the user is authenticated

```
...
User.findOne({
  id: +req.session.userId                    ◁──┐  Finds the currently
}).exec(function (err, foundUser) {                authenticated user
  if (err) {
    return res.negotiate(err);
  }                                           ┌──  Handles if the user
                                              │    is not found
  if (!foundUser) {                      ◁────┘
    sails.log.verbose('Session refers to a user who no longer exists');
    return res.view('show-video', {
      me: null,
      video: foundVideo,
      tutorialId: req.param('tutorialId'),
      chats: foundVideo.chats
    });
  }

  return res.view('show-video', {          ◁──┐  Renders the
    me: {                                        show-video
      username: foundUser.username,              view
      gravatarURL: foundUser.gravatarURL,
      admin: foundUser.admin
    },
    video: foundVideo,
    tutorialId: req.param('tutorialId'),
    chats: foundVideo.chats
  ...
```

Now that you're adding real `chat` records to the video player page, you need to be able to chat! You'll start to implement that next.

14.3.3 *Subscribing a socket to a room*

Each chat is associated with a particular video and a particular user. When the rendered brushfire/views/show-video.ejs view loads, you display any existing chats associated with the video. You'll need a way to send new chats created for the period between page refreshes. To accomplish this task, you'll send an event as each new chat is created. But you don't want to send the event to all connected WebSockets. Instead, you want to limit sending the event to those WebSockets that are currently on the video player page of a particular `video` record. You can accomplish this by creating a room unique to that `video` record, joining the WebSockets that are on this page to the room, and then sending an event to the room. But what room are we talking about?

Socket.io uses the metaphor of a *room* to group WebSockets together. From the backend, you can then broadcast messages to the room. You can also subscribe and unsubscribe WebSockets from the room. There's no need to create a room explicitly. The first user who joins a room automatically creates the room in the process. So, by loading the show-video view, the frontend Angular controller makes a PUT request to /videos/2/join. This, in turn, triggers the joinChat action, which you'll implement now. In Sublime, open brushfire/api/controllers/VideoController.js, and add the following code to the joinChat action.

Listing 14.11 Joining the video room

```
joinChat: function (req, res) {

  if (!req.isSocket) {                        Ensures that this is a
    return res.badRequest();                  WebSocket request
  }

  sails.sockets.join(req, 'video'+req.param('id'));      Joins the current
                                                         WebSocket (req)
  return res.ok();                                       to a video room
},
```

The sails.sockets.join() method is one of the low-level methods Sails provides that allows realtime communication with the frontend. The method has two required arguments: a WebSocket and a roomName. The WebSocket refers to the client Web-Socket that made the request, and the roomName is the name of the room to join. You'll pass the req dictionary as the first argument, and use a combination of the word *video* with the id of the video record to create a unique room name for each video as the second argument. Now that you've joined the WebSocket to the video room, let's set up a mechanism for sending a chat.

14.3.4 Sending a chat notification

You want to send the contents of the input field of the chat form in the show-video view to the backend send-chat endpoint. When the user clicks the Send button, the chat action is triggered. In Sublime, open brushfire/api/controllers/VideoController.js, and add the following code to the chat action.

Listing 14.12 Saving the chat and then broadcasting it to the video room

```
Chat.create({                               Creates a
  message: req.param('message'),            chat record
  sender: req.session.userId,
  video: +req.param('id')
}).exec(function (err, createdChat){
  if (err) return res.negotiate(err);

  User.findOne({                            Finds the currently
    id: req.session.userId                  authenticated user
  }).exec(function (err, foundUser){
    if (err) return res.negotiate(err);
    if (!foundUser) return res.notFound();

    sails.sockets.broadcast('video'+req.param('id'), 'chat', {    Broadcasts the
      message: req.param('message'),                              chat event to
      username: foundUser.username,                               the video room
```

```
    created: 'just now',
    gravatarURL: foundUser.gravatarURL
  });

  return res.ok();
```

Initially, the chat record is created. Next, you'll query for the currently authenticated user using the userId found in the session. You'll use a combination of the results of your created chat record and user query as the required Brushfire API reference values in the chat event that you'll send to the room. To accomplish this, you send the event using another Sails low-level WebSocket method: sails.sockets.broadcast(). This method can be executed with three different function signatures, as shown in figure 14.9.

1 `sails.sockets.broadcast(roomName, eventName, data);`

2 `sails.sockets.broadcast(roomName, data, socketToOmit);`

3 `sails.sockets.broadcast(roomName, eventName, data, socketToOmit);`

Figure 14.9   The broadcast method can be executed using the roomName, eventName, and data as arguments **1**. The method can also be executed without the eventName **2**, in which case the default event name is used. In addition, the currently requesting WebSocket can be omitted by adding the WebSocketToOmit argument, req. Finally, all four arguments **3** can be used.

If an eventName isn't provided, a default event name of message is used. You want the requesting WebSocket to be included in those WebSockets that will receive the event, so you'll leave out the WebSocketToOmit argument. The final step is adding an event listener on the frontend configured for the chat event.

14.3.5 *Adding a chat event listener to the frontend*

Although we're concentrating on the backend, it's important to review what's being incorporated into the frontend regarding WebSocket requests. Figure 14.10 illustrates an overview of the significant exchanges between the frontend and backend as it relates to chat.

When the user-agent clicks a video, the showVideo action is triggered **1**, which finds and displays any existing chats using Video.findOne() and populates the chats to the view on the backend. When the rendered view is displayed on the browser, the user-agent connects to the Sails WebSocket server automatically **2** via a link to sails.io.js in the show-video view. The Angular controller **3** also joins the newly created WebSocket to a unique video room. When a user clicks the Send button on the chat form **4**, the backend broadcasts the chat message to any listening WebSockets in

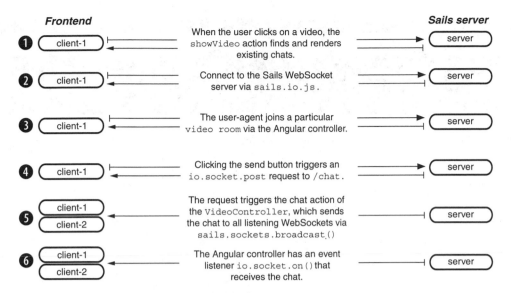

Figure 14.10   The significant interactions between the frontend and backend relating to chat

the video room ❺. The listening WebSocket can hear the broadcasted event because of an event listener ❻ in the showVideoPageController.js controller file, which is displayed in the following listing.

Listing 14.13   The `chat` event listener

```
...
io.socket.on('chat', function (e) {          ◁─┐  Listens for a
  console.log('new chat received!', e);          │  chat event

  $scope.chats.push({            ◁─┐
    created: e.created,              │  Adds the new chat
    username: e.username,           │  to the chats array
    message: e.message,
    gravatarURL: e.gravatarURL
  });
                                        ┌ The $apply method is
  $scope.$apply();          ◁──────────┤ required so that Angular
});                                     └ realizes the $scope is dirty.
```

When a chat event is sent to the client, an event handler is triggered and the newly created chat is added to the chats array on the Angular $scope, which updates the UI displaying the chat, similar to figure 14.11.

Our old friend Chad has an additional request for the chat. He wants a user to know when another user is typing in the message field of the chat form. You'll implement this last piece of chat functionality in the next section.

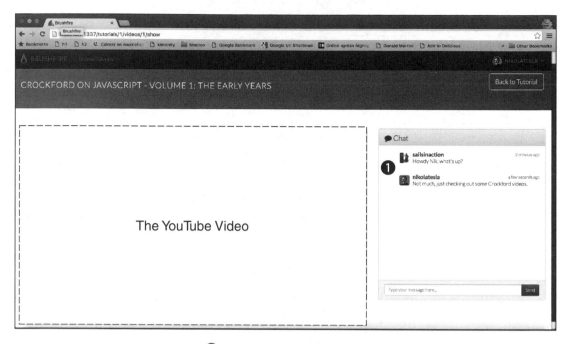

Figure 14.11   The `chat` event listener ❶ displays the chat event message contents.

14.4   *Sending typing and stoppedTyping notifications*

Figure 14.12 provides an overview of the typing message feature you're going to implement.

When a `user` is typing in the `message` field of the `chat` window ❶, you want the frontend to make a PUT request to `/videos/:id/typing` ❷. That request ❸ matches a route that triggers the `typing` action ❹ in the video controller, which broadcasts a `typing` event. An event handler listens for the `typing` event ❺, which triggers the

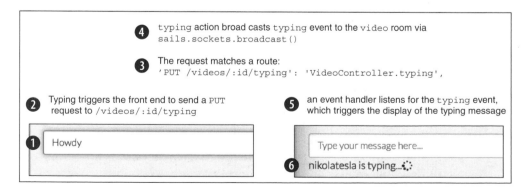

Figure 14.12   The steps the frontend and backend must fulfill in order to display a message when a user is typing in the message field of the chat window

display of the typing animation ❻. Reviewing the API Reference reveals that this feature will require the following on the backend:

- A `typing` action that broadcasts a `typing` event to all WebSocket members of the `video` room
- A `stoppedTyping` action that broadcasts a `stopTyping` event to all WebSocket members of the `video` room
- A route connecting a PUT request to /videos/:id/typing to the `typing` action
- A route connecting a PUT request to /videos/:id/stoppedTyping to the `stoppedTyping` action

On the frontend, you'll need to generate two requests when the user starts typing in the message input field and when the user stops typing, as well as event handlers to listen for the `typing` and `stoppedTyping` events. Let's get busy.

14.4.1 *Listening for different kinds of notifications*

First, let's add the two requests for the typing and stopped-typing states. Remember, you're now dealing with the frontend and not the backend API. In Sublime, open brushfire/assets/js/controllers/showVideoPageController.js, and add the `whenTyping` and `whenNotTyping` methods shown here.

Listing 14.14 Adding the `whenTyping` and `whenNotTyping` methods

```
...
$scope.whenTyping = function (event) {

  io.socket.request({
    url: '/videos/'+$scope.fromUrlVideoId+'/typing',
    method: 'put'
  }, function (data, JWR){
      // If something went wrong, handle the error.
      if (JWR.statusCode !== 200) {
        console.error(JWR);
        return;
      }
  });
};

$scope.whenNotTyping = function (event) {

  io.socket.request({
    url: '/videos/'+$scope.fromUrlVideoId+'/stoppedTyping',
    method: 'put'
  }, function (data, JWR){
      // If something went wrong, handle the error.
      if (JWR.statusCode !== 200) {
        console.error(JWR);
        return;
      }
  });
};
}]);
```

You use the io.socket.request() method, which provides you with lower-level access to the request headers, parameters, method, and URL of the request. Both methods are triggered within the show-video view in brushfire/views/show-view.ejs using a combination of ng-blur, ng-focus, and ng-keypress. Now let's add the event handlers that will listen for the typing and stoppedTyping events. Back in Sublime, open brushfire/assets/js/controllers/ showVideoPageController.js, and add the event handlers for the typing and stoppedTyping events shown in the next listing.

> **Listing 14.15 Adding the event handlers for typing and stoppedTyping events**

```
...
io.socket.on('typing', function (e) {
  console.log('typing!', e);

  $scope.usernameTyping = e.username;
  $scope.typing = true;

  $scope.$apply();
});

io.socket.on('stoppedTyping', function (e) {
  console.log('stoppedTyping!', e);

  $scope.typing = false;
  $scope.$apply();
});
...
```

14.4.2 *Excluding the sender from a broadcast*

Now that you have the frontend implemented, let's start with backend implementation of the two routes that will trigger the typing and stoppedTyping actions. In Sublime, open brushfire/config/routes.js, and add the two routes shown here.

> **Listing 14.16 Adding two routes that trigger the typing and stoppedTyping actions**

```
...
'PUT /videos/:id/join': 'VideoController.joinChat',
'PUT /videos/:id/typing': 'VideoController.typing',
'PUT /videos/:id/stoppedTyping': 'VideoController.stoppedTyping',
...
```

Next, let's implement the typing action. In Sublime, open brushfire/api/controllers/ VideoController.js, and add the typing action as follows.

> **Listing 14.17 Broadcasting a typing event excluding the sender's WebSocket**

```
typing: function(req, res) {
    if (!req.isSocket) {
      return res.badRequest();
    }
```
◁── **Only socket requests should hit this endpoint.**

```
User.findOne({                                    ←⎤ Finds the currently
    id: req.session.userId                           ⎦ authenticated user
}).exec(function (err, foundUser){
    if (err) return res.negotiate(err);
    if (!foundUser) return res.notFound();

    sails.sockets.broadcast('video'+req.param('id'), 'typing', {    ←
        username: foundUser.username
    }, (req.isSocket ? req : undefined) );      ←

    return res.ok();          Adding the sender's WebSocket      Sends the typing
});                            id prevents the sender from      event to all users in
},                                receiving the event.          the video chat room
```

Earlier, you used the `sails.sockets.broadcast()` method without sending an optional WebSocket to be omitted. It's not necessary for the user who's typing in the chat window to receive the `typing` event. You'll pass the requesting WebSocket as the WebSocket to be omitted from receiving the event. Last, you'll implement the action that will stop the animation. The `stoppedTyping` action doesn't require a query to the user model because you're not displaying a message that a particular user stopped typing. In Sublime, open brushfire/api/controllers/VideoController.js, and add the stopTyping action shown in the following listing.

Listing 14.18 Broadcasting a `stoppedTyping` event excluding the sender's WebSocket

```
stoppedTyping: function(req, res) {
  if (!req.isSocket) {
    return res.badRequest();
  }

  sails.sockets.broadcast('video'+req.param('id'),
    'stoppedTyping', (req.isSocket ? req : undefined) );

  return res.ok();
}
```

Let's see this in action. Restart Sails via `sails lift`, and navigate two different authenticated browsers, one in regular mode and one in incognito mode, to the same video. You can use the users that were created by the bootstrap file, `nikolatesla` and `sails-inaction`, both of which have the password `abc123`. Use ShiftIt to line up the browsers side by side. Browse to the same video, for example, http://localhost:1337/tutorials/1/videos/1/show. Begin typing in one of the chat windows, and you should see something similar to figure 14.13.

> **NOTE** We used an incognito browser, which creates a browser with a different session cookie than the regular browser. If we had used two regular browsers, the same session cookie would be used and, therefore, both browsers would access the same authenticated user.

Figure 14.13   When two user-agents are on the same video and one begins to type a chat message ❶, the other user-agent has a typing message displayed ❷.

Typing in the message input field triggers a PUT request to /videos/:id/typing, which triggers the typing action. Within this action, you broadcast a typing event to any WebSocket ids that have joined the video room ('video' + video id) and have an event handler listening for a typing event.

14.4.3 *Other useful methods in sails.sockets*

Brushfire doesn't require using all of the backend low-level WebSocket methods, so let's take a quick look at the remaining methods:

- .addRoomMembersToRooms(sourceRoom, destRooms, cb) subscribes all members of a room to one or more additional rooms.
- sails.sockets.blast(data) sends a message/event to all WebSockets connected to the Sails WebSocket server regardless of what rooms they've joined.
- sails.sockets.leave(socket, roomName) unsubscribes a WebSocket from a room.
- sails.sockets.leaveAll(roomName, cb) unsubscribes all members of a room from that room *and* every other room they're currently subscribed to.
- .removeRoomMembersFromRooms() unsubscribes all members of a room from one or more other rooms.

For a complete reference to each method, head over to http://mng.bz/2jH2.

14.5 *Understanding resourceful pubsub*

In addition to the WebSocket client and low-level backend WebSocket methods, Sails provides an automation layer called *resourceful pubsub*. Each model, also referred to as a *resource*, is automatically equipped with methods for joining connected WebSockets to event notifications when records are created, updated, and/or deleted. In Brushfire, you want each `video` record to have its own unique room such as `video1`. Currently, you're creating the room name by concatenating the word `video` with the `id` of each record. When the browser user-agent's WebSocket accesses a particular video player page, you join the WebSocket to the room with the concatenated name.

Resourceful pubsub methods create and maintain the room names for you. RPS rooms also add an additional layer of detail. In addition to using a model record's `id` as the basis for a room name, pubsub rooms are generated for `create`, `update`, and `delete` actions, as well as additions to and removals from associations. For example, you have the fidelity of joining a requesting WebSocket to a room that limits events to the updates of that record.

> **NOTE** These RPS methods follow a pattern referred to as the publish/subscription model. If a WebSocket is subscribed to a resource, then events are published to the subscribing WebSockets.

In the previous section, you used three backend low-level WebSocket methods:

- `sails.sockets.getId(req)` returns the WebSocket `id` found on the `req` dictionary.
- `sails.sockets.join(req, roomName)` joins the WebSocket to a room.
- `sails.sockets.broadcast(roomName, data)` sends an event to a room.

RPS provides additional backend methods that extend their low-level counterparts to a specific resource—the model. There are ten pubsub methods in total. Four of the methods replace and enhance the low-level `.join()` method:

- `.subscribe()` joins a requesting WebSocket to the *update, destroy, add,* and *remove* rooms of one or more record(s) of a model. Behind the scenes, Sails takes care of creating and managing these room names. For example, a room named `sails_model_user_33: update` is the `update` action room for a user record with an `id` of 33. You don't have to remember the room names. Instead, you pass various pubsub methods, including `.subscribe()`, the `id` of a record or records you want to join the room.
- `.unsubscribe()` removes a requesting WebSocket from the room of one or more record(s) of a model.
- `.watch()` joins a requesting WebSocket to a model's class room whose name is derived behind the scenes by concatenating the word *create* with the model name, like `sails_model_create_user`. This is a room that will watch for new records of a particular model.
- `.unwatch()` removes a requesting WebSocket from the model's class room.

The remaining six pubsub methods replace and enhance the low-level `.broadcast()` method that sends events to WebSockets:

- `.publishCreate()` sends an event to subscribers of the model class room like `sails_model_create_video`.
- `.publishUpdate()` sends an event to subscribers of the `update` instance room like `sails_model_video_44:update`.
- `.publishDestroy()` sends an event to subscribers of the `destroy` instance room like `sails_model_video_44:destroy`.
- `.publishAdd()` sends an event to subscribers of the `add` instance room like `sails_model_video_44:add:chats`.
- `.publishRemove()` sends an event to subscribers of the `remove` instance room like `sails_model_video_44:add:chats`.
- `.message()` sends an event to all WebSockets that are listening for an event based on the model name like `sails_model_video_44:message`.

14.5.1 *Using .subscribe()*

The `.subscribe()` pubsub method subscribes the requesting client WebSocket to one or more database records. In our example, we have a single `video` record for each video player page. The `Video.subscribe()` method will automatically create video `update` and `destroy` rooms, as well as rooms affecting the `chats` association, adding and removing associated records and then joining the requesting WebSocket to those rooms. In the next section, we'll explore methods that send events to these rooms. For now, in Sublime, open brushfire/api/controllers/VideoController.js, and change the `joinChat` action similar to the following listing.

> **Listing 14.19 Adding the `.subscribe()` method with `.join()` in the `joinChat` action**

```
...
joinChat: function (req, res) {
  if (!req.isSocket) {
    return res.badRequest();
  }

  sails.sockets.join(req, 'video'+req.param('id'));

  Video.subscribe(req, req.param('id'));         ◁─┐  Subscribes the requesting
                                                   │  WebSocket to the provided
  return res.ok();                                 │  video record instance
},
...
```

By using `Video.subscribe()`, you're not responsible for managing room names for the chat messages. Instead, you'll refer to the `id` of the record you want to subscribe a WebSocket to or to send an event to. Next, let's incorporate pubsub methods to send events to these rooms.

14.5.2 Using .publishUpdate()

The requesting WebSockets are now joined to unique rooms whose names reflect the id of the record of the `video` model as well as the type of action being performed: `create`, `update`, `destroy`, and so on. Now, you need a way of sending events to the appropriate rooms. `Video.publishUpdate()` accepts an `id` or array of `ids` of `video` records as the first argument in its method signature. It then uses that information to broadcast an `update` event to the `update` room of those records.

> **TIP** Ironically, the `.publishUpdate()` method doesn't update any model records. Instead, it provides a mechanism for you to broadcast the fact that an `update` event has occurred within a controller action to those WebSockets that are subscribed to the `model` room and have event listeners configured to listen for a particular event.

In Sublime, open brushfire/api/controllers/VideoController.js, and substitute `sails .sockets.broadcast()` in the `chat` action with `Video.publishUpdate()` similar to the following.

Listing 14.20   Substituting `.broadcast()` with `.publishUpdate()` in the `chat` action

```
chat: function(req, res) {
  ...
    User.findOne({
      id: req.session.userId
    }).exec(function (err, foundUser){
      if (err) return res.negotiate(err);
      if (!foundUser) return res.notFound();

    Video.publishUpdate(+req.param('id'), {          Provides the id of
      message: req.param('message'),                 the video record to
      username: foundUser.username,                  broadcast the event
      created: 'just now',
      gravatarURL: foundUser.gravatarURL             The message dictionary
    });                                              to be passed with the
  ...                                                video event
```

Now, when a user sends a chat, a `video` event is broadcast to all WebSockets subscribed to that particular `video` record. Finally, let's change the event name of your event listener from `chat` to `video`.

14.5.3 RPS methods and event names

The pubsub publish methods `.publishUpdate()`, `.publishCreate()`, and `.publish-Destroy()` share the same event name derived from the model. In this case, the event name is `video`. You currently have the event listener configured for a `chat` event. So let's change it to `video`. In Sublime, open brushfire/assets/js/controllers/showVideo-PageController.js, and change the event listener event name to `video`, as shown here.

Listing 14.21   Updating the event listener to the `video` event

```
...
  io.socket.on('video', function (e) {

    $scope.chats.push({
      created: e.data.created,
      username: e.data.username,
      message: e.data.message,
      gravatarURL: e.data.gravatarURL
    });

    $scope.$apply();
  });
...
```

> Substitutes the video event for the chat event

> Notice you're also adding a data property to the event.

The listener will now be triggered when a `video` event is sent. Also, the contents of the event will have a `data` property similar to the following.

Listing 14.22   A typical `video` event

```
{
  data: {
    created: "just now",
    gravatarURL:
    ➥ "http://www.gravatar.com/avatar/c06112bbecd8a290a00441bf181a24d3?",
    message: "How are you?",
    username: "nikola-tesla",
  },
  id: 6,
  verb: "updated"
}
```

Even though you use the same event name for each method, you can differentiate between event types by checking the `verb` property, in this case, `updated`.

For Brushfire chat, you need to transform some of the values before they're sent as part of an event to the frontend. Therefore, you use the publish methods in your custom actions. There are cases, however, when you don't need a custom controller action and can instead rely on blueprint actions. In these cases, you can use built-in pubsub features of blueprint actions to automate the process of managing WebSockets.

14.6 *Understanding how the blueprint API uses RPS methods*

Eight blueprint actions are available to each controller unless overwritten by a custom action using the same name:

- `find`
- `findOne`
- `create`
- `update`

- destroy
- add
- remove
- populate

In chapter4, we introduced some of these actions and how they can be triggered by blueprint routes or custom routes to provide prebuilt CRUD operations to controllers. What we haven't discussed is that these actions also contain built-in RPS features.

14.6.1 *The find and findOne actions*

The blueprint `find` and `findOne` actions automatically subscribe requesting WebSockets to various pubsub rooms of existing records of a model. The blueprint `find` action automatically subscribes the requesting WebSocket to any records that match the results of a `find` query, including any records that are part of an association. For example, let's say you want to track the position of each user's cursor in the browser. You'll first create a `cursor` model. You'll then use the Sails WebSocket client to make a virtual `GET` request to `/cursor`. This virtual request will trigger the blueprint `find` action executing `Cursor.subscribe()`, which will automatically subscribe the requesting WebSocket to various rooms. `Cursor.subscribe()` will join the requesting WebSocket to the `update`, `destroy`, `add`, and `remove` rooms for each record found by the `find` query and generated by the first WebSocket joining the room. In addition, the `find` action will execute `Cursor.watch()`. `Cursor.watch()` joins the requesting WebSocket to a room that combines the model name with the word *create*: `sails_model_create_cursor`. Adding the requesting WebSocket to the various rooms will enable the pubsub publish methods to automatically send events within the blueprint `create`, `update`, `destroy`, `add`, `remove`, and `populate` actions. Unlike the blueprint `find` action, the `findOne` action subscribes the requesting client to the record rooms—`update`, `destroy`, `add`, and `remove`—but not to the `create` class room.

14.6.2 *The create action*

After the blueprint `create` action creates a record or records, it subscribes the requesting WebSocket to the created record or records. It then subscribes all of the WebSockets that are members of the model's `create` room to the newly created record or records. Finally, by using `.publishCreate()`, the blueprint `create` action will send an event to the subscribers of the model's `create` room. For example, `sails_model_create_cursor` would be the `create` room for `cursor` model. A typical event from the blueprint `create` action's automatic use of the `.publishCreate()` method will look similar to this.

Listing 14.23   A typical event from the `.publishCreate()` method

```
{
  data: {          ⟵─┤ The record that
    id: 1,             was created
```

```
    createdAt: "2015-12-13T22:48:50.328Z",
    updatedAt: "2015-12-13T22:48:50.328Z",
  },
  id: 1,
  verb: "created"
}
```

The id of the record that was created

The type of publish pubsub method used

14.6.3 *The update action*

After the blueprint `update` action updates a record, it subscribes the requesting Web-Socket to the updated record. Using `.publishUpdate()`, the blueprint `update` action sends an event to the subscribers of the updated record's `update` room. For example, `sails_model_cursor_24:update` would be the `update` room for a `cursor` record with an `id` of 24. A typical event from the blueprint `update` action's automatic use of the `.publishUpdate()` method will look similar to the following.

Listing 14.24 A typical event from the `.publishUpdate()` method

```
{
  data: {
    name: "john",
    updatedAt: "2015-12-13T23:20:34.560Z",
  },
  id: 32,
  previous: {
    createdAt: "2015-12-13T23:20:34.560Z",
    updaedAt: "2015-12-13T23:20:34.570Z",
    id: 32,
    name: "joe"
  },
  verb: "updated"
}
```

The record that was updated

The previous values of the record before it was updated

The type of publish pubsub method used

14.6.4 *The destroy action*

After the blueprint `destroy` action destroys a record, it executes `.publishDestroy()`, sending an event to the subscribers of the deleted record's `delete` room. For example, `sails_model_cursor_24:destroy` would be the `destroy` room for a `cursor` record with the `id` of 24. The action then unsubscribes the requesting WebSocket and any existing subscribers from the deleted record's `update`, `destroy`, `add`, and `remove` rooms. A typical event from the blueprint `destroy` action's automatic use of the `.publishDestroy()` method will look similar to this.

Listing 14.25 A typical event from the `.publishDestroy()` method

```
{
  previous: {
    createdAt: "2015-12-13T23:20:34.560Z",
    updaedAt: "2015-12-13T23:20:34.570Z",
```

The previous values of the record before it was deleted

```
    id: 32,
    name: "joe"
  },
    id: 32,                          The type of publish
    verb: "deleted"         ◁──┘    pubsub method used
}
```

14.6.5 *The populate action*

After the blueprint `populate` action populates an association, it subscribes the requesting WebSocket to the record or records returned after populating the association. Using this blueprint method doesn't produce any events.

14.6.6 *The add action*

After the blueprint `add` action adds the associated record, it executes `.publishAdd()`, sending an event to the subscribers of the add room. For example, `sails_model_video_32:add:cursors` would be the `add` room for the `cursor` record with the `id` of 32. A typical event from the blueprint `add` action's automatic use of the `.publishAdd()` method will look similar to the following.

> **Listing 14.26 A typical event from the `.publishAdd()` method**

```
                              The id of the         The type of publish
  id: 32,              ◁──    parent record         pubsub method used
  verb: "addedTo",                        ◁──
  attribute: "cursors",                         ◁──
  addedId: "5"     ◁──┐  The id of the           The association
}                      added record              attribute
```

14.6.7 *The remove action*

After the blueprint `remove` action removes the associated record, it executes `.publish-Remove()`, sending an event to the subscribers of the remove room. For example, `sails_model_video_32:remove:cursors` would be the `remove` room for the `cursor` record with the `id` of 32. A typical event from the blueprint `remove` action's automatic use of the `.publishRemove()` method will look similar to this.

> **Listing 14.27 A typical event from the `.publishRemove()` method**

```
{                              The id of the        The type of publish
  id: 32,              ◁──     parent record        pubsub method used
  verb: "removedFrom",                     ◁──
  attribute: "cursors",                        ◁──
  removedId: "5"   ◁──┐  The id of the           The association
}                      removed record            attribute
```

14.7   *Summary*

- Once a WebSocket makes a connection with the WebSocket server, the server can send events to the connected WebSocket at will.

- Sails provides virtual request methods similar to AJAX but with the addition of exposing the WebSocket `id` to the backend.

- Sails provides resourceful pubsub, which automatically equips models with methods for joining connected WebSockets to event notifications when records are created, updated, and/or deleted.

Deployment, testing, and security

This chapter covers

- Deploying Brushfire to a PaaS
- Distinguishing between development and production
- Incorporating testing into Brushfire
- Understanding XSS and CSRF attacks and protection

In this final chapter, we'll address deploying Brushfire into the wild. This will require us to choose a deployment destination, and will include deploying and configuring a remote PostgreSQL instance for our main database and a Redis instance for our session and WebSocket stores. We'll separate Brushfire into three different environments: development, production, and test. We'll use the environments as a way to configure Brushfire separately based on one of the three environments chosen. Testing is a vital step in the development process. We'll show you how to set up tests for endpoints and model methods. We'll wrap up the chapter with a discussion of the most prevalent security vulnerabilities and steps you can take to protect against them.

405

15.1 Obtaining the example materials for this chapter

If you've followed along in chapter 14 with an existing project, you can continue to use that project in this chapter. But if you want to start from this chapter and move forward, clone the following repo: https://github.com/sailsinaction/brushfire-ch14-end. After cloning the repo, install the Node module dependencies via `npm install`. You'll also want to add the local.js file that you created in chapter 14. In Sublime, copy and paste your local.js file that you created in chapter 14, or create a new file in brushfire/config/local.js, and add the following code.

> **Listing 15.1 Adding to the local.js file**

```
module.exports.blueprints = {
  shortcuts: true,
  prefix: '/bp',
};

module.exports.connections = {
  myPostgresqlServer: {
    adapter: 'sails-postgresql',
    host: 'localhost',
    database: 'brushfire'
  }
};

module.exports.mailgun =  {
  apiKey: 'ADD YOUR MAILGUN API KEY HERE',
  domain: 'ADD YOUR MAILGUN DOMAIN HERE',
  baseUrl: 'http://localhost:1337'
};
```

15.2 Deploying your Sails app

You have many options when deploying a Sails application into the wild. A significant choice is whether to deploy the application to a server located on your own hardware, on a cloud computing service (CCS), or to one of the many *platform as a service* (PaaS) providers. Creating your own server, whether locally or virtually, is beyond the scope of this book. Instead, we'll use a PaaS called Heroku to deploy Brushfire. The techniques we'll employ, however, will be generally applicable to any PaaS you choose. We'll also use Heroku to host remote versions of our existing PostgreSQL database and new databases for the session and WebSockets databases. In this section, we'll create destinations for Brushfire and our main PostgreSQL database on Heroku.

15.2.1 About Heroku

Like other PaaS providers, Heroku frees you from having to manage much of the infrastructure involved in deploying and maintaining your application. This infrastructure includes the hardware and software related to servers, storage, and networking. Heroku uses lightweight Linux containers called *dynos* to run instances of an application.

> **DEFINITION** A *container* is part of a technology generally termed *containerization*, where multiple isolated instances of an operating system can run on a single shared host. Each container can, in turn, run individual instances of an application.

15.2.2 Scaling to multiple dynos

For many applications, one server is enough to handle the expected traffic—at least at first. Chad is thinking big, so we're planning for growth. We'll assume Brushfire could be deployed on multiple containerized dynos similar to figure 15.1.

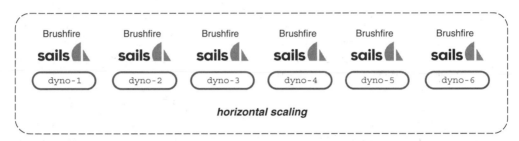

Figure 15.1 Horizontal scaling of an application on Heroku is accomplished by adding additional dynos to a given project.

Adding dynos in this way is known as *horizontal scaling*. This is opposed to adding resources to an individual node or dyno, known as *vertical scaling*. Horizontal scaling has the advantage that (in principle) you aren't limited by the maximum amount of resources you can add to a single machine. Instead, the load can be spread across multiple machines/dynos. You also have the advantage of reducing the risk of a single source of failure. Configuring Brushfire so that it can be successfully deployed using horizontal scaling on multiple dyno instances requires a few application configuration considerations, including the following:

- How do you route incoming requests to multiple dynos?
- Where will your database reside, and how will each dyno be configured to connect to it?
- How do you implement a centralized storage regime for WebSockets and sessions?

First, Heroku has its own load-balancing router that sits between an incoming request and the dyno instances. Incoming requests are automatically routed for you similar to figure 15.2.

It's also worth pointing out that the traffic from the browser to this load balancer is using HTTPS. Therefore, you don't need to worry about configuring TLS. We'll discuss TLS in the security section later in this chapter.

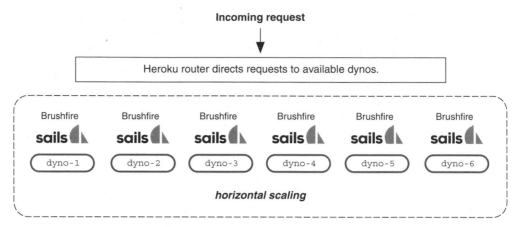

Figure 15.2   Heroku's load-balancing router automatically routes incoming requests to multiple instances of Sails within multiple dynos.

> **DEFINITION**   *TLS* stands for *transport layer security* and is responsible for encrypting traffic between the browser and server. Its purpose is to ensure that traffic between the browser and server remains private.

Second, for your database, you'll have one remote PostgreSQL instance that covers all current and subsequent dynos. You'll also move your sessions and WebSockets store from an individual per-instance memory store to one central Redis location, similar to figure 15.3.

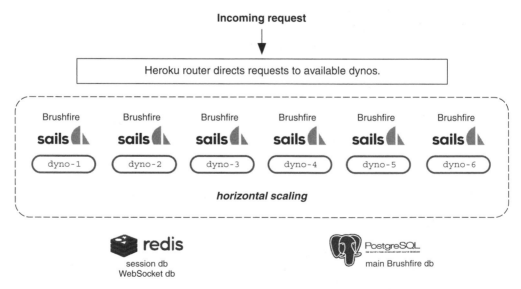

Figure 15.3   The Brushfire dynos will use a centralized PostgreSQL instance for the main database and a Redis instance for session and WebSocket storage.

DEFINITION   *Redis* is an *in-memory* datastore using key/value pairs similar to a dictionary. We'll take a much closer look at Redis later in the chapter.

The goal here is to make each dyno stateless and therefore independent of holding things in memory like a session id. But before you transition your PostgreSQL database, session, and WebSocket store, you'll create an initial Heroku dyno for Brushfire. The remaining configuration steps involve setting up instructions for Heroku and Sails to follow when each dyno is created.

15.2.3   Installing the Heroku tool belt

Heroku uses Git to actually deploy Brushfire. Therefore, you'll need to create another remote that's pointing to Heroku.

DEFINITION   A *remote* is the label for the destination (URL) of a remote repository.

Instead of using Git directly from the command line, Heroku has its own tool belt that wraps Git functionality. We assume that you've already created a free account on http://heroku.com. Once you've created the account, you'll want to install the Heroku tool belt found here: https://toolbelt.heroku.com/. After the tool belt is installed, head over to the command line, and from the root of your Brushfire project type

```
~/brushfire $ heroku create
```
◁─┤ **Creates an application on Heroku and adds a heroku alias that points to a remote Heroku repo**

If this is the first time you've used the Heroku tool belt from the command line, you'll be prompted for your Heroku account credentials. After you enter your credentials, a Heroku application will be created with an alias to a remote Heroku repo:

```
~/brushfire $ heroku create
https://still-retreat-63077.herokuapp.com/ | https://git.heroku.com/still-
➥ retreat-63077.git
~/brushfire $
```

You now have a place for Brushfire, but you haven't pushed anything yet, so the Brushfire application has not, as yet, been deployed.

Heroku will provide a random name for your application. For example, it named ours *still-retreat-63077,* which doesn't exactly roll off your tongue. You can change the name by navigating your browser to the Heroku dashboard and selecting the randomly assigned name. Select the Settings option, similar to figure 15.4.

NOTE   Heroku application names must be unique, so *your* application name will be different from ours.

Heroku application names are unique. We suggest using *brushfire* in the name, followed by some other identifier. For example, we renamed our application brushfire-sailsinaction.

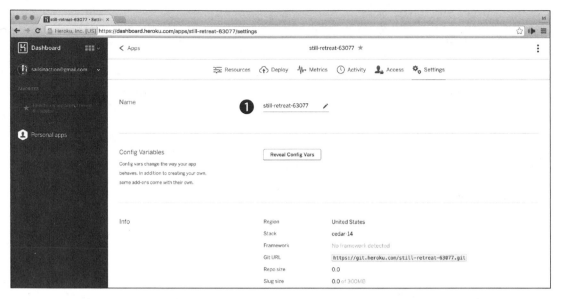

Figure 15.4   You can rename an application directly from the Heroku dashboard under Settings ❶.

To change the name, click the pencil icon next to the name in the dashboard. Changing the name of the application does have an implication with respect to the Heroku remote repo. To review, Brushfire will be using three Git repositories, as illustrated in figure 15.5.

Figure 15.5   Brushfire is stored in a local GIT repo ❶ on your local machine with two remote repos, one each on Heroku ❷ and GitHub ❸.

We have our local repo on our machine and a remote repo on GitHub. When we created an application on Heroku, another remote repository was created pointing to our application still-retreat-63077. Therefore, we need to change the name of the remote repository. In our case, we renamed it from still-retreat-63077 to brushfire-sailsinaction. Rename the application using the unique name you created earlier. Heroku makes this easy to do from the command line:

> **This updates the name of the Heroku remote repository to the new name.**

```
~/brushfire $ heroku git:remote -a brushfire-sailsinaction
```

You've created a place for Brushfire on Heroku, but before you actually deploy it, you also need to create a place for your PostgreSQL database.

15.2.4 *Using a remote PostgreSQL database*

During development, you used a local running version of PostgreSQL as your main database for Brushfire. This works for development. But now that you're transitioning to a production environment, you need a more stable place to store your data. Your PaaS provider, Heroku, also provides remote PostgreSQL instances as an add-on *database as a service* (DaaS). This will allow you to separate the location of your application from the underlying database. To add the service, return to Heroku and select your application from the dashboard, and then select Find More Add-ons, similar to figure 15.6.

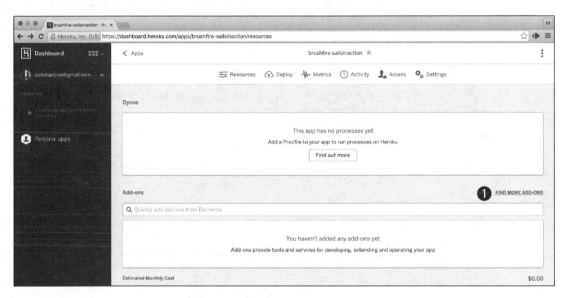

Figure 15.6 Heroku offers a variety of add-ons as a service, including PostgreSQL. To obtain a list of all services, click Find More Add-ons ❶ on the dashboard.

After clicking the link, you'll go through several steps, as illustrated in figure 15.7.

Heroku has created a PostgreSQL instance that will serve as your production database. More on what *production* means in a moment. Now that you have destinations for the application and database, you need to provide the configuration instructions that Heroku and Sails will use each time Brushfire is deployed and started.

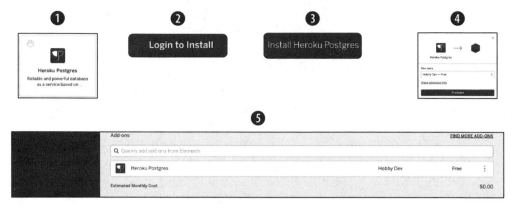

Figure 15.7   Locate and click Heroku Postgres ❶ from the list of available services. Click Login to Install ❷, and then Install Heroku Postgres ❸. You'll want to choose the zero-cost Hobby Dev ❹ and click the Provision button. Finally, you'll see the Heroku Postgres instance ❺.

15.3   *Using environment variables with Sails*

Environment variables are values kept in memory that can be accessed by a particular running instance of Sails. They're useful for temporarily storing sensitive credentials to databases and services like Mailgun. They can also be used as a way of configuring Sails when the Sails server lifts. In this section, we'll show you how to use environment variables with Heroku to configure and store credentials for your remote PostgreSQL database, as depicted in figure 15.8.

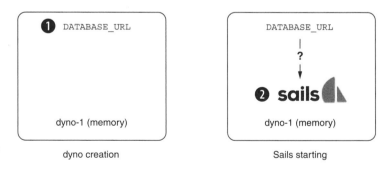

Figure 15.8   When Heroku starts the dyno, an environment variable is created in memory ❶. When Sails starts ❷, how do you get the value of the environment variable into Sails?

We'll also show you the mechanism for accessing environment variables within Sails. As always, instead of discussing these concepts theoretically, we'll dive in with an example.

15.3.1 Storing credentials in environment variables

Using brushfire/config/local.js during development was a convenient way of storing credentials locally. That, combined with using `brushfire/.gitignore`, prevented the local.js file from being pushed to your remote repository, thereby effectively preventing sensitive data from being pushed to a public repository. Now that you're deploying Brushfire to Heroku, there's an issue of where and how to store these credentials. You'll store the credentials on Heroku and access them securely in Sails using environment variables.

> **NOTE** Remember that *environment variables* are values that are stored in memory and can be accessed by a particular running instance of Sails.

When you created the PostgreSQL instance on Heroku, a configuration variable named `DATABASE_URL` was generated for you. *Configuration variable* is Heroku's term for a potential environment variable. We say *potential* because it doesn't become an environment variable until the dyno is started and the configuration variables are loaded into the environment's memory. The value for the `DATABASE_URL` environment variable contains the credentials for your remote PostgreSQL database instance outlined in figure 15.9.

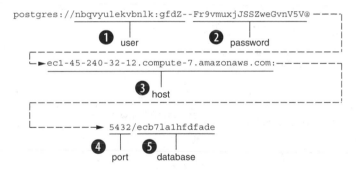

Figure 15.9   The value of the `DATABASE_URL` contains the database credentials including the user ❶, password ❷, host ❸, port ❹, and database ❺ to the PostgreSQL instance.

If you're curious where to find the configuration variables set by Heroku, click the Settings menu of your Brushfire application in Heroku, and then click Reveal Config Vars. Your browser should look similar to figure 15.10.

Once you deploy Brushfire to Heroku, this `DATABASE_URL` can be used within Sails to configure the connection to the remote PostgreSQL instance. At this point, you have a remote PostgreSQL database and the necessary credentials in an environment variable that you can access. But Sails has only a connection to your local PostgreSQL instance. Let's create a separate connection for the remote database instance.

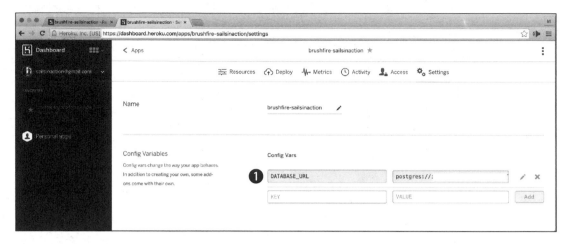

Figure 15.10   Heroku allows you to create environment variables, which are set prior to launching Brushfire. When you create the PostgreSQL instance, the DATABASE_URL config var ❶ is also created.

15.3.2   *Configuring a connection to a remote database*

You're currently using a connection named myPostgresqlServer, defined in brushfire/config/local.js, to connect your local Brushfire application to your local PostgreSQL database, similar to the following listing.

Listing 15.2   Credentials to your local PostgreSQL database

```
...
exports.connections = {
  myPostgresqlServer: {
    adapter: 'sails-postgresql',        A connection to the
    host: 'localhost',                  local PostgreSQL
    database: 'brushfire'               database
  }
};
...
```

Let's create another connection named productionPostgresqlServer to connect your soon-to-be deployed version of Brushfire to your remote PostgreSQL database on Heroku. In Sublime, open brushfire/config/connections.js, and add the following connection.

Listing 15.3   Adding a connection to the remote Heroku PostgreSQL instance

```
...
productionPostgresqlServer: {           This points to the Heroku
  adapter: 'sails-postgresql',          DATABASE_URL environment
  url: process.env.DATABASE_URL,        variable set by Heroku.
  ssl: true                             Heroku requires that this
}                                       property be set to true.
...
```

Notice that you reference the `DATABASE_URL` environment variable that holds the remote PostgreSQL credentials using Node's `process` dictionary to access it when Sails starts. Let's take a closer look at using the `process` dictionary as a conduit to access environment variables.

15.3.3 *Accessing environment variables in custom code*

In the previous section, you created a new connection to your remote PostgreSQL instance and used the `DATABASE_URL` environment variable that Heroku sets when Brushfire is deployed to access the database credentials. You'll access the environment variable using the global `process` dictionary of Node. Let's examine the `process` dictionary in action. From the command line, start the Sails REPL by typing

```
~/brushfire $ DATABASE_URL=example sails console    ⟵——— Sets the DATABASE_URL
                                                         environment variable to example
                                                         and starts the Sails REPL
```

> **DEFINITION**   The *read-eval-print loop* (REPL) is a program that allows you to interactively execute JavaScript and immediately see the results within a running Node application in the Sails console. It functions similarly to executing a command in the console of your browser on the frontend.

To log the contents of the `process` dictionary, return to the command line and type

```
sails> process    ⟵——— This logs the global process
                       dictionary to the console.
```

There's quite a bit of information attached to the `process` dictionary, so you can make it more manageable by looking at a portion of the `process` dictionary by next typing

```
sails> process.env    ⟵——— This logs the environment variables
                           collected by Node to the Sails console.
```

You should see the `DATABASE_URL` as one of the environment variables logged to the terminal window. When Heroku starts an instance of Sails, it also sets the `DATABASE_URL` environment variable automatically. Now, configure Brushfire to use a connection to the local PostgreSQL instance while you're developing on your local machine. Use the new remote connection configuration when you deploy Brushfire to Heroku using Sails runtime modes. To exit the Sails REPL, press Ctrl-C twice.

15.4 *Runtime environments*

Currently, when you start Brushfire using `sails lift`, you initiate a runtime environment in development mode.

> **DEFINITION**   A *runtime environment* loosely refers to the computer or container in which an application is currently running.

A runtime mode enables you to configure Sails based on a mode by setting the NODE_ENV environment variable.

> **DEFINITION**   NODE_ENV is the holy grail of environment variables for third-party Node applications. Many Node applications, including Sails, use NODE_ENV to set up the initial runtime mode of an application.

The different configurations based on the mode are accomplished through configuration files in brushfire/config/env/. Sails creates two runtime-specific files with each new project: development.js and production.js. These files work like the other Sails configuration files found in brushfire/config/. The settings in these files, however, override any other settings in brushfire/config/ (except for brushfire/config/local.js). In addition to being able to configure Sails differently based on the mode through the contents of these environment-specific files, development and production modes also have special significance in Sails. In development mode, your Sails app will go out of its way to help you. For example, Sails will provide you with more-descriptive error and debugging output. In contrast, production mode configures itself (and its dependencies) to optimize performance.

You have a variety of ways to set the runtime mode when Sails starts:

- Using `sails lift` without any command-line parameters or environment variables will set Sails' runtime mode to development.
- Using `sails lift --prod` sets Sails' runtime mode to production.
- Using `NODE_ENV=production node app.js` sets Sails' runtime mode to production.
- Setting the environment variable `NODE_ENV=production` in the terminal window before starting Sails will set Sails' runtime mode to production.

To ensure that Sails will run in production mode when deployed to Heroku, we'll create a Heroku config variable that will set NODE_ENV to `production` when a dyno starts. You can create the variable from the terminal window by typing the following commands on the command line:

```
~/brushfire $ heroku config:set NODE_ENV=production
```

> **NOTE**   We could have created the config variable from within the Heroku dashboard. Earlier, we showed you how to access DATABASE_URL from Heroku config variables. You can also add variables directly from the Heroku user interface instead of the command line.

Heroku will now set NODE_ENV to `production` each time Sails is deployed and before Sails starts up. Now that you can set Sails' runtime mode, let's instruct Sails to execute particular commands based on a particular mode.

15.4.1 Setting a default datastore for production

When Sails starts, all models are currently configured to use the local PostgreSQL instance connection in brushfire/config/models.js, similar to the next listing.

Listing 15.4 Setting the default connection for all models

```
module.exports.models = {
  connection: 'myPostgresqlServer',    ◁──  All models will use the
...                                          myPostgresqlServer
                                             connection.
```

You can override brushfire/config/models.js with another configuration file found at brushfire/config/env/production.js.

NOTE   Recall that brushfire/config/env/production.js is executed if Sails is set to production mode via the NODE_ENV environment variable.

From this file, you can set the default connection for all models when Sails is in production mode. In Sublime, open brushfire/config/env/production.js, and add a new models property that uses the productionPostgresqlServer connection, similar to this.

Listing 15.5 Setting the default connection for all models in production

```
module.exports = {
  models: {
    connection: 'productionPostgresqlServer'    ◁──  All models will use the
  },                                                 productionPostgresqlServer
...                                                  connection in production.
```

Now you have all models configured to use either the myPostgresqlServer connection or the productionPostgresqlServer connection, depending on Sails' runtime mode, as illustrated in figure 15.11.

on startup

...without command-line parameters or environment variables

...using `sails lift --prod`

...using `NODE_ENV=production node app.js`

...using `NODE_ENV=production` in the terminal window before starting Sails

development mode
brushfire/config/local.js

local database

production mode
brushfire/config/env/production.js

remote database

Figure 15.11   The runtime mode dictates which database connection is used at startup.

> **WARNING**   Without `brushfire/.gitignore`, `brushfire/config/local.js` *will* overwrite the configuration settings in brushfire/config/production.js. The reason it's not overwriting it on Heroku is that `.gitignore` blocks local.js from the remote repository. If you were deploying Brushfire by a method other than a remote Git repository, `brushfire/.gitignore` wouldn't block local.js, and thus its configuration would overwrite your production configuration. Therefore, if you're deploying using a method other than a remote Git repository, you'll need to make sure brushfire/config/local.js is not also deployed.

Finally, let's move the `productionPostgresqlServer` connection you created earlier to brushfire/config/env/production.js so that all your production configuration is in one place. In Sublime, open brushfire/config/connections.js, and move the `production-PostgresqlServer` connection to brushfire/config/env/production.js like so.

> **Listing 15.6   Adding the `productionPostgresqlServer` connection to production.js**

```
module.exports = {
  models: {
    connection: 'productionPostgresqlServer'
  },
  connections: {                              Adds connections
    productionPostgresqlServer: {             specifically for
      adapter: 'sails-postgresql',            production mode
      url: process.env.DATABASE_URL,
      ssl: true
    }
  }
};
```

15.4.2   *Configuring auto-migration settings*

When we first started developing Brushfire, changes to our database schema could happen ad hoc because we weren't concerned with preserving the underlying data. In fact, we have migrations within brushfire/config/models.js set to drop the database tables each time we restart Sails. Needless to say, in production, you're very concerned with preserving your data each time you restart Sails. In production mode, Sails will override all configuration files regarding migrations and automatically set migrations to safe mode to prevent inadvertent deletion of data.

In development mode, allowing database tables to be dropped each time Sails is restarted is compatible with your existing bootstrap file that creates test data each time Sails lifts. For production mode, however, the existing bootstrap file will attempt to create users that potentially exist, causing an error and preventing Sails from starting up. Let's change the bootstrap file to add test user records only if no users exist. In Sublime, open brushfire/config/bootstrap.js, and add the following code.

Listing 15.7 Changing the bootstrap file to check for existing users

```
module.exports.bootstrap = function(cb) {
  User.find().limit(1).exec(function(err, user) {        ◁──  Finds all users, but
    if(err) { return cb(err); }                               limits the number of
    if(user.length > 0) { return cb(); }          ◁──────     records found to 1

    var FixtureBootstrapper = require('../fixtures');        If a user exists, continues
    return FixtureBootstrapper(cb);                          lifting Sails without
  });                                                        creating test users
};
```

You'll use the `find` method to look for records in the `user` model. Because there could be millions of users, you'll limit the query to the first record found. If a record is found, you'll pass control back to Sails without adding any test data.

15.4.3 *Creating tables in PostgreSQL*

Because production mode will set migrations to `safe`, meaning no schema changes can be made to database tables, you need a mechanism to configure both the initial and ongoing configuration of the remote PostgreSQL database. To accomplish this, you'll temporarily connect your local version of Brushfire, which runs in development mode, to your remote instance of PostgreSQL on Heroku. That way, when the local Sails version starts, the remote instance of PostgreSQL will be configured with the initial schema attributes for each table. To do this, however, you need to comment out the existing connection in your local version of Sails and add a temporary connection to your remote database. In Sublime, open brushfire/config/local.js, and make a copy of the `myPostgresqlServer` connection, as shown here.

Listing 15.8 Connecting the local Brushfire to the remote PostgreSQL database

```
...
module.exports.connections = {
  // myPostgresqlServer: {                   ◁──  Adds comment tags
  //   adapter: 'sails-postgresql',               to existing local
  //   host: 'localhost',                         PostgreSQL connection
  //   database: 'brushfire'
  // }

  myPostgresqlServer: {                          Adds the connection
    adapter: 'sails-postgresql',                 credentials to the
    url: 'ADD YOUR OWN HEROKU POSTGRESQL URL HERE',  ◁──  remote PostgreSQL
    ssl: true                                    connection on Heroku
  }
};
...
```

NOTE We also added comments to the existing local PostgreSQL instance.

Start the Sails server using `sails lift`. The table schemas will be set up according to the configuration of Brushfire models. It's important to note that because your local instance of Brushfire has migrations set to drop, you need to exercise *extreme* caution when using this technique to initialize the remote PostgreSQL instance. Once Sails loads, you can confirm that the tables and test data were created by navigating your browser to localhost:1337 and signing in as sailsinaction with the password abc123. After confirming that the tables are configured properly, head back to brushfire/config/local.js, and remove the connection to the remote PostgreSQL instance and restore the connection to the local PostgreSQL database, similar to this.

Listing 15.9   Restored local Brushfire PostgreSQL database

```
...
module.exports.connections = {
    myPostgresqlServer: {
    adapter: 'sails-postgresql',
    host: 'localhost',
    database: 'brushfire'
  }

  // myPostgresqlServer: {
  //    adapter: 'sails-postgresql',
  //     url: 'ADD YOUR OWN HEROKU POSTGRESQL URL HERE',
  //     ssl: true
  // }
};
...
```

Once you add real production data into the database, you should use only one of the many third-party clients to access your remote production database. We currently use a third-party client called Postico.

15.4.4 *Runtime vs. build-time process*

Now that you're about to deploy Brushfire into production, it's necessary to distinguish between *runtime process* and *build-time process*. This distinction is important because there are some tasks you want to run each time the Sails server starts. For example, the bootstrap is a runtime process because you use it to execute when the Sails server starts. Some tasks you want performed only when Brushfire is deployed. For example, you want the production Grunt tasks to execute when you deploy and not each time the Sails server starts. Therefore, you need to change the Grunt tasks to execute when Brushfire is deployed instead of every time the Sails server is started.

15.4.5 *Setting up Grunt for production*

By default in production mode, Sails will perform different Grunt tasks on your static assets. The production Grunt tasks include concatenating asset files as well as minification of some assets. These tasks can take a few minutes, depending on the size of the project. Heroku has a default 60-second boot timeout. This means that Brushfire needs to start within 60 seconds or it will fail.

NOTE In development mode, Sails doesn't wait for the Grunt tasks to be completed before lifting. In production mode, Sails does wait until all Grunt tasks are completed.

Therefore, you want the static asset preparation tasks to happen at build time to avoid any potential timeout issues. In order to run these tasks during build time and not during runtime, you must make a few configuration changes. First, you'll turn off Grunt when you're in production mode. Next, you'll alter the name of the Grunt task that Heroku will use to build your static assets during build time. Finally, you'll install an alternative set of scripts that incorporates Grunt into Heroku's build-time process.

To turn off Grunt in production, you need to alter the Sails startup file named app.js. In Sublime, open brushfire/app.js, and make the following changes.

Listing 15.10 Preventing Grunt tasks on startup if Sails is in production mode

```
    ...
      console.error('npm install rc --save');
      rc = function () { return {}; };
    }
  }

  var config = rc('sails');                                   Checks if you're
                                                              in production
                                                                    mode
  if (process.env.NODE_ENV === 'production' || process.env.nogrunt) {
    config.hooks = config.hooks || {};

    config.hooks.grunt = false;         Turns off
  }                                     Grunt tasks

  sails.lift(config);          Lifts Sails with your
})();                          new configuration
```

NOTE The changes you make to the brushfire/app.js file won't be executed locally using `sails lift` because app.js is executed only when starting Sails via Node app.js. Heroku, however, starts Sails using Node app.js, and thus the file will be executed on the remote instance of Sails.

In production mode, Grunt is set up by default to run a task named prod located in brushfire/tasks/register/prod.js. Instead, you'll change the name of the existing production Grunt task to the name Heroku will use when building your static assets. In Sublime, open brushfire/tasks/register/prod.js, and rename the registered task to `heroku:production`, similar to the following listing.

Listing 15.11   Renaming the registered Grunt task for Heroku

```
module.exports = function (grunt) {
  grunt.registerTask('heroku:production', [        ◁─┐   Changes the registered
      'compileAssets',                                  │   task name from prod to
      'concat',                                         │   heroku:production
      ...
```

Heroku will execute this Grunt task when building a Sails dyno. Finally, the scripts Heroku will use to build your Sails dyno are called *buildpacks*. Default Heroku build-packs don't support Grunt, so let's set the buildpack location to an alternative set of buildpacks that do support Grunt. Head back over to the terminal window and type the following commands on the command line:

```
~/brushfire $ heroku buildpacks:set https://github.com/mbuchetics/heroku-
buildpack-nodejs-grunt.git
```

Heroku will now execute your Grunt tasks as part of its build-time process.

15.4.6 *Deploying to Heroku*

You're now ready to deploy Brushfire to Heroku. Save your changes to the local Git repository by returning to the terminal window and typing the following commands on the command line:

```
                                                    ┌─   Stages all your changes
                                                    │    for the next commit
~/brushfire $ git add .                          ◁─┘
~/brushfire $ git commit -am 'added deployment configuration'   ◁─┐
                                                                    Commits changes to
                                                                    the local repository
```

Now that you've committed your changes to the local repo, deploying Brushfire to Heroku is as simple as pushing your local repository to the Heroku remote repository. Again, from the command line type

```
~/brushfire $ git push heroku master
```

At the end of the build process, Heroku will display the URL of the Brushfire instance. Navigate your browser to the logged URL, which should look similar to figure 15.12.

Although Brushfire has been deployed, you still have some work to do. Chad has high hopes for growth and wants you to plan for Brushfire to use multiple Heroku dynos. Therefore, you need to transition from individual session and WebSocket stores on each Brushfire instance to a central store for all dynos.

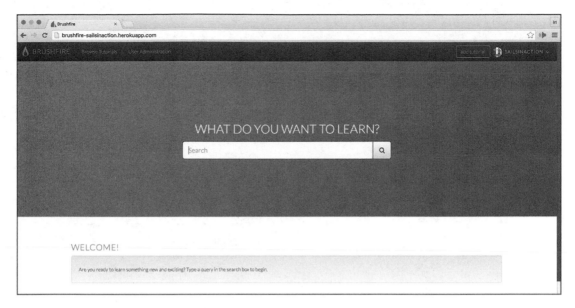

Figure 15.12   Brushfire deployed and running on Heroku

15.5   Configuring sessions and sockets for production

During development, you stored session information in memory on your local machine. Now that you have the potential for multiple instances of Brushfire in production, you need to configure a centralized session store for any potential number of Heroku dynos. You'll use Redis as the database to store sessions. Recall that Redis is an in-memory datastore using key/value pairs similar to a dictionary. Similar to PostgreSQL, Heroku provides remote Redis instances as a DaaS. Let's set up Redis in Heroku.

15.5.1   Provisioning a remote Redis To Go instance

To add a remotely hosted Redis database on Heroku, navigate your browser to the Heroku dashboard Resources page. You should see the existing remote PostgreSQL instance as one of the add-ons. The process of adding Redis is similar to what you did with PostgreSQL. From the Resources page, click Find More Add-ons. Next, click the Redis To Go service, followed by the Login to Install button, followed by the Install Redis To Go button. Select your Brushfire instance and click Submit. Finally, ensure you're using the free Nano plan and click the Provision button. Similar to the remote PostgreSQL instance, Heroku creates a configuration variable named `REDISTOGO_URL` that contains the credentials for the Redis To Go datastore. You'll use this variable and its value when configuring sessions and WebSockets.

15.5.2 *Configuring a remote session store*

Sessions are currently stored in memory in each instance of Sails. Now that you have a remote Redis database, you can configure each Sails dyno to use this single remote instance. In Sublime, open brushfire/config/env/production.js, and add the following to enable the Sails session store to Redis.

Listing 15.12   Configuring Redis To Go for sessions in production

```
...
connections: {
  productionPostgresqlServer: {
    adapter: 'sails-postgresql',
    url: process.env.DATABASE_URL,
    ssl: true
  }
},
session: {                             ◁── Configuring
  adapter: 'redis',                        sessions to use
  url: process.env.REDISTOGO_URL           the redis adapter
},
...
```

Now that you have the connection configured, let's install the adapter. From the terminal window, type

```
~/brushfire $ npm install connect-redis --save
```

Once it's installed, sessions will now be configured to use the Redis To Go instance on Heroku for Brushfire in production mode.

15.5.3 *Using Redis to deliver notifications*

Similar to sessions, WebSockets are currently stored in memory for each instance of Sails. You need to configure each Sails dyno to use this remote instance. In Sublime, open brushfire/config/env/production.js, and add the following code to enable the Sails WebSocket store to Redis.

Listing 15.13   Configuring Redis To Go for WebSockets in production

```
...
session: {
  adapter: 'redis',
  url: process.env.REDISTOGO_URL
},
sockets: {                             ◁── Configuring
  adapter: 'socket.io-redis',              WebSockets to use the
  url: process.env.REDISTOGO_URL,          redis socket adapter
},
...
```

Now that you have the connection configured, you need to install the adapter. From the terminal window, type

```
~/brushfire $ npm install socket.io-redis --save
```

Once it's installed, WebSockets will be configured to use the Redis To Go instance on Heroku for Brushfire in production mode.

15.5.4 Using Redis in development (so you don't have to log in all the time)

There's no real performance or scalability advantage to using Redis for WebSockets in development. But there is a benefit to using Redis with sessions. Sessions are stored in memory on your local machine. Therefore, any time you restart Sails, the sessions are lost because they're stored in memory on the same machine. Installing a local instance of Redis and configuring Sails to use it during development eliminates the need to sign in after restarting the Sails server. In Sublime, open brushfire/config/session.js, and uncomment the adapter, similar to the following listing.

> **Listing 15.14 Configuring a local Redis database for sessions in development**

```
...
  module.exports.session = {
  secret: '[YOUR SECRET] ',
  ...
adapter: 'redis',
  ...
```

Specifies the redis adapter in development mode

Information about installation can be found at http://redis.io/download. For OS X, we used the package manager Homebrew. Once installed, the Redis server can be started by typing the following from the command line:

```
~/ $ redis-server
```

Sails will now use the local Redis instance in development mode and the remote instance in production mode. To confirm that Redis is running locally, restart Sails using `sails lift`. Navigate your browser to localhost:1337 and sign in to Brushfire using `sailsinaction` and the password `abc123`. Now, restart the Sails server using `sails lift`. If you go back to your browser and refresh, you should be logged in. This is because the session database is now separate from your Sails instance.

15.5.5 Configuring Mailgun for email delivery

You need a way to configure the Mailgun service credentials you implemented earlier in chapter 11. You can configure Heroku to set environment variables, much like you configured your PostgreSQL database credentials by storing them securely on Heroku. Add the environment variables by navigating your browser to the Heroku dashboard for your Brushfire instance and clicking Settings. Then, from the Settings page,

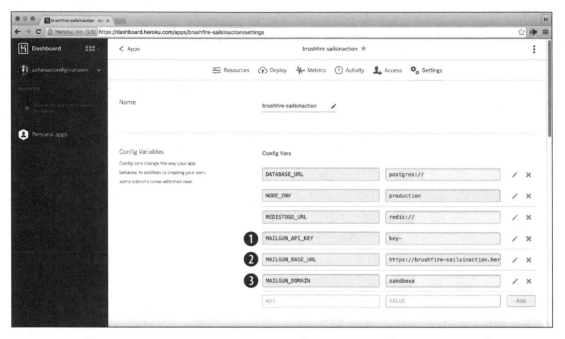

Figure 15.13 The Mailgun credentials include the API key ❶, the base URL ❷, and the domain ❸.

click Reveal Config Vars. After you add the environment variables, your browser should look similar to figure 15.13.

Next, you'll add these environment variables to the production configuration file. In Sublime, open brushfire/config/env/production.js, and add the following Mailgun settings.

Listing 15.15 Configuring Mailgun credentials for production

```
...
session: {
  adapter: 'redis',
  url: process.env.REDISTOGO_URL
},

mailgun: {
  apiKey: process.env.MAILGUN_API_KEY,       Mailgun credentials
  domain: process.env.MAILGUN_DOMAIN,        via environment
  baseUrl: process.env.MAILGUN_BASE_URL      variables
}
};
```

In production, Brushfire is now properly configured for Mailgun. Commit the changes from the terminal window by typing

```
~/brushfire $ git commit -am 'added mailgun credentials'
```

And then push the results to Heroku by typing

```
~/brushfire $ git push heroku master
```

Let's move on to a very important topic: testing.

15.6 Testing

The amount of testing needed for a project can be a highly contentious subject. In this section, we'll show you how to implement and configure a testing environment that supports many different testing styles. When planning for this book, we considered using test-driven development (TDD) and realized that including that discussion could double the length of the manuscript. In the end, we compromised on providing this discussion that allows you to implement your own style of testing.

You can use many libraries and frameworks to test Sails, but in this book you'll use a JavaScript testing framework named Mocha. Mocha allows you to create test cases, execute those cases, and receive the results via reports. You'll also use SuperTest, another testing library, which allows you to easily create test cases that make requests to your routes and controller/actions. SuperTest also provides a way to make requests using existing sessions.

15.6.1 Installing dependencies for your test suite

In this section, you'll install Mocha and SuperTest as well as configure the folder structure that will contain your tests. From the command line, install Mocha by typing

```
~/brushfire $ npm install mocha --save-dev
```

By using the –dev tag, you'll install Mocha as a development dependency, and, therefore, it won't be installed when Brushfire is deployed in production mode. You'll do something similar for SuperTest. From the command line, type

```
~/brushfire $ npm install supertest --save-dev
```

Now that both frameworks are installed, you can create a folder structure for your tests. From the root of the Brushfire project, create a folder named brushfire/test/. You'll add all your tests, helper functions, and fixtures to this folder.

15.6.2 Using before() and after()

Mocha provides functions where you can set up preconditions before tests as well as clean up after tests. In Sublime, create a new file named brushfire/test/bootstrap.test.js, and add the following code.

> **Listing 15.16 Adding before and after hooks to Mocha**

```
var Sails = require('../node_modules/sails');
var sails = require('sails');
```

```
before(function(done) {
  Sails.lift({
    log: {
      level: 'error'
    },
    hooks: {
      grunt: false
    }
  }, done);
});

after(function(done) {
  Sails.lower(done);
});
```

> **The before method allows you to lift Sails before a test is executed.**

> **Starts Sails without loading Grunt**

> **The after method allows you to close Sails after tests are completed.**

This Mocha bootstrap file is very useful for running tasks before and after a test and should not be confused with brushfire/config/bootstrap.js, which is executed when the Sails server starts. Next, let's see how you can use npm to start your tests from the command line.

15.6.3 *Running tests from the command line*

You'll use npm from the command line to initiate tests. To set this up, open brush-fire/package.json in Sublime, and add the following to the `scripts` dictionary.

> **Listing 15.17   Configuring npm to initiate tests from the command line**

```
...
  "scripts": {
    "debug": "node debug app.js",
    "start": "node app.js",
    "test": "NODE_ENV=test mocha --recursive -t 5000"
  },
...
```

> **Initiates the test environment by setting NODE_ENV and starting Mocha**

Let's see this in action. From the command line, start Mocha by typing

```
~/brushfire $ npm test
```

Because you don't have any tests yet, you should see something like `0 passing (1ms)` from the command line. This will not only initiate Mocha tests but also set the run-time mode of Sails to `test`. Before you start testing, you'll set up a test environment mode file similar to what you did for production and development modes.

15.6.4 *Configuring your test environment*

You currently have configuration files for development and production modes. Let's add one for your test environment. In Sublime, create a file named brushfire/config/env/test.js, and add the following code.

Listing 15.18 Configuring npm to initiate tests from the command line

```
module.exports = {
  models: {
    connection: 'memory',          Configures all models to use the
    schema: true,                  memory connection, enforce
    migrations: 'drop'             schema, and drop tables
  },
  connections: {
    memory: {                      Configures the memory
      adapter: 'sails-memory',     connection to use the
    }                              sails-memory adapter
  },
  session: {                       Configures sessions to
    adapter: 'memory'              use the in-memory
  },                               adapter
};
```

It sometimes works well to use the `sails-memory` adapter to speed up testing. So, during testing, you'll configure models and sessions to use the `sails-memory` adapter instead of the PostgreSQL and Redis adapters. To install the `sails-memory` adapter, head over to the terminal window, and type

```
~/brushfire $ npm install sails-memory --save-dev
```

You're now ready to add your first test case.

15.6.5 *Understanding tests*

Before diving into an actual test of Brushfire, we thought it would be easier to start our discussion with a simple test case that isolates the structure of a test. In the brushfire/test/ folder, create a subfolder named integration/. This is where you'll aggregate your tests. Create the test in Sublime by creating a file named brushfire/test/integration/test.js and adding the following code.

Listing 15.19 Fundamentals of a test

```
                                            Adds Node's native
var assert = require('assert');             assert module

describe('Personal Heros :: ', function(){
  describe('Nikola Tesla :: ', function(){          Name spacing your test
    it('everyone should think Nikola Tesla is a genius!', function() {
      // Since there are no errors, this test will pass!
      assert.equal(1,1);                                      First test
    });                          First                        case
  });                           assertion
});
```

The `assert` library is a core module in Node. One of the purposes of the library is to provide methods that you can use to test whether something is true. The `describe()`

method is a way to group multiple tests under a particular namespace often referred to as a *test suite*. You can also nest the `describe()` method in another `describe()` to create subgroups. Observing the results of a test will provide greater clarity on how and why you use these methods. The `it()` method creates an actual test case. Anything that throws an error within the `it()` method will cause the test to fail. Execute your first test by heading to the terminal window and typing the following from the command line:

```
~/brushfire $ npm test
```

The result of the test should look similar to the following.

Listing 15.20   The results of executing test.js

```
brushfire@0.0.0 test /brushfire
> NODE_ENV=test mocha --recursive -t 5000

  Personal Heros ::                                    From the description() method
    Nikola Tesla ::
      ✓ everyone should think Nikola Tesla is a genius!   From the it()
                                                          method
  1 passing (2s)        ◁──── The test passed.
```

Looking at the log results of the test, you can see that your first test passed.

15.6.6   *Testing an endpoint*

Now that you have an initial test under your belt, let's create a test for a portion of your signup-a-user endpoint. The route consists of a `POST` request to `/signup` that triggers the `signup` action of the `user` controller. There's a policy on this action that requires a `user` to be logged out and therefore not authenticated in order to access the action. In order to test whether this policy is working, you need to create and authenticate a user as part of the setup for the test. In Sublime, create a new file name brushfire/test/integration/create-user.js, and add the following code.

Listing 15.21   Creating the user before the test

```
var assert = require('assert');
var request = require('supertest');

describe('User Controller :: ', function() {          Establishes the
  describe('POST /user/signup :: ', function() {       test suite group
    describe('When logged in :: ', function() {        and subgroups
      var agent;
      before(function(done) {
        agent = request.agent(sails.hooks.http.app);      Returns a dictionary
                                                           you can use to make
        Passwords.encryptPassword({       Encrypts the    requests with cookies
          password: 'abc123'              test user
        })                                password
```

```
          .exec({
            error: done,
            success: function(password) {
              User.create({
                username: 'testtest',              ◄─┐  Creates
                email: 'test@test.com',               │  the user
                encryptedPassword: password
              })
              .exec(function(err, user) {
                if(err) { return done(err); }

                agent                              ◄─┐  Makes a request using the
                .put('/login')                        │  agent to authenticate the
                .send({                               │  test user
                  username: 'testtest',
                  password: 'abc123'
                })
                .set('Content-Type', 'application/json')
                .end(function(err, res) {
                  if(err) { return done(err); }
                  console.log('res.status', res.status);
                  return done();
                });
              });
            }
          });
        });
      });
    });
  });
```

Again, you use the `before()` method. But this time you use it within a `describe()` method. Therefore, instead of the `before` code executing prior to all tests, as it did in bootstrap.test.js, this code will execute before the tests within this particular `describe()`.

> **NOTE** We've made this `before()` method asynchronous by adding `done` as an argument in the callback. Thus, no tests will be run until `before()` returns control.

Next, you'll configure SuperTest's `agent` dictionary, which allows you to make requests with persisted cookies.

> **NOTE** There are many ways to make client requests of a server. You can rely on a browser to make a request, or you can rely on a library that uses methods that issue requests on your behalf. The SuperTest agent allows you to simulate a browser request, including things like cookies used with sessions.

You encrypt the test user password and then create the user before making a request with your `agent` dictionary. The request authenticates the test user and then passes control back to Mocha to execute the remainder of the tests.

Now that you have an authenticated test user, let's use it to test the policy. Head back to Sublime, and add the following code to brushfire/test/integration/create-user.js.

Listing 15.22   Testing the signup-a-user endpoint

```
...
  it('should return a 403 response code', function(done) {        ← Creates an
                                                                     asynchronous
    agent                          ← Attempts to                     test case
    .post('/user/signup')            create a user
    .send({
      username: 'foo',
      email: 'foo@foo.com',
      password: 'barbaz'
    })
    .set('Content-Type', 'application/json')
    .end(function(err, res) {
      if(err) { return done(err); }

      assert.equal(res.statusCode, 403);        ← Confirms the
                                                   correct returned
      return done();                             status code
    });
  });
 });
});
```

First, you create an asynchronous test case by adding done as an argument to the callback of the it() method. Then, you make a request that will trigger an attempt to create a user using the agent method.

NOTE   The policy should prevent an authenticated user from reaching the signup action and produce the 403 status code.

Finally, you confirm that the returned status code is 403 by using the assert() method. Let's see this in action. From the terminal window, type the following on the command line:

```
~/brushfire $ npm test
```

You should now have two passing tests.

15.6.7   *Refactoring a test using fixtures and helper functions*

At times, you'll want to refactor some repeated aspects of a test into a reusable component. For example, let's refactor the test-user properties into their own fixture. Within brushfire/test/, create a subfolder named fixtures. In Sublime, create a new file named brushfire/test/fixtures/user.js similar to the following listing.

Listing 15.23 Refactoring the test user data into fixtures

```
module.exports = {
  username: 'testtest',
  password: 'abc123',
  email: 'test@test.com'
};
```

You can now `require` this `fixture` any time you need it. Next, let's refactor the creation and authentication of a test user into its own utility method. In Sublime, open brushfire/test/integration/create-user.js, and replace the bulk of creating and authenticating a user with a new method appropriately named `createTestUser-AndAuthenticate(agent, done)` similar to the following.

Listing 15.24 Introducing a new helper function in a test

```
var assert = require('assert');
var request = require('supertest');

describe('User Controller :: ', function() {
  describe('POST /user/signup :: ', function() {
    describe('When logged in :: ', function() {
      var agent;
      before(function(done) {

        var createTestUserAndAuthenticate = require('../utils/create-logged-
        ➡ in-user');
        agent = request.agent(sails.hooks.http.app);

        createTestUserAndAuthenticate(agent, done);
      });

      it('should return a 403 response code', function(done) {
        ...
```

Requires the soon-to-be refactored code →

Executes the new method, passing in the agent and callback from the before() method ←

Next, let's implement the `createTestUserAndAuthenticate()` method. Within brushfire/test/, create a subfolder named utils. You'll use the utils subfolder as a place for your utility test methods. In Sublime, create a new file named brushfire/test/utils/create-logged-in-user.js, and add the following code.

Listing 15.25 Implementing the `createTestUserAndAuthenticate` method

```
var request = require('supertest');
var Passwords = require('machinepack-passwords');
var USER_FIXTURE = require('../fixtures/user');

module.exports = function(agent, cb) {
  Passwords.encryptPassword({
    password: USER_FIXTURE.password
  })
  .exec({
    error: cb,
```

Adds access to test user fixtures ←

Passes in the agent dictionary and callback ←

Syntax for accessing the fixture dictionary |

```
      success: function(password) {
        User.create({
          username: USER_FIXTURE.username,
          email: USER_FIXTURE.email,
          encryptedPassword: password
        })
        .exec(function(err, user) {
          if(err) { return cb(err); }

          agent
          .put('/login')
          .send({
            username: USER_FIXTURE.username,
            password: USER_FIXTURE.password
          })
          .set('Content-Type', 'application/json')
          .end(function(err, res) {
            if(err) { return cb(err); }
            return cb();
          });
        });
      }
    });
};
```

Let's again see this in action. From the terminal window, type the following on the command line:

```
~/brushfire $ npm test
```

After the refactor, you should still have two passing tests, except you now have a utility function you can use throughout your test suites. Next, let's do some validation testing on the user model.

15.6.8   *Testing model methods and validations*

The POST /user/signup endpoint has several initial validations. Let's test one of the validations: when a user hasn't supplied an email address. In Sublime, open brushfire/test/integration/create-user.js, and add the following code.

Listing 15.26   Testing the missing email validation

```
...
describe('When logged out ::', function() {
  describe('With an invalid email address', function() {          ◁——  Group tests as
    it('should return a 400 status code when missing', function(done) {    email validations
      request(sails.hooks.http.app)          ◁——┐
      .post('/user/signup')                     │  Makes request with
      .send({                                   │  missing email property
        username: 'foo',
        password: 'barbaz'
      })
```

```
        .set('Content-Type', 'application/json')
        .end(function(err, res) {
          if(err) { return done(err); }
          assert.equal(res.statusCode, 400);        ◁──┐  Tests for 400
          return done();                                 │  response
        });
      });
    });
  });
```

These tests will require a new user that is unauthenticated, so you don't need any test user creation and authentication setup. The validation requires an email address, so you'll make a request to sign up a new user without an email address. The test is expecting a 400 Bad Request status code. Give it a try. Start the test from the terminal window via npm test. You should now have three passing tests. Finally, create a test for a successful signup. In Sublime, open brushfire/test/integration/create-user.js, and add the following test.

Listing 15.27   Testing for a successful signup

```
        ...
        describe('With valid properties', function() {
        var userResponse;                         ◁──
                                                        userResponse will hold
Creates  ┌▷ before(function(done) {                     the res dictionary you'll
a user    │    request(sails.hooks.http.app)            use later within the
          │    .post('/user/signup')                    assert() method.
          │    .send({
          │      username: 'foofoo',
          │      password: 'barbaz',
          │      email: 'foo.bar@baz.com'
          │    })
          │    .set('Content-Type', 'application/json')
          │    .end(function(err, res) {
          │      if(err) { return done(err); }
          │      userResponse = res;
          │      done();                                        Tests whether
          │    });                                              the user was
          │  });                                                successfully
          │                                                     created
             it('should return a 200 response code', function() {
                assert.equal(userResponse.statusCode, 200);   ◁──┘
     Tests    });
whether the
   username   it('should return the username of the user in the body', function() {
was created ┌▷   assert.equal(userResponse.body.username, 'foofoo');
            │  });
            │
             it('should set the gravatar on the user record', function(done) {
     Tests ┌▷   User.findOne({ username: 'foofoo' }).exec(function(err, user) {
whether the │    if(err) { return done(err); }
 gravatarURL │    assert(user);
was created │    assert(user.gravatarURL);
            │    assert.notEqual(user.gravatarURL, '');
```

```
            done();
        });
      });
    });
  });
});
```

Here, you're testing whether the user was created successfully in various ways:

- Did you receive a 200 status response?
- Did you receive a valid username?
- Did you receive a valid gravatarURL?

Once again, let's execute the test via npm test. You should now have six passing tests. With these testing components, you have the tools necessary to test all aspects of your controller/actions.

15.7 Security

Although we've been working on Brushfire security concepts throughout the book, we wanted to extend our discussion with a section that identifies an application's core security vulnerabilities as well as the various steps you can take to protect against them. Figure 15.14 focuses on the top vulnerabilities of each layer of Brushfire's technical stack.

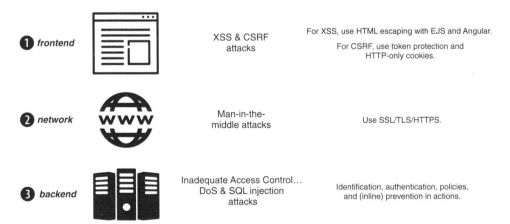

Figure 15.14   An overview view of the security vulnerabilities of Brushfire's technical stack includes attacks related to the frontend, attacks related to the network, and attacks related to the backend.

First, we'll address frontend vulnerabilities due to cross-site scripting (XSS) and cross-site request forgery (CSRF) attacks ❶, as well as preventive measures to protect against them. Next, we'll look at how to protect against man-in-the-middle (MITM) network attacks ❷. We'll end with addressing backend vulnerabilities and protections ❸. We encourage you to explore the Sails security site at http://sailsjs.org/documentation/concepts/security as well as the Open Web Application Security Project (OWASP) site at http://mng.bz/yXd3. Each destination provides a wealth of timely information pertaining to many aspects of application security.

15.7.1 *Frontend, network, and backend security*

Before addressing specific vulnerabilities, it's important to discuss your control or lack thereof of each layer. Relative control is directly tied to a layer's exposure to changes without your consent. For example, on the client side, you've provided validation logic through Angular that prevents the creation of a user that contains characters other than spaces (the letters Aa–Zz, or the numbers 0–9). But anyone can circumvent those validations because you have no control over changes to the browser user-agent. You have to design your security around an assumption that anything you do on the browser user-agent is subject to change and, therefore, any data from the frontend layer is untrusted and possibly malicious. In the validation example, because frontend validations can be thwarted, you must also create the same validations on the backend.

The network layer is also outside your control and subject to changes. Again, you have to protect against the possibility that someone could intercept and change your requests/responses before they reach the user-agent or server. Finally, unlike the browser user-agent or network, you can reasonably expect that what you create on the backend won't change without your consent. That doesn't mean you can't create unwanted vulnerabilities. It just means that whatever you've baked in won't be subject to change.

15.7.2 *Understanding cross-site scripting attacks*

Cross-site scripting (XSS) attacks occur when an attacker injects malicious scripts into an otherwise benign web page, causing the browser to do things counter to the best interest of the user. These malicious scripts can be injected in a variety of ways. The most prevalent way is a stored or *persistent* attack.

> **TIP** Once stored, a persistent attack can occur any time a user renders the injected page.

A persistent attack occurs when the malicious script is stored in a database. It's then executed when the stored data is injected and rendered on a page.

15.7.3 *Protecting against XSS attacks*

The best defense against an XSS attack is to *HTML escape* any untrusted data that's inserted into a page.

> **DEFINITION** *HTML escaping* is a process of replacing the characters of potentially harmful scripts with an HTML entity. For example, you don't want the

<script> tag to be executed in any data you inject in the page. HTML escaping replaces the less-than (<) sign with the HTML entity < and the greater-than (>) sign with the HTML entity >. Therefore, the <script> tag becomes <script> which renders as <script> but does not execute as <script>.

Figure 15.15 illustrates HTML escaping of potentially malicious user-provided data.

Figure 15.15   After HTML escaping, the malicious script ❶ is rendered harmless ❷ before it's injected into a page.

Brushfire uses EJS template tags, <%= %>, *and* Angular template tags, {{ }}, to HTML escape data on a page. For example, these tags automatically escape characters like the less-than (<) and greater-than (>). A majority of the time, you'll use the EJS <%= %> template tag that HTML escapes content. There are two instances, however, where you want to inject data into a page without HTML escaping. In brushfire/views/layout.ejs, you use <%- body %> and <%- partial() %> to inject other views into the layout. These tags don't do HTML escaping and instead pass the responsibility of HTML escaping untrusted data to the views they inject. You also use the EJS <%- %> template tag when bootstrapping data on a page. Any time you inject user content without HTML escaping, you open yourself to risk, so it's important that you can trust whatever you're injecting without HTML escaping it first.

> **NOTE**   As of the publish date of this book, Sails v1.0 hasn't been released. But when it is, you'll be able to take advantage of an easier approach for injecting data on the page using script tags. Take a look at the Sails v1.0 release notes at http://sailsjs.org/support for more information.

15.7.4   *Understanding cross-site request forgery attacks*

A typical cross-site request forgery (CSRF) attack occurs when a user who has authenticated to a trusted site and has a valid session unwittingly executes a script that uses the existing browser session to perform a malicious act as an authenticated user, as shown in figure 15.16.

For example, a user navigates their browser to a site they trust and then logs in. The login process establishes a session between the browser user-agent and the trusted website. Any subsequent request made from the browser user-agent while the session

NO CSRF Protection

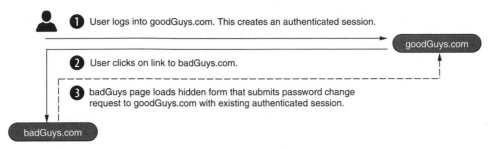

① User logs into goodGuys.com. This creates an authenticated session.

goodGuys.com

② User clicks on link to badGuys.com.

③ badGuys page loads hidden form that submits password change request to goodGuys.com with existing authenticated session.

badGuys.com

Figure 15.16 A typical CSRF attack begins with a user ① logging in to a trusted site. The user ② clicks a malicious link that appears to be legitimate but is actually a page on an untrusted site ③ that uses the existing session to do bad things.

is active, regardless of whether the request is made from a new window or tab, will appear from the perspective of the server to be from that authenticated user. An attacker could, for example, use the hijacked session for a malicious act that changes the user's password. This type of attack does require that the application have an XSS vulnerability or that the user click a malicious link from some other source such as a link in an email that triggers a request from the authenticated browser.

Sails provides protection against this style of attack using a CSRF token. Whereas a session tells the server that a user is *who* they say they are, a CSRF token tells the server that a user is *where* they say they are. When enabled, all non-GET requests to the Sails server must be accompanied by a special token, identified as the csrf parameter, similar to figure 15.17.

This time-stamped secret CSRF token is generated by the server and made available via either a local variable named csrf in a view or via a GET request to the /csrf-Token route, where the token will be returned as JSON. Without this token, the would-be attacker will be prevented from making non-GET requests. Let's enable

WITH CSRF Protection

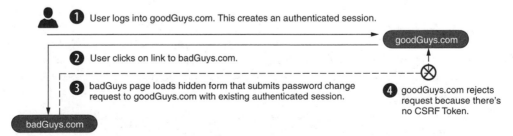

① User logs into goodGuys.com. This creates an authenticated session.

goodGuys.com

② User clicks on link to badGuys.com.

③ badGuys page loads hidden form that submits password change request to goodGuys.com with existing authenticated session.

④ goodGuys.com rejects request because there's no CSRF Token.

badGuys.com

Figure 15.17 With CSRF protection enabled, a user ① logs in to a trusted site. The user ② clicks a malicious link that appears to be legitimate but is actually a page on an untrusted site ③ that uses the existing session to attempt to do bad things. Without the csrf token, a malicious request ④ will be rejected by goodGuys.com.

CSRF protection in Brushfire and then look at the various ways of obtaining and including it in non-GET requests.

15.7.5 *Enabling CSRF token protection*

Enabling CSRF token protection is simple. In Sublime, open brushfire/config/csrf.js, and change the csrf property value to true, similar to the next listing.

Listing 15.28 Enabling `csrf` token protection

```
module.exports.csrf = true;
```

The Brushfire backend will now expect a csrf token in every non-GET request. If no token is provided, the request will fail.

15.7.6 *Sending the CSRF token*

Now that you've enabled the use of CSRF tokens, you need to make sure the token is passed into all non-GET requests. You can either add the token to each request manually or utilize an automated method to add a header to all HTTP and Web-Sockets requests.

> **NOTE** HTTP and WebSockets use headers to communicate configuration properties of requests and responses.

Angular provides a way to set common headers in HTTP requests for a given application. In Sublime, open brushfire/assets/js/app.js, and add the following code.

Listing 15.29 Adding a common `csrf` token header to Angular HTTP requests

```
...
angular.module('brushfire').run(['$http', function($http) {
  if (window.SAILS_LOCALS._csrf) {
    $http.defaults.headers.common['X-CSRF-Token'] = window.SAILS_LOCALS._csrf;   ◁─┐
  }
}]);                                                            This adds the csrf token
                                                               to every HTTP request.
```

Now all HTTP requests will contain a header with the csrf property to Sails. Next, you need to bootstrap the csrf token to the window dictionary using the csrf local variable Sails provides you from a view. In Sublime, open brushfire/views/layout.ejs, and add the following code.

Listing 15.30 Establishing the `csrf` token as a property on the `window` dictionary

```
...
<!--TEMPLATES END-->
<script src="/js/dependencies/sails.io.js" headers='{"x-csrf-token":<%-
⮡ typeof _csrf !== 'undefined' ? JSON.stringify(_csrf) : 'null'
```

```
➥ %>}'></script>
<!--SCRIPTS-->
<script src="/js/dependencies/sails.io.js"></script>
  ...
```

> The generated token is now available via the window dictionary.

Because you add sails.io.js manually outside the Grunt SCRIPTS tag, you need to remove sails.io.js from the Grunt pipeline. In Sublime, open brushfire/tasks/pipeline.js, and comment out the sails.io.js dependency, similar to this.

Listing 15.31 Removing sails.io.js from the pipeline.js file

```
...
// 'js/dependencies/sails.io.js',
'js/dependencies/angular.js',
'js/dependencies/jquery.min.js',
...
```

> Removing sails.io.js from the Grunt pipeline.js dependency

This takes care of non-GET HTTP requests, but you also need to bootstrap the csrf token for all WebSocket requests. In Sublime, open brushfire/views/layout.ejs, and add the following code near the bottom of layout.ejs.

Listing 15.32 Adding the csrf token as a common header for WebSocket requests

```
    ...
    <script type="text/javascript">
      io.sails.headers = {
        'x-csrf-token': window.SAILS_LOCALS._csrf
      }
    </script>
  </div>
</body>
</html>
```

> Adds the _csrf token in the header of each WebSocket request in Brushfire

All of Brushfire's non-GET requests use either Angular or WebSockets. But there may be times when you want to access the csrf token from some other AJAX request via a GET request to /csrfToken. For example, the next listing illustrates how to incorporate the token request as part of a series of AJAX requests.

Listing 15.33 Inserting a csrf token via a hidden input field

```
$(document).ready(function(){

  var _csrf;
  $.get('/csrfToken', function( data ) {
    _csrf = data._csrf;
  });

  $('#loginButton').click(function(){

    $.ajax({
      url: '/user/login',
      type: 'POST',
```

> Gets the CSRF token

```
      data: {
        _csrf: _csrf
      },                              ◁——  Uses the CSRF
      success: function(result){            token in a POST
        console.log('result: ', result);    request
      },
      error: function(xhr, status, err){
        console.log(err);
      }
    });
  });
});
```

Although we don't recommend using HTML form requests in your application, the following listing illustrates how to configure them for CSRF tokens.

Listing 15.34 Inserting a `csrf` token via a hidden input field

```
<form>
  <input type="hidden" name="_csrf" value="<%= _csrf %>" />
</form>
```

When the form is submitted, the `csrf` token is also submitted, allowing the request and form fields to be passed through to the controller action.

15.7.7 *Disabling CSRF protection in tests*

You need to disable CSRF tokens in your test environment because your goal is not to test the framework but instead to test your application. In Sublime, open brush-fire/config/env/test.js, and add the following property.

Listing 15.35 Disabling `csrf` tokens in the test environment

```
...
session: {
    adapter: 'memory'
  },
  csrf: false        ◁——  Disabling csrf tokens in
};                         the test environment
```

Let's commit your changes and push them to Heroku. From the terminal window, type

```
~/brushfire $ git add .          ◁——  Stages all your changes
                                       for the next commit
~/brushfire $ git commit -am 'added csrf protection'   ◁——  Commits changes
                                                             to the local
~/brushfire $ git push heroku master    ◁——               repository
                                         Pushes the changes to the
                                         Heroku remote repository
```

15.7.8 *Understanding cross-origin resource sharing*

A page obtained from a server and rendered by a browser user-agent that contains a script can't successfully make a request using that script to a server from a different domain. This is because the request violates the browser's same-origin policy.

> **DEFINITION** A browser's *same-origin policy* restricts access of scripts, specifically AJAX, from accessing data on a different web server than what originally delivered the script.

This prevents malicious script attacks across domains.

> **NOTE** If the malicious link triggers a form submission request as opposed to an AJAX request, the browser's same-origin policy doesn't restrict the form request. Because a form request isn't subject to the same-origin policy, the request is allowed. But the form request can't receive a JSON response like an AJAX request, so the endpoint is protected.

There are very limited occasions, however, when you might need to divide your application across multiple domains and use cross-origin resource sharing (CORS) to open cross-domain access. Sails can be configured to allow cross-origin requests from a list of domains you specify or from every domain. This can be done on a per-route basis or globally for every route in your app. Unless you completely trust the domain, we highly recommend against using CORS. And if you use CORS, you should limit the domains that can access it. CORS is beyond the scope of the book, but additional details about configuring it can be found at http://mng.bz/555D.

15.7.9 *Understanding man-in-the-middle attacks*

Man-in-the-middle attacks occur because of your inherent lack of control over the network. You can't be certain that a request traveling over the network between the frontend and the backend hasn't been intercepted and altered. Protecting against MITM attacks is straightforward. You need to encrypt the data that passes between your requests and responses. To do this, you need transport layer security (TLS), which is beyond the scope of the book. But Brushfire is currently piggybacking on top of Heroku's TLS via https://brushfire-sailsinaction@herokuapp.com.

15.7.10 *Denial of service attacks*

When you think about a denial of service (DoS) attack, you're most likely thinking about thousands of nodes making requests to a particular endpoint, interrupting service of the application. In reality, a DoS attack is any attempt to interrupt service of an application. Ironically, many times the interruption of service isn't intentional. At the application level, you can write things in your code that make you vulnerable to DoS attacks. As we said, in many cases these are accidental DoS attacks!

For example, if you write code that doesn't use `.limit()` in your queries, you're going to get all of the records. So, for the first few months of your application, there are no problems. But as your application grows, and you have a few hundred thousand records or a few million, every time a request is sent to that controller action, it will load all the records. Once again, that might be okay for a few requests, but as those requests build, you're now loading 20 or 30 million records. This can quickly take down your application due to running out of RAM and then disk, and finally you have a pile of hot liquid metal. The way to work around this is to always use `.limit()` in `find`, `update`, and `destroy` methods that use criteria that could generate an unlimited number of records.

Another possible attack can occur by not limiting the number of things that can be created. For example, a tutorial can currently have an unlimited number of videos. But let's put an arbitrary limit of 25 videos per tutorial. The limit would need to be set in the `newVideo` action of the page controller as well as the `addVideo` action of the tutorial controller. The following listing depicts some initial code to set a limit for the `newVideo` action.

Listing 15.36   Limiting the number of videos in a tutorial

```
...
var MAX_NUM_VIDEOS_PER_TUTORIAL = 25;

Tutorial.findOne({
  id: +req.param('id')
})
.populate('owner')
.populate('ratings')
.populate('videos')
.exec(function (err, foundTutorial){
  if (err) return res.negotiate(err);
  if (!foundTutorial) return res.notFound();

  if (foundTutorial.videos.length >= MAX_NUM_VIDEOS_PER_TUTORIAL) {
    return res.badRequest("Tutorials may have no more than 25
    ➥ videosYou've Maxium videos reached!"          ◁────┐   If the number of videos
    );                                                       exceeds the maximum,
  }                                                          inform the frontend.
  ...
```

The final type of unintentional attack is failure to wrap synchronous functions in a `try/catch`, which can cause the server to crash. Remember to not only wrap the synchronous function with `try/catch` but also to handle the underlying error. The next listing illustrates the correct use of `try/catch` with a synchronous function.

Listing 15.37 Wrapping synchronous functions in `try/catch`

```
...
try {
  var randomString = Strings.unique({}).execSync();
} catch (err) {
  return res.serverError(err);
}
...
```

15.7.11 SQL injection attacks

There are times when you may need to go beyond the features of the ORM. Sails and Waterline don't restrict you from accessing the database directly using the `.query()` method. But you do have much more responsibility in protecting the way user data interacts with the query and the database directly. Waterline provides these types of protections if you're using model methods like `find`, `create`, `update`, and `destroy`. But you have the responsibility when using `.query()`. For more information on using `.query()`, see http://mng.bz/N4z3.

15.8 Summary

- You now understand containerization and horizontal/vertical scaling of an application.
- Sails uses development, production, and test environments that enable different configurations of Sails, depending on the environmental mode.
- Environment variables allow you to control Sails' startup configuration as well as security transmit credentials within Sails when it's deployed.
- Sails can use Mocha and SuperTest to test controller actions and models.
- Sails uses tokens to protect requests against CSRF attacks.

index

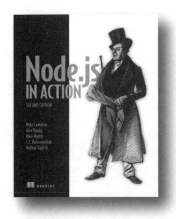

Node.js in Action, Second Edition
by Mike Cantelon, Alex Young, Marc Harter,
    T.J. Holowaychuk, and Nathan Rajlich

ISBN: 9781617292576
450 pages
$49.99
February 2017

Node.js in Practice
by Alex Young and Marc Harter

ISBN: 9781617290930
424 pages
$49.99
December 2014

hapi.js in Action
by Matt Harrison

ISBN: 9781633430211
384 pages
$44.99
December 2016

For ordering information go to www.manning.com

MORE TITLES FROM MANNING

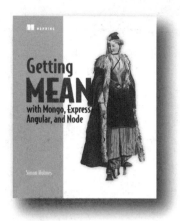

*Getting MEAN with Mongo, Express,
Angular, and Node*
by Simon Holmes

> ISBN: 9781617292033
> 440 pages
> $44.99
> November 2015

Express in Action
Writing, building, and testing Node.js applications
by Evan M. Hahn

> ISBN: 9781617292422
> 256 pages
> $39.99
> April 2016

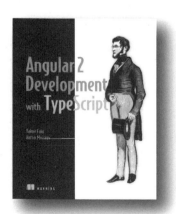

Angular 2 Development with TypeScript
by Yakov Fain and Anton Moiseev

> ISBN: 9781617293122
> 456 pages
> $44.99
> December 2016

For ordering information go to www.manning.com